Perspectives

ON ETHNICITY IN CANADA
A READER

D1450505

Perspectives
ON ETHNICITY IN CANADA
A READER

MADELINE A. KALBACH
Chair of Ethnic Studies
Professor of Sociology
University of Calgary

WARREN E. KALBACH
Professor Emeritus
University of Toronto

Adjunct Professor
Department of Sociology
University of Calgary

THOMSON

NELSON

Australia   Canada   Mexico   Singapore   Spain   United Kingdom   United States

For more information contact
Nelson Thomson Learning,
1120 Birchmount Road,
Scarborough, Ontario,
M1K 5G4.
Or you can visit our Internet site at http://www.nelson.com

Canadian Cataloguing in Publication Data

Main entry under title:
Perspectives on ethnicity in Canada: a reader

ISBN 0-7747-3658-5

1. Minorities – Canada. 2. Ethnicity – Canada. 3. Canada – Ethnic relations.
I. Kalbach, Madeline A. II. Kalbach, Warren E., 1922-

FC104.P467 2000   305.8'00971   C99-931477-7
F1035.A1P467 2000

Senior Acquisitions Editor: Heather McWhinney
Developmental Editor: Camille Isaacs
Production Editor: Linh Vu
Production Coordinator: Cheryl Tiongson

Copy Editor: Beverley Endersby
Cover Design: Sonya V. Thursby, Opus House Incorporated
Interior Design: Brett Miller/Sonya V. Thursby, Opus House Incorporated
Typesetting and Assembly: Carolyn Hutchings Sebestyen
Printing and Binding: Webcom Limited

Cover art: Copyright © David Griffith. Used with permission.

This book was printed in Canada.

2 3 4 5   05 04 03

*To those at the University of Calgary who made the Chair
in Ethnic Studies a reality*

PREFACE

Race and ethnic relations have been a prominent feature of the news in the
1980s and 1990s. South Africa, for example, has gained its independence; the
Berlin wall has fallen; and ethnic conflict in Asia, and in the former
Yugoslavia, has been in the news over the past five years or more. In Canada,
our two Quebec-sovereignty votes; Aboriginal land claims; acceptance of
refugees from Kosovo, as well as from other parts of the world, have become
an important part of ethnic relations in our society. In addition, since 1967
the immigrant stream to Canada has undergone a major change as a result of
the removal of the discriminatory aspects of immigration policy; that is,
Canada's immigrants are now mainly from non-European sources. Current
events both international and national underline the importance of doing
research in the area of race and ethnic relations, and of imparting the knowledge garnered to students of the subject so that they might gain insight,
knowledge, and an understanding of other cultures and the problems that
immigrants coming to Canada face.

As individuals whose research and teaching in the area of race and ethnic relations are inexorably intertwined, we felt that there was a need for a
book of readings such as this one. This volume is made up of five sections,
ranging in focus from theory to empirical studies of specific research questions. Each section contains some articles that have been previously published
and some that were written especially for this volume. The articles focus on
what we see as some of the important areas of race and ethnic relations,
including theory, definitions, ethnic persistence, assimilation, integration,
power, and discrimination. Space limitations made it impossible to include
articles on every area of importance. Perhaps those subjects can be addressed
in a future volume. The contributing authors are among the most prominent
researchers in the field.

Part One addresses race and ethnicity in terms of definitions and basic
theory; it is where the study of race and ethnic relations begins. Part Two consists of three articles that focus on the changing mosaic of Canada, the emergence of "Canadian" as an answer to the Canadian census ancestry question,
and ethnic self-identity. Part Three deals with ethnic persistence and integration, while Part Four examines power and inequality in Canadian society. Part
Five focusses on prejudice and discrimination in its examination of contemporary issues involving attitudes toward non-white ethnic groups, and the
maintenance of a multicultural policy in Canada and other parts of the world.

ACKNOWLEDGEMENTS
▼

Many people contributed to this book of readings. We would like to thank all the contributors for the time, effort, and thought they put into their articles. Ten articles were written especially for this volume; we are grateful to the authors of those chapters for their contributions. Ten articles were selected from previously published works. We would like to thank the authors and their publishers for granting permission to include their work in this book of readings. Harcourt Canada has been professional in every way and facilitated the book from beginning to end. Heather McWhinney convinced us to do the book, and Camille Isaacs kept us on track from the early stages to final submission. Camille's advice was always sound and very helpful. Our appreciation is also extended to the reviewers — Augie Fleras, University of Waterloo; Tanya Basok, University of Windsor; Mirelle Cohen, University of British Columbia — for their helpful suggestions. Last, but not least, we thank our research assistants Alison Sabo, Irene Smolik, and Karen Murphy.

Madeline A. Kalbach
Warren E. Kalbach

A NOTE FROM THE PUBLISHER
▼

Thank you for selecting *Perspectives on Ethnicity in Canada: A Reader* by Madeline A. Kalbach and Warren E. Kalbach. The authors and publisher have devoted considerable time to the careful development of this book. We appreciate your recognition of this effort and accomplishment.

We want to hear what you think about *Perspectives on Ethnicity in Canada: A Reader*. Please take a few minutes to fill in the stamped reader reply card at the back of the book. Your comments and suggestions will be valuable to us as we prepare new editions and other books.

CONTENTS

PART FIVE
▼

PREJUDICE AND DISCRIMINATION

PART ONE

ETHNICITY

A MATTER OF DEFINITION AND THEORY

INTRODUCTION

Part One consists of four chapters, each of which brings the reader up to date on the current thinking about theory, methods, and definitions in the context of ethnic relations. In Chapter One, Alan Anderson and James Frideres develop a model to explain race and ethnic relations in Canada. In so doing, they draw on the sociological factors that individuals encounter on a daily basis. In essence, they incorporate both the micro and the macro perspectives in their model. Whereas the macro perspective focusses on the structure of society, the micro perspective focusses on the individual. Anderson and Frideres argue that one must use both perspectives to understand ethnic relations in Canada.

In Chapter Two, Robert Miles and Rudy Torres focus on the question of whether it is necessary for social scientists to have a concept of race just because there is a belief that races exist in the world. They explore the reasons for asking this question, and they answer it "by suggesting that social scientists do not need to, and indeed should not, transform the *idea* of race into an analytical category and use 'race' as a *concept*." To make their point, Miles and Torres present many of the perspectives on race espoused by social scientists in Britain and the United States. Their discussion is current and brings us up to the end of the 1990s.

Raymond Breton's landmark study (1964) was the first to develop and measure the notion of institutional completeness. Since then, it has played an integral part in the study of Canada's ethnic communities. In Chapter Three, Sheldon Goldenberg and Valerie Haines link the notion of institutional completeness to the study of social networks. They show how this linkage enhances Breton's theory by expanding it to include the theoretical advances in community and urban sociology.

In Chapter Four, Edit Petrovic looks at the emergence of gender, race, and ethnicity as a field of study in its own right. She argues that, having evolved from a variety of approaches and disciplinary interests, and therefore a diversity of theoretical and ideological foundations, the subject has a broad theoretical base. She discusses several models: the cumulative or additive model, the "matrix of domination" model, and the voice metaphor or model. In addition, she argues that gender, race, and ethnicity research in the Canadian context tends to be informed by other models as well, such as colonialism, nativism, multiculturalism, and diversity.

3

1

▼

EXPLAINING CANADA'S ETHNIC LANDSCAPE: A THEORETICAL MODEL

ALAN B. ANDERSON AND JAMES S. FRIDERES

INTRODUCTION

As a society, we are in the midst of a pervasive and profound crisis in Canada, forcing us to deal with a host of social problems, including ethnic inequality, prejudice, racism, systemic discrimination, and ethnic conflict. While this essay focusses on ethnic issues, the reader must understand that the problems related to ethnicity are only part of a large range of social issues facing Canadians. In short, ethnic differentiation co-exists with other aspects of inequality that are beyond the scope of this analysis (see also Berry & Laponce, 1994). A review of intergroup behaviour in Canada and elsewhere in the world provides ample evidence that ethnicity has become the peak of the pyramid and can no longer be accorded a secondary theoretical or practical significance. Anyone who wishes to better understand Canadian society must view ethnicity as one of the most important factors (Wanner, 1999). This situation is not uniquely Canadian. Elsewhere in the world, whether in Africa, South America, or Europe, ethnicity has become a central element in the way individuals and groups interact (Breton et al., 1990). Conflict, so prevalent in today's society, usually has an ethnic dimension. Thus, it is important that ethnicity be acknowledged as a major factor in group dynamics, not only in Canada, but also throughout the world.

The important issues of our day are matters of human behaviour. Almost all the problems currently facing individuals, organizations, or societies are the result, more or less, of the way people behave toward one another. Humans obtain their principal satisfactions and motivations from their relationships with other people. As the twenty-first century approaches, the diverse attitudes, opinions, motivations, and contextual constructs that underlie social behaviour are only beginning to be understood. As our society becomes more complex, the need to advance this knowledge of human behaviour becomes even greater. A better understanding of ethnic issues provides a basis for predicting and explaining group dynamics, including ethnic conflict (see also Driedger, 1996).

It is obvious to many that Canadians are experiencing a crisis in social relations. The tensions between English and French, whether inside or outside Quebec, are evident, and are made more so by the mass media every day. Television and newspapers depict ethnic conflicts in a variety of contexts, for example, in police, housing, educational, and playground settings. What is even more remarkable is that today's leaders in Canada fail to acknowledge this crisis, a failure that reflects an inability to deal with real social issues or problems. Our leaders are lacking the intellectual and political will to carry out social analysis of human behaviour and to develop policies that could ameliorate the tensions and potential conflicts among ethnic groups. It is in this area that social scientists can add to the study of human behaviour.

In this chapter, we limit our focus to ethnic or race relations in Canada. We discuss how social scientists are able to identify specific historical, contextual, and individual attributes that signal how people of different ethnicities act toward one another, and the consequences of such actions (see also James, 1996).

THE CENTRALITY OF ETHNIC RELATIONS: CANADIAN SOCIETY
▼

Few, if any, countries in the world today can legitimately claim to have a population consisting entirely of a single ethnic group. Most societies are pluralistic, or multi-ethnic, consisting of a variety of ethnic groups, each comprising a different proportion of the total population and controlling its own destiny, to differing degrees (Isajiw, 1999). Canada is no exception; over the past three decades, the pluralistic diversity of our society has become a major practical and policy issue, and one that is hotly debated by nearly all Canadians.

This fact alone makes ethnic relations a prominent area of study within the social sciences, particularly sociology, covering a wide range of topics of relevance in most of the traditional fields of sociological inquiry. Whether you are studying residential patterns, intermarriage patterns, youth conflict, criminal behaviour, or employment equity, issues of ethnicity are in the foreground. Nearly all state activities and institutions, such as religion, education, and bureaucracies, shape the social behaviour of individuals and groups (Li, 1999; Marger, 1996).

THE COMPLEXITY OF CANADIAN SOCIETY
▼

A single model of ethnic relations is impossible to formulate. The difficulty lies in the fact that almost every ethnic group within Canadian society is a minority (where "minority" denotes a lack of power and "majority" indicates power), at least at the national level. Moreover, there are well over a hundred clearly defined ethnic groups (some native born, others of immigrant origin) in Canada, not to mention distinctive subgroups. Cross-cutting these delineations, we find some groups that exhibit "visible minority" attributes, for example, skin pigmentation, that allow for quick identification (real or mistaken) and categorical placement. These ethnic/racial populations range in number from hundreds to millions. Many of them are exclusively urban; others are primarily rural. Virtually all embrace a wide range of opinions among their members as to exactly what constitutes ethnic identity, to what extent this identity should be stressed, and how it might be sustained (Driedger, 1996).

Ethnic relations in Canada are unique, even though some parallels with other countries are evident (Reitz & Breton, 1994). As Canada exists within its own historically formed social/economic/political framework, it must be examined in that context. For example, Canadian society has chosen, in many forms and manners of expression, to enact a "liberalist" position rather than a conservative perspective. Moreover, in dealing with ethnic relations, Canada has focussed on two aspects: removing institutional barriers in the economic sphere, and developing strategies to help integrate people into Canadian society, for example, language, social skills, and job training programs. In short, Canadians adopt a liberal position which argues that state intervention is required to deal with the sociological and institutional barriers that prevent non-British (and non-white) groups from achieving necessary education and employment.

More than twenty years ago, academic observers of the Canadian social scene suggested that the following characteristics were peculiarly relevant to an understanding of Canadian society:

- A weak sense of national identity accompanied by a strong sense of regional identification. In the case of certain provinces, such as Quebec, regional identification is interlinked with particular ethnic group loyalties.
- A hierarchical social structure which is associated with the existence of class-based inequalities in educational and occupational opportunities.
- An ethnic stratification system based on familial, religious and linguistic allegiances that is intertwined with existing class structure.
- An official ideology that espouses the doctrine of cultural pluralism rather than assimilation. (Pike & Zureik, 1975: viii–ix)

Nothing that has happened over the past-quarter century suggests that these attributes of Canadian society have changed. With the introduction of more than 200 000 immigrants from non-traditional countries over the past two decades, Canada has become more culturally diverse, and the mosaic has taken on many different hues. Those ethnic groups who were considered recent immigrants have now become "old," and recent arrivals have the status of "new" members of Canadian society. The third force (non-French, non-British) now makes up a substantial proportion of the Canadian population (nearly 20 percent), and an even greater proportion of the population of large urban areas, for example, over 40 percent of Toronto residents, is made up of immigrants, thus adding to the complexity of ethnic relations. The arrival of visible minorities has further complicated intergroup relations by introducing "race" as an additional factor when trying to explain behaviour.

ETHNIC RELATIONS: UNDERSTANDING AND MAKING PREDICTIONS
▼

Most Canadians find ethnic issues complex and seemingly without resolution. They continually ask questions such as: Why don't "ethnics" integrate into Canadian society? How come "ethnics" seem to want to maintain their ancestral ethnic linkages? Why don't immigrants become more like "regular" Canadians? Canadians look to social scientists for answers. In this chapter, we want to situate the issues and sort out the various positions in the current debate, and give you, the reader, some idea of what is at stake. We want to map the activities, and then give you the means to discover explanations for the role and function of specific actions taken by individuals and ethnic groups. A number of theoretical perspectives have been put forward to explain ethnic relations (Richmond, 1994). One of the oldest theoretical perspectives is the biological model. The central thesis of this perspective is that non-whites are, in some sense, genetically or biologically different from whites. A. Jensen (1969) was one of the first contemporary social scientists in the United States to take such a stand, and the publication of his article in the *Harvard Educational Review* gave instant international exposure to his ideas. Hernstein and Murray (1994) expanded and developed Jensen's ideas, but their conclusions were rejected once other scholars undertook methodological and statistical analyses of their data. In Canada, P. Rushton and A. Bogaert (1987), utilizing data bases with suspect validity, continued this line of thinking and argued that Asians were the brightest of "races," followed by whites, and then Blacks and aboriginals. Jensen's initial findings were widely publicized in the media, and it was quickly recognized that he had used flawed methodologies; ultimately, his research was published only in obscure, ideologically biased journals, his work having being discredited by scholars and policy-makers. Nevertheless, it is important for the reader to realize that these contemporary researchers have tried to resurrect biological theories as an explanation of why ethnic or racial groups behave in the way they do and as a means to predict interethnic/interracial relations. Thus, many individuals' aversion to non-whites is an opinion based on "scientific" grounds, and, for them, the oppression of non-whites is simply part of nature.

Cultural theorists, extending this general thesis, argue that the character and content of non-white (read non–British/French origin) cultures inhibit them from successfully competing with other whites in the areas of education, business, and occupation (McRobbie, 1994). The attributes noted as leading to success in these areas, for example, motivation, deferred gratification, work ethic, are missing from non-white ethnic groups. These culturalists and post-modernists note that, while the educational and occupational differences among ethnic groups seemed to be decreasing between the turn of the century and the 1960s, in more recent times, the differences have been increasing (Li, 1999; Lian & Matthews, 1998). These differences are a result, according to the cultural theorists, of the influx of non-white immigrants into Canadian society. They argue that only when non-whites are able to overcome these deficiencies will they be able to compete equally with whites. We reject such models or explanations of behaviour and note that there is no empirical evidence to support such claims. However, these biological and cultural models have been evident in the literature for many years and seem to have undergone some resurgence of popularity in the recent past. The model we utilize to explain ethnic and race relations reflects the sociological imagination, drawing upon the macro and micro sociological factors that surround all of us each day.

MACRO AND MICRO MODELS
▼

Two perspectives make up the theoretical model we use to explain human behaviour — macro and micro variables. The former focus on the structure of society; the latter focus on the individual. The first of these perspectives is usually associated with Karl Marx; the second, with Sigmund Freud. Macro theorists attempt to explain social behaviour by looking at how the structure of society impinges upon the individual. For example, people living on an Indian reserve will, because of the social conditions and social structure that predominates there, behave in ways almost unthinkable for those living in the Mount Royal area of Montreal. Likewise, individuals living in ethnic enclaves in the city of

Toronto behave in ways that individuals living in rural Newfoundland cannot fathom. There are many variations of a macro perspective, some focussing solely on demographic factors or economic issues, and others using a combination of different structural factors to explain human behaviour.

At the other end of the continuum, the micro theorists focus solely on the individual to explain human behaviour. For them, individuals are capable of transcending the structural conditions in which they operate (sometimes referred to as the exercise of "free will"), and thus behaviours can be best explained by looking at the attributes of the individual. For these theorists, the individual personality or sociodemographic attribute of the individual, for example, age or sex, is the key to explaining behaviour.

To our way of thinking, attempts to utilize one or the other perspective produce an infertile theory, incapable of fully understanding or predicting human behaviour. We argue that a social-psychological perspective has to be employed in order to explain and predict human behaviour. We define a social-psychological perspective as one that attempts to explain behaviour as a result of the intersection of society and the individual. Figure 1.1 identifies the principal components of this perspective and how they link.

As is evident from Figure 1.1, we agree with West (1993) when he argues that a full theory of race/ethnic relations has to have three conceptual conditions if adequate explanation and prediction are to occur:

- an understanding of the historical conditions which produced the logic of discrimination and prejudice in Canadian society;

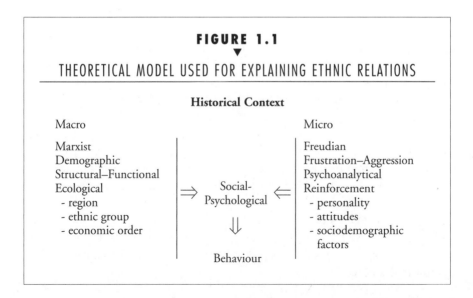

FIGURE 1.1
▼
THEORETICAL MODEL USED FOR EXPLAINING ETHNIC RELATIONS

Historical Context

Macro		Micro
Marxist		Freudian
Demographic		Frustration–Aggression
Structural–Functional		Psychoanalytical
Ecological	$\Rightarrow$ Social- $\Leftarrow$	Reinforcement
- region	Psychological	- personality
- ethnic group	$\Downarrow$	- attitudes
- economic order		- sociodemographic factors
	Behaviour	

- a micro understanding of how people operate in their day-to-day lives;
- and an understanding of the social structure of society (institutional linkage) and how this relates to ethnic group relations.

This model provides a map of how individuals participate in the institutional network of society on an ongoing basis. It shows that many factors impinge upon the individual or group, restricting or enlarging the behavioural repertoire. Some of these are external to the individual, and others are internal; some are psychological, and others are structural. Adding to the complexity and dynamics of this model is the variable of "context," or situational determinants. All behaviour, to some extent, is situationally determined, and this context must be taken into account if we are to explain behaviour. The context in which behaviour takes place gives logic, consistency, and legitimacy to the behaviour we engage in. The "weight" or importance of these situational determinants will vary and needs to be taken into account when assessing the matrix of possible behaviours that can be exhibited by the individual. In short, individual (micro) and structural (macro) factors need to be identified within a field of context if we are to make predictions and explain social behaviour.

It is clear that the macro and micro perspectives need to be integrated if ethnic relations in Canadian society are to be explained. Whether one begins with the micro or macro is of little importance, as long as both are taken into consideration in explaining ethnic relations. For example, some researchers argue that individuals operate within a social structure, and thus their individual actions are constrained by these structural conditions; for example, social class imposes certain limits on an individual's behaviour (Bourdieu, 1989; Satzewich, 1992). Thus they prefer to begin with the macro factors, and then move to an analysis of the micro elements. In more practical terms, this means that one must look at both structural variables and individual factors in order to explain social behaviour.

In summary, the micro or psychological approach focusses on personality factors, for example, those behind racial prejudice. It neglects the social context in which these attitudes have developed, are reinforced, and operate. We argue that if one focusses solely on the individual as the major operative force in explaining human behaviour, the very concept of society tends to be destroyed. On the other hand, the macro models tend to ignore the individual and focus on the social system. One problem with these approaches is, for example, their treatment of social change. While there is nothing inherent in sociological approaches that precludes their treatment of social change, previous work using these models tended to ignore change or treated it in a most simplistic fashion.

THE HISTORICAL CONTEXT
▼

The reader is reminded that, to fully understand and predict ethnic relations, we need to accept the principle of historical specificity. This principle forces us to understand the conditions under which non-British (and non-French) groups have been treated over time, and the structural constraints under which these people have to live. Put another way, one cannot adopt an ahistorical approach to studying ethnic relations. One must fully appreciate the history of the relations, whether myth or reality, that impinges upon the views, attitudes, and behaviour of ethnic-group members. The recent events in Yugoslavia and Kosovo reveal animosities that can be traced back to the fourteenth century. Irish–British antagonisms reflect real and imagined atrocities occurring nearly 800 years ago. Thus, the historical collective conscience of the ethnic group is an important contextual factor that will give us fertile ground upon which to build a theoretical explanation of today's behaviour.

The reader must also understand that ethnic relations change over time and context. Aboriginals were once military allies of the British, the French promoted an intermarriage policy with Aboriginal peoples, Eastern European immigrants to Canada were treated as though they were only just a step above farm animals, Blacks and Jews were refused entrance to Canada, and Chinese and Japanese were deported from Canada. As McVey and Kalbach (1995) point out, the population composition of Canada has revealed a chameleon trend over the past century. Thus, ethnic relations have a dynamic that must be fully appreciated, and the reader must understand that, while the relationships among the groups may change, the underlying explanatory model remains the same. Moreover, it is important to remember that the salience of the macro or micro factors may also vary over time. Nevertheless, social-psychological analysis must ferret out the salience and importance of each factor.

CONCEPTUAL MODELS
▼

The goal of theory is to predict and understand. It is important to note that these are separate goals, and achieving one may not mean achieving the other. The student is reminded to keep these differences in mind. You see these differences all the time. For example, when the weather person predicts rain for the day and it does not occur, the audience does not reject further weather predictions. Undaunted, the weather person is able to explain why her or his prediction did not come true. We feel that taking a solely micro approach will allow you to achieve some prediction of behaviour. On the other hand, if you take a macro approach you will be able to achieve some understanding of the relations between and among various ethnic groups. It is only when an integration of the two approaches is utilized that you, the analyst, will be able to achieve both prediction and explanation with sufficient accuracy to warrant the acceptance of social psychology as a valuable discipline for policy-makers, social leaders, and others who have to make decisions that have an impact upon individual and group behaviour.

Our assumptions are simple. We believe, first, that humans are social animals who live and learn in human groups. Second, individuals become human through social interaction with others. Third, while society has an impact upon individual behaviour, individuals have an impact upon the social structure. In short, the relationship between individuals and society is reciprocal. Using these assumptions, we believe that models of ethnic relations can be constructed that will yield a better understanding of how and why ethnic groups act in particular ways. One has to view how an individual behaves in a particular social structure during a specific time and place if a full understanding of human behaviour is to be achieved.

We argue for a sociohistorical theoretical approach. Theorists adopting this approach have developed elaborate models of ethnic-group reactions at the time of contact that have far-reaching effects on the relationships today. Only through the use of such an approach will we be able to integrate the individual, societal factors, and the situational contexts in which the events are occurring (Isajiw, 1999). Such an approach offers the reader a full and informative understanding of social reality.

CONCLUSION
▼

By using a theoretical model that incorporates both the micro and the macro, we hope to integrate different theoretical perspectives. Such a model allows us to incorporate the local community, and the regional, national, and global context, in explaining ethnic relations. In doing so, we can make sense out of the enormous complexity of our country, which is at once unicultural, bicultural, and, at another level, multicultural. The intersection of the different units of analysis provides for a more complete explanation of how such factors as globalized capitalism simultaneously integrate and segment the workforce by ethnicity, and it allows us to situate local cases within the global context.

Using this model allows us to explain why "assimilation" was the preferred manner in which dominant groups dealt with minority groups at the turn of the century. It also leads us to an understanding of how this policy changed over time and has resulted in today's championing of "multiculturalism" (Kymlicka, 1998). Ethnicity as a salient component of an individual's life changes over time, and its impact upon behaviour is equally variable. Ethnic and racial groups are gradually incorporating into Canadian society, and these structural events need to be taken into consideration if an understanding of intergroup behaviour is to be achieved. Nevertheless, all these factors must be part of the "calculus" if adequate and illuminating explanations of ethnic and race relations are to emerge.

Focussing upon the individual and structural factors also allows us to assess both the internal dynamics of an ethnic group and the interaction among two or more ethnic communities in a given locale. The integration of these factors will demystify the ways in which different forms of relationships among ethnic groups are produced and reproduced. This model allows us to assess the meaning, identity, and ideology of ethnic relations, and to show how they have continually been created, contested, and transformed. Finally, such a perspective allows us to assess the way "mediating institutions" shape, structure, and constrain interrelations, often within hierarchies that assert the dominance of established groups. In this way, issues of class and power are brought into the analysis of ethnic relations. In the end, to fully understand ethnic relations in any pluralistic society, we must pursue a historical frame of reference, both a micro and a macro perspective as well as an interdisciplinary approach.

REFERENCES
▼

Berry, J., & J.A. Laponce (Eds.). (1994). *Ethnicity and culture in Canada: The research landscape.* Toronto: University of Toronto Press.

Bourdieu, P. (1989). Social space and symbolic power. *Sociological Theory, 7,* 14–21.

Breton, R., Isajiw, W., Kalbach, W., & Reitz, J. (1990). *Ethnic identity and equality: Varieties of experience in a Canadian city.* Toronto: University of Toronto Press.

Driedger, L. (Ed.). (1996). *Multi-ethnic Canada: Identities and inequalities.* Toronto: Oxford University Press.

Hernstein, R., & Murray, C. (1994). *The bell curve: Intelligence and class structure in American life.* New York: The Free Press.

Isajiw, W. (1999). *Understanding diversity: Ethnicity and race in the Canadian context.* Toronto: Thompson Educational.

James, C. (1996). *Seeing ourselves: Exploring race, ethnicity and culture.* Toronto: Thompson Educational.

Jensen, A. (1969). How much can we boost IQ and scholastic achievement? *Harvard Educational Review, 39*(3), 1–123.

Kymlicka, W. (1998). *Finding our way: Rethinking ethnocultural relations in Canada.* Toronto: Oxford University Press.

Li, P. (1999). *Race and ethnic relations in Canada* (2nd ed.), Toronto: Oxford University Press.

Lian, J., & Matthews, D. (1998). Does the vertical mosaic still exist? Ethnicity and income in Canada, 1991. *Canadian Review of Sociology and Anthropology, 35,* 461–482.

Marger, M. (1996). *Race and ethnic relations: American and comparative perspectives.* Belmont, CA: Wadsworth.

McRobbie, A. (1994). *Postmodernism and popular culture.* New York: Routledge.

McVey, W., & Kalbach, W. (1995). *Canadian population.* Toronto: Nelson Canada.

Pike, R., & Zureik, E. (Eds.). (1975). *Socialization and values in Canadian society.* Toronto: McClelland & Stewart.

Reitz, J., & Breton, R. (1994). *The illusion of difference: Realities of ethnicity in Canada and the United States.* Toronto: C.D. Howe Institute.

Richmond, A. (1994). *Global apartheid: Refugees, racism and the new world order.* Toronto: Oxford University Press.

Rushton, P., & Bogaert, A. (1987). Race differences in sexual behavior: Testing and evolutionary hypotheses. *Journal of Research in Personality, 21,* 529–551.

Satzewich, V. (Ed.). (1992). *Deconstructing a nation: Immigration, multiculturalism and racism in '90's Canada.* Halifax: Fernwood.

Wanner, R. (1999). Prejudice, profit or productivity: Explaining returns to human capital among male immigrants to Canada. *Canadian Ethnic Studies, 30*(3), 24–55.

West, C. (1993). *Keeping faith: Philosophy and race in America.* New York: Routledge.

2

▼

DOES "RACE" MATTER?
TRANSATLANTIC PERSPECTIVES
ON RACISM AFTER
"RACE RELATIONS"

ROBERT MILES AND RUDY TORRES

> The discourse promoting resistance to racism must not prompt identification with and in terms of categories fundamental to the discourse of oppression. Resistance must break not only with *practices* of oppression, although its first task is to do that. Resistance must oppose also the *language* of oppression, including the categories in terms of which the oppressor (or racist) represents the forms in which resistance is expressed. (Goldberg, 1990: 313–314)

INTRODUCTION
▼

In April 1993, one year after the Los Angeles civil unrest, a major United States publisher released a book with the creatively ambiguous title *Race Matters* by the distinguished scholar Cornel West. The back cover of the slightly revised edition published the following year categorized it as a contribution to both African-American studies and current affairs. The latter was confirmed by the publisher's strategy of marketing the book as a "trade" rather than as an "academic" title: this was a book for the "American public" to read. And the American public was assured that they were reading a quality product when they were told that its author had "built a reputation as one of the most eloquent voices in American's racial debate."

Some two years later, the *Los Angeles Times* published an article by its science writer under the headline "Scientists Say Race Has No Biological Basis." The opening paragraph ran as follows:

> Researchers adept at analyzing the genetic threads of human diversity said Sunday that the concept of race — the source of abiding cultural and po-

litical divisions in American society — simply has no basis in fundamental human biology. Scientists should abandon it.

And on the same day (20 February 1995), the *Chronicle of Higher Education* reproduced the substance of these claims in an article under the title "A Growing Number of Scientists Reject the Concept of Race." Both publications were reporting on the proceedings of the American Association for the Advancement of Science in Atlanta.

If "the concept of race ... simply has no basis in fundamental human biology," how are we to evaluate Professor West's assertion that "race matters"? If "race" matters, then "races" must exist! But if there are no "races," then "race" cannot matter. These two contributions to public political debate seem to reveal a contradiction. Yet within the specific arena of academic debate, there is a well-rehearsed attempt to dissolve the contradiction, which runs as follows. It is acknowledged that, earlier this century, the biological and genetic sciences established conclusively in the light of empirical evidence that the attempt to establish the existence of different types or "races" of human beings by scientific procedures had failed. The idea that the human species consisted of a number of distinct "races," each exhibiting a set of discrete physical and cultural characteristics, is therefore false, mistaken. The interventions reported as having been made in Atlanta in February 1995 only repeat what some scientists have been arguing since the 1930s. Yet the fact that scientists have to continue to assert these claims demonstrates that the contrary is still widely believed and articulated in public discussion.

Because this scientific knowledge has not yet been comprehensively understood by "the general public" (which not only persists in believing in the existence of "races" as biologically discrete entities, but also acts in ways consistent with such a belief), it is argued that social scientists must employ a *concept* of "race" to describe and analyze these beliefs, and the discrimination and exclusion that are premised on this kind of classification. In other words, while social scientists know that there are no "races," they also know that things believed to exist (in this case "races") have a real existence for those who believe in them, and that actions consistent with the belief have real social consequences. In sum, because people believe that "races" exist (i.e., because they utilize the *idea* of "race" to comprehend their social world), social scientists need a *concept* of "race."

Or do they? This chapter will explore the reasons why this question needs to be asked. It will also answer it by suggesting that social scientists do not need to, and indeed should not, transform the *idea* of "race" into an analytical category and use "race" as a *concept*. Pre-eminent among the reasons for such an assertion is that the arenas of academic and political discourse cannot be clinically separated. Hence Professor West, in seeking to use his status as a leading Afro-American scholar to make a political intervention in current affairs by arguing that "race matters," is likely to legitimate and reinforce the widespread public belief that "races" exist, irrespective of his views on this issue. For if this belief in the existence of "races" was not widespread, there would be no news value in publishing an article in a leading daily United States newspaper that claims that "Race Has No Biological Basis."

CRITICIZING "RACE" AS AN ANALYTICAL CATEGORY
▼

We begin this exploration by crossing the Atlantic in order to consider the issue as it has been discussed in Britain since the early 1950s. As we shall see, the development of the British discussion has in fact been influenced substantially by the preconceptions and language employed in the United States: the use of "race" as an analytical category in the social sciences is a transatlantic phenomenon.

It is now difficult to conceive, but 40 years ago no one would have suggested that "race matters" in Britain. The idea of "race" was employed in public and political discussion, but largely only in order to discuss "the colonies": the "race problem" was spatially located beyond British shores in the British Empire, and especially in certain colonies, notably South Africa. It is relevant to add that this, too, had not always been so. During the nineteenth and early twentieth centuries, it was widely believed that the population of Britain was composed of a number of different "races" (e.g., the Irish were identified as being "of the Celtic race") and, moreover, migration to Britain from central and eastern Europe in the late nineteenth century was interpreted using the language of "race" to signify the Jewish refugees fleeing persecution (e.g., Barkan, 1992: 15–165). But, as the situation in the port city of Liverpool after World War I suggested (e.g., Barkan, 1992: 57–165), the language of "race" used to refer to the interior of Britain was to become tied exclusively to differences in skin colour in the second half of the twentieth century. What, then, was the "race" problem that existed beyond the shores of Britain?

Briefly expressed, the problem was that, or so it was thought, the colonies were spatial sites where members of different "races" (Caucasian, White, African, Hindu, Mongoloid, Celtic: the language to name these supposed "races" varied enormously) met and where their "natures" (to civilize, to fight, to be lazy, to progress, to drink, to engage in sexual perversions, etc.) interacted, often with tragic consequences. This language of "race" was usually anchored in the signification of certain forms of somatic difference (skin colour, facial characteristics, body shape and size, eye colour, skull shape) which were interpreted as the physical marks that accompanied, and that in some unexplained way determined, the "nature" of those so marked. In this way, the social relations of British colonialism were explained as being rooted simultaneously in the biology of the human body and in the cultural attributes determined by nature.

But the "race" problem was not to remain isolated from British shores, to be contained there by a combination of civilization and violence. All Her Majesty's subjects had the right of residence in the Motherland, and increasing numbers of them chose to exercise that right as the 1950s progressed. Members of "coloured races," from the Caribbean and the Indian subcontinent in particular, migrated to Britain largely to fill vacancies in the labour market but against the will of successive governments (Labour and Conservative), who feared that they carried in their cheap suitcases not only their few clothes and personal possessions, but also the "race problem" (e.g., Joshi & Carter, 1984; Solomos, 1989; Layton-Henry, 1992). By the late 1950s, it was widely argued that, as a result of "coloured immigration," Britain had imported a "race" problem: prior to this migration, so it was believed, Britain's population was "racially homogeneous," a claim that neatly dispensed with not only earlier racialized classifications of both migrants and the population of the British Isles, but also the history of interior racisms.

The political and public response to immigration from the Caribbean and the Indian subcontinent is now a well-known story (e.g., Solomos, 1989; Layton-Henry, 1992), although there are a number of important byways still to be explored. What is of more interest here is the academic response. A small number of social scientists (particularly sociologists and anthropologists) wrote about these migrations and their social consequences, using the language of everyday life: *Dark Strangers* and *The Colour Problem* were the titles of two books that achieved a certain prominence during the 1950s, and their authors subsequently pursued distinguished academic careers. Considered from the point of view of the 1990s, these titles now seem a little unfortunate, and perhaps even a part of the problem, insofar as they employ language that seems to echo and legitimate racist discourses of the time.

But can the same be said for two other books that became classic texts within the social sciences: Michael Banton's *Race Relations* (1967) and John Rex's *Race Relations in Sociological Theory* (1970)? Both were published in the following decade and were widely interpreted as offering different theoretical and political interpretations of the consequences of the migration to, and settlement in, Britain of British subjects and citizens from the Caribbean and the

Indian subcontinent. And indeed they did offer very different analyses. Notably, Rex sought to reinterpret the scope of the concept of racism to ensure that it could encompass the then contemporary political discourses about immigration. Such discourse avoided any direct references to an alleged hierarchy of "races" while at the same time referring to or implying the existence of different "races." Banton interpreted this shift in discourse as evidence of a decline in racism, a conclusion that was to lead him to eventually reject the concept of racism entirely (1987).

But what is more remarkable is that, despite their very different philosophical and theoretical backgrounds and conclusions, they shared something else. Both Banton and Rex mirrored the language of everyday life, incorporated it into academic discourse and thereby legitimated it. They agreed that Britain (which they both analyzed comparatively with reference to the United States and South Africa) had a "race relations" problem, and Rex in particular wished to conceptualize this problem theoretically in the discipline of sociology. In so doing, both premised their arguments on the understanding that scientific knowledge proves that "races" do not exist in the sense widely understood in everyday common-sense discourse: if "race" was a problem, it was a social and not a biological problem, one rooted, in part at least, in the continued popular belief in the existence of "races." Indeed, John Rex had been one of the members of the team of experts recruited by UNESCO to officially discredit the continuing exploitation of nineteenth-century scientific knowledge about "race" by certain political groups and to educate the public by making widely known the more recent conclusions of biological and genetic scientists (Montagu, 1972).

The concept of "race relations" seemed to have impeccable credentials, unlike the language of "dark strangers," for example. This is in part because the notion was borrowed from the early sociology of the "Chicago School" in the United States which, among other things, was interested in the consequences of two contemporaneous migrations: the early twentieth-century migration from the Southern to the Northern states of "Negroes" fleeing poverty (and much more besides) in search of wage labour, and the continuing large-scale migration from Europe to the United States. As a result of the former migration, "Negro" and "white races" entered, or so it was conceptualized, into conflicting social relations in the burgeoning industrial urban areas of the Northern states, and sociologists had named a new field of study. "Coloured migration" to British cities after 1945 provided an opportunity for sociologists to import this field of study into Britain: Britain, too, now had a "race relations" problem.

Moreover, for Rex at least, "race relations situations" were characterized by the presence of a racist ideology. Hence, the struggle against colonialism could now be pursued within the Mother Country "herself": by intervening in the new domestic race-relations problem on the side of the colonized victims of racism, one could position oneself against the British state now busily seeking a solution to that problem through the introduction of immigration controls intended specifically to prevent "coloured" British subjects from entering the country. Such was the rush to be on the side of the angels that few, if any, wondered about what the angels looked like and whether there was any validity in the very concept of angel.

There was a further import from the United States that had a substantial impact on the everyday and academic discourses of race relations in the late 1960s and early 1970s in Britain: the struggle for civil rights and against racism on the part of "the Blacks" in the United States (the notion of "Negro" had now run its course and, like "coloured" before it, it had been ejected into the waste-bin of politically unaccepted language). This movement had the effect of mobilizing not only many Blacks in Britain, but also many whites politically inclined toward one of several competing versions of socialist transformation. And if radical Blacks were busy "seizing the time" in the names of antiracism and "Black autonomy," there was little political or academic space within which radically-inclined white social scientists could wonder about the legitimacy and the consequences of seizing the language of "race" to do battle against racism. For it was specifically in the name of "race" that Black people were resisting their long history of colonial oppression: indeed, in some versions of this vision of liberation, contemporary Blacks were the direct descendants and inheritors of the African "race" that had been deceived and disinherited by the "white devils" many centuries ago. In this "race war," the white race was soon to face the day of judgement.

Possession of a common language and associated historical traditions can blind as well as illuminate. It is especially significant that both the Left and the Right in Britain looked across the Atlantic when seeking to analyze and to offer forecasts about the outcome of the "race relations" problem that both agreed existed within Britain. The infamous speeches on immigration made by the MP Enoch Powell in the late 1960s and 1970s contained a great deal of vivid imagery, refracting the current events in American cities and framing them as prophecies of what was inevitably going to happen in due course in British cities if the "alien wedge" was not quickly "repatriated." At the same time, the Left drew political inspiration from the Black struggle against racism and sought to incorporate aspects of its rhetoric, style, and politics. Hence, while there was disagreement about the identity of the heroes and the villains of race relations in the United States, there was fundamental agreement that race relations there provided a framework with which to assess the course of race relations in Britain. Even legislation intended to regulate race relations and to make racialized discrimination illegal refracted the "American experience."

As a result, the academic response to the "race relations" problem in Britain was largely isolated both from the situations elsewhere in Europe — and particularly in northwest Europe, which was experiencing a quantitatively much more substantial migration than that taking place in Britain — and from academic and political writing about those situations. Two features of those situations are pertinent to the argument here.

First, the nation-states of northwest Europe had recently experienced either fascist rule or fascist occupation, and therefore had suffered the direct consequences of the so-called final solution to the Jewish question, which sought to eliminate the "Jewish race." Hence, the collective historical memory of most of the major cities of northwest Europe was shaped by the genocide effected against the Jews and legitimated in the name of "race," even if that historical memory was now the focus of denial or repression. Second, this experience left the collective memory especially susceptible to the activities of UNESCO and others seeking to discredit the idea of "race" as a valid and meaningful descriptor. Hence, the temporal and spatial proximity of the Holocaust rendered its legitimating racism (a racism in which the idea of "race" was explicit and central) an immediate reality: in this context, few people were willing to make themselves vulnerable to the charge of racism, with the result that suppressing the idea of "race," at least in the official and formal arenas of public life, became a political imperative.

The political and academic culture of mainland northwest Europe has therefore been open to two developments which distinguish it from that existing in the British Isles. First, in any debate about the scope and validity of the concept of racism, the Jewish experience of racism is much more likely to be discussed, and even to be prioritized over any other. Second, the idea of "race" itself became highly politically sensitive. Its very use as a descriptor is more likely to be interpreted in itself as evidence of racist beliefs and, as a result, the idea is rarely employed in everyday political and academic discussion, at least not in connection with domestic social relations. However, in Britain, given the combination of the colonial migration and the multiple ideological exchange with the United States, there were far fewer constraints on the everyday use of the idea of "race" and on a redefinition of the concept of racism. As a result, the latter came to refer exclusively to an ideology held by "white" people about "Black" people that was rooted in colonial exploitation and in capitalist expansion beyond Europe.

Having recognized the relative distinctiveness of the political and academic space in northwest Europe and then having occupied that space, one can view those social relations defined in Britain and the United States as race relations from another point of view. For there is no public or academic reference to the existence of race relations in contemporary France or Germany. It then becomes possible to pose questions that seem not to be posed from within these intimately interlinked social and historical contexts. What kinds of social relations are signified as race relations? Why is the idea of "race" employed in everyday life to refer only to certain groups of people and to certain social situations? And why do social scientists unquestioningly import everyday meanings into their reasoning and theoretical frameworks in defining "race" and "race relations" as a particular field of study? As a result, what does it mean for an academic to claim, for example, that "race" is a factor in determining the structure of social inequality or that "race" and gender are interlinked forms of oppression? What is intended and what might be the consequences of asserting as an academic that "race matters"?

These are the kinds of questions that one of the present authors has been posing for nearly fifteen years (e.g., Miles, 1982, 1984, 1989), influenced in part by the important writing of the French theorist Guillaumin (1972, 1995). The answers to these questions lead to the conclusion that one should follow the example of biological and genetic scientists and refuse to attribute analytical status to the *idea* of "race" within the social sciences, and thereby refuse to use it as a descriptive and explanatory *concept*. The reasoning can be summarized as follows (cf. Miles, 1982: 22–43; 1993: 47–9).

First, the idea of "race" is used to effect a reification within sociological analysis insofar as the outcome of an often complex social process is explained as the consequence of some thing named "race" rather than of the social process itself. Consider both the recent publication of *The Bell Curve* (1994) by Richard J. Hernstein and Charles Murray and the authors' assertion that "race" determines academic performance and life chances. The assertion can be supported with statistical evidence which demonstrates that, in comparison with "Black people," "white people" are more likely to achieve top grades in school and to enter the leading universities in the United States. The determining processes are extremely complex, including among other things parental class position, active and passive racialized stereotyping, and exclusion in the classroom and beyond. The effects of these processes are all mediated through a previously racialized categorization into a "white/Black" dichotomy that is employed in everyday social relations. Hence, it is not "race" that determines academic performance; rather, academic performance is determined by an interplay of social processes, one of which is premised on the articulation of racism to effect and legitimate exclusion. Indeed, given the nineteenth-century meanings of "race," this form of reification invites the possibility of explaining academic performance as the outcome of some quality within the body of those racialized as "Black."

Second, when academics who choose to write about race relations seek to speak to a wider audience (an activity that we believe to be fully justified) or when their writings are utilized by non-academics, this unwittingly legitimates and reinforces everyday beliefs that the human species is constituted by a number of different "races," each of which is characterized by a particular combination of real or imagined physical features or marks and cultural practices. When Professor West seeks to persuade the American public that "race matters," there is no doubt that he himself does not believe in the existence of biologically defined "races," but he cannot control the meanings attributed to his claim on the part of those who identify differences in skin colour, for example, as marks designating the existence of Blacks and whites as discrete "races." Unintentionally, his writing may then come to serve as a legitimation not only of a belief in the existence of "race" as a biological phenomenon, but also of racism itself. He could avoid this outcome by breaking with the "race relations" paradigm.

Third, as a result of reification and the interplay between academic and common-sense discourses, the use of "race" as an analytical concept incorporates a notion that has been central to the evolution of racism into the discourse of antiracism, thereby sustaining one of the conditions of the reproduction of racism within the discourse and practice of antiracism.

For these reasons, the idea of "race" should not be employed as an analytical category within the social sciences, and it follows from this that the object of study should not be described as "race relations." Hence, we reject the race-relations problematic as the locus for the analysis of racism. But we do not reject the concept of racism. Rather, we critique the race-relations problematic in order to retain a concept of racism that is constructed in such a way as to recognize the existence of a plurality of historically specific racisms, not all of which employ explicitly the idea of "race." In contrast, the race-relations paradigm refers exclusively to either Black/white social relations or social relations between "people of colour" and "white people," with the result that there is only one racism, the racism of whites, which has as its object and victim people of colour (e.g., Essed, 1991). Moreover, as is increasingly recognized in the academic literature of the past decade, many recent and contemporary discourses that eschew use of the idea of "race" nevertheless advance notions that were previously a referent of such an idea. We can only comprehend contemporary discourses that dispense with the explicit use of the idea of "race" and those discourses that naturalize and inferiorize white populations if we rescue the concept of racism from the simultaneous inflation and narrowing of its meaning by the intersection of the academic and political debates that have taken place in Britain and the United States since the end of World War II.

REFLECTIONS ON THE RACIALIZATION OF THE UNITED STATES BY THE AMERICAN ACADEMY
▼

When one views the contemporary academic debate about racism in the United States both from this analytical position and from Europe, one is struck by the following things. First, when compared with the mid- and late 1960s, it is now an extremely contested debate, and one in which many voices are heard arguing different positions. One the one hand, writers such as Wellman (1993) continue to assert that racism remains the primary determinant of social inequality in the United States, while, on the other, writers such as Wilson (1987) claim that the influence of racism has declined substantially, to the point where it cannot be considered to be a significant influence on current structure of inequality. Between these two positions, one finds writers such as West who assert that the continuing impact of racism has to be assessed in terms of its relationship with the effects of class, sexism, and homophobia (e.g., 1994: 44). Moreover, it is a debate in which the voices of "Afrocentrists" (e.g., Karenga, 1993) and "Black feminists" (e.g., hooks, 1990) have become extremely influential over the past two decades, while at the same time a "Black" conservative intellectual tradition has emerged and attracted increasing attention (e.g., Sowell, 1994).

Second, it remains a debate in which it is either largely taken for granted or explicitly argued that the concept of racism refers to an ideology, and (in some cases) a set of practices, of which Black people are the exclusive victims: racism refers to what "white" people think about and do to "Black" people. While the concept of institutional racism goes further by eschewing any reference to human intentionality, it retains the white/Black dichotomy in order to identify beneficiary and victim. Thus the scope of the concept of racism is very narrowly defined: the centrality of the white/Black dichotomy denies by definition the possibility that any group other than white people can articulate, practise, or benefit from racism, and suggests that only Black people can be the objects or victims of racism.

Some of West's writing illustrates this difficulty. He clearly distinguishes himself from those he describes as Black nationalists when he argues that their obsession with white racism obstructs the development of the political alliances that are essential to effecting social changes, changes that will alleviate the suffering of Black people in the United States, and that white racism alone cannot explain the socio-economic position of the majority of Black Americans (1994: 82, 98–99). Moreover, he goes so far as to suggest that certain Black nationalist accounts "simply mirror the white supremacist ideals we are opposing" (1994: 99). Yet he seems reluctant to identify any form of racism other than white racism. In his carefully considered discussion of what he describes as "Black–Jewish relations," he employs a distinction between Black anti-Semitism and Jewish anti-Black racism (1994: 104; see also Lerner & West, 1995: 135–156), which suggests that these are qualitatively different phenomena: Jews *articulate* racism, while Blacks *express* anti-Semitism. This interpretation is reinforced by his assertion that Black anti-Semitism is a form of "xenophobia from below" that has a different institutional power when compared with "those racisms that affect their victims from above" (1994: 109–110), even though he claims that both merit moral condemnation.

A similar distinction is implicit in the recent writing of Blauner (1992), who, partly in response to the arguments of one of the present authors, has revised his position significantly since the 1960s. Blauner returns to the common distinction between "race" and ethnicity, arguing that the "peculiarly modern division of the world into a discrete number of hierarchically ranked races is a historic product of Western colonialism" (1992: 61). This, he argues, is a very different process from that associated with ethnicity. Hence, Blauner refrains from analyzing the ideologies employed to justify the exclusion of Italians and Jews in the United States in the 1920s as racism: these populations are described as "white ethnics" who were "viewed racially" (1992: 64). Concerning the period of fascism in Germany, Blauner refers to genocide "where racial imagery was obviously intensified" (1992: 64), but presumably the imagery could never be intensified to the point of warranting description as racism because the Jews were not "Black." Yet, as we shall see shortly in the case of West's writing, Blauner comes very close to breaking with the race-relations problematic when he argues that "much of the popular discourse about race in America today goes awry because ethnic realities get lost under the racial umbrella. The positive meanings and potential of ethnicity are overlooked, even overrun, by the more inflammatory meanings of race" (1992: 61). It is a debate which is firmly grounded in the specific realities of the history and contemporary social structure of the United States, or rather a particular interpretation of those particular realities. It is perhaps not surprising therefore that scholars of racism in the United States have shown so little interest in undertaking comparative research, although there are important exceptions. Some comparative work has been undertaken that compares the United States with South Africa (e.g., van den Berghe, 1978; Fredrickson,

1981), and a comparison between the United States and England achieved prominence some twenty years ago (Katznelson, 1976; for a recent analysis, see Small, 1994). More recently, the "neo-conservative" Sowell (1994) has chosen a comparative international arena to demonstrate what he sees as the explanatory power of his thesis, although it is arguable whether this constitutes a contribution to the sociology of racism. But the vast bulk of work on racism by scholars in the United States focusses on the United States itself. This may be explained as the outcome of a benign ethnocentrism, but one wonders whether it is not also a function of the limited applicability of a theory of racism that is so closely tied to the race-relations paradigm and a Black/white dichotomy that it has limited potential to be used to analyze social formations where there is no "Black" presence.

Yet there is evidence of an increasingly conscious unease with this race-relations paradigm and the Black/white dichotomy. For example, as we have already noted, West argues in a recent book that "race matters": "Race is the most explosive issue in American life precisely because it forces us to confront the tragic facts of poverty and paranoia, despair and distrust. In short, a candid examination of race matters takes us to the core of the crisis of American democracy (1994: 155–156). But he also argues that it is necessary to formulate new frameworks and languages in order not only to comprehend the current crisis in the United States, but also to identify solutions to it (1994: 11). Indeed, he asserts that it is imperative to move beyond the narrow framework of "dominant liberal and conservative views of race in America," views that are formulated with a "worn-out vocabulary" (1994: 4). But it seems that West does not accept that the idea of "race" itself is an example of this exhausted language, for he employs it throughout with apparently little hesitation, despite the fact that he believes that the manner in which "we set up the terms for discussing racial issues shapes our perception and response to these issues" (1994: 6). Later in the book, he seems to be on the verge of following through the logic of this argument to its ultimate conclusion when he argues that the Clarence Thomas/Anita Hill hearings demonstrate that "the very framework of racial reasoning" needs to be called into question in order to reinterpret the Black freedom struggle not as an issue of "skin pigmentation and racial phenotype," but, instead, as an issue of ethics and politics (1994: 38). And yet West cannot follow through the logic of this argument to the point of acknowledging that there cannot be a place for the use of "race" as an analytical concept in the social sciences.

But there is a transatlantic trade in theories of racism and this is now a two-way trade. Not only are some scholars in the United States aware of debates and arguments generated in Europe (including those contributions that question some of the key assumptions which characterize the debate in the United States), but some have also acknowledged and responded to one of the present authors, who has criticized both the use of "race" as an analytical concept and the way in which the concept of racism has been inflated (e.g., Miles, 1982, 1989, 1993). Recent contributions by Wellman (1993), Blauner (1992), Omi and Winant (1993, 1994), and Goldberg (1993) all refer to and comment on these arguments, with varying degrees of enthusiasm. Interestingly, they all seem to ignore the writing of Lieberman and his associates (e.g., Lieberman, 1968; Reynolds, 1992) in the United States, who argue for a position that overlaps in important respects the one outlined here.

Goldberg offers perhaps the most complex and thoughtful response in the course of a wide-ranging and, in part, philosophically inspired analysis of contemporary racisms and of the conceptual language required to analyze them. His important analysis requires a more extended evaluation than is possible in the limited space available here, so we have chosen to focus instead on the work of Omi and Winant. This is in part because their writing has already had considerable influence in both the United States and Britain, partly because of the way in which some of their key concepts have parallels in the equally influential work of Gilroy (1987). And this influence is deserved. There is much to admire and to learn from their theoretical and conceptual innovations. We prefer to employ a concept of *racialized* formation (rather than racial formation), but we agree that racialized categories are socially created, transformed, and destroyed through historical time (see Omi & Winant, 1994: 55). We can recognize that it is essential to differentiate between "race" (although we do not use "race" as a *concept,* but, rather, we capture its use in everyday life by referring to the *idea* of "race") and the concept of racism, a distinction that allows us to make a further distinction between racialization and racism (although Omi and Winant refer to this as a distinction between racial awareness and racial essentialism (compare Omi & Winant, 1994: 71 with Miles, 1989: 73–84). And we also agree that it is essential to retain the concept of racism to identify a multiplicity of historically specific racisms, with the consequence that there is "nothing inherently white about racism" (Omi & Winant, 1994: 72; see also 1994: 73, and compare with Miles, 1989: 57–60; 1993). Wellman (1993: 3) is simply mistaken when he claims that Miles argues that racism is not a useful concept.

It is important to highlight these areas of agreement prior to considering Omi and Winant's defence of the use of the idea of "race" as an analytical concept in the social sciences in order to indicate both the innovations that they have effected within the discussion in the United States about racism, and their failure to pursue the logic of these innovations to their ultimate conclusion. Partly as a result of their emphasis upon the way in which the idea of "race" has been socially constructed and reconstructed, there is now a debate within the literature in the United States about the theoretical and analytical status of the idea of "race." Other scholars in the United States have made important contributions to the development of this debate, notably Lieberman (1968), Fields (1990), and Roediger (1994). Fields's work is especially significant because it reaches a conclusion that is close to that reached by one of the present authors (see Miles, 1982; 1993: 27–52). Omi and Winant have criticized Fields's conclusions in the course of defending their continued use of "race" as analytical concept, and it is therefore important to reflect upon the arguments and evidence that they have employed.

Omi and Winant offer two criticisms of the position that the idea of "race" should be analyzed exclusively as a social or ideological construct (1993: 5). First, they suggest that it fails to recognize the social impact of the longevity of the concept of "race." Second, they claim that, as a result of this longevity, "race is an almost indissoluble part of our identities," a fact which is not recognized by those who argue that "race" is an ideological construct. They are mistaken on both counts. The writing of Miles highlights the historical evolution of the meanings attributed to the idea of "race" and, for example, in his discussions of colonialism and of the articulation between racism and nationalism, stresses the way in which the idea of belonging to the "white race" was central to the construction of the identity of the British bourgeoisie and working class (1982, 1993). Indeed, these claims can be refuted simply by citing a quotation from Fields (1990: 118) that Omi and Winant themselves reproduce (1993: 5). Fields writes:

> Nothing handed down from the past could keep race alive if we did not constantly reinvent and re-ritualise it to fit our own terrain. If race lives on today, it can do so only because we continue to create and re-create it in our social life, continue to verify it, and thus continue to need a social vocabulary that will allow us to make sense, not of what our ancestors did then, but of what we choose to do now.

Thus, Fields certainly does not deny that in the contemporary world people use the idea of "race" to classify themselves and others into social collectivities and act in ways consistent with such a belief, actions that collectively produce structured exclusion. And, hence, Omi and Winant's critique is shown to be vacuous. Fields's key objective is to critique the way in which historians invoke the idea of "race" to construct explanations for events and processes in the past, and her critique applies equally to the work of sociologists such as Omi and Winant, who have reinvented and re-ritualized the idea of "race" to fit their own terrain within the academy (which is after all only one more arena of social life). Let us examine how Omi and Winant reinvent and thereby reify the idea of "race" in the course of their sociological analysis. Consider the following claim: "One of the first things we notice about people when we meet them (along with their sex) is their race" (1994: 59). Elsewhere, they argue that "to be raceless is akin to being genderless. Indeed, when one cannot identify another's race, a microsociological 'crisis of interpretation' results ..." (1993: 5). How are we to interpret this assertion? While they also claim that "race is ... a socially constructed way of differentiating human beings" (1994: 65), the former assertion is at the very least open to interpretation as suggesting that "race" is an objective quality inherent in a person's being, that every human being is a member of a "race," and that such membership is inscribed in a person's visible appearance. It is in the interstices of such ambiguity that the idea of "race" as a biological fact does not just "live on" but is actively re-created by social scientists in the course of their academic practice.

This argument commonly stimulates incomprehension on the part of scholars in the United States, who echo arguments employed in some critiques of this position in Britain. Thus, it is often said, "How can you deny analytical status to the idea of race and ultimately the existence of race when blacks and whites are so obviously different and when all the evidence demonstrates that their life chances differ too?" In responding to this question, it is necessary first to problematize what it takes for granted, specifically that the "Black/white" division is *obvious*. The quality of obviousness is not inherent in a phenomenon, but is the outcome of a social process in the course of which meaning is attributed to the phenomenon in a particular historical and social context. The meaning is learnt by those who are its subject and object. They therefore learn to habitually recognize it, and perhaps to pass on this signification and knowledge to others, with the result that the quality of obviousness attributed to the phenomenon is reproduced through historical time and social space.

Skin colour is one such phenomenon. Its visibility is not inherent in its existence but is a product of signification: human beings identify skin colour to mark or symbolize other phenomena in a historical context in which other significations occur. When human practices include and exclude people in the light of the signification of skin colour, collective identities are produced and social inequalities are structured. It is for this reason that historical studies of the meanings attributed to skin colour in different historical contexts and through time are of considerable importance. And it is in relation to such studies that one can inquire into the continuities and discontinuities with contemporary processes of signification that sustain the obviousness of skin colour as a social mark. Historically and contemporarily, differences in skin colour have been and are signified as a mark, which suggests the existence of different "races." But people do not see "race": rather, they observe certain combinations of real and sometimes imagined somatic and cultural characteristics that they attribute meaning to with the idea of "race." A difference of skin colour is not essential to the process of marking: other somatic features can be and are signified in order to racialize. Indeed, in some historical circumstances, the absence of somatic difference has been central to the powerful impact of racism: the racialized "enemy within" can be identified as a threatening presence even more effectively if the group is not "obviously different," because "they" can be imagined to be everywhere.

Omi and Winant reify this social process and reach the conclusion that all human beings belong to a "race" because they seek to construct their analytical concepts to reproduce directly the common-sense ideologies of the everyday world. Because the idea of "race" continues to be widely used in everyday life in the United States (and Britain) to classify human beings and to interpret their behaviour, Omi and Winant believe that social scientists must employ a *concept* of race. This assumption is the source of our disagreement with them. We argue that one of the contemporary challenges in the analysis of racisms is to develop a conceptual vocabulary that explicitly acknowledges that people use the *idea* of "race" in the everyday world while simultaneously refusing to use the idea of "race" as an analytical *concept* when social scientists analyze the discourses and practices of the everyday world. It is not the *concept* of "race" that "continues to play a fundamental role in structuring and representing the social world" (Omi & Winant, 1994: 55) but, rather, the *idea* of "race," and the task of social scientists is to develop a theoretical framework for the analysis of this process of structuring and representing that breaks completely with the reified language of biological essentialism. Hence, we object fundamentally to Omi and Winant's project of developing a critical theory of the concept of "race" (1993: 6–9) because we also recognize the importance of historical context and contingency in the framing of racialized categories and the social construction of racialized experiences (cf. Omi & Winant, 1993: 6): we believe that historical context requires us to criticize all concepts of "race," and this can be done by means of a concept of racialization. Omi and Winant's defence of the concept of "race" is a classic example of the way in which the academy in the United States continues to racialize the world.

Furthermore, the concept of racialization employed by Omi and Winant is not fully developed, nor do they use it in a sustained analytical manner, because it is grounded in "race relations" sociology, a sociology that reifies the notion of "race" and thereby implies the existence of "racial groups" as monolithic categories of existence. Additionally, they fail to take into account the impact of the social relations of production within the racialization process. We, on the other hand, advance the position that the process of racialization takes place and has its effects in the context of class and production relations and that the idea of "race" may indeed not even be explicitly articulated in the racialization process (see Miles, 1989, 1993).

CONCLUSION
▼

West begins the first essay in his book *Race Matters* with a reference to the Los Angeles riots of April 1992. He denies that they were either a "race riot or a class rebellion." Rather, he continues,

> ... this monumental upheaval was a multi-racial, trans-class, and largely male display of social rage.... Of those arrested, only 36 percent were black, more than a third had full-time jobs, and most claimed to shun political affiliation. What we witnessed in Los Angeles was the consequence of a lethal linkage of economic decline, cultural decay, and political lethargy in American life. Race was the visible catalyst, not the underlying cause. (1994: 3–4)

And he concludes by claiming that the meaning of the riots is obscured because we are trapped by the narrow framework imposed by the dominant views of "race" in the United States.

The *Los Angeles Times* Opinion Editor, Jack Miles, rendered a different version of the narrow framework of the Black/white dichotomy. In an essay in the October 1992 issue of the *Atlantic Monthly* entitled "Blacks vs Browns," Miles suggested that Latinos were taking jobs that the nation, by dint of the historical crimes committed against them, owed to African Americans. He blamed Latinos for the poverty in African-American communities — a gross misattribution of responsibility — while reinforcing "race" as a relevant category of social and analytical value. His confusion was revealing: the "two societies, one black, one white — separate and unequal" dichotomy made famous by the 1968 report of the National Advisory Commission on Civil Disorders cannot provide an analytical framework to deconstruct the post-Fordist racialized social relations of the 1990s.

The meaning of West's argument is constructed by what is not said as much as by what is. There is a silence about the definition of "race riot": presumably, the events of April 1992 would have been a race riot if the principal actors had been "Blacks" and "whites." Hence, West refers only to "race" as the visible catalyst. Rodney King was "obviously black" and the policemen who arrested him were "obviously white." But the riots themselves did not fit the race-relations paradigm because the rioters and those who became the victims of the riot were not exclusively Blacks and whites. Indeed, as the media were framing the events of April 1992 in Black/white terms in the great melodrama of race relations, the first image across the airwaves was of men atop a car waving the Mexican flag! Thus, "Hispanic" may signify presumptively as "white" in the ethno-"racial" dynamics that rest on a system of neat racialized categories, but this has little to do with the popular understanding and experience of Latinos. The outcome of such practices has led to superficial analysis of the full impact of the riots within the context of a changing political economy. The analytical task is therefore to explain the complex nature of the structural changes associated with the emergence of the post-Fordist socioeconomic landscape and the reconfigured city's racialized social relations.

Perhaps half of the businesses looted or burned were owned by Korean Americans and another third or so were owned by Mexican Americans/Latinos and Cuban Americans. Those engaged in the looting and burning certainly included African Americans, but poor, recent, and often undocumented immigrants and refugees from Mexico and Central America were equally prominent. Of those arrested, 51 percent were Latinos and 36 percent were African Americans. And, of those who died in the civil unrest, about half were African Americans and about a third were Latinos. All this is only surprising if one begins with the assumption that the events were or could have been "race riots." But such an assumption is problematic for two reasons.

First, academics, media reporters, and politicians "conspired" to use the vocabulary of "race" to make sense of the Los Angeles riots because it is a central component of everyday, common-sense discourse in the United States. And when it became overwhelmingly apparent that it was not a Black/white riot, the language of "race" was nevertheless unthinkingly retained by switching to the use of the notion of "multiracial" in order to encompass the diversity of historical and cultural origins of the participants and victims. Therefore, while the race-relations paradigm was dealt a serious blow by the reality of riots, the vocabulary of "race" was retained. But — and here we find the source of West's unease — the idea of "race" is so firmly embedded in common sense that it cannot easily encompass a reference to Koreans or Hispanics or Latinos, for these are neither Black nor white. It is thus not surprising that pundits and scholars such as West stumble over "racial" ambiguity. The clash of racialized language with a changing political economy presents challenges for scholars and activists alike.

Second, if one had begun with an analysis grounded simultaneously in history and political economy rather than with the supremely ideological notion of race relations, one would have quickly concluded that the actors in any riot in central Los Angeles would probably be ethnically diverse. Large-scale inward migration from Mexico and Central America and from Southeast Asia into California has coincided with a restructuring of the Californian economy, the loss of major manufacturing jobs, and large-scale internal migration within the urban sprawl of "greater" Los Angeles, with the consequence that the spatial, ethnic, and class structure that underlay the Watts riots of 1965 had been transformed into a much more complex set of relationships. The most general conditions were structural in nature, and thus the decline and shift in the manufacturing base in Los Angeles was not unique but represented a shift in the mode of capital accumulation worldwide (from Fordist to Flexible). In order to analyze those relationships, there is no need to employ a concept of "race": indeed, its retention is a significant hindrance. But it is also necessary to draw upon the insights consequent upon the creation of the concept of racisms. The complex relationships of exploitation and resistance, grounded in differences of class, gender, and ethnicity, give rise to a multiplicity of ideological constructions of the racialized Other. For, while the idea of "race" does not matter outside the process of racialization, to which academics are active contributors, the racisms employed in Los Angeles and elsewhere to naturalize, inferiorize, exclude, and sustain privilege certainly *do* matter.

REFERENCES
▼

Banton, M. (1967). *Race relations*. London: Tavistock.

———. (1987). *Racial theories*. Cambridge: Cambridge University Press.

Barkan, E. (1992). *The retreat of scientific racism: Changing concept of race in Britain and the United States between the wars*. Cambridge: Cambridge University Press.

Blauner, B. (1992). Talking past each other: Black and white languages of race. *The American Prospect, 10*, 55–64.

Essed, P. (1991). *Understanding everyday racism: An interdisciplinary theory*. Newbury Park, CA: Sage.

Fields, B.J. (1990). Slavery, race and ideology in the United States of America. *New Left Review, 181*, 95–118.

Fredrickson, G.M. (1981). *White supremacy*. New York: Oxford University Press.

Gilroy, P. (1987). *There ain't no black in the Union Jack: The cultural politics of race and nation*. London: Hutchinson.

Goldberg, D.T. (1990). The social formation of racist discourse. In D.T. Goldberg (Ed.), *Anatomy of racism* (pp. 295–318). Minneapolis: University of Minnesota Press.

———. (1993). *Racist culture: Philosophy and the politics of Meaning*. Oxford: Blackwell.

Guillaumin, C. (1972). *L'Idéologie raciste*. Paris: Mouton.

————. (1995). *Racism, sexism, power and ideology.* London: Routledge.

Hernstein, R.J., & Murray, C. (1994). *The bell curve: Intelligence and class structure in American life.* New York: The Free Press.

hooks, b. (1990). *Yearning: Race, gender and cultural politics.* Boston: South End.

Joshi, S., & Carter, B. (1984). The role of labour in the creation of a racist Britain. *Race and Class, 25*(3), 53–70.

Karenga, M. (1993). *Introduction to Black studies.* Los Angeles: University of Sankore Press.

Katznelson, I. (1976). *Black men, white cities.* Chicago: University of Chicago Press.

Layton-Henry, Z. (1992). *The politics of immigration.* Oxford: Blackwell.

Lerner, M., and West, C. (1995). *Jews and Blacks: Let the healing begin.* New York: G.P. Putnam's Sons.

Lieberman, L. (1968). The debate over race: A study in the sociology of knowledge. *Phylon, 39,* 127–141.

Miles, R. (1982). *Racism and migrant labour: A critical test.* London: Routledge & Kegan Paul.

————. (1984). Marxism versus the sociology of race relations. *Ethnic and Racial Studies, 7*(2), 217–237.

————. (1989). *Racism.* London: Routledge.

————. (1993). *Racism after "race relations."* London: Routledge.

Montagu, A. (1972). *Statement on race.* London: Oxford University Press.

Omi, M., & Winant, M. (1993). On the theoretical status of the concept of race. In C. McCarthy & W. Crichlow (Eds.), *Race, identity and representation.* New York: Routledge.

————. (1994). *Racial formation in the United States: From the 1960s to the 1990s* (2nd ed.). New York: Routledge.

Rex, J. (1970). *Race relations in sociological theory.* London: Weidenfeld & Nicolson.

Reynolds, L.T. (1992). A retrospective on 'race': The career of a concept. *Sociological Focus, 25*(1), 1–14.

Roediger, D. (1994). *Towards the abolition of whiteness: Essays on race, politics and working class history.* London: Verso.

Small, S. (1994). *Racialized barriers: The Black experience in the United States and England in the 1980s.* London: Routledge.

Solomos, J. (1989). *Race and racism in contemporary Britain.* London: Macmillan.

Sowell, T. (1994). *Race and culture: A world view.* New York: Basic.

van den Berghe, P.L. (1978). *Race and racism: A comparative perspective.* New York: John Wiley.

Wellman, D. (1993). *Portraits of white racism* (2nd ed.). Cambridge: Cambridge University Press.

West, C. (1994). *Race matters.* New York: Vintage.

Wilson, W.J. (1987). *The truly disadvantaged.* Chicago: University of Chicago Press.

SOCIAL NETWORKS AND INSTITUTIONAL COMPLETENESS: FROM TERRITORY TO TIES

SHELDON GOLDENBERG AND VALERIE A. HAINES

INTRODUCTION
▼

Ever since its introduction in 1964 by Raymond Breton, the concept of "institutional completeness" has played an important role in the study of ethnic communities in Canadian sociology (Driedger & Church, 1974; Balakrishnan, 1976; 1982; Makabe, 1979; Brym, Gillespie, & Gillis, 1985; Pineo, 1988). Yet, despite its popularity, the concept itself and the assumptions that underpin it have not been investigated systematically.[1] To begin to fill this gap, we locate studies of institutional completeness against the backdrop of changing views of the nature of community. After documenting the shift from an ecological to a network conception of community that occurred in community and urban sociology, we (1) establish that the current framing of the concept of institutional completeness rests on an ecological foundation, and then (2) investigate the implications for studying institutional completeness of shifting from an ecological to a network concept of community.

COMPETING CONCEPTIONS OF COMMUNITY
▼

The concept of community has been the subject of an ongoing debate in the sociological literature (Hillery, 1955; Effrat, 1973; Poplin, 1973; Wellman, 1979; Wellman, Carrington, & Hall, 1988). In his analysis of competing definitions of community, Hillery (1955: 118) identified three points of convergence among them: social interaction, a geographical area, and a common tie or ties. The best-developed and most influential formulation of this approach to community is found in the writings of the members of the Chicago School of Sociology and their followers (cf. Hawley, 1950; Duncan, 1961). According to their ecological conception, communities are clearly discernible, spatially delimited entities with well-defined boundaries (Haines, 1985). Spatial proximity is assumed to be the basis of commonality in outlook and action of community members.[2]

The ecological conception of community was widely accepted at the time that Breton was writing. Even at this time, however, it was not without its critics. Webber's (1963, 1964) concepts of "community without propinquity" and "nonplace urban realm" challenged its domain assumption of spatial proximity as the basis of commonality in outlook and action in human communities. This call for a shift from territory to interaction as the defining characteristic of community was reinforced and extended by Martindale and Hanson's (1969) community as a "systematic unity of life," Tilly's (1973) "community of interest," Effrat's (1973) "nonspatial community of limited liability," and, most recently, by the development of network conceptions of community, including Craven and Wellman's (1973) network city, Wellman and Leighton's (1979) network analytic approach to the community question, and Fischer's (1982) personal networks in towns and cities. Most explicit in the case of the network formulations, this approach defines communities "by links among members rather than by criteria external to the networks, such as geographical mapping" (Craven & Wellman, 1973: 82).

Proponents of the aspatial approach to community do not deny the reality of the place community. But by treating place communities as a special case of community (Webber, 1964; Berry & Kasarda, 1977; Wellman & Leighton, 1979), they avoid the standard ecological assumption that spatial proximity is a sufficient condition for community. Once this assumption is discarded, the spatiality of any community becomes an empirical question (Craven & Wellman, 1973) and the issue of boundary specification becomes a central concern.

THE ECOLOGICAL FRAMING OF INSTITUTIONAL COMPLETENESS
▼

In community and urban sociology, the network approach has been taken seriously. What was once accepted without question by community and urban sociologists as the proper focus for their studies — bounded local areas — must now be defended as a legitimate object of study (cf. Guest & Lee, 1983; Campbell, 1990). But, despite widespread acceptance of the case for aspatial communities, the discussion that follows makes it clear that it has proven difficult to link the network approach to studies of institutional completeness. Like studies of Canadian ethnic communities more generally, most such studies remain firmly grounded in the ecological tradition. In these cases, the ethnic institutions and their participants are studied within geographically defined communities.

In Breton's original formulation, the concept of institutional completeness was used to explain the integration of immigrants in the receiving country; that is, into the community of their own ethnicity, the native/receiving community, or other ethnic communities. Integration in all directions is understood to occur through the formation of informal social networks of companionship ties (e.g., visiting friends, meeting socially with co-workers). When an immigrant is "transplanted from one country to another, he has to reconstruct his interpersonal 'field.' He will rebuild in a new community a network of personal affiliations" (Breton, 1964: 194). To satisfy other needs such as making a living and attending church, immigrants must use existing social institutions. Thus, the "social organization of the communities which the immigrant contacts in the receiving community" is a "crucial" factor "bearing on the absorption of immigrants" (Breton, 1964: 193). In the case of the ethnic communities of immigrants, Breton's primary focus, integration is a function of the degree of institutional completeness of these communities: the higher the degree of institutional completeness of an ethnic community, the more institutional services (e.g., religious, educational, political, national, professional, welfare and mutual aid, communication) it can provide for its members and, therefore, the greater "its capacity to attract the immigrant within its social boundaries" (Breton, 1964: 194). "Institutional completeness would be at its extreme," then, "whenever the ethnic community could perform all the services required by its members. Members would never have to make use of native institutions for the satisfaction of any of their needs, such as education, work, food and clothing, medical care, or social assistance" (Breton, 1964: 194).

Breton's strategy for conceptualizing and operationalizing the ethnic composition of immigrants' interpersonal relations moved his analysis of the effects of community characteristics on the integration of immigrants in a network direction. The focus on ties among individuals rather than territory that this approach to the study of integration entails is reinforced by his suggestion that institutional completeness could be treated as the extent to which members "make use" of ethnic institutions to satisfy their needs (Breton, 1964: 194).[3] But because Breton assumed that the social boundaries of the ethnic communities that he studied were coterminous with the spatial boundaries of the city of Montreal, he did not exploit these network metaphors. Instead of measuring actors' participation in ethnic institutions wherever it takes place,[4] he measured the degree of institutional completeness of ethnic communities by counting the number of churches, welfare organizations, newspapers, and periodicals that were found in each Montreal-based ethnic community.[5] Breton's conception of ethnic community reproduces the ecological view of the nature of community both in its focus on social relationships within a local area (the city of Montreal) and in its lack of concern for the problem of boundary specification.

This ecological conception of ethnic community became a hallmark of subsequent studies of institutional completeness. Like Breton (1964) before them, Driedger & Church (1974) studied institutional completeness within spatially defined communities. But, unlike Breton, who randomly sampled census tracts of Montreal, they chose census tracts of the city of Winnipeg that were characterized by particularly high ethnic concentrations. To examine the institutional completeness of these places, they focussed on three local services that were available to members of each ethnic group: churches, voluntary organizations, and schools. This focus cleared the way for their demonstration of the importance of residential segregation for the maintenance of institutional completeness and, through this, ethnic solidarity.

This ecological conception of community also underpins Driedger's (1979, 1980) ethnic-enclavic perspective on the maintenance of urban ethnic boundaries. Presented as the ethnic equivalents of Gans's urban villages, ethnic-enclavic communities develop when "minorities wish to develop a means of control over a population in a specific area" (Driedger, 1979: 74). They are maintained by the joint operation of ethnic-enclavic factors (e.g., residential segregation, institutional completeness, cultural identity, social distance) and social and psychological factors (e.g., ideological vision, historical symbols, charismatic ethnic leadership, social status). For Drieger, then, ethnic enclavity and institutional completeness are logical corollaries of each other.

TOWARD A NETWORK FRAMING OF INSTITUTIONAL COMPLETENESS
▼

Under its ecological framing, institutional completeness is an attribute of an ethnic community that, by virtue of its ecological grounding, is a place community. Because social network analysts view and classify the various aspects of the social world according to their relationships rather than according to their attributes (Knoke & Kuklinski, 1982), grounding the study of institutional completeness in a network concept of community would shift the focus of attention away from attributes of places to the relations among actors in one or more aspatial networks. And, because the spatiality of communities that are defined in this way is an empirical question, defining their boundaries is of theoretical and practical importance. Actors or nodes for the network must be selected and the types of social relationships to be studied must be specified (Laumann, Marsden, & Prensky, 1983).

In the case of institutional completeness, the appropriate nodes and types of social relations have been identified by ecologically based studies: co-ethnics for the nodes, and ethnic educational, religious, political, recreational, national, professional, welfare society, and communication affiliations for the social relationships. Instead of counting the number of ethnic institutions in a particular geographical area, the network framing measures levels of participation of co-ethnics in ethnic institutions regardless of their geographical location.[6]

Studies like the one by Driedger and Church (1974) have demonstrated the importance of residential segregation for the maintenance of institutional completeness and, through this, ethnic identity. The network conception of community does not deny the importance of residential segregation in these processes. What it does suggest is that if ethnic communities can be aspatial communities, then residential segregation may be neither necessary nor sufficient for either process. Because individuals can belong to an ethnic community without living in a particular locality, "residence in an ethnically segregated neighbourhood is one of the least sensitive indicators of a person's ties to an ethnic group" (Reitz, 1980: 117).

Interactions can and do take place within geographically circumscribed areas (e.g., neighbourhoods, census tracts, cities, regions, countries). But not all of the co-ethnics residing in such an area participate in these ethnic institutions, nor does any particular local concentration of ethnic institutions preclude participation by co-ethnics who are widely dispersed in space. As Hawley (1950, 1986) in human ecology, Yancey, Ericksen, and Juliani (1976), in the study of ethnicity, and Wellman (1979), in the study of the community question, have stressed, advances in transportation and communication technologies have "liberated" community from spatial constraints.[7] Spatial boundaries and social boundaries need not be and frequently are not coterminous. Once the aspatiality of ethnic communities is recognized, then, non-participation in local ethnic institutions and participation in non-local ethnic institutions become two sides of the same coin. Boissevain's (1971) analysis of the Italian community of Montreal provides a strategic illustration of the former; Bruser Maynard's (1972) work *Raisins and Almonds* illustrates the latter.

Building on the element of Breton's work that focussed on the participation of individuals in ethnic institutions, Boissevain (1971) viewed the

Italian community of Montreal as "a viable whole, composed of multiple overlapping networks of social relations originating in the fields of kinships, friendship, neighbourhood and the marketplace, which are given a certain territorial unity by the parish structure of the Italian national church" (1971: 164). It is largely a geographically concentrated community. Most Italians live near relatives, and see a good deal of them on a frequent basis: "57% of the Canadian born (and 52% of the immigrants) in our general sample chose to buy houses in neighbourhoods with which they were already familiar and in which relatives and other Italians lived" (1971: 155). But this means that 43 percent of the second generation, most of whom grew to adulthood in a community exhibiting high levels of institutional completeness,[8] chose to buy houses elsewhere. This suggests that residential concentration does not necessarily guarantee a strong commitment to the ethnic community and participation in ethnic institutions, although we would be the first to agree with Boissevain that non-local residents can also participate in ethnic services and institutions. Boissevain also notes that only 57 percent of the Canadian born attend church services in Italian at least once a year, and 53 percent of this sample use no Italian at work. This seems to further confirm our contention that, at least for some of those living in predominantly Italian neighbourhoods, it is still not the case that spatial proximity assures meaningful participation in ethnic institutional life.

Boissevain's focus on multiple overlapping networks and his conclusion that the Italians of Montreal form a community linking "people who are geographically separated and who may even belong to different socio-economic classes" (1971: 152) moved his study of ethnic communities in the direction that our network reconceptualization of institutional completeness calls for. His observations that 70 percent of immigrants and 28 percent of those born in Canada receive letters from Italy at least once a fortnight and that, for many, both immigration to Canada in the first place and subsequent settlement patterns reflect financial and other help obtained from kin at some considerable distance, are consistent with an aspatial conception of community. But because his focus is "The Italians of Montreal," Boissevain does not capitalize on the implicit aspatiality of his conception of community. Like Breton before him, he grafts aspatial networks of social relationships onto an ecological foundation.

This description applies equally to Brettell's (1981) comparison of the extent of Portuguese ethnic-community formation in Toronto and Paris. Framed by the contrast between a geographical (ecological) conception of community and its network-based counterpart, Brettell (1981: 13) used data on the timing of Portuguese immigration to Toronto and Paris, the numbers of immigrants, their settlement patterns within these cities, their contact with co-ethnics in Toronto and Paris, and the levels of institutional completeness of their ethnic communities in these cities to sustain the conclusion that " 'community' in either a geographical sense or an ethnic network sense does not exist for Portuguese immigrants in Paris as it does among Portuguese immigrants in Toronto." The evidence that Brettell uses to support this conclusion does establish the absence of a geographically based ethnic community in Paris. At the same time, however, it counters her argument for the absence of a network-based community for Portuguese immigrants in Paris, if the aspatiality of a network conception of community is taken seriously. The fact that "annual religious festivals are celebrated with fellow villagers during the summer visits to Portugal, not on the streets of Paris" (1981: 13), the fact that for Paris immigrants the community of orientation is "in Portugal itself, in the village they have left" (1981: 13), and the fact that this "community is sustained by a long distance social network" (1981: 14) through village newspapers sent by village priests; visits with fellow villagers during summer vacations in Portugal; and travel by fellow villagers to Paris for visits or jobs, all point to ties among co-ethnics that span national boundaries and, through them, to community in an ethnic-network sense.

The importance of taking the aspatiality of communities seriously is made even clearer in Bruser Maynard's autobiographical *Raisins and Almonds* (1972). This is her account of growing up in various small towns in Saskatchewan and Manitoba in the 1920s. Her family was most often the only Jewish family in town. Nonetheless, she was able to retain her Jewish identity by virtue of her father's willingness to send away for mail-order Sunday school leaflets from a rabbi in Winnipeg (1972: 20), and through her family's occasional stays with relatives in that city (1972: 66). Other important non-local connections included a subscription to a Jewish newspaper from New York (1972: 163), Sunday in-gatherings of Jewish families from other nearby Prairie towns (1972: 29), and even her family's collection of Jewish works of theology and literature (1972: 163). Bruser Maynard's illustrations can easily be supplemented by others that reflect the importance of non-local institutional support for ethnic identity. Maintenance of Jewish identity has been related to taking jobs at remote Jewish summer camps, attendance at religious services on special holidays in a town down the highway or only when an itinerant rabbi passes through, memberships in national or even international welfare organizations such as the B'nai B'rith, or even having Jewish pen-pals in New York or Israel. In all of these cases, the services required to maintain ethnic identity are provided by ethnic institutions that are non-local.

Studies of institutional completeness that are grounded in the ecological conception of community can account for situations where localized social ties comprise a majority of urbanites' social relationships. What shifting to a social-network conception of community allows and, in fact, demands is the investigation of the impact of non-local ties on the processes of ethnic identification and assimilation. Localized social interaction does occur, but the evidence (Craven & Wellman, 1973; Wellman, 1979; Wellman & Leighton, 1979; Fischer, 1982) suggests that "such ties, while real and important, comprise a minority of most urbanites' social relationships" (Guest & Lee, 1983: 218). Social ties with co-ethnics can link them to one another across geographical space, maintaining a situation in which ethnicity remains important even without spatial proximity.

CONCLUSION
▼

Studies of institutional completeness have focussed primarily on the implications of co-ethnic affiliations for ethnic identification and assimilation. In its ecological formulation, where spatial proximity is key, participation in ethnic institutions presupposes residence in the area in which these institutions are found. This assumption of the coterminality of ethnic communities and place communities has been challenged by research using aspatial conceptions of community. Advances in transportation and communication technologies have expanded opportunities for maintaining ethnic identification through ties with geographically dispersed co-ethnics. To adapt Wellman's (1988: 37–38) phrasing, the network framing of institutional completeness confronts head on "the existence of ramified, spatially dispersed networks of 'community ties,' even when they do not fit within bounded neighborhood or kinship solidarities."

Where networks of community ties do fit within bounded neighbourhoods, the ecological and network conceptions of institutional completeness converge. In these instances, the structure of institutionally complete ethnic enclaves is, as Craven and Wellman (1972: 71) point out, "reminiscent of the dense 'village' networks," networks which they suggest are defined by a proliferation of interactional ties among members that are contained within the boundaries of the village and neighbouring farms. It does not follow, however, that only "self-contained urban villages" (Wellman, 1979: 1207) are institutionally complete, as the ecological approach suggests.[9] If ethnic communities can be aspatial communities, then institutionally complete communities can assume other network configurations. Linking the study of institutional completeness with the study of social networks not only sensitizes researchers to this possibility, but also provides them with the concepts and techniques with which to investigate it.

"Urban villages" or "ethnic enclaves" can be studied using the network approach. In network terms, such communities exhibit high density, relatively small size, and low diversity, where "diversity" refers both to geographic range and to heterogeneity of alter's attributes (e.g., religion, sex).[10] Unlike its ecological counterpart, however, the network approach can also handle other network configurations of institutionally complete communities such as those illustrated by Brettell's Portuguese and Bruser Maynard's Jews. Size, density, and diversity are not the only network concepts that can be used to characterize the structure of ethnic communities. Institutionally complete communities may also vary across other properties of networks such as reachability, anchorage, and composition, on the one hand, and features of individual ties such as frequency, intensity, multiplexity, and duration, on the other. Which measures are most appropriate is an empirical question. By tapping the number and the nature of ties that connect co-ethnics, the network approach can avoid the limitations of the enumerative approach to the measurement of institutional completeness and, at the same time, bring studies of institutional completeness into line with recent developments in community and urban sociology.

NOTES
▼

1. Discussions of institutional completeness routinely appear in textbook treatments of ethnic communities, but the concept often seems to be ritualistically cited rather than examined. It is not without its critics, however. Roberts and Boldt (1979) and Baureiss (1981) have criticized the "enumerative approach" that Breton and others have used to operationalize the concept of institutional completeness. Roberts and Boldt do not deny the value of counting the number of ethnic institutions, but argue that the nature or quality of these institutions must also be considered. Working from a distinction between social organizations (the objects of Breton's enumerative approach) and social institutions, Baureiss extends this critique to suggest that ethnic institutional structure (i.e., kinship, language retention) must also be assessed.

2. Other views of community as a social group with a territorial dimension include Hiller's (1941) community as a local social group, Janowitz's (1952) community of limited ability, and Warren's (1963) functional definition of community.

3. Providing ethnic services and making use of ethnic services are not independent phenomena. A viable ethnic community requires participants; empty schools and churches are presumably not to be considered to be indicators of a high degree of institutional completeness.

4. Using data collected by O'Bryan, Reitz, and Kuplowska (1976), Reitz (1980) measures ethnic participation for a sample of respondents from ten ethnic groups and five major Canadian cities. He presents an interesting discussion of institutional completeness that translates the concept into "institutional strength" and compares members of the various ethnic groups with respect to participation in ethnic institutions. Unfortunately, Reitz cannot tell us where the institutions are with which his respondents are variably connected. It is easy to assume that they are in all cases local institutions, but they need not be so, and it is just this possibility of non-local affiliations with ethnic institutions that is addressed by our network reconceptualization.

5. Even in ecological terms, this operational definition of the relevant community is problematic. Should one use the Montreal metropolitan boundaries or Montreal proper? Should one try to identify the boundaries of ethnic communities within the larger city? Is it relevant how diffused or concentrated ethnic institutions may be within the overall urban area? Driedger and Church (1974) give such issues more attention than is apparent in Breton's original formulation of institutional completeness.

6. Network analysts distinguish between analysis of whole networks and egocentric (personal) networks (Wellman, 1988; Marsden, 1990). Because the whole network approach presupposes closed populations, our network reframing calls for the collection of egocentric network data.

7. Keller (1968: 61) attempts to capture this distinction in her discussion of a "shift from a neighboring of *place* to a neighboring of *taste*."

8. The social organization of this Italian community includes newspapers printed in Italian, stores in which service people and customers ordinarily speak Italian, workplaces in which supervisors and employees customarily speak Italian, churches in which services are conducted in Italian, and Italian ethnic voluntary organizations and associations. An enumeration of ethnic organizations would result in the classification of this community as relatively high in terms of institutional completeness.

9. Wellman's (1979: 1207) comments on institutional completeness can be read as a variation on this suggestion: "The argument suggests that primary ties are often dispersed among multiple, sparsely interconnected social networks. These networks, by their very nature, are not 'institutionally complete' (Breton, 1964), self-contained 'urban villages.' "

10. Many network analysts (Burt, 1983; Campbell, Marsden, & Hurlbert, 1986; Marsden, 1987) treat size, density, and diversity as dimensions of network range.

REFERENCES

▼

Balakrishnan, B.R. (1976). Ethnic residential segregation in the metropolitan areas of Canada. *Canadian Journal of Sociology, 1*(4), 481–498.

———. (1982). Changing patterns of ethnic residential segregation in the metropolitan areas of Canada. *Canadian Review of Sociology and Anthropology, 19*(1), 92–110.

Baureiss, Gunter. (1981). Institutional completeness: its use and misuses in ethnic relations research. *Journal of Ethnic Studies, 9*(2), 101–110.

Berry, Brian, J.L., & Kasarda, John D. (1977). *Contemporary urban ecology.* New York: Macmillan.

Boissevain, Jeremy. (1971). The Italians of Montreal. In W.E. Mann (Ed.), *Canada: A sociological profile* (pp. 150–165). Toronto: Copp Clark.

Breton, Raymond. (1964). Institutional completeness of ethnic communities and the personal relations of immigrants. *American Journal of Sociology, 70*(2), 193–205.

Brettell, Caroline B. (1981). Is the ethnic community inevitable? A comparison of the settlement patterns of Portuguese immigrants in Toronto and Paris. *Journal of Ethnic Studies, 9*(3), 1–17.

Bruser Maynard, Fredelle. (1972). *Raisins and almonds.* Toronto: Doubleday.

Brym, Robert J., Gillespie, Michael W., & Gillis, A.R. (1985). Anomie, opportunity, and the density of ethnic ties: Another view of Jewish outmarriage in Canada. *Canadian Review of Sociology and Anthropology, 22*(1), 102–112.

Burt, Ronald S. (1983). Range. In Ronald S. Burt and Michael J. Minor (Eds.), *Applied network analysis: A methodological introduction* (pp. 176–194). Beverly Hills, CA: Sage.

Campbell, Karen E. (1990). Networks past: a 1939 Bloomington neighborhood. *Social Forces, 69*(1), 139–155.

Campbell, Karen E., Marsden, Peter V., & Hurlbert, Jeanne S. (1986). Social resources and socioeconomic status. *Social Networks, 8*(1), 97–117.

Craven, Paul, & Wellman, Barry. (1973). The network city. *Sociological Inquiry, 43*(3/4), 57–88.

Driedger, Leo. (1979). Maintenance of urban ethnic boundaries: The French in St. Boniface. *The Sociological Quarterly, 20*(1), 89–108.

———. (1980). Jewish identity: the maintenance of urban religious and ethnic boundaries. *Ethnic and Racial Studies, 3*(1), 67–88.

Driedger, Leo, & Church, Glenn. (1974). Residential segregation and institutional completeness: A comparison of ethnic minorities. *Canadian Review of Sociology and Anthropology, 11*(1), 30–52.

Duncan, Otis Dudley. (1961). From social system to ecosystem. *Sociological Inquiry, 31*(2), 140–149.

Effrat, Marcia Pelly. (1973). Approaches to community: Conflicts and complementarities. *Sociological Inquiry, 43*(3/4), 1–32.

Fischer, Claude S. (1982). *To dwell among friends: Personal networks in town and city.* Chicago: University of Chicago Press.

Guest, Avery M., & Lee, Barrett A. (1983). The social organization of local areas. *Urban Affairs Quarterly, 19*(1), 217–240.

Haines, Valerie A. (1985). From organicist to relational human ecology. *Sociological Theory, 3*(1), 65–74.

Hawley, Amos H. (1950). *Human ecology: A theory of community structure.* New York: Ronald Press.

———. (1986). *Human ecology: A theoretical essay.* Chicago: University of Chicago Press.

Hiller, E.T. (941) The community as a social group. *American Sociological Review, 6*(2), 189–202.

Hillery, George A. (1955). Definitions of community: Areas of agreement. *Rural Sociology, 20*(2), 111–123.

Janowitz, Morris. (1952). *The community press in an urban setting.* Chicago: University of Chicago Press.

Keller, Suzanne. (1968). *The urban neighborhood: A sociological perspective.* New York: Random House.

Knoke, David, & Kuklinski, James H. (1982). *Network analysis.* Beverly Hills, CA: Sage.

Laumann, Edward O., Marsden, Peter V., & Prensky, David. (1983). The boundary specification problem in network analysis. In Ronald S. Burt & Michael J. Minor (Eds.), *Applied network analysis: A methodological introduction* (pp. 18–34). Beverly Hills, CA: Sage.

Makabe, Tomoko. (1979). Ethnic identity scale and social mobility: The case of the Nisei in Toronto. *Canadian Review of Sociology and Anthropology, 16*(2), 136–146.

Marsden, Peter V. (1987). Core discussion networks of Americans. *American Sociological Review, 52*(1), 122–131.

———. (1990). Network data and measurement. *Annual Review of Sociology, 16,* 435–463.

Martindale, Don, & Hanson, R. Galen. (1969). *Small town and the nation: The conflict of local and translocal forces.* Westport, CT: Greenwood.

O'Bryan, G., Reitz, J.G., and Kuplowska, O. (1976). *Non-official languages: A study in Canadian multiculturalism.* Ottawa: Supply & Services Canada.

Pineo, Peter C. (1988). Socioeconomic status and the concentric zonal structure of Canadian cities. *Canadian Review of Sociology and Anthropology, 25*(3), 421–438.

Poplin, Dennis E. (1973). *Communities: A survey of theories and methods of research.* New York: Macmillan.

Reitz, Jeffrey G. (1980). *The survival of ethnic groups.* Toronto: McGraw-Hill Ryerson.

Roberts, Lance W., & Boldt, Edward D. (1979). Institutional completeness and ethnic assimilation. *Journal of Ethnic Studies, 7*(2), 103–108.

Tilly, Charles. (1973). Do communities act? *Sociological Inquiry, 43*(3/4), 209–240.

Warren, Roland L. (1963). *The community in America.* Chicago: Rand McNally & Co.

Webber, Melvin. (1963). Order in diversity: Community without propinquity. In L. Wingo, (Ed.), *Cities and space: The future use of urban land* (pp. 23–54). Baltimore: Johns Hopkins University Press.

———. (1964). The urban place and the nonplace urban realm. In Melvin M. Webber, (Ed.), *Explorations into urban structure* (pp. 79–153). Philadelphia: University of Pennsylvania Press.

Wellman, Barry. (1979). The community question: The intimate networks of East Yorkers. *American Journal of Sociology, 84*(5), 1201–1231.

———. (1988). Structural analysis: From method and metaphor to theory and substance. In Barry Wellman & S.D. Berkowitz, (Eds.), *Social structures: A network approach* (pp. 19–61). Cambridge: Cambridge University Press.

Wellman, Barry, & Leighton, Barry. (1979). Networks, neighborhoods, and communities. *Urban Affairs Quarterly, 14*(3), 363–390.

Wellman, Barry, Carrington, Peter J., & Hall, Alan. (1988). Networks as personal communities. In Barry Wellman & S.D. Berkowitz, (Eds.), *Social structures: A network approach* (pp. 130–184). Cambridge: Cambridge University Press.

Yancey, William L., Ericksen, Eugene P., & Juliani, Richard N. (1976). Emergent ethnicity: A review and reformulation. *American Sociological Review, 41*(3), 391–403.

CONCEPTUALIZING GENDER, RACE, AND ETHNICITY AS A FIELD OF STUDY

EDIT PETROVIC

INTRODUCTION

▼

Since World War II, and especially from the 1960s onward, race and ethnic studies has become a major field of inquiry. Anticolonial and antiracist discourse, as well as the phenomenon of ethnic revival and the spread of ethnic conflicts in different parts of the world, have helped to make race and ethnic relations one of the major areas of research within the social sciences. In addition, different feminist traditions also emerged out of an ideological and operational movement since the 1960s. Fundamental premises of Western society, and women's position within the existing structures of oppression and domination, were openly criticized and, as a result, gender issues became more central to social research. While class is also linked to gender, race, and ethnicity, it is not discussed in depth here.

Since the late 1970s, postmodernist theory has opened the doors to new ways of looking at major social concepts such as gender, class, race, and ethnicity. Along with different minority groups in North America struggling for recognition, feminists became vocal, pointing out that there are many unique concerns, as well as differences, in the way men and women experience and respond to social inequalities. Sexism and racism were eventually linked and explained as two separate but mutually related systems of patriarchal domination (Ng, 1991).

THEORETICAL OVERVIEW

▼

Several crucial ideas emerged from the work of Foucault (1972), Derrida (1978), and Lyotard (1984), Clifford (1988), Jameson (1991), West (1991),

Harraway (1994), and Taylor (1994). These ideas helped to create gender, race, and ethnicity as a new, interdisciplinary field of study. As postmodern theorists like to point out, disciplinary boundaries became blurred, for example, those between humanities and social sciences, and universal theories failed to explain the increasing complexity of social relations. According to Seidman, the value of postmodernist knowledge lies in making us aware of and tolerant toward social differences, ambiguity, and conflict (1994: 5). Such a fractured approach to knowledge allowed the investigation of the linkages between previously detached domains, including gender, race, and ethnicity. They were no longer perceived as categorical phenomena (What is gender? What is ethnicity?), but rather as relational phenomena (What is the meaning of ethnicity in relation to gender and social class?). Such an approach turned social analysts into social interpreters or mediators between different social worlds (Bauman, 1987).

The work of Derrida (1978), Foucault (1972), and Rorty (1979) suggested that there are links between knowledge and power. In addition, the idea of the pragmatic, political nature of knowledge, perceived as a strategy serving diverse interests and goals, was contextualized within the feminist discourse. All knowledge was perceived as being situated or located within the context of individuals and groups who produce it through interaction. This view turned the attention to knowledge producers in an attempt to understand how the relationships of power and domination generate knowledge as a public commodity.

It became important to know who speaks and why, who gave one the authority to speak, and who is represented by a particular voice. This was subsequently referred to as "the voice metaphor." This concern became particularly important in the critique by minority women of white, middle-class, feminist modes of representation. These writers criticized the false notions of sisterhood and common womanhood promoted by mainstream feminist groups. Audre Lorde pointed out: "As white women ignore their built-in privilege of whiteness and define woman in terms of their own experience alone, the women of colour become *other*, the outsider whose experience and tradition is too alien to comprehend" (1995: 535). This valid point that Lorde and others are making allows us to also re-examine class relations built on the notion of "common (white) sisterhood." How much are white, lower-class women represented within the common sisterhood?

Postmodernist theory also introduced the notion of fragmented, shifting, and constructed identities. Without the notion of identity as a measure of how people feel about themselves, the entire gender, race, and ethnicity project could end up in abstract and detached theorizing. It became possible to look at gender or race, not as things that people possess (Messner, 1997: 204), but as an analytical technique probing the process of gendering or racializing one's identities. This process has been described particularly well by Pon (1996). Pon considers the ways in which Chinese men in the 1920s in Canada were portrayed as people of a feminine race or as people who, according to white perception, possessed feminine racial characteristics. Their femininity was perceived to be derived from their work in feminine occupations such as domestics. Inherent in such negative identification is a devaluation of femininity and a non-white racial background.

RESEARCH MODELS OF GENDER, RACE, AND ETHNICITY
▼

An examination of the scope of gender, race, and ethnic research and its characteristics is a useful way to shed light on the three predominant approaches elaborated on by Anderson and Hill Collins (1995). The first two models of their typology of gender, class, and ethnicity studies are informed by the Marxist critique of the modes of production and their role in reproducing oppression and domination. The first, called the "cumulative," or "additive" model, basically adds components as it describes individual and group experiences with oppression and domination. Little attempt is made to relate and link those experiences or to ground them in a particular historical period. When we interpret oppressions as separate domains, we help perpetuate the belief that sexism, racism, and ethnic chauvinism, or nationalism are distinct and unrelated mechanisms of domination. This static and passive approach offers little in terms of linking the cumulative effects of multiple oppressions.

The second tradition in which gender, class, and race studies are written is defined by the "matrix of domination" model, which explains and historically contextualizes multiple sources of domination and oppression, but fails to look more closely at the concept of domination itself. Instead, the metaphor portrays a worldview in which one either dominates or is dominated. A more dynamic model would consider the multiple levels or variations that the matrix of domination can generate. One can be oppressed in one domain and yet be an oppressor in another, for example. Another problem with this model is that, when focussing on those who are oppressed (minorities), one tends not to focus on the oppressor(s) (majority), and therefore fails to understand the dynamics of the domination /subordination process. Finally, not all aspects of race, ethnic, and gender relations are reducible to relations of oppression and domination. Relationships of complementarity and empowerment should also be incorporated into the model.

The "matrix of domination" approach can be credited for bringing attention to the process by which minority women are placed vis-à-vis their own group and the majority group. Sometimes the group to which they belong subordinates them. Yet criticizing one's own group or culture while struggling for recognition is often perceived as non-acceptable. Loudre talked about such internal silencing in her explanation of how heterosexual Black men and women reject the very existence of Black lesbians because lesbianism has traditionally been seen as a white woman's problem and something that will discredit Black people's struggle for recognition (1995: 538).

The third model in the field of gender, race, and ethnicity is that of the voice metaphor, which focusses on individual stories and experiences, and the role that gender, race, and ethnicity play in individual-identity construction. Such stories appear unrelated and fragmented, and are told with little attempt to contextualize them with other individual or group experiences. As Dilthey (1976) pointed out, this leads to fixed expressions. In the context of "voice editing," it implies passivity. To affirm that one is affected and disadvantaged by recognized race, gender, class, or ethnic differences does not go beyond such realization. Voice metaphor appears to be more like a souvenir collection or a bricolage of oppressed voices. Nevertheless, it has been an important technique in consciousness-raising or in improving awareness of the concerns and conditions of minority groups.

THE CANADIAN CONTEXT
▼

Gender, race, and ethnic research in the Canadian context are framed by the colonialism, nativism, multiculturalism, and diversity models. The "matrix of domination" and the "voice metaphor" models described above are also used in this regard. The "matrix of domination" model, for example, is used by Calliste (1994) in her historical account of Canadian immigration policies and the way they created, reflected, and helped to perpetuate existing negative stereotypes about Caribbean domestic workers. Similarly, Bourgeault's (1991) work on the colonial domination of Indian women dealt with the impact of early colonialism on economic and social subordination of Indian women in Canada.

The "voice metaphor" approach is used by Yee (1993). Yee combines narrative with poems and ethnographic descriptions relevant to the recognition of her own identity. A somewhat different perspective, not readily reduced to either of the two models, is found in Carter's (1996) study of Indian women in the early settlement era in Western Canada. Although patterns of domination are an implicit part of her historical analysis, her approach offers a more dynamic look at relationships between different segments of majority–minority groups. Central to Carter's analysis is the process of the construction of Native women's identities as their responses to the predominance of negative images.

The colonial/postcolonial model created a seemingly uniform or universal Native identity. Such power to impose and sustain identities and to construct a Native community to which such identities belong recently has been challenged by both Native and non-Native writers. For example, Vibert (1996) exposes the cultural logic of colonial practice in constructing a Native hunter as a standard bearer of manly Indianness in a contrast to middle-class British masculinity. In unpacking the fur-trader narratives, she demonstrates how the image of the buffalo-hunting Indian came to be identified as the Indian of Euro-American imagination (1996: 51). Seen in such light, narratives become a part of a political project: de-colonizing struggles to control and correct hegemonic images of Native people in Canada.

The colonial model continues to be exploited in Canada in the areas of multiculturalism and diversity, especially in the domain of immigrant subcultures. Multiculturalism as an ideological construct in Canada can itself be seen as a form of hybridization. The ideology is built on a premise of recognition and appreciation of differences, incorporating at the same time the notion of power relations. It defines both the other and the mainstream. Critics pointed out that multiculturalism Canadian-style often nourishes non-threatening cultural differences. Distinct cultural traditions are often defined in terms of culture-specific gender relations wherein the experiences of immigrant women and men significantly differ. Multiculturalism introduces the metaphor of an individual caught between cultures. For writers in this field, vacillation between the two meta-narratives — one of homogenization, and the other of emergence or becoming — became inevitable (Clifford, 1988: 17).

In Canada, it is important to realize that the conceptualization of an immigrant almost always leaves out English- and French-speaking white immigrants. Gender, race, and ethnicity research of immigrants are usually grounded in minority/majority relations. Palmer Seiler (1996) uses the voice model to talk about the double vulnerability of immigrant women. She argues that their marginalization is based on gender and ethnicity. On the other hand, Tastosglou (1997) interprets intergenerational immigrant narratives from the standpoint of women. The interconnectedness of gender, ethnicity, and class in mediating immigrant women's identities and cultures and the multiple uses of the voice strategy are crucial aspects of her analysis, although such voice-editing implies questions about selectivity and representation.

CONCLUSION
▼

Out of the diversity of writing styles, research methodologies, and disciplinary backgrounds that contributed to the consolidation of gender, race, and ethnicity as a field of study, it is possible to argue that something new has emerged. It is a field of study in which the domains of many disciplines, such as history, sociology, English, anthropology, and linguistics, inform each other and provide needed new perspectives on gender, race, and ethnicity. A combination of writing styles, documentary and non-documentary sources, disciplinary and interdisciplinary approaches, as well as theoretical perspectives, does not set grounds for the creation of a coherent theoretical framework in a traditional sense. Instead, it allows for the constant reinvention of the object of study. Gender, race, and ethnicity as a field of study, then, provides a much-needed experiential, interpretive perspective, but at the same time incorporates the more traditional analytical social sciences methodology.

REFERENCES
▼

Anderson, Margaret, & Hill Collins, Patricia (Eds.). (1995). *Race, class and gender: An anthology.* Belmont, CA: Wadsworth.

Bauman, Zygmund. (1987). *Legislators and interpreters.* Cambridge: Polity Press.

Bourgeault, Ron. (1991). Race, class and gender: Colonial domination of Indian women. In Jesse Vorst (Ed.), *Race, class, gender: Bonds and barriers* (pp. 88–117). Toronto: Garamond.

Calliste, Agnes. (1994). Race, gender and Canadian immigration policy: Blacks from the Caribbean, 1900–1932. *Journal of Canadian Studies, 28*(4), 131–148.

Carter, Sarah. (1996). Categories and terrains of exclusion: Constructing the "Indian women" in the early settlement era in Western Canada. In Joy Parr & Mark Rosenfeld (Eds.), *Gender and history in Canada* (pp. 30–49). Toronto: Copp Clark.

Clifford, James. (1988). *The predicament of culture: Twentieth-century ethnography, literature and art.* Cambridge, MA: Harvard University Press.

Derrida, Jacques. (1978). *Writing and difference.* Chicago: University of Chicago Press.

Dilthey W. (1976). *Dilthey: Selected writings* (H.P. Rickman, Ed.). Cambridge: Cambridge University Press.

Foucault, Michel. (1972). *The order of things.* New York: Pantheon.

Gunew, Sneja. (1990). *Feminist knowledge: Critique and construct.* London: Routledge.

Harraway, Donna. (1994). A manifesto of cyborgs: Science, technology and socialist feminism. In Steven Seidman (Ed.), *Postmodern turn* (pp. 82–115). Cambridge: Cambridge University Press.

Hartsock, Nancy. (1983). The feminist standpoint: Developing the ground for a specifically feminist historical materialism. In Sandra Harding & Merrill B. Hintikka (Eds.), *Discovering reality: Feminist perspectives on epistemology* (pp. 283–310). Dordrecht, Holland; Boston: D. Reidel; Hingham, MA.

Jameson, Frederic. (1991). *Postmodernism or the cultural logic of late capitalism.* Durham, NC: Duke University Press.

Lorde, Audre. (1995). Age, race, class and sex: Women redefining difference. In Margaret Anderson & Patricia Hill Collins (Eds.), *Race, class and gender: An anthology* (pp. 532–540). Belmont, CA: Wadsworth.

Lyotard, Jean-François. (1984). *The postmodern condition.* Minneapolis: University of Minnesota Press.

Messner, Michael. (1997). Boyhood, organized sport, and the construction of masculinities. In Diana Kendall (Ed.), *Race, class and gender: A reader* (pp. 203–217). Boston: Allyn & Bacon.

Ng, Roxana. (1991). Sexism, racism and Canadian nationalism. In Jesse Vorst (Ed.), *Race, class and gender: Bonds and barriers* (pp. 12–26). Toronto: Garamond.

Palmer Seiler, Tamara. (1996). Including the female immigrant story: A comparative look at narrative strategies. *Canadian Ethnic Studies.* Special issue: *Ethnic Themes in Literature, 28*(1), 51–66.

Pon, Madge. (1996). Like a Chinese puzzle: The construction of Chinese masculinity in Jack Canuck. In Joy Parr & Mark Rosenfeld (Eds.), *Gender and history in Canada* (pp. 88–100). Toronto: Copp Clark.

Rasporich, Beverly. (1996). Native women writing: Tracing the patterns. *Canadian Ethnic Studies.* Special issue: *Ethnic Themes in Literature, 28*(1), 37–50.

Rorty, Richard. (1979). *Philosophy and the mirror of nature.* Princeton: Princeton University Press

Seidman, Steven (Ed.). (1994). *Postmodern turn: New perspectives on social theory.* Cambridge: Cambridge University Press.

Tastsoglou, Evangelia. (1997). The margin at the center: Greek immigrant women in Ontario. *Canadian Ethnic Studies, 29*(1), 119–160.

Taylor, Charles. (1994). The politics of recognition. In David Goldberg (Ed.), *Multiculturalism: A critical reader* (pp. 75–106). Boston: Blackwell.

Vibert, Elizabeth. (1996). Real men hunt buffalo: Masculinity, race and class in British fur traders' narratives. In Joy Parr & Mark Rosenfeld (Eds.), *Gender and history in Canada* (pp. 50–67). Toronto: Copp Clark.

West, Cornel. (1994). The new cultural politics of difference. In Steven Seidman (Ed.), *Postmodern turn: New perspectives on social theory* (pp. 65–81). Cambridge: Cambridge University Press.

Yee, May. (1993). Finding the way home through issues of gender, race, and class. In Himani Bannerji (Ed.), *Returning the gaze: Essays on racism, feminism and politics* (pp. 3–37). Toronto: Sister Vision.

Yuval-Davis, Nira. (1997). *Gender and nation.* London: Sage.

PART TWO

THE CHANGING
MOSAIC

INTRODUCTION

The three chapters in Part Two address some of the complexities and ramifications of the various attempts to conceptualize and measure the ethnic and cultural origins of the population from data collected in Canada's periodic national censuses. There are a number of reasons why it is difficult to develop a historical record of Canada's evolving ethnic-origin mosaic that is consistent, valid, and unambiguous. The main difficulty arises from the fact that the methods and questions used to elicit information on ethnic and cultural origins of the population have changed over the years; further, the lack of historical comparability and the increasing ambiguity of the questions' intent are raising new challenges for those attempting to monitor and interpret the significance of changes that are occurring in Canada's ethnic and cultural composition.

In Chapter Five, Warren Kalbach describes the extent of ethnic diversity in Canada's population that has evolved since the early period of scattered and relatively homogeneous French, British, and Native Indian settlements, when the French and English were in direct competition for trade and colonization in the New World. The transition from French to British political control and cultural dominance, and the impact of the subsequent increase in immigration of other Europeans to Canada, are examined from the late nineteenth through the first half of the twentieth century. The author draws attention to the fact that the picture of Canada's changing cultural mosaic during the hundred years following Confederation, being based on assumptions of patrilineal descent and minimal ethnic intermarriage, probably has resulted in an underestimation of the amount of ethnic diversity in Canada's mosaic. The possible effects of changes in the format of the ethnic-origin question that have allowed and encouraged respondents to indicate whether or not their ancestry involved multiple ethnic origins are also considered. Analysis of the nature and increasing numbers of multiple-origin combinations resulting from ethnic intermarriage provides some evidence as to the extent to which this marriage pattern, rather than weakening the British/French bicultural base of Canadian society, continues to strengthen it.

In Chapter Six, Ravi Pendakur and Fernando Mata are concerned with assessing the validity and usefulness of data collected in the 1996 census for analyzing trends in the ethnic- and cultural-origin composition of the population. The authors consider the consequences of including "Canadian" for the first time, as one of a number of possible acceptable responses to the traditional ethnic-origin question. The significant increase in the numbers reporting a "Canadian" origin (identity?) in both the 1993 National Census Test and in the 1996 census raises concerns that a significant component of those claiming to be "Canadian" might be coming from the non-British or non-French origin groups. Using a comparative analysis of the social and cultural characteristics of those who indicated they were "Canadian" with groups reporting British and French origins, and those reporting origins other than French or British, the authors attempt to determine which groups were more likely to report themselves as being "Canadian" when given the opportunity to do so. Their work clearly shows the difficulties that can arise with slight changes in the wording and format of census questions, and the importance of clarifying the intent of the ethnic-origin question, that is, whether it is to elicit a current ethnic "identity" or "origin" response. In either case, Pendakur and Mata's article would suggest that information on both "identity" and "ethnic origin" would be necessary to better understand the processes by which immigrants and their descendants begin to acquire new "identities" as they become integrated and assimilated into Canadian (or Canadien) society.

Chapter Seven, written by Rudolph Kalin and John Berry, deals with a more subjective and less tangible and changing type of ethnic/cultural mosaic than that based on the ethnic-origin (ancestry) question. The authors' interests are focussed not so much on the ethnic identities of the newly arrived immigrants as on tracking the transformation of immigrants' original ethnic identities as they are gradually integrated and assimilated into Canadian society. Using survey data, the authors identify various types of identities prevalent between 1974 and 1991, and note differences in anglophone and francophone communities, as well as for "Other Ethnics." Their research suggests that, over time, "civic" identity eventually supersedes self-identity based on ethnic origins. The process of transformation is described as varying in complexity by region, especially in Quebec, where considerable conflict exists between the civic identities of Québécois and Canadian. The importance of Kalin and Berry's article lies in its focus on the transformation of the ethnic identities of immigrants from their heritage identities to hyphenated forms, and ultimately to such civic identities as "Canadian" or "Canadien." Their analysis suggests the importance of looking not only at the ethnic origins of recent immigrants, but also at the current identities of the older and longer-established immigrant populations that reflect the years of integration and assimilation into the dominant bicultural British-/French-Canadian society. Kalin and Berry point to the need for much more research on the meaning of "Canadian" as an identity and as an emergent ethnic group.

▼

ETHNIC DIVERSITY: CANADA'S CHANGING CULTURAL MOSAIC

WARREN E. KALBACH

INTRODUCTION
▼

Before the Europeans began to arrive in North America, the continent had been occupied for thousands of years by widely scattered but relatively small aboriginal bands characterized by a diversity of language and culture. This was the setting into which the major European powers of the time had ventured in their search for a more direct route to the riches of the East Indies. The French and the English were the major rivals in the seventeenth and eighteenth centuries, competing to establish their "presence" through exploration and settlement, and to achieve political and economic control through colonization and domination of trade in the region.

Canadian society today is the result of four centuries of exploration and settlement, cultural conflict, and economic development to exploit its vast natural resources. An understanding of the nature of Canadian society can be achieved through an examination of the cultural heritage of its founding groups and their descendants, as well as the demographic processes that have significantly affected the relative sizes and character of both its early populations and the immigrants that followed.

THE BEGINNINGS OF CULTURAL DIVERSITY
▼

When the first European explorers began to appear off the shores of North America, they knew next to nothing about the nature of the continent that confronted them. Their first general impressions of the New World were of a wilderness barrier of indeterminate proportions, grossly underpopulated by relatively small numbers of widely scattered, basically "uncivilized," and sometimes hostile Native Indians. In their early contacts with the indigenous population, they sought access to this cornucopia of natural resources through trade as well as by claiming, in the name of "God and Country," any land thought to be rich in natural resources or necessary for the security and defence of their trading routes and settlements.

The aboriginal population existing in North America during the period prior to the arrival of the Europeans has been estimated at nearly 1 million, and approximately 220 000 to 350 000 were thought to have been in that part of North America that is now Canada (Pointing, 1997). From prehistoric to recent times, they appear to have been widely scattered across the continent, but clustered in at least five major cultural areas, with distinctively different environments — the Northwest Coast, the Plains, the Plateau, the Eastern Woodlands, and the Northern Area — with a variety of distinct indigenous languages, 52 of which are still spoken in Canada today (*Canadian Encyclopedia*, 1999).

The first Europeans to have extended contact with the Native Indians were the French and English, the dominant political and economic powers of the seventeenth and eighteenth centuries. As they were the main competitors for new lands and trading routes, it was their exploration and trading activities, involving the aboriginal populations, that began a process of cultural change affecting both the Native and foreign-born populations that has continued to this day.

More than a century after Cabot's first voyage to the New World, Champlain established the first French trading post, which was later to become Quebec City. France was initially more interested in the exploration and establishment of trading routes and posts, and in converting the Native Indians to Christianity, than in establishing permanent settlements. Yet, during these early years, in spite of the harsh climate, recurring food shortages, epidemics, and intermittent hostilities with both the English and Native Indians, France did manage to settle sufficient numbers to maintain a foothold, albeit a tenuous one, to carry on with its fur-trading and soul-saving activities as a French colony. Under these difficult conditions, the population of New France managed to increase from a mere 28 in 1608 to 3215 in 1665 (Kalbach & McVey, 1971: 11–12).

DIVERSITY OF ETHNIC ORIGINS IN THE PRE-CONFEDERATION ERA
▼

Migration to New France had been the main source of its early population growth. But, as conditions improved, fertility became the significant factor, as

Quebec's population increased from 3215, to 70 000 in 1760. Under British control after 1763, Quebec experienced a further population growth, attributable to continuing high fertility among the Catholic population and continuing improvement in mortality conditions, increasing to slightly more than 1.1 million in 1861, just prior to Confederation.

The character of the population in the rest of British North America was basically set by the large-scale immigration of the British Empire Loyalists from the British colonies after the American Revolution, when they settled in the Maritimes, the Eastern Townships, and Upper Canada. The first estimates of Upper Canada's population in 1784 placed it at about 10 000. In another 40 years, it had reached 150 000; and, as a result of large-scale immigration from Europe during the post-Napoleonic era, its population's total had passed Quebec's, reaching 950 000 by mid-century, and 1.4 million in 1861 (Kalbach & McVey, 1979).

Prior to Confederation, the population of Quebec had been able to maintain its cultural homogeneity because of the continuing high fertility of its French Catholic population and negligible immigration. Under British Colonial rule, the early homogeneity of Upper Canada's British population would weaken over time as the Irish and Scots came in increasing numbers, and immigrants continued to come from the United States and countries outside the British Isles.

In 1851, just prior to Confederation, Lower Canada had a fairly high degree of cultural homogeneity, with 75 percent of its native-born population of French origin. This contrasted sharply with the situation in Upper Canada, where both the native- and foreign-born French accounted for only 3 percent of the population. In Upper Canada, the foreign-born British (35 percent) and the native-born of British origins (almost 55 percent), together accounted for 90 percent of its population. The remaining 7 percent of the population consisted mainly of a few Germans and some 44 000 immigrants who had come from the United States, plus another 6500 from areas of earlier settlement in Atlantic Canada (Census, 1851–52).

Using the data either on country of origin or on ethnic origin as a basis for determining the degree of cultural diversity can provide only a rough approximation of its extent in any given population. While either the ethnic or the country-of-origin data can identify major ethnocultural groups in a population, neither, alone, can identify any of the major subcultural groups that may exist within the major ethnic groups, which are not culturally homogeneous. To understand the nature of Canada's cultural diversity, it is necessary to look beyond data identifying ethnic origin or countries of origin, and examine religious composition as well.

RELIGIOUS DIVERSITY IN CANADA PRIOR TO 1867
▼

Early settlement in New France, and later in British North America, reflected the cultural complexion of the residents' national origins. French settlements, reflecting the early and dominating influence of the Roman Catholic Church, were relatively homogeneous in terms of both the ethnic origins and the religion of the populace. Settlements established by immigrants from the British Isles and later augmented by the migration of British Empire Loyalists after the Peace of Paris in 1783 were characteristically Protestant, but more heterogeneous with respect to both their ethnic origin and their religion because of the many denominations and sects that characterized Protestantism. However, those of English origin and Anglican faith, while not always the majority, represented the dominant social, economic, political, and cultural power base, and thus gave early Canada its distinctive Anglo-Saxon character.

Early censuses in other areas of British North America did not reveal the same degree of dominance exhibited by the Roman Catholic Church in Quebec. A Nova Scotia census in 1767 reported 85 percent of its population as Protestant, while a more detailed census, 60 years later, showed the Presbyterians, at 30 percent, to be the largest Protestant denomination, followed by the Church of England with 23 percent; Baptist, at 16 percent; Methodist, at 8 percent; Dissenter, at 4 percent; and Lutherans, at 2 percent (Government of Canada, 1870–71).

CULTURAL DIVERSITY SINCE CONFEDERATION
▼

The first census of Canada following Confederation included Nova Scotia and New Brunswick, in addition to the provinces of Ontario and Quebec (Government of Canada, 1870–71). The number of groups large enough to be reported in terms of their ethnic or country of origins had not increased from the 16 reported in the 1851 census. In contrast, the number of religions and denominations identified in published reports increased from 16 to 25 (Secretary of the Board of Registration and Statistics, 1853; Government of Canada, 1870–71). There is little question that Canada's population has become more culturally diverse as it has grown through natural increase and net migration, as have the numbers and size of the various ethnic-origin and religious groups that comprise it. But, just how much this diversity has increased and how significant it is for Canadian society are difficult to assess with any certainty, because the perception of diversity depends on the way ethnic-origin and religious groups are identified and combined during any analysis of cultural diversity (Kalbach, 1976).

For practical reasons alone, not all of the ethnic origins or religions identified during an enumeration can be separately identified and published in public releases of census results. Consequently, much of the combining of ethnic and religious categories that occurs in data processing and presentation tends to convey an overly simplified picture of an exceedingly complex ethnoreligious structure that comprises hundreds of distinctively different groups. While results of analyses based on more heterogeneous groupings of ethnic origins or religions can still have general sociological validity, such analyses tend to obscure the true complexity and richness of the ethnoreligious structure and its significance for Canadian society.

CHANGES IN CANADA'S ETHNOCULTURAL MOSAIC, 1871–1971
▼

An analysis of post-Confederation trends in Canada's ethnocultural origins must take cognizance of the changes in census definitions and procedures that may have affected the comparability of the data over time. The census definition and the procedures for obtaining ethnic origin data were essentially unchanged prior to 1971; but significant changes were made in both the definition of ethnic origin and census procedures (Statistics Canada, 1997), and in the legislative acts and regulations governing the selection and admission of immigrants, starting late in the 1960s (McVey & Kalbach, 1995).

Trends in the relative sizes of Canada's ethnic origin populations for the historical period 1871 to 1971 are shown in Figure 5.1. As described in the census of 1871, Canada's population was 60 percent British origins, and 31 percent French. Together, they formed the bicultural base, comprising 91 percent of the population. One hundred years later, the 1971 census showed that their respective shares had declined, to 45 and 29 percent, respectively, shrinking their bicultural base by seventeen percentage points, to 74 percent of the total (see Table 5.1). The decline in proportions of the founding populations was primarily due to the faster-growing populations of other European origins, fed by the heavy immigration to Canada in response to its efforts to settle the West, develop its natural resources and transportation networks, and industrialize and expand its economy, all without significantly changing the basic nature of Canada's bicultural and bilingual society.

The population of British origins grew from 2.1 million to 9.6 million, an increase of 356 percent, while the population of French origin increased by 464 percent, from 1.1 million to 6.2 million. Yet, in spite of these significant increases, both groups lost ground because the population of origins other than

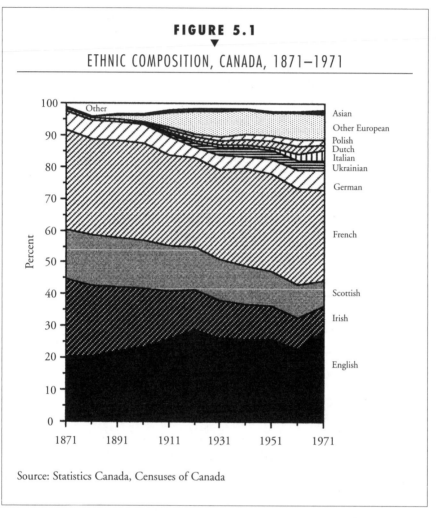

FIGURE 5.1

▼

ETHNIC COMPOSITION, CANADA, 1871–1971

Source: Statistics Canada, Censuses of Canada

British or French increased at a faster rate, particularly during the early years of the twentieth century and the immediate post–World War II period. Among the faster-growing "other" Europeans, whose proportions had increased from 7 to 23 percent by 1971, those of German origin were the largest group, with 1.3 million. The Italians, with 731 000, were second largest, followed by 581 000 Ukrainians, 42 000 Dutch, 385 000 Scandinavians, and 316 000 of Polish origin. The presence of Asians was first noted in the 1881 census, when they comprised only 0.1 percent of Canada's total. After 90 years, and at about the time of liberalization of the immigration laws, the 1971 census reported that their share had increased to 1.3 percent. Other non-Europeans and non-Asians accounted for 2.4 percent of Canada's total by 1971, up from 1.5 percent in 1871.

TABLE 5.1
▼
PERCENTAGE AND NUMERICAL DISTRIBUTION OF THE POPULATION BY SELECTED ETHNIC ORIGINS, CANADA, 1971, 1981, AND 1991

Ethnic Origin Group	1971		1981		1991	
	Number (000s)	Percent	Number (000s)	Percent	Number (000s)	Percent
British[a]	9 624	44.6	9 674	40.2	7 595	28.1
French[b]	6 180	28.7	6 439	26.7	6 159	22.8
British and French	—	—	430	1.8	1 072	4.0
Other European	4 960	23.0	4 649	19.3	4 146	15.4
Asian	286	1.3	785	3.3	1 463	5.4
Other single origins	519	2.4	697	2.9	1 833	6.9
Other multiples	—	—	1 408	5.8	4 726	17.5
Total	21 568	100.0	24 083	100.0	26 994	100.0

[a] Includes British-only multiples in 1991.
[b] Includes French-only multiples in 1991.

Source: *1971 Census*, Cat. 99-709, May 1977; *1981 Census*, Cat. 92-911, February 1984; and *1991 Census*, Cat. 93-315, February 1993.

In terms of the three major, but broadly defined, general groupings of the population by ethnic origins, that is, British, French, and "all others," Canada's ethnic composition changed relatively slowly between Confederation and 1971. The proportion of those of British origins declined steadily, while the French remained fairly constant, and the more heterogeneous "all others" steadily increased. At the time of the 1971 census, it was thought that, "if the present trend continues, it appears likely that the ethnic origins of the population will probably be divided between the 'French' ethnic group and 'All Other' ethnic groups each having about 30% of the total population and the other 40% being of British origins" (Statistics Canada, 1977: 45).

Given the increase in the numbers and size of the ethnic-origin groups relative to the British and French charter groups, both ethnic differentials in rates of immigration and natural increase contributed significantly to Canada's growing sense of cultural diversity during the hundred years following Confederation. The number of ethnic-origin groups that had increased in size enough to be recognized and counted by the time of the 1971 census had more than doubled, from 16 to 38.

TRENDS IN RELIGIOUS AFFILIATION, 1871-1971
▼

After a century of population growth under an increasingly restrictive immigration policy designed to encourage immigration from only those countries whose cultures were not significantly different from those of the founding French and British charter groups, the overall religious composition would not have been expected to have changed to any great extent. Primarily concentrated in Quebec, Roman Catholics have continued to maintain their dominant position in Canadian society. As may be seen in Figure 5.2, their

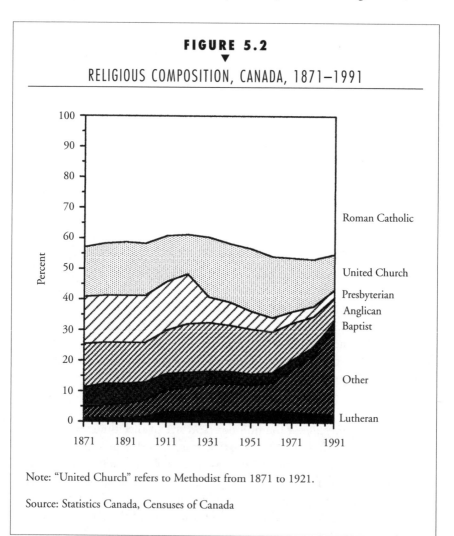

FIGURE 5.2
▼
RELIGIOUS COMPOSITION, CANADA, 1871–1991

Note: "United Church" refers to Methodist from 1871 to 1921.

Source: Statistics Canada, Censuses of Canada

share of the total population, at 43 percent in 1871, remained relatively unchanged for a hundred years, increasing only slightly, to 46 percent, by 1971. The major change occurred within the Protestant group as a whole, with the five major Protestant denominations combined declining from 53 to just under 40 percent in 1971. During the same period, the smaller Protestant denominations, the Jews, Eastern non-Christian religions, and those indicating no religion increased from approximately 4 to 15 percent.

Similar to the increase in the number of ethnic-origin groups reported in the censuses during this period, the number of religious affiliations for which data were collected and reported also increased from about 26 in the 1871 census to almost 30 by 1971. The balance between Roman Catholics and the major Protestant groups and the general level of religious diversity remained relatively unchanged during this period. However, after 1961 there is some evidence that the changes in religious composition, shown in Figure 5.2, are the direct consequence of changes in the procedures by which data on religious affiliation were obtained.

REFOCUSSING THE IMAGE OF CANADA'S CULTURAL MOSAIC
▼

Around the time of the 1971 census, two major developments occurred that had the potential to profoundly affect Canada's image as a multicultural nation. Changes were beginning to be made in the format and content of census questions and procedures to improve both the quality and the validity of census data; however, these changes would reduce the comparability of these data with those gathered earlier, and also alter the conceptualization of Canada's multicultural character. The sudden increase in the proportion of "Other Religions" after the 1961 census, indicated in Figure 5.2, while reflecting valid increases in the smaller Protestant denominations, Eastern non-Christian, and Jews, also reflected a very significant rise in those reporting "no religion." While an increase would be expected in a secularizing society, the suddenness of its appearance might be called into question. In this case, it was the direct consequence of changes in the format of the religion question used in the 1971 census. It was the first time that "no religion" had been offered as a possible option, and the first time that those being enumerated in urban areas were given the opportunity to respond to the census under the condition of relative anonymity offered by self-enumeration census forms.

More serious obstacles to a better understanding of the sociodemographic nature of Canada's cultural mosaic have been the changes in definitions and procedures by which information on ethnic and cultural origins of the population have been obtained. As recently as the 1971 census, only one response was allowed to the ethnic-origin question, generally the one indicating ancestry on the paternal side before coming to this continent. Not until 1981 was a multiple-origin ancestry either considered or accepted as an acceptable answer. More recent censuses have actively encouraged the multiple-origin response by specifically asking for as many origins as apply and providing four spaces for "write-in" answers. The number of multiple responses, initially low, at 7 percent, in 1981, dramatically increased, to 29 percent in 1991 and 36 percent five years later, at the time of the 1996 census.

To further complicate matters, the numbers reporting "Canadian" as their ethnic ancestry continued to increase in spite of specific and continuing efforts to explicitly state in the census instructions that "Canadian" was not a valid answer to the ethnic-origin question. In 1991, 2.8 percent had reported "Canadian" as a single origin, while another 1 percent included "Canadian" as part of a multiple-ancestry response. In 1996, after including "Canadian" as one of a list of 24 examples of ethnic origins provided in the actual question on the census form, more than 5 million respondents, or 19 percent, gave "Canadian" as their only origin, while another 14 percent included "Canadian" as one of their multiple ancestries (Statistics Canada, 1993, 1998).

The implications of these changes and the nature of the responses suggest that, prior to 1971, Canada has been depicted as a society composed of a number of ethnic-origin groups maintaining a relative degree of cultural homogeneity through ethnic endogamy and immigration. However, such attempts to depict Canada as a model of "cultural pluralism" can be sustained only by ignoring the extent of assimilation that has occurred, as reflected by the increasing levels of ethnic intermarriage, which has characterized Canada's population over the years (Richard, 1991). Based on the traditional notion that every person has only a single ethnic origin, usually on the paternal side, trend analysis continues to point to the declining influence of the British/French bicultural base. The British Isles single-origin data have shown a major decline, from 61 percent in 1871 to 45 percent in 1971, along with a much smaller decline in the population of French origins in the same period, from 31 to just under 29 percent.

Extending the analysis to 1991 on the basis of the single-origin concept employed in the censuses prior to 1971 and identifying the French–British multiples that were first reported in the 1981 census, shows, in Table 5.1, that the bicultural base declined further by 1991, barely maintaining a slight bicultural majority of 51 percent. The absurdity of maintaining the myth of cultural homogeneity for the founding ethnic groups becomes readily apparent in the results of the 1996 census showing the percentage distribution of the population by ethnic origin, in Table 5.2. When persons are not only encour-

TABLE 5.2
▼
TOTAL POPULATION BY ETHNIC ORIGIN, CANADA, 1996

Ethnic Origin	Number	Percent
Single Origins: Total	18 303 625	64.4
Multiple Origins: Total	10 224 500	35.6
Some British ancestry		
Single British Isles	3 267 525	11.5
British-only multiples	1 606 445	5.6
British and Canadian	1 179 725	4.1
British and Other	2 217 370	7.8
British, Canadian, and Other	598 635	2.1
Some British and French ancestry		
British and French multiples	856 985	3.0
British, French, and Canadian	280 595	1.0
British, French, and Other	518 480	1.8
British, French, Canadian, and Other	121 870	0.4
Some French ancestry		
Single French origin	2 683 840	9.4
French-only multiples	12 430	0
French and Canadian	597 605	2.1
French and Other	435 205	1.5
French, Canadian, and Other	121 805	0.4
Mostly French or British[a]		
Single Canadian origin	5 326 995	18.7
Canadian and Other	579 045	2.0
No British or French ancestry		
Single European origin	3 742 895	13.1
Single Arab origin	188 430	0.7
Single West Asian	106 865	0.4
Single South Asian	590 150	2.1
Single East or Southeast Asian	1 271 450	4.5
Single African origin	137 315	0.5
Single Pacific Islander	5 765	0.0
Single Latin, Central, and South American	118 635	0.4
Single Caribbean origin	305 290	1.1
Single Aboriginal origin	477 635	1.7
Other single origins	80 845	0.3
Multiple origins	1 098 295	3.8
Total Population	28 528 125	100.0

[a] Although the increase in reporting of "Canadian" ethnic origins may have had an impact on the reporting of single origins for many groups, British Isles origins and French origins appear to have been particularly affected.

Source: Statistics Canada, *1996 Census of Canada.* See http://www.statcan.ca

aged, but instructed, to provide multiple origins, where applicable, only 12 and 9 percent persisted in giving single British or French origins, respectively — hardly a realistic portrait of Canada's cultural mosaic.

Assuming that most of those with multiple origins, including either of or both British and French, or even Canadian, origins, have experienced some degree of assimilation by the bicultural dominant population, a significantly different picture of Canada's cultural mosaic emerges. Rather than withering away, the British and French bicultural base can be seen to have been augmented through the intermarrying of members of minority ethnic origins with members of the two culturally dominant groups. Canada appears to still have a strong bicultural base, with 75 percent of its population having only or some British or French ancestry. Just 13 percent have "other European" single ancestry, 8 percent Arab or Asian, and 4 percent other single origins or multiple origins other than British, French, Acadian, or Canadian (Statistics Canada, 1998).

CONCLUSION
▼

Canada has been touted as a multicultural nation where minority ethnic groups can become successfully integrated into society without becoming totally assimilated and losing all their distinctive cultural characteristics. Demographically, our population has multi-ethnic and multi-racial origins and has experienced a considerable amount of cultural assimilation through ethnic and religious intermarriage and/or from the acculturation pressures from peer groups or schools in subsequent generations of immigrant families. For some, for example, the foreign-born from non-western-European or non-European countries, this level of integration may not be possible in their lifetimes, or even for their second generation. There is considerable evidence that the more different one's culture is perceived to be from that of either of Canada's founding charter groups, and the stronger one's ethnic identity and "ethnic connectedness" to one's ethnic community in Canada, the longer it may take to become sufficiently integrated and assimilated to become a fully participating member of Canadian society on a basis of equality (Kalbach & Kalbach, 1996).

After some twenty years of experience under the country's multicultural policies, support has begun to weaken for the policy of maintaining heritage cultures as a means of reducing discrimination and promoting social cohesion in Canadian society (Economic Council of Canada, 1991). The policy was meant to encourage the preservation of "as much of ethnic culture as is compatible with Canadian customs" (Economic Council of Canada, 1991). The persistence of some differences may be seen as helping to maintain the social cohesiveness of the ethnic community, on the one hand, while, on the other hand, providing the basis for the continuing discrimination and prejudice experienced by individuals of some ethnic origins. Clarifying the nature of Canada's cultural mosaic and the extent to which acculturation has been an essential part of the process of integration into Canadian society should help in the development of multicultural policies to reduce those interethnic cultural differences underlying the persistence of ethnic and racial discrimination.

REFERENCES
▼

Canadian Encyclopedia. (1999). *The Canadian encyclopedia.* Deluxe Edition (7 CD-ROM set). Toronto: McClelland & Stewart.

Economic Council of Canada. (1991). *New faces in the crowd.* Ottawa: Minister of Supply & Services Canada.

Government of Canada. (1870–71). *Census of Canada,* Vol. 2, Tbls. II & III. Ottawa: Department of Agriculture, December 1873.

Kalbach, W.E. (1976). Canada: A demographic analysis. In G. Ramu & S. Johnson (Eds.), *Introduction to Canadian society* (pp. 11–76). Toronto: Macmillan of Canada.

Kalbach, M.A, & Kalbach, W.E. (1996). Ethnic diversity and persistence as factors in socioeconomic inequality: A challenge for the twenty-first century. In the Proceedings of the 1995 Symposium "Towards the XXI Century: Emerging Socio-Demographic Trends and Policy Issues in Canada." Ottawa, St. Paul University.

Kalbach, W.E., & McVey, W.W. (1971). *The demographic basis of Canadian society.* Toronto: McGraw-Hill.

———. (1979). *The demographic basis of Canadian society* (2nd ed.). Toronto: McGraw-Hill Ryerson.

McVey, W.W., & Kalbach, W.E. (1995). *The population of Canada.* Toronto: Nelson Canada.

Pointing, R.J. (1997). *First Nations in Canada: Perspectives on opportunity, empowerment, and self determination.* Toronto: McGraw-Hill Ryerson.

Richard, M.A. (1991). *Ethnic groups and marital choices.* Vancouver: University of British Columbia Press.

Secretary of the Board of Registration and Statistics. (1853). *Census of the Canadas for 1851–52,* Appendix 4. Quebec: John Lovell at His Steam Printing Establishment, Mountain Street.

Statistics Canada. (1977). *1971 Census of Canada: "Ethnic Origins of Canada."* Cat. 99-709. Ottawa: Minister of Industry, Trade & Commerce, May.

————. (1984). *1981 Census of Canada: "Ethnic Origins."* Cat. 92-911. Ottawa: Minister of Supply & Services, February.

————. (1993). *1991 Census of Canada: "Ethnic Origins: The Nation."* Cat. 93-315. Ottawa: Minister of Industry, Science & Technology, February.

————. (1997). *1996 Census Dictionary,* Ottawa: Minister of Industry.

————. (1998). *1996 Census of Canada* [On-line]. Available at http://www. statcan.ca.

PATTERNS OF ETHNIC IDENTIFICATION AND THE "CANADIAN" RESPONSE

RAVI PENDAKUR AND FERNANDO MATA

INTRODUCTION
▼

There has been a great deal of discussion in both the popular press and the political arena regarding the validity of the ethnicity question and the reporting of "Canadian" as an ethnic origin. The purpose of this study is to understand the patterns of ethnic identification and assess the impact of an increased "Canadian" response rate on the validity of the ethnicity question. Our central question is to determine the degree to which the reporting of "Canadian" as an ethnic origin distorts the reporting of other origins (i.e., to what degree are people reporting "Canadian" at the expense of their other ethnic identifications).

The impetus for this study stems from two sources. First, in the 1996 census, the format of the ethnicity question was changed substantially, and "Canadian" was added to the list of examples. The new question format means that it will be very difficult, if not impossible, to compare 1996 data with those from previous census years. As well, it has been shown in previous National Census Tests that including "Canadian" as an example markedly increases the number of people who report "Canadian" as an ethnic origin. Second, presentations made by representatives from Statistics Canada suggested that Statistics Canada wishes to remove the question from the 2001 census on the grounds that it is difficult and expensive to code, it imposes a response burden, and it is politically sensitive. Further, given that there is a marked increase in the proportion of respondents writing in "Canadian" as an ethnic origin, the interpretations of the results are seen as ambiguous.

Because data from the 1996 Census were not available at the time of analysis, we used the National Census Test that was conducted in 1993. The

National Census Test was administered to a representative sample of Canadian households and tests the 1996 census questionnaire and methodology. It contains all the relevant information to undertake such an analysis.

This paper is divided into two parts. Part One reviews the way in which ethnicity data are collected by the census and the changes to the question between 1991 and 1996. Part Two examines the responses to the ethnic-origin question from the 1993 National Census Test, using descriptive and discriminant analysis in order to determine the degree to which people responding "Canadian" are similar or not similar to people reporting other origins.

THE ETHNIC-ORIGIN QUESTIONS IN THE CENSUS
▼

Ethnicity is a multifaceted concept. Criteria for membership in an ethnic group can include, among other things, self-categorization or identification, descent, specific cultural traits such as custom or language, and a social organization for interaction both within the group and with people outside the group. Past censuses have asked a number of questions that attempt to tap into these facets of cultural origin. Such questions include those on place of birth, period of immigration, mother tongue, and home language, in addition to the more general question on ethnic origin. In the absence of a question on ethnic origin, it would therefore be possible to capture at least some information on Canada's ethnic dimension. However, a question that probes more generally for ethnic origin casts a wider net than is evident in the questions above by capturing people who are not immigrants and do not speak a heritage language, but nevertheless are part of a minority ethnic group.

The 1991 ethnic-origin question captured information through the use of fifteen check-in boxes as well as two write-in boxes (see Figure 6.1). The question format allowed respondents to provide more than one ethnic origin (in fact, a respondent could tick all fifteen check-in boxes and write in up to three additional responses). It could be argued that this format led respondents to choose the tick-off boxes rather than writing in an origin because it was easier to do so. For this reason, although the ability of the question format to pick up multiple origins was advantageous, the pattern of responses may have suppressed detail (for example, it is possible that people simply ticked off "Italian" rather than responding with a more detailed answer of "Sicilian").

In 1996, the response format to the question was changed dramatically (see Figure 6.2). Check-in boxes were removed, and the respondent was provided with four write-in boxes. As well, "Canadian" was added to the list of examples in the question. Up to six origins were captured. In one sense, the 1996

FIGURE 6.1
▼
1991 QUESTION ON ETHNIC ORIGIN

---

15. To which ethnic or cultural group(s) did this person's
    ancestors belong?

    Mark or specify as many as applicable

    Note:
    While most people of Canada view themselves
    as Canadian, information on their ancestral
    origins has been collected since the 1901
    Census to reflect the changing composition of
    the Canadian population and is needed to
    ensure that everyone, regardless of his/her
    ethnic or cultural background, has equal
    opportunity to share fully in the economic,
    social, cultural and political life in Canada.
    Therefore, this question refers to the origins of
    the person's ancestors

    See Guide
    Examples of other ethnic or cultural groups are:
    Portuguese, Greek, Indian from India, Pakistani,
    Filipino, Vietnamese, Japanese, Lebanese,
    Haitian, etc.

French
English
German
Scottish
Italian
Irish
Ukrainian
Chinese
Dutch (Netherlands)
Jewish
Polish
Black
North American Indian
Métis
Inuit/Eskimo

Other ethnic or
cultural group(s) -
Specify

_____

_____

FIGURE 6.2
▼
1996 CENSUS QUESTION ON ETHNIC ORIGIN (QUESTION 17)

To which ethnic of cultural group(s) did this person's **ancestors** belong?

For example, French, English, German, Scottish, Canadian, Italian, Irish, Chinese,
Cree, Micmac, Métis, Inuit (Eskimo), Ukrainian, Dutch, East Indian, Polish,
Portuguese, Jewish, Haitian, Jamaican, Vietnamese, Lebanese, Chilean, Somali, etc.

_____

_____

_____

format could provide a more accurate picture of ethnic identity in Canada because it did not lead the respondent to the same degree as the 1991 question. Previous census tests, however, have shown that the addition of "Canadian" as an example category may lead more respondents to simply write in "Canadian," rather than thinking more deeply about their ethnic origins. Our research question is to determine the degree to which this is the case.

THE "CANADIAN" RESPONSE
▼

Statistics Canada has always accepted "Canadian" as an ethnic category. In censuses previous to 1991, the proportion of people responding "Canadian" was relatively low. In 1991, three-quarters of a million people reported only Canadian origins, with another quarter-million reporting "Canadian" in combination with other origins, most often "British" or "French" (see Table 6.1). What is interesting is that the reporting of "Canadian," even by more than 1 million people, did not really affect the number of people reporting origins other than British or French.[1] Because of this reporting pattern, the reporting of "Canadian" was not an issue in determining the number of people reporting minority origins.

In 1996, the reporting of "Canadian" as an ethnic origin increased more than eightfold. One in five respondents reported "Canadian" as his or her only

TABLE 6.1
▼
PATTERN OF CANADIAN RESPONSE, CANADA, 1991, 1996

Ethnic Origin	1991	1996
Canadian only	765 095	5 326 995
British and Canadian	116 530	1 179 925
British, Canadian, and Other	40 160	598 635
French and Canadian	20 825	597 605
French, Canadian, and Other	5 280	121 805
Canadian and Other	58 030	579 050
British, French, and Canadian	13 545	121 870
British, French, Canadian, and Other	13 560	280 595
Total	1 033 025	8 806 480

Source: 1991, Statistics Canada publication 93-315; 1996, *Census Release on Ethnic Origin.*

ethnic origin. An additional 3.5 million people reported "Canadian" in combination with other origins (usually either "British" or "French"). If reporting of "Canadian" is largely restricted to those of British and French origin, such reporting should not pose a problem in determining the composition of Canada's minority population. If however, reporting of "Canadian" is misinterpreted by respondents to be a test of nationality or loyalty to Canada, the validity of the question could be jeopardized. This is because it is possible that people will respond "Canadian" even though their origins include other ancestries as well.

DATA ANALYSIS
▼

Our strategy for data analysis follows several steps. Using the 1993 National Census Test, we first explore the sociodemographic, residential, linguistic, and economic indicators of respondents reporting different ethnic origins. Second, we conduct a discriminant analysis of the data.[2] Through the discriminant function calculated by the procedure, differences between groups are captured. The separation between those who report only "Canadian" as an origin, combinations of "Canadian" with other origins, and the remaining origins is paramount. Third, to establish differences between groups using the information contained in the major discriminant functions, we perform a hierarchical cluster analysis with a minimal number of solutions. All these analyses are carried out to determine the degree to which respondents identifying themselves as Canadian are substantively different from those reporting other ethnic origins.

The 1993 National Census Test (NCT) data base includes members of the labour force from a pool of approximately 32 000 individuals. Initial analysis determined that this data base provided enough cases to conduct an analysis on the patterns of ethnic identification. From this data base, we examined responses from questions concerning mother tongue, ethnic origin, place of birth, province of residence, citizenship, age, education, labour force characteristics, and income. Statistically, all these sociodemographic characteristics can be summarized by simpler measures such as functions or linear combinations of variables. Orthogonal measures (independent of each other) allow for the estimation of the average positions of different ethnic groups in a spatial plane spanned by the measures. Closer proximity of particular groups in such a plane can be interpreted as a rough measure of similarity between groups. Conversely, greater distance between the groups could be interpreted as a greater magnitude of dissimilarity in their characteristics.

If the reporting of "Canadian" as an ethnic origin is randomly distributed across all groups, it is expected that the average position of the "Canadian" group will be relatively equidistant from all the other groups. If, on the contrary, the "Canadian" group clusters with the British, French, or British and French group, this result could be interpreted as a sign that these respondents come mostly from "majority" backgrounds. Finally, if the "Canadian" group clusters with non–British or French ethnicities, this can be interpreted as an indication that people from these origins are likely to report "Canadian" as an ethnic origin.

Twelve mutually exclusive ethnic categories are included in the analysis:

1. Canadian single origin
2. British single origin
3. French single origin
4. European single origin
5. Non-European single origin
6. Aboriginal single origin
7. Canadian, British and French
8. Canadian and Other
9. British and French
10. British and Other
11. French and Other
12. Residual (all other groups, including other multiple combinations)

The analysis of basic sociodemographic characteristics suggests that there are differences between those who report "Canadian" as an ethnic origin and those who do not. Table 6.2 describes the major characteristics of the twelve groups studied. While there are few differences in average age and gender composition, those who identify themselves as Canadian are predominantly citizens by birth, with relatively low levels of schooling. Half of people reporting "Canadian" report English as mother tongue, and half report French, this despite the fact that only 23 percent of the total population report French as mother tongue. Forty-three percent of people reporting "Canadian" live in Quebec. Just over 60 percent of those reporting only "Canadian" are active in the labour force. However, labour force participation is higher for those reporting "Canadian" in combination with other origins. The same is true for income characteristics. The average total income of people reporting only "Canadian" is $22 355, which is low in comparison with other groups, and lower in comparison with those reporting "Canadian" with other origins. The descriptive statistics suggest that there are differences between those reporting "Canadian" and those reporting other origins that are worth pursuing using discriminant analysis.

TABLE 6.2
SOCIODEMOGRAPHIC INDICATORS OF THE ETHNIC GROUPS EXAMINED

Indicators	Canadian Only	Canadian, British, and French	Canadian and Other	British	French	European (single origin)	Non-European (single origin)	British and French	British and Other	French and Other	Aboriginal (single origin)	Residual
Mean Age	40.0	40.4	34.9	47.2	44.2	48.5	39.6	38.3	38.1	36.5	35.5	42.6
% Males	49.4	47.1	42.1	48.7	51.1	50.7	49.4	47.5	46.6	46.3	47.8	47.9
PROVINCIAL REPRESENTATION												
% Atlantic	22.1	24.3	11.6	41.8	19.4	4.3	5.8	40.1	12.7	12.6	11.2	23.6
% Quebec	43.0	19.1	8.3	1.9	58.9	4.5	5.9	9.2	1.4	16.7	11.9	15.6
% Ontario	18.7	29.6	31.1	29.6	13.0	37.0	28.5	31.7	33.5	30.0	16.4	30.0
% Prairies	11.1	18.0	28.5	17.6	6.5	43.0	43.7	13.1	36.9	32.0	53.7	22.2
% B.C.	5.0	9.1	20.5	9.1	2.2	11.2	16.1	5.8	15.5	8.6	6.7	8.5
SOCIO-ECONOMIC CHARACTERISTICS												
% with Post-Secondary Degrees	7.9	13.1	10.9	12.7	12.0	11.0	18.3	11.5	15.7	9.9	0.7	7.3
% in Labour Force	60.9	64.9	68.9	57.6	58.2	59.2	65.1	65.7	69.7	66.3	50.7	48.0
Average Total Income ($)	22 355	33 004	39 872	36 161	18 059	41 993	29 387	34 031	33 595	25 249	10 243	64 184

(continued)

(Table 6.2 continued)

Indicators	Canadian Only	Canadian, British, and French	Canadian and Other	British	French	European (single origin)	Non-European (single origin)	British and French	British and Other	British French and Other	Aboriginal (single origin)	Residual
CITIZENSHIP												
% Citizens by Birth	98.8	97.3	98.0	88.9	97.5	64.8	49.7	97.0	92.4	92.4	97.0	78.7
% Naturalized Citizens	0.6	1.6	1.3	8.5	1.6	28.7	29.6	1.9	4.4	4.4	1.5	5.6
% Non-Citizens	0.2	0.4	0	1.5	0.5	5.0	18.0	0.3	2.0	1.7	0.7	1.2
IMMIGRANT STATUS												
% Immigrants	0.6	1.0	1.6	0.9	0.7	34.1	47.3	0.2	1.9	3.9	0.7	17.7
% U.K. and U.S. born	0.5	1.2	1.0	9.4	0.6	1.3	3.1	1.6	5.2	2.2	1.5	2.4
% European born	0	0.3	0	0.2	1.2	31.4	3.5	0	0.3	3.2	0	1.8
% Other	0.5	0.6	0.7	0.8	0.4	2.7	43.7	0.2	1.5	0.7	0.7	15.9
MOTHER TONGUE												
% English	50.4	71.0	89.7	98.5	12.7	45.4	49.7	82.5	97.7	68.5	62.7	64.3
% French	48.2	26.3	9.3	1.0	86.3	1.3	1.4	14.8	0.6	25.1	14.9	17.7
% English and French	0.3	0.5	0	0.1	0.5	0.1	0.1	2.3	0.1	0.5	0	0.4
% Other	0.8	1.8	0.3	0.1	0.3	52.8	48.5	0.3	1.4	5.9	21.6	5.5
Weighted N*	3 560 000	2 020 000	250 000	4 590 000	2 300 000	3 210 000	2 250 000	670 000	1 430 000	340 000	80 000	850 000

For the discriminant analysis, seventeen variables were used: age, income, and fifteen dummy variables representing sociodemographic, residential, educational, citizenship-status, linguistic, and place-of-birth individual characteristics. To avoid "closure" errors leading to multiple collinearity, dummy variables corresponding to Atlantic-region residence, non-citizen status, and immigrant status were excluded from the discriminating variables list.

A total of eleven functions were extracted from the data (see Table 6.3). Each discriminant function has a corresponding Wilks' lambda. This statistic (which is X^2 distributed) is the proportion of total variance not accounted for by differences between groups with respect to the function. Smaller lambdas are associated with a better reduction of error variance. The eleven functions accounted for a combined Wilks' lambda of 0.18, which produced a X^2 of 43 348, found to be statistically significant at the $p < .001$ level.

In discriminant analysis, eigenvalues can be used to describe the separation between groups. The eigenvalue is defined as the between sum of squares to the within sum of squares ratio where discriminant scores are treated as dependent variables, and group categories as independent ones. Large eigenvalues in functions reflect better discriminatory power. The first function, the most important, has the greatest eigenvalue (1.11), accounting for almost half of the variation in the data. The second function, almost half as powerful, has an eigenvalue of 0.60 and explains less in terms of the between-group variance present in the data.

What did the first two discriminant functions measure? The first function clearly separated groups whose were mostly made up of Canadian-born (particularly those whose mother tongue is French) from those groups in which immigrants were more numerous. The variable that had the positive loadings on this function was "Other" mother tongue (.73). French mother tongue had a negative loading of –.38. The second function maximized the differences between Quebec residents and non-Quebec residents, and their corresponding associated characteristics (e.g., English mother tongue). Calculated structure coefficients (correlations between the discriminant function and binary coefficients representing the groups) reinforced this pattern of differentiation.

More than three quarters of the group's separation was captured by the first two functions, and, consequently, the bulk of the separation between the groups across the discriminating variables can be readily summarized by their positions along the functions. The orthogonal property (non-correlation) of the discriminant functions allows us to map the average position of groups (also known as "centroids") on a plane spanned by the two discriminant functions. This graphic representation of the differences between groups is presented in Figure 6.3. Such a presentation allows us to describe the differences

TABLE 6.3
▼
DISCRIMINANT ANALYSIS RESULTS

Panel A

VARIABLES AND DISCRIMINANT COEFFICIENTS

Discriminant Variables	Mean	Standard Deviation	Standardized Discriminant Coef. Function		Structure Coef. Function	
			1	**2**	**1**	**2**
Age	43.15	18.17	0.01	-0.12	0.06	-0.02
Male	0.49	0.50	0	0.03	0	0.03
Post-Secondary Degree	0.12	0.32	0.02	-0.02	0.03	-0.02
Total Income	32 571	28 526	0	0	0.02	0
In Labour Force	0.61	0.49	0.02	0.01	0.01	0.01
Quebec Resident	0.18	0.39	-0.11	0.10	-0.46	0.46
Ontario Resident	0.27	0.45	0.15	0.22	0.13	-0.08
Prairies Resident	0.22	0.42	0.33	0.38	0.28	0.08
B.C. Resident	0.09	0.28	0.13	0.17	0.11	-0.04
Citizen by Birth	0.87	0.34	-0.13	0.05	-0.4	-0.20
Citizen by Naturalization	0.09	0.28	0	-0.01	0.33	0.16
English Mother Tongue	0.66	0.47	0.37	-0.17	0.17	-0.90
French Mother Tongue	0.22	0.41	-0.38	0.62	-0.71	0.66
Other Mother Tongue	0.11	0.31	0.73	0.47	0.65	0.60
Born in U.K. or U.S.	0.04	0.19	-0.04	-0.15	0.04	-0.21
Born in Europe	0.05	0.21	-0.02	0.09	0.35	0.36
Born in Other Countries	0.04	0.20	0.06	0.02	0.30	0.22

Panel B

SUMMARY STATISTICS

Major Functions	Eigenvalue	% Variance	Canonical
1 (Immigrant Status)	1.11	49.2	0.72
2 (Quebec vs. outside Quebec)	0.60	26.5	0.61

Significance of Functions

WILKS' LAMBDA

Test of Function(s)	Wilks' Lambda	Chi-Square	d.f.	Significance
1 through 11	0.18	43478	187	0
2 through 11	0.38	24438	160	0
3 through 11	0.61	12469	135	0
4 through 11	0.84	4574	112	0
5 through 11	0.90	2737	91	0
6 through 11	0.96	1116	72	0
7 through 11	0.98	471	55	0
8 through 11	0.99	205	40	0
9 through 11	1	59	27	0
10 through 11	1	25	16	0.06
11	1	6	7	0.51

FIGURE 6.3
▼
RELATIVE POSITION OF GROUPS IN DISCRIMINANT SPACE

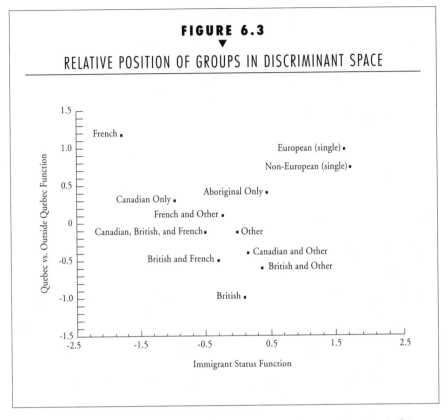

between those who identify themselves as Canadian or combinations of Canadian with other ethnicities in the form of spatial distance.

Visual inspection of the points in Figure 6.3 suggest that those who identify solely as Canadian are far away from those reporting European and non-European origins (located in the far left of the figure) while occupying intermediate positions between those reporting "French" (upper left) or multiple ethnicities (central cluster of the figure). Those who report "Canadian" in combination with other origins appear to be indistinguishable from the members of the central cluster of the chart. In the same way, those who report "Canadian" are fairly close to those who report either British origins, or French origins, in combination with other origins. This clustering process suggests that these groups have similar characteristics, whereas they are dissimilar from those reporting European and non-European origins.

To move from plain visual inspection to statistical testing aimed at determining if there are clustering patterns present in the data, we also conducted a homogeneity test using post hoc comparisons of means applying the Scheffé criteria. Results of these tests (presented in Table 6.4) reveal that there are statistically significant differences between the means of the groups. At

TABLE 6.4
▼
HOMOGENEITY SUBSETS FOUND USING SCHEFFÉ TESTS ON GROUP'S CENTROIDS

Discriminant Scores from Function 1 for Analysis 1

SUBSET FOR ALPHA = .05

Groups	1	2	3	4	5	6	7	8
French (single origin)	-1.78							
Canadian (single origin)		-1.03						
Canadian, British, and French			-0.56					
British and French			-0.46					
French and Other			-0.34	-0.34				
Canadian and Other				-0.17				
Residual category				-0.14	-0.14			
British (single origin)				-0.12	-0.12			
British and Other					0.08	0.08		
Aboriginal (single origin)						0.19		
European (single origin)							1.25	
Non-European (single origin)								1.84
Level of Significance	1	1	0.07	0.08	0.06	0.95	1	1

Discriminant Scores from Function 2 for Analysis 1

SUBSET FOR ALPHA = .05

Groups	1	2	3	4	5	6
British (single origin)	-1.09					
British and Other	-0.88	-0.88				
British and French		-0.69				
Canadian and Other		-0.67				
Canadian, British, and French			-0.32			
French and Other			-0.24			
Aboriginal (single origin)			-0.21			
European (single origin)			-0.21			
Residual category			-0.16			
Canadian (single origin)				0.2		
Non-European (single origin)				0.77		
French (single origin)						1.1
Level of Significance	0.14	0.15	0.58	1	1	1

least eight homogeneous subsets were found for the first discriminant function, and six were found for the second discriminant function.

The next and final stage involves cluster analysis of a twelve-by-twelve dissimilarity matrix between the groups. We conducted a hierarchical cluster analysis using standardized Euclidean distances as dissimilarity measures between average discriminant scores. Our primary goal was to determine the extent to which people who claimed only Canadian origin would form clusters with other groups. Given that we have twelve groups, a maximum of a four-cluster solution was considered optimal. Results of the clustering solutions are presented in Table 6.5. The two-cluster solution clearly separates European and non-European single origins from the other groups. In the three-cluster solution, the Canadian and French single-origin groups form a separate cluster different from the remaining groups. In the four-cluster solution, the Canadian and French single-origin groups remain separate, while the Aboriginal group separates from the central cluster of groups. In short, those who declare a single Canadian ethnic identity in the NCT have more in common with those who declare a French single origin (or at the most multiples of British and French) and very little in common with those reporting Aboriginal or specific European or non-European origins.

TABLE 6.5
▼
HIERARCHICAL CLUSTER ANALYSIS SOLUTIONS*

Case	4 Clusters	3 Clusters	2 Clusters
Canadian (single origin)	1	1	1
British (single origin)	2	2	1
French (single origin)	1	1	1
Canadian, British, and French	2	2	1
Canadian and Other	2	2	1
European (single origin)	3	3	2
Non-European (single origin)	3	3	2
British and French	2	2	1
British and Other	2	2	1
French and Other	2	2	1
Aboriginal (single origin)	4	2	1
Residual category	2	2	1

* Based on a dissimilarity matrix of standardized Euclidean distances.

CONCLUSION
▼

The goal of this study was to explore the degree to which the data collected in the 1996 census question on ethnicity are valid for the study of minority groups in Canada. We set out to examine the pattern of ethnic identification in Canada, particularly with respect to those reporting "Canadian" as an ethnic origin. Our strategy for analysis of the 1993 National Census Test data base followed several steps. First, we explored the sociodemographic, residential, linguistic, and economic indicators of respondents according to their responses to the ethnic-origin question. Second, we conducted a discriminant analysis of the data. Third, to establish differences between groups, using the information contained in the major discriminant functions, we performed a hierarchical cluster analysis with a minimal number of solutions.

We found that people reporting "Canadian" as an ethnic origin are more similar to those who report either British or French origins. They are, however, less similar to those reporting origins other than British or French. It appears therefore that, despite the relatively high proportion of people reporting "Canadian," it does not have a measurable impact on the reporting of minority ethnic groups.

Ethnicity encompasses a wide range of concepts. If we are limited to questions concerning language knowledge or place of birth, we would be unable to capture information on the cultural origins of individuals who are born in Canada (which would not be captured by the "place of birth" question) or those who speak only an official language. This would result in an information vacuum pertaining to a large and growing portion of the population.

In our view, despite the limitations of trying to tap a multidimensional concept such as ethnic origin through a single question, and the difficulties posed by the increased Canadian count, the ethnic question of the census continues to provide solid information on Canada's diverse population. The substantial reporting of "Canadian" as an ethnic origin has not invalidated the data collected concerning minorities in Canada.

NOTES
▼

1. We say this because a comparison of the number of people reporting origins other than British or French in 1986 and 1991 suggested that, in many cases, the counts went up rather than down. This suggests that the "Canadian" response is

probably coming from the majority, British and French groups, rather than the minority groups.

2. Discriminant analysis is a multivariate technique that determines if a particular combination of variables is able to separate individuals in terms of their group membership. In this case, a respondent's age, education, place of birth, mother tongue, citizenship status, province of residence, and income are used to see the degree to which these characteristics are successful in separating people into different ethnic groups.

ETHNIC AND CIVIC SELF-IDENTITY IN CANADA: ANALYSES OF 1974 AND 1991 NATIONAL SURVEYS[1]

RUDOLF KALIN AND JOHN W. BERRY

INTRODUCTION
▼

Self-identity in the context of multiculturalism is an interesting and important topic. Individuals living in a diverse society may choose to identify themselves in a variety of ways. They may view themselves in national (e.g., Canadian), provincial (e.g., Manitoban), or ethnic (e.g., Ukrainian-Canadian or Ukrainian) terms. In Canada, a good deal of attention has been focussed on ethnic self-identity (e.g., Kalin & Berry, 1979; Aboud, 1981; Driedger, 1989). Ethnic identity, however, has to be understood in the context of regional and national affiliations. In a plural society like Canada, a fragmentation of identities and allegiances is possible (Cairns, 1993). One way to reconcile possible fragmentation is to think of a person's orientation to different groups as being nested. Individuals can feel pride in, and allegiance to, smaller communities (e.g., ethnic groups) nested within the larger community of the nation-state.

Another creative suggestion on how possibly fragmented loyalties can coalesce into a unitary allegiance to a large community is provided by Breton (1988) in his discussion of two types of nationalism. According to Breton, *ethnic nationalism* (which can also be called "cultural" or "primary") is founded on cultural unity. Here, inclusion in or exclusion from a community is based on ethnic factors, such as common ancestry, language, religion, and cultural distinctiveness. *Civic nationalism* (also called "political," "territorial," or "secondary"), on the other hand, is founded on pragmatic and utilitarian factors that form the basis of the collectivity. In civic nationalism, culture is dissociated from the political aspects of the state. It is Breton's thesis that in anglophone Canada, as well as in francophone Quebec, there has been a historical change from ethnic to civic nationalism, and that civic nationalism has come to incorporate cultural pluralism. Breton, however, also considers the shift from ethnic to civic nationalism to be further along in English Canada than in Quebec.

Ethnic identity becomes significant in Canada because Canadians have a variety of ethnic origins. However, ethnic identity is clearly not the same as ethnic origin. The question of how closely the two are related has been debated in the literature. For example, Lupul (1984) has taken Isajiw (1983) to task for suggesting that "everyone is ethnic." Lupul has suggested that the designation of Canadians as "ethnic" is accomplished primarily by social scientists, but this designation may have little reality in the minds of Canadians. Lupul has argued that many Canadians, primarily those of Anglo-Celtic origin, do not want to be considered ethnic. The late John Porter (1979) has suggested that "ethnicity may well be an artifact of the census rather than the social reality it is claimed to be ..." (p. 181).

There are other considerations that make the study of ethnic identity a significant issue in Canada. Many Canadians are of mixed ethnic heritage, and for these individuals it becomes an interesting question of how they resolve the question of ethnic identity. Others have ancestors who have been in Canada for many generations; hence, their ethnic origin, as opposed to their civic allegiance to Canada, may not be a significant feature of their self-identity.

The question of the subjective importance of ethnic identity is also significant for understanding the likely fate of multiculturalism, both as social fact and as public policy. Ethnic identity is a possible measure of the involvement in, and commitment of Canadians to, multiculturalism. If ethnic identity is strong and widespread, then most Canadians will have a stake in multiculturalism. On the other hand, if ethnic identity is weak and significant only to relatively few Canadians, public interest in and support for multiculturalism may be weak. We may even expect some opposition if a large number of Canadians feel that multiculturalism does not apply to them and therefore feel left out.

Ethnic identity has been defined by Driedger (1989) as "a positive personal attitude and attachment to a group with whom the individual believes he [sic] has a common ancestry based on shared characteristics and shared socio-cultural experiences" (p. 162). This definition refers essentially to "symbolic" ethnicity, which Gans (1979) describes as "love for and a pride in a tradition that can be felt without having to be incorporated in everyday behaviour" (p. 9). In contrast to "symbolic" is "behavioural" ethnic identity (Kalin & Berry, 1994), which consists of outward expressions of ethnicity, such as being able to speak a heritage language and use it frequently, choosing best friends primarily from one's own group, practising endogamy, and belonging to ethnic and/or religious organizations of one's group. Driedger's (1975, 1976) Ethnic Cultural Identity (ECI) index is a good measure of behavioural ethnic identity. The behavioural versus the symbolic aspects of ethnic identity are part of the insightful conceptualization of multiculturalism provided by Roberts and Clifton (1990), who differentiate between institutionalized, ritualistic, and symbolic multiculturalism, and assimilation. When both symbolic and behavioural ethnic identity are present, we have "institutionalized multiculturalism," where ethnic groups have a relatively high level of institutional completeness (Breton, 1964). Members have a strong sense of identity, and they conform to cultural norms and traditions. Where there is behavioural, but not symbolic, identity, we have "ritualistic multiculturalism." In "symbolic multiculturalism," members have a sense of symbolic identity, but they show no behavioural conformity with the cultural traditions. In the absence of any of the three types of multiculturalism, assimilation to a mainstream culture prevails.

Most social/psychological research on ethnic identity has addressed the assessment and interpretation of the symbolic form. This article follows in this tradition. Several different kinds of questions have been employed in studies assessing symbolic ethnic identity. Respondents can be provided with response alternatives, as in the national survey by Berry, Kalin, and Taylor (1977). After respondents were queried about their fathers' and mothers' ethnic origin, they were asked, "Do you think of yourself as a Canadian, ethnic origin–Canadian (e.g., Italian-Canadian), or ethnic origin (e.g., Italian, etc.)"? Berry et al. (1977) found that, in the total sample, 59 percent identified as Canadian. But there were substantial variations in ethnic identity according to ethnic origin. Among respondents of Anglo-Celtic origin, 80 percent identified as Canadian; among those of French origin, the most frequent response was French-Canadian (44 percent) followed by Canadian (26 percent), followed by Québécois (22 percent). Among Canadians of other ethnic origin, 59 percent identified as Canadian, 28 percent as ethnic Canadians, and 5 percent in terms of their ethnic origin without a hyphen.[2] In the survey by O'Bryan, Reitz, and Kuplowska (1976), 35 percent identified as Canadian, 45 percent had a dual identity, consisting either of ethnic-Canadian or a Canadian of other ethnic origin, and 17 percent identified with an ethnic-only label (e.g., Chinese). In a study of a large sample of Canadians, Boyd et al. (1981) discovered that 86 percent identified as Canadian. Frideres and Goldenberg (1977) studied ethnic identity in a sample of University of Calgary students. In their investigation, 67 percent identified as Canadian, 12 percent responded with a hyphenated identity, and 11 percent gave an ethnic-only response.

When respondents are given identity alternatives from which to select, it may well be possible that investigators suggest an appropriate response to respondents. In order to overcome this problem, Mackie (1978) asked a sample of adults from Calgary the following question: "Canada is made up of many people who have come from all over the world, like the Irish, Italian, Norwegian, Chinese, etc. Do you identify with any of these people? If so, which one?" Thirty-two percent in this sample gave an ethnic-only response (e.g., Italian), less than 1 percent gave a hyphenated response, but a substantial majority of 67 percent gave a response of "none." Mackie (1978) assessed ethnic identity in a second way. She asked respondents to provide twenty statements to the question "Who am I?" If ethnicity is salient to an individual's sense of self, it should appear in one of the statements. However, results showed that only 3 percent mentioned ethnic origin. Other factors, for example, religion with 18 percent, and being Canadian with 10 percent, were much more frequently mentioned.

In commenting on these results, Driedger, Thacker, and Currie (1982) wondered whether respondents might have missed the "etc." in Mackie's first question, and not finding their ethnic group among any of those mentioned, responded with none. Driedger et al. (1982) therefore proposed that an open-ended question would be a more suitable way to assess people's identity. They conducted studies in Winnipeg and Edmonton, where they asked respondents: "How would you define your ethnicity?" The three responses were then coded into one of three categories — namely, Canadian, hyphenated Canadian, and ethnic. In Winnipeg, 30 percent identified as Canadian, 10 percent gave a hyphenated response, and 50 percent gave an ethnic response. In Edmonton, 49 percent identified as Canadian, 8 percent gave a hyphenated response, and 37 percent responded with an ethnic group only. Driedger reasoned that in Western Canada ethnicity plays a greater role than in the East and felt that the higher ethnic or hyphenated response, as compared with the national sample by Berry et al. (1977), was primarily a result of difference in the region of respondents.

Mackie and Brinkerhoff (1984) completed a comprehensive study comparing different methods of soliciting ethnic-identity responses and measuring ethnic salience, and concluded that, in their sample of Calgary residents of primarily European origin, ethnic identity had low salience. Mackie and Brinkerhoff (1988) conducted a comparative study of Canadian and American students. They expected ethnic identity to be more salient in the Canadian sample because of the mosaic orientation, as opposed to the melting-pot ideology of the United States. Results did not follow these expectations: the salience of ethnic identity was equally low in both countries.

A study assessing both behavioural and symbolic identity was reported by Weinfeld (1981). Using data from a 1970 survey of Toronto household heads, he examined the ethnic identification of Slavic, Jewish, and Italian respondents who were either immigrants or Canadian-born. Ethnic self-identification (as opposed to identifying as Canadian) was high among this sample (e.g., 80 percent of Slavic immigrants had an ethnic identity versus only 20 percent with a Canadian identity). Weinfeld also noted, however, that behavioural ethnic identity lagged behind symbolic (which he called "affective") and followed more of an "assimilationist" versus a "survivalist" pattern.

Past studies, then, reveal somewhat variable results regarding the distribution of identity choices among Canadians. Some indicate that "Canadian" is by far the predominant choice, this result being obtained primarily from national or non-selected samples. Another set of studies reveals a lower prevalence of Canadian identity and a more frequent choice of some form of heritage identity. Such results were obtained primarily in studies where respondents were drawn from ethnic groups. To get an accurate sense of the distribution of identity choices in the Canadian population, it seems appropriate to study national and representative samples.

The purpose of this article was to examine ethnic- and civic-identity choices obtained in representative national surveys conducted in 1974 and 1991; to probe the distribution nationally, by region and by ethnic origin; to discover changes between surveys conducted in 1974 and 1991; to identify attitudinal characteristics associated with different identity choices. In brief, three basic questions were asked: How do Canadians identify? Is a civic identity of "Canadian" compatible with multiculturalism? Is an ethnic identity compatible with a civic allegiance to the country as a whole?

METHOD
▼

The present study examined results from two national surveys, conducted primarily to investigate attitudes toward multiculturalism and related topics. The assessment of identity was an important but limited part of these surveys.

1974 SURVEY

This survey has been reported in full by Berry et al. (1977). For that study, 1849 respondents 16 years of age or older and able to speak French or English were interviewed in person during June and July 1974. Interviews were concerned with attitudes toward ethnic groups, immigration, and multiculturalism. The assessment of identity was derived from two sets of questions.

In the first, respondents were asked about the national origins of their fathers and mothers. Following this question, they were asked how they usually thought of themselves. They were given the following options: (1) as a (Father origin)-Canadian (e.g., Greek-Canadian), (2) as a (Mother-origin)-Canadian (e.g., Italian-Canadian), (3) as a Canadian, (4) as an English-Canadian, (5) as a French-Canadian, (6) as a Québécoise (asked in Quebec only), (7) as a Father-origin national (e.g., Greek), or (8) as a Mother-origin national (e.g., Italian). All eight responses were read out and the respondent selected one of them.

For the present analyses,[3] respondents were placed in identity categories as follows: (1) Canadian, if they selected the Canadian response; (2) British-Canadian, if they selected English-Canadian, or if either parent was of English, Scottish, or Irish origin and they selected a hyphenated identity in terms of British ancestry; (3) French-Canadian, if they chose French-Canadian, or if either parent was of French origin and they picked a hyphenated identity; (4) Provincial, for respondents in Quebec who selected Québécois; (5) Other Ethnic–Canadian, if self-identity was hyphenated and the ancestral origin was other than British or French; (6) Other National, (7) Other National, if respondents assigned to themselves a national identity other than Canadian, but including British, French, and Other Ethnic.

1991 SURVEY

In this survey, the instrument consisted of 130 attitude, 3 identity, and 22 demographic questions. They were grouped in various ways, separating attitudes, values, beliefs, knowledge, perceptions, evaluations, and self-characterizations (see Berry & Kalin, 1995, for an overview of selected results from this survey) and prepared in both English- and French-language versions. A copy of the interview schedule is available from Multiculturalism and Citizenship Canada. A total of 3325 respondents answered the survey, consisting of a national sample of 2500 adults (over the age of 18), and over-samples in Montreal, Toronto, and Vancouver, to ensure a sample of 500 in each of these three cities. The survey was carried out in late June and July 1991, using a random-telephone-dialling procedure. A quota system ensured proportional representation of males and females, as well as of the regions of Canada. The analysis by Berry and Kalin (1995) suggests that the sample was reasonably representative of the Canadian population.

The questions forming the basis of the assessment of identity were somewhat different from those used in the 1974 survey. In 1991, three identity questions were asked in the following sequence, near the end of the interview. The first asked, "To which ethnic or cultural group(s) did your ancestors belong?" (If Canadian mentioned, probe: "Other than Canadian, to which ethnic or cultural group[s] did your ancestors belong?") All responses were recorded, and were tracked as first mention, second mention, and later mention. In a second question, respondents were told, "People may describe themselves in a number of ways. If you had to choose one, generally speaking, do you think of yourself as: (1) First origin reported (in the first question, e.g., Dutch), (2) First origin-Canadian (e.g., Dutch-Canadian), (3) Second origin, if reported (e.g., Italian), (4) Second origin-Canadian (e.g., Italian-Canadian), (5) a Province of residence (e.g., Manitoban), (6) a Canadian, (7) Other (coded as missing in subsequent analyses). All seven choices were read out by the interviewer before respondents gave their choice.

From this question, respondents were placed in the following identity categories: (1) "Canadian," if they selected the Canadian alternative; (2) "British-Canadian," if they assigned themselves a hyphenated identity in terms of their first or second origin and that origin was British; (3) "French-Canadian," if they picked a hyphenated identity in terms of first or second origin, and that origin was French; (4) "Provincial," if they described themselves in terms of a province; (5) "Other Ethnic–Canadian," if they selected a hyphenated identity in terms of their first or second origin, and that origin was other than French or British; (6) Other National, if they described themselves in terms of their first or second origin without qualifying it with "Canadian." Canadian and Provincial can be regarded as civic identities, while British-Canadian, French-Canadian, Other Ethnic–Canadian, and Other National qualify as ethnic identities.

In a third question, respondents were asked, "Using a 7-point scale where 1 is very weak and 7 is very strong, how strongly do you identify with being ...?" Each of the first six options was read out again to the respondents. This third question was used to assess the strength of each of the identities.

RESULTS
▼

The distribution of ethnic self-identity in the two national surveys is shown in Table 7.1, for the total samples as well as grouped by the ethnic origin of respondents. By far the most frequently selected self-identity in both surveys was Canadian. This was particularly true among respondents of British (80 percent in both surveys) and Other Ethnic origin (59 and 65 percent). The most frequent response among those of French origin, however, was different. In the 1974 survey, it was French-Canadian (47 percent) and, in the 1991 survey, Provincial (i.e., Québécois with 47 percent). Note, however, that a sizable

TABLE 7.1
▼
SELF-IDENTITY (IN PERCENT) OF RESPONDENTS IN TWO NATIONAL SURVEYS BY ETHNIC ORIGIN[a]

Self-Identity	MAS 74 Ethnic Origin				MAS 91 Ethnic Origin			
	Total	British	French	Other Ethnic	Total	British	French	Other Ethnic
Canadian/ Canadien	59	80	26	59	64	80	32	65
British-Canadian	7	13	3	3	2	6	0	0
French-Canadian	15	3	47	3	4	1	16	0
Provincial[b]	7	1	22	1	19	9	47	9
Other Ethnic– Canadian	8	0	0	28	7	1	1	20
Other National	3	2	2	5	4	3	4	5
N =	1810	708	376	541	3276	1392	746	1027

[a] All analyses weighted by respondent weight.
[b] In the 1974 survey, respondents in Quebec were the only ones given the provincial-identity option. In 1991, survey respondents in all provinces had this option.

proportion of respondents of French origin still identified as Canadian (26 percent in 1974 and 32 percent in 1991).

Provincial identity was the second most frequent response in the 1991 survey. The 1974 survey is not strictly comparable to the one in 1991 because a Provincial response was available only to residents of Quebec in the earlier survey.

A hyphenated identity was a sizable choice for those of a given ethnic origin, but it seems to have declined between 1974 and 1991. Among respondents of British origin, 13 percent selected some form of British-Canadian identity in 1974. This dropped to 6 percent in 1991. Among those of French origin, 47 percent selected French-Canadian in 1974 and this dropped to 16 percent in 1991. Among those of Other Ethnic origin, 28 percent had a hyphenated identity in 1974 and this dropped to 20 percent in 1991.

Other National identity (e.g., Greek) was selected by very few respondents in both surveys. In other words, despite the relatively popular use of nationality as a description of others, Other National is virtually non-existent as a self-identity category.

The distribution of ethnic self-identity by region of resident in the two surveys is shown in Table 7.2. Canadian was uniformly the highest response

TABLE 7.2

▼

SELF-IDENTITY (IN PERCENT) OF RESPONDENTS IN TWO NATIONAL SURVEYS BY REGION OF RESIDENCE[a]

	MAS 74					MAS 91				
Self-Identity	Atlantic	Quebec	Ontario	Prairies	B.C.	Atlantic	Quebec	Ontario	Prairies	B.C.
Canadian/ Canadien	73	20	72	74	76	68	28	78	76	79
British-Canadian	18	2	7	8	8	4	1	3	2	4
French-Canadian	3	45	6	2	2	1	12	1	2	1
Provincial[b]	NA	27	NA	NA	NA	22	50	2	11	9
Other Ethnic– Canadian	1	2	4	1	13	1	5	11	7	5
Other National	5	3	–	–	2	4	4	5	3	3
N =	161	479	684	289	196	298	856	1178	569	375

[a] All analyses weighted by respondent weight.
[b] In the 1974 survey, respondents in Quebec were the only ones given the provincial-identity option. In 1991, survey respondents in all provinces had this option.

in all regions except Quebec, where Québécois was the most frequent choice. The shift in the most popular self-identity from French-Canadian in the 1974 survey to Québécois in the 1991 survey is again evident in Table 7.2.

A Provincial identity was the second most frequent choice in all regions except Ontario, where Other Ethnic–Canadian identity was second. British-Canadian and French-Canadian identities show a general decline between the two survey years, as does Other Ethnic–Canadian in the Prairies and British Columbia.

In addition to assigning themselves to an ethnic self-identity category, respondents were also asked to rate the *strength* of identification with several identities. To simplify data analyses, the highest-strength rating given by a respondent to any of the ethnic-origin categories (first- or second-origin nationality, or hyphenated Canadian; French and British were included as ethnic for the purpose of these analyses) was taken as the strength of ethnic-origin identity.

Table 7.3 shows the mean strength of identification ratings in the total 1991 survey and broken down by region of residence. The strength of Canadian identity was uniformly high and near the maximum possible rating of 7 in all regions except Quebec, where it was still relatively high. The strength of Provincial identity was second highest in all provinces except Quebec, where it was the highest. Provincial identity was also stronger than identity in terms

TABLE 7.3
▼
MEAN STRENGTH OF IDENTIFICATION WITH THREE IDENTITIES BY REGION OF RESIDENCE IN 1991 SURVEY[a]

REGION

Identity	Total	Atlantic	Quebec	Ontario	Prairies	B.C.
Canadian/Canadien[b]	6.3	6.7	5.2[d]	6.6	6.6	6.7
Provincial	5.3	5.8	6.0	4.4[e]	5.5	5.5
"Ethnic" Origin[c]	4.1	3.5	4.6[f]	3.9	4.1	4.0
N =	3 320	300	863	1 191	584	382

[a] All analyses weighted by respondent weight.
[b] Response to "How strongly do you identify as (given identity)?"
[c] Ethnic-origin identity consists of the highest strength of identity rating given by a respondent to an identity option containing an "ethnic" component (e.g., Dutch, Dutch-Canadian). British and French count as "ethnic" options here.
[d] Quebec is significantly lower than each of the other regions.
[e] Ontario is significantly lower than each of the other regions.
[f] Quebec is significantly lower than the Atlantic provinces, Ontario, and B.C.

of ethnic origin. Ethnic-origin identity, including any British, French, or Other Ethnic origin, was the weakest in all regions.

The relative weakness of ethnic-origin identity has to be qualified by results shown in Table 7.4, however. Respondents who identified themselves as Ethnic in some way (British-Canadian, French-Canadian, Other Ethnic–Canadian, and Other National) had a relatively strong ethnic-origin identity. What is notable, in addition, however, is that the respondents with some ethnic self-identity had a relatively strong Canadian identity. It appears, then, a Canadian identity is quite compatible with a self-identity in terms of an ethnic origin.

Yet a different pattern applies to those respondents with a Provincial self-identity. As expected, their strongest identification was with Provincial identity. In comparison with respondents from the other self-identity categories, those with a Provincial self-identity scored the lowest on strength for Canadian identity, and near the lowest on strength for ethnic-origin identity.

In addition to describing self-identity and strength of identification in the country as a whole, as well as in regions, a second major purpose of this article was to examine the attitudinal characteristics of individuals with different identities. Is self-identity as Canadian, as compared with Ethnic or Provincial, compatible with multiculturalism? Also, is an ethnic identity congruous with feeling Canadian? In order to answer these questions, respondents were divid-

TABLE 7.4
▼
MEAN STRENGTH OF IDENTIFICATION WITH THREE IDENTITIES
BY SELF-IDENTITY IN 1991 SURVEY[a]

Identity	Total	Canadian	British Canadian	French Canadian	Provincial	Other Ethnic Canadian	Other National
Canadian/Canadien[b]	6.3	6.8	6.6	5.8	4.8	6.2	5.4
Provincial	5.3	4.9	5.4	5.8	6.8	4.8	4.7
"Ethnic" Origin[c]	4.1	3.5	6.2	6.4	4.0	6.3	5.9
N =	3 269	2 087	78	130	613	233	128

[a] All analyses weighted by respondent weight.
[b] Response to "How strongly do you identify as (given identity)?"
[c] Ethnic origin identity consists of the highest strength of identity rating given by a respondent to an identity option containing an "ethnic" component (e.g., Dutch, Dutch-Canadian). British and French count as "ethnic" options here.

ed according to their first-mentioned ethnic origin into those of British, French, or Other Ethnic origin. Within each of these groups, respondents were again divided into those who identified as Canadian, Provincial (in the 1991 survey), or any of the ethnic-origin categories. For these groupings, the means of the major attitude scales were calculated and displayed in Tables 7.5 and 7.6. These attitude scales are described in detail in Berry et al. (1977) and Berry and Kalin (1995). Based on results in Tables 7.5 and 7.6, the question of whether having a Canadian, as opposed to an Ethnic or Provincial, identity is compatible with multiculturalism can be answered as follows.

For respondents of British origin, the answer to this question appears to be yes, because on specific multicultural attitudes, respondents with a Canadian identity were no different from those with an Ethnic identity (in 1974), or with an Ethnic or Provincial identity (in 1991). In fact, in the 1974 survey, those of British origin with a Canadian identity were higher in multicultural ideology than those with an Ethnic British identity. On the measure of ethnocentrism, which can be thought of as the opposite of tolerance, those of British origin with a Canadian, as opposed to an Ethnic, identity were less ethnocentric in the 1974 survey. A similar result obtained in 1991. Respondents with a Canadian identity were approximately the same as those with an Ethnic identity and both groups were more tolerant than respondents with a Provincial identity. For respondents of British origin, it seems safe to conclude that having a Canadian identity is no barrier to accepting multiculturalism. On the contrary, those with a Canadian identity have attitudes that are quite compatible with multiculturalism.

TABLE 7.5
▼
MEANS OF ATTITUDES BY SELF-IDENTITY AMONG RESPONDENTS OF BRITISH, FRENCH, AND OTHER ETHNIC ORIGIN IN 1974 SURVEY[a]

Ethnic Self-Identity

Attitudes	Canadian	Provincial	"Ethnic"[b]	F
BRITISH ORIGIN				
MC Program Attitudes	4.9	NA	4.6	3.6
MC Perceived				
Consequences	4.7	NA	4.4	3.9
MC Ideology	4.7	NA	4.3	13.3**
Ethnocentrism	3.3	NA	3.9	16.3**
N =	568	–	128	–
FRENCH ORIGIN[c]				
MC Program Attitudes	4.6	4.3	4.3	0.7
MC Perceived				
Consequences	4.4	4.0	4.1	1.0
MC Ideology	4.5	4.1	3.9	5.8*
Ethnocentrism	3.7	3.6	4.1	4.3**
N =	43	84	147	–
OTHER ETHNIC ORIGIN				
MC Program Attitudes	4.7	NA	5.1	9.0*
MC Perceived				
Consequences	4.7	NA	4.9	3.1
MC Ideology	4.6	NA	4.8	1.6
Ethnocentrism	3.1	NA	3.4	8.1*
N =	318	–	208	–

* $p < .01$
** $p < .001$

[a] All analyses weighted by respondent weight.
[b] "Ethnic" identity consists of the following responses to the identity question: British–Canadian, French-Canadian, Other Ethnic–Canadian, or some Nationality other than Canadian.
[c] As "Provincial" identity was provided to respondents in Quebec only, this analysis is restricted to French-origin respondents in Quebec.

For respondents of French origin, a similar conclusion applies in that those with a Canadian identity are at least as positive, if not more positive, than respondents with either a Provincial or an Ethnic identity. In 1974, they had a higher multicultural ideology than respondents with a Provincial or

TABLE 7.6
▼
MEANS OF ATTITUDES BY SELF-IDENTITY AMONG RESPONDENTS OF BRITISH, FRENCH, AND OTHER ETHNIC ORIGIN IN 1991 SURVEY[a]

Ethnic Self-Identity

Attitudes	Canadian	Provincial	"Ethnic"[b]	F
BRITISH ORIGIN				
MC Program Attitudes	5.9	6.0	6.1	2.3
MC Perceived				
Consequences	4.9	4.8	5.2	3.3
MC Ideology	4.6	4.6	4.7	1.2
Tolerance	5.5	5.1	5.4	6.8*
Canadianism	5.8	5.3	5.7	24.3**
N =	1112	125	150	–
FRENCH ORIGIN				
MC Program Attitudes	6.1	6.1	5.9	1.6
MC Perceived				
Consequences	5.3	4.9	5.0	8.6*
MC Ideology	4.6	4.3	4.5	5.6*
Tolerance	5.4	5.2	5.1	3.4
Canadianism	5.8	4.4	5.4	121.9**
N =	237	349	160	–
OTHER ETHNIC ORIGIN				
MC Program Attitudes	5.9	5.7	6.1	7.1**
MC Perceived				
Consequences	5.0	4.7	5.2	7.3**
MC Ideology	4.6	4.4	5.0	15.5**
Tolerance	5.5	5.1	5.4	6.2*
Canadianism	5.8	4.9	5.7	36.0**
N =	671	96	260	–

* $p < .01$
** $p < .001$

[a] All analyses weighted by respondent weight.
[b] "Ethnic" identity consists of the following responses to the identity question: British-Canadian, French-Canadian, Other Ethnic–Canadian, or some Nationality other than Canadian.

Ethnic identity. In 1991, Canadian identifiers were higher in multicultural ideology than those with a Provincial identity. In 1974, they were also less ethnocentric than respondents with an Ethnic identity.

Among respondents of Other Ethnic origin, those with a Provincial identity were the least favourable toward multiculturalism in 1991. Those with a Canadian identity were very similar to respondents with an Ethnic identity in terms of attitudes toward multiculturalism. In 1974, those with an Ethnic, as opposed to a Canadian, identity had somewhat more favourable program attitudes. Respondents of Other Ethnic origin with a Canadian identity were less ethnocentric than Ethnic identifiers in 1974, and more tolerant than Provincial identifiers in 1991.

Canadianism was a scale developed specifically from eight items in the 1991 survey. It measures a sense of attachment and commitment to Canada. As expected, respondents with a Canadian self-identity among all three origin categories score the highest on Canadianism. While this result is as expected, the results for respondents having an Ethnic identity are less obvious. For all origin categories, those with a Ethnic identity have a Canadianism score that is nearly as high as those with a Canadian identity. Relatively lower scores were obtained for those who had a Provincial identity. These results, as well as those from Table 7.4, suggest that having an Ethnic identity is quite compatible with having a strong Canadian identity and having a strong commitment and attachment to Canada.

CONCLUSION
▼

Self-identity takes different forms in anglophone and francophone Canada. Among anglophones, the civic identity of "Canadian" is by far the most prevalent identity in all regions. Various forms of heritage identity (including British-Canadian, French-Canadian, Other Ethnic–Canadian, and Other National) are relatively uncommon. Heritage identity was also on the decline from 1974 to 1991. These results are in line with earlier findings (Berry et al., 1977; Boyd et al., 1981; Frideres & Goldenberg, 1977; Mackie, 1978; Mackie & Brinkerhoff, 1984, 1988), suggesting that ethnic identity in Canada does not have high salience and that there has been a decline of ethnic, in favour of a civic, identity. Results by other investigators (Driedger et al., 1982; O'Bryan et al., 1976; Weinfeld, 1981), showing substantial ethnic as opposed to civic identity, can be explained by the samples used in these studies (drawn from actively ethnic communities). Results from the present investigation mirror those findings in the sense that respondents of Other Ethnic, as compared with British, origin were more likely to choose a heritage identity.

In contrast to the low salience and relative unimportance of heritage identity, Canadian identity is very strong in anglophone Canada. A large majority selected it and, when given the opportunity to rate its strength in the 1991 survey, even respondents selecting a different identity rated Canadian identity as being strong. In a related paper (Kalin, 1995), the identity and citizenship attitudes of Canadians from twelve ethnic origins were analyzed. Outside of Quebec, Canadian identity and attachment to Canada were found to be strong among all twelve groups, with few differences existing among them. The findings obtained in the present surveys fit in well with the conclusions reached by Kalin and Berry (1994) that in anglophone Canada ethnic identity is of substantial significance for only one third or fewer Canadians.

These conclusions regarding the salience and strength of Canadian identity do not apply to francophone Canadians. In this portion of the population, the most prevalent response changed from French-Canadian in the 1974 survey to Québécois in 1991. This change is possibly the result of the rise of Quebec nationalism over the past twenty years. It may also simply reflect the greater popularity of "Québécois" over this time period. It is noteworthy, however, that in 1991 the strength of Canadian identity predominates over that of heritage identity even in Quebec. These results suggest that there has been a shift from ethnic to civic identity in Quebec over the past 25 years. In Quebec, of course, there is a conflict between the civic identities of Québécois and Canadian.

Provincial identity probably has a different meaning in the rest of Canada, as compared with Quebec. Rather than indicating a particular type of nationalism, it may well be a reflection of regionalism. But, nevertheless, it is an allegiance to a civic as opposed to an ethnic entity. Sizable minorities selected a Provincial identity in all regions except Ontario, and this identity also received reasonably high-strength ratings everywhere except Ontario.

A question in this paper concerns the compatibility of a Canadian identity and multiculturalism, on the one hand, and ethnic identity and national unity, on the other. This question can be answered in the affirmative on both fronts. Tolerance and multicultural attitudes among those with a Canadian identity are at least positive as (and in some cases more positive than) among Canadians with other identities. In anglophone Canada, those with an ethnic identity rate the strength for their Canadian identity as strong and they score high on Canadianism. In francophone Canada, the lower scores on Canadianism and the lower-strength ratings for Canadian identity may represent challenges to Canadian national unity.

What are the implications of these findings for the multiculturalism policy? The strong and prevalent Canadian identity among anglophone Canadians found in the surveys clearly does not mean a rejection of multiculturalism.

The present results on identity, as well as more detailed analyses of multicultural attitudes offered elsewhere (Berry & Kalin, 1995), suggest that Canadians are largely supportive of multiculturalism. Whether this support is active, as opposed to permissive, is another question. The prevalent and strong Canadian identity, coupled with the relatively non-salient and weak ethnic identity suggests that civic identity in Canada is more important than ethnic identity.

NOTES
▼

1. This paper is an expansion of presentations given at Annual Meetings of the Canadian Psychological Association, in Quebec City, 14 June, 1979, and 11–13 June, 1992. It reports on two national surveys. One was carried out in 1974 and reported in Berry et al. (1977). The other was conducted in June 1991 by Angus Reid and commissioned by Multiculturalism and Citizenship Canada. It included questions developed by the present authors. We acknowledge the contributions of Serge Guimond, Doug Palmer, and Jim Cameron to the development of the original items. However, the interpretations expressed in this paper are those of the authors and do not necessarily reflect the views of Multiculturalism and Citizenship Canada.

2. It should be noted in this context that there must have been some misunderstanding of the results of Berry et al. (1977) by Driedger et al. (1982) and Driedger (1989) about the precise meaning of the response categories. What Berry et al. (1977) labelled "other ethnic" was an ethnic-Canadian identity (e.g., Polish-Canadian). Driedger interpreted that as an ethnic-only (e.g., Polish) identity. Consequently the figures reported by Driedger et al. (1982) and Driedger (1989) are at variance with what was actually found by Berry et al. (1977).

3. The identity categories used in the present analyses were somewhat different from those reported by Berry et al. (1977). In the earlier report "English-Canadian" was coded only if the respondent selected the English-Canadian alternative provided by the interviewer. Respondents who gave their paternal or maternal origin as Scottish, Welsh, or Irish, and chose a hyphenated identity, were counted as "Other Ethnic." In the coding used for the present investigation, such respondents were counted as "British-Canadians." Similarly, in the earlier report "French-Canadian" was counted only if respondents checked the French-Canadian alternative provided. Those who gave one origin as French and used that origin to modify the hyphenated Canadian response were counted as "Other Ethnic" in the report by Berry et al. (1977), but as French-Canadians in the present paper. The net result of the slight differences in coding was that the present category of British-Canadian is larger than the earlier one of English-Canadian. The same applies to the category of French-Canadian. The category of Other Ethnic–Canadian as used in the present investigation is consequently smaller than that used by Berry et al. (1977).

REFERENCES
▼

Aboud, F. (1981). Ethnic self-identity. In R.C. Gardner & R. Kalin (Eds.), *A Canadian social psychology of ethnic relations* (pp. 37–56). Toronto: Methuen.

Berry, J.W., & Kalin, R. (1995). Multicultural and ethnic attitudes in Canada: An overview of the 1991 national survey. *Canadian Journal of Behavioural Science,* 27(3), 301–320.

Berry, J.W., Kalin, R., & Taylor, D. (1977). *Multiculturalism and ethnic attitudes in Canada.* Ottawa: Supply & Services Canada.

Boyd, M., Goyder, J., Jones, F.E., McRoberts, H.A., Pineo, P., & Porter, J. (1981). Status attainment in Canada: Findings of the Canadian mobility study. *Canadian Review of Sociology and Anthropology, 18,* 657–673.

Breton, R. (1964). Institutional completeness of ethnic communities and personal relations to immigrants. *American Journal of Sociology, 70,* 193–205.

———. (1988). From ethnic to civic nationalism: English Canada and Québec. *Ethnic and Racial Studies, 11*(1), 85–102.

Cairns, A.C. (1993). The fragmentation of Canadian citizenship. In W. Kaplan (Ed.). *Belonging: The meaning and future of Canadian citizenship* (pp. 181–220). Montreal and Kingston: McGill-Queen's University Press.

Driedger, L. (1975). In search of cultural identity factors: A comparison of ethnic minority students in Manitoba. *Canadian Review of Sociology and Anthropology, 12,* 150–162.

———. (1976). Ethnic self-identity: A comparison of ingroup evaluations. *Sociometry, 39,* 131–141.

———. (1989). *The ethnic factor: Identity in diversity.* Toronto: McGraw-Hill Ryerson.

Driedger, L., Thacker, C., & Currie R. (1982). Ethnic identification: Variations in regional and national preferences. *Canadian Ethnic Studies, 14*(3), 57–68.

Frideres, James S., & Goldenberg, Sheldon. (1977). Hyphenated Canadians: Comparative analysis of ethnic, regional and national identification of Western Canadian university students. *Journal of Ethnic Studies, 5,* 91–100.

Gans, H.J. (1979). Symbolic ethnicity: The future of ethnic groups and culture in America. *Ethnic and Racial Studies, 2,* 1–20.

Isajiw, W.W. (1983). Multiculturalism and the integration of the Canadian community. *Canadian Ethnic Studies, 14*(2), 107–117.

Kalin, R. (1995). Ethnic and citizenship attitudes in Canada: Analyses of a 1991 national survey. *Nationalism and Ethnic Politics, 1*(3), 26–44.

Kalin, R., & Berry, J.W. (1979). Social and attitudinal correlates of ethnic identity in Canada. Paper presented at Annual Meeting of Canadian Psychological Association, Quebec.

———. (1994). Ethnic and multicultural attitudes. In J.W. Berry & J. Laponce (Eds.). *Ethnicity and culture in Canada: The research landscape* (pp. 293–321). Toronto: University of Toronto Press.

Lupul, M. (1984). On being analytically or scientifically ethnic. *Canadian Ethnic Studies, 16*(2), 116–117.

Mackie, M. (1978). Ethnicity and nationality: How much do they matter to Western Canadians? *Canadian Ethnic Studies, 10*(2), 118–129.

Mackie, M., & Brinkerhoff, M.B. (1984). Measuring ethnic salience. *Canadian Ethnic Studies, 16*(1), 114–131.

———. (1988). Ethnic identification: Both sides of the border. *Canadian Ethnic Studies, 20*(2), 101–113.

O'Bryan, K., Reitz, J., & Kuplowska, O. (1976). *Non-official languages: A study in Canadian multiculturalism.* Ottawa: Supply & Services Canada.

Porter, J. (1979). *The measure of Canadian society.* Toronto: Gage.

Roberts, L.W., & Clifton, R.A. (1990). Multiculturalism in Canada: A social perspective. In Peter S. Li (Ed.), *Race and ethnic relations in Canada* (pp. 120–147). Toronto: Oxford University Press.

Weinfeld, M. (1981). Myth and reality in the Canadian mosaic: "Affective ethnicity." *Canadian Ethnic Studies, 13*(3), 80–100.

PART THREE

ETHNIC PERSISTENCE
AND INTEGRATION

INTRODUCTION

Canada presents itself as a multicultural society, open to immigrants from any place in the world, in which those of diverse ethnic origins are encouraged to retain their distinctive cultural characteristics as they seek to become successfully integrated into Canadian society. The study of intergroup relations, especially between minority and dominant ethnic cultural groups, has long been concerned with the processes of integration and assimilation that tend to weaken or reinforce their distinctive cultural characteristics and behaviour patterns. Chapter Eight, by Madeline Kalbach, focusses on the patterns and trends of ethnic intermarriage as an index of marital assimilation from 1871 to 1991. Census data for husbands and wives are used to show an increasing trend in ethnic intermarriage, and variations in propensities for ethnic exogamy by region and period of immigration. A tendency for ethnic minority groups to marry into the culturally dominant British and French groups emphasizes the importance of intermarriage as a facilitator of assimilation into Canadian society.

Chapter Nine, by T.R. Balakrishnan, deals with ethnic residential concentration and segregation by examining the relevance of social class, ethnic origin, social distance, and increasing ethnic diversity for residential segregation in Canada's census metropolitan areas (CMAs). Using standard measures of spatial concentration and ethnic segregation, he examines the effects of recent heavy immigration of visible minorities during the period 1986–96. While increases in ethnic diversity seem not to have contributed to higher levels of segregation, or greater concentration, their patterns still vary among the various CMAs. Declines in the concentration of some ethnic groups are attributed in part to changes in immigrant-selection policies and to a greater degree of heterogeneity among visible-minority immigrants. Trends in occupational segregation are suggestive of increased economic assimilation, portending future declines in residential segregation.

In Chapter Ten, Monica Boyd reviews the mobility studies of the offspring of various ethnic immigrant groups with an eye to their relevance for the Canadian situation. The 1991 census data are used to show that the living situation of young immigrant offspring in Canada varies substantially according to their ethnic origin. Boyd examines the various "integrative" models, mainly developed in the United States, to test their relevance for the various ethnic groups in the Canadian context. Revised versions of the "straight-line" assimilation model, suggesting that pathways to assimilation also can include assimilation to ethnic enclaves or absorption into the under-class, remain to be tested on the offspring of post-1960s immigrant groups in Canada.

Chapter Eleven, by M. Reza Nakhaie, examines the basic question of the relationship between ethnic origin and socio-economic status, defined in the Marxian sense of "ownership of the means of production." The analysis of the results of two national surveys reveals that only those of Jewish origins are overrepresented in the ownership class. Those of English ancestry are not overrepresented in ownership positions, only in managerial positions, where the overrepresentation was found to have declined between 1973 and 1983. Italian and French origins were found to be mostly overrepresented in the working class. Nakhaie suggests, as a result of his analysis, that the relation-ship between ethnic origin and class position in Canada was in a state of flux during this period.

Madeline Kalbach and Warren Kalbach, the authors of Chapter Twelve, address the continuing debate over the socio-economic consequences of the retention of distinctive ethnic characteristics for immigrants and their chil-dren while becoming integrated into Canadian society. The analysis of a num-ber of recent European and non-European immigrant groups is shown to gen-erally support the findings of earlier studies, as well as establishing the importance of age at immigration for socio-economic achievement. Those whose characteristics show some "ethnic connectedness," that is, indicate re-tention of an ethnic religious identity, and who report that they still mostly use an ethnic language in the home, tend to be more disadvantaged in terms of their socio-economic status in a secular society than the less ethnically con-nected individuals. The findings appear to be significant only for the foreign-born immigrant, but have important consequences for immigration policies that would encourage immigrant groups to maintain their ethnic and cultur-al distinctiveness.

ETHNICITY AND THE ALTAR[1]
MADELINE A. KALBACH

INTRODUCTION
▼

Intermarriage had been widely accepted as an indicator of assimilation and as a method of assimilation (Drachsler, 1920; Hurd, 1929; Nelson, 1943; Kalbach, 1975, 1983; Lieberson & Waters, 1988; Richard, 1991). By definition, it means the crossing of some well-defined line such as ethnic origin or religion. Hence, ethnic intermarriage, or ethnic exogamy, for example, occurs when an individual marries a spouse of an ethnic origin different from his or her own. On the other hand, ethnic intramarriage, or ethnic endogamy, occurs when an individual marries a person of the same ethnic or cultural origin as him- or herself. Similarly, religious intermarriage occurs when a person marries a spouse of a different religion than his or her own. Persons who marry within their own ethnic or religious group are more ethnically connected than their counterparts who marry someone of a different ethnic origin or religion. Thus, those who marry exogamously are said to be more assimilated than those who remain ethnically or religiously connected through marriage (Richard, 1991).

The purpose of this research is to look at ethnic intermarriage in Canada. More specifically, it reviews the Canadian literature on ethnic intermarriage and looks at the trends of ethnic exogamy from 1871 to 1991. The analysis examines the level of intermarriage for both husbands and wives, regardless of ethnic origin, as well as for selected ethnic-origin groups at the time of the 1991 census and the pattern of mate selection for husbands and wives.

ETHNIC INTERMARRIAGE: THE CANADIAN EXPERIENCE
▼

Much of the research on ethnic intermarriage in Canada employs census data. These data reveal the prevalence of intermarriage rather than the incidence because they tell only about those marriages still in existence at the time the data were collected (Lieberson & Waters, 1985). Moreover, information is not given on marriages that have been dissolved by death or divorce, or previous marriages (Lieberson & Waters, 1988: 171). Hence, the amount of intermarriage tends to be underestimated.

Relatively few Canadian researchers have examined assimilation through ethnic intermarriage in detail. Burton Hurd (1929, 1942, 1964) is one of the few who did. Hurd's research focussed on intermarriage between ethnic minorities and the British and French in order to determine the correlates of intermarriage, and the extent and speed of assimilation in Canada. His research reflected the concern for assimilation that prevailed in the early twentieth century. Because the census did not publish data on the ethnic origins of husbands and their wives, Hurd used the vital statistics that provided the ethnicity of the parents of children born in 1921, 1931, and 1941. In general, Hurd's work indicated increasing intermarriage and significant differences between geographic and linguistic groups from 1921 to 1941. More specifically, he concluded that intermarriage increased for all groups between the three decades, but more so between 1931 and 1941. This was particularly true for the Southern, Central, and Eastern Europeans, but most true for the Northern and Western Europeans (1964: 99). The Jewish were found to be least exogamous, followed by the French, British, and Asiatics. In addition, Hurd's data indicated that assimilation by intermarriage with the British increased over the 30-year period and that a substantial increase had occurred with the French between 1931 and 1941. One of the shortcomings of Hurd's analysis was that he was unable to differentiate between foreign- and native born. However, it provides evidence of increasing intermarriage and significant differences between ethnic groups.

Hurd's analysis was extended by Kalbach (1983) using data from special tabulations from the 1961 and 1971 censuses of Canada. In general, ethnic intermarriage for native-born husbands was found to have increased during the period, but at a relatively slow rate. This is consistent with Hurd's earlier findings. Another study that used census data to examine intermarriage trends in Canada showed that ethnic intermarriage increased between 1951 and 1971 (Jansen, 1982). Like Hurd, Jansen found the Jewish to be the least exogamous of any group. An examination of Nova Scotia marriage licence data from 1946 to 1966 revealed that the Irish exhibited the highest rates of intermarriage, followed by the Germans, French, Scottish, English, and Blacks (Campbell & Neice, 1979). An examination of patterns of ethnic intermarriage in Canada using census data for 1871 and 1971 clearly demonstrates advances in marital assimilation for native-born husbands over the century, and found significant differences between English, Irish, Scottish, French, and German husbands' propensities to intermarry (Richard, 1991). These variations were found to be greater in the twentieth century than in the nineteenth century. The major finding was the historical shift in marriage patterns exhibited by native-born Irish, Scottish, and German husbands, from being overwhelmingly endogamous in 1871 to being overwhelmingly exogamous by 1971 (Richard, 1991). The French remained largely endogamous over the century, but an increase in marital assimilation did occur. The overall level of ethnic intermarriage increased from 17.1 percent in 1871 to 24 percent in 1971 (Richard, 1991). This means that a significant amount of assimilation occurred through marriage and for most ethnic groups over the century between 1871 and 1971.

DATA SOURCES
▼

The data for this analysis come from the 1871 and 1951–1991 federal censuses of Canada, and for 1921, 1931, and 1941 from Hurd's monographs (1929, 1942, 1964). The 1871 data are taken from the Canadian Historical Mobility Project (CHMP) conducted by Darroch and Ornstein. The CHMP is a stratified, random sample of more than 60 000 individuals who were members of approximately 10 000 households drawn from the original 1871 census schedules. Hurd was unable to get ethnic-origin data for husbands and wives, and so based his analysis on the vital statistics that provided the ethnicity of parents of the children born in 1921, 1931, and 1941. Data from the 1971 census are taken from special tabulations, and the 1971 Public Use Sample Tape (family file). Similarly, the 1981 census data are taken from family files of the 1981 Census Public Use Microdata File.

DEFINITIONS OF VARIABLES
▼

Ethnic Origin: In 1871, "ethnic origin" referred to racial origin and was a mixture of various cultural, geographic, and biological attributes (Richard, 1991). In 1971, it referred to the ethnic or cultural ancestry traced through the paternal side. In 1981, "ethnic origin" referred to ethnic or cultural origin traced through either parent's side. By 1991, the same definition applied, but multiple origins were accepted and encouraged. Hence, to make the data comparable to those for earlier years, only the single origins were used in 1991.

Nativity: This term refers to whether a person was born outside of or inside Canada (i.e., is foreign- or native born).

Ethnic Exogamy/Ethnic Intermarriage: This analysis uses rates of intermarriage as defined by the percentage of husbands who married wives of different ethnic origins, or conversely, the percentage of wives who married husbands of different ethnic origins.

PATTERNS AND TRENDS OF ETHNIC INTERMARRIAGE, 1871–1991
▼

Table 8.1 reveals that the trend from 1871 to 1991 has been one of increasing ethnic intermarriage for husbands of husband–wife families in Canada. The same general trend has been exhibited by husbands of specific ethnic-origin populations with some exceptions. Scandinavian husbands exhibited a slight decline in ethnic intermarriage in 1951, down from their levels a decade earlier. The upward trend, however, was evident again by 1961. Italian husbands' level of ethnic exogamy reached a high of 45 percent in 1941, declined to about 34 percent by 1951, and to 23 percent by 1961 and 1971. This decline in the level of ethnic exogamy for Italian husbands can probably be explained by an increase in immigration of Italians after World War II. As immigration began to fall off and third-generation Italians reached the marriageable ages, levels of ethnic exogamy began to increase in 1981 and 1991. Similarly, a decline in Polish ethnic intermarriage between 1981 and 1991 can probably be attributed to an influx of Poles into Canada in the 1980s. In both cases, the decline in ethnic exogamy likely reflects the effect of an influx of foreign-born husbands and their wives because most immigrant husbands who were already married upon arrival in Canada would have most likely been married to a spouse of the same ethnic origin as himself — hence, raising the level of endogamy and, conversely, lowering the level of exogamy.

Figure 8.1 reveals the percentage of husbands and wives of single origins with wives and husbands of a different origin than themselves. It can be seen that wives had lower levels of ethnic exogamy at the time of the 1991 census than husbands, regardless of ethnic origin. In addition, native-born husbands and native-born wives have significantly higher levels of ethnic exogamy than their foreign-born counterparts.

TABLE 8.1

▼

PERCENTAGE OF FAMILY HEADS WITH WIVES OF A DIFFERENT ETHNIC ORIGIN, FOR SELECTED ORIGINS, CANADA, 1871, 1921–1991

Ethnic Origin of Family Head	1871	1921	1931	1941	1951	1961	1971	1981	1991
British	4.0	8.0	–	–	14.9	18.8	19.1	24.7	37.3
French	3.3	15.1	5.0	6.6	10.3	11.7	13.8	14.3	14.5
German	27.1	24.8	27.5	41.4	48.0	48.0	50.8	56.1	60.2
Italian	–	19.3	23.0	44.8	–	23.4	23.5	28.3	32.8
Dutch	–	53.0	45.4	48.9	57.3	45.1	47.5	51.5	55.2
Polish	–	20.0	22.0	48.2	44.3	51.0	56.8	63.5	49.6
Scandinavian	–	42.7	54.0	66.6	63.5	68.8	73.1	82.8	81.4
Ukrainian	–	7.5	9.8	20.7	25.2	38.2	46.0	58.1	63.8
Total	17.1	11.6	–	–	19.8	22.3	23.9	27.3	35.0

Source: Historical Mobility Project, *1871 Census of Canada*. 1921, 1931, and 1941 data based on the parentage of children born in the Registration Area 1921, and in Canada in 1931 and 1941, as reported in Hurd's Census Monographs. Hurd, W.B., *Origin, Birthplace, Nationality and Language of the Canadian People*, *1921 Census of Canada*, Dominion Bureau of Statistics, Ottawa: King's Printer, 1929; *1931 Census of Canada*, Vol. XIII, Dominion Bureau of Statistics, Ottawa: King's Printer, 1942, Table XLVI; and *Ethnic Origin and Nativity of the Canadian People*, *1941 Census of Canada*, Dominion Bureau of Statistics, Ottawa: Queen's Printer, Table XLV; *1951 Census of Canada*, Dominion Bureau of Statistics, Ottawa: King's Printer, Vol. III, Table 144; Canada, Report of the Royal Commission on Bilingualism and Biculturalism, Book IV, Ottawa: Queen's Printer, 1966, Table A-40, p. 279, and Special Tabulations from the *1971 and 1991 Census of Canada* provided by Statistics Canada. Statistics Canada, *1981 Census of Canada*, 2% Public Use Microdata File, Family File. *1991 Census of Canada*. Special Tabulations.

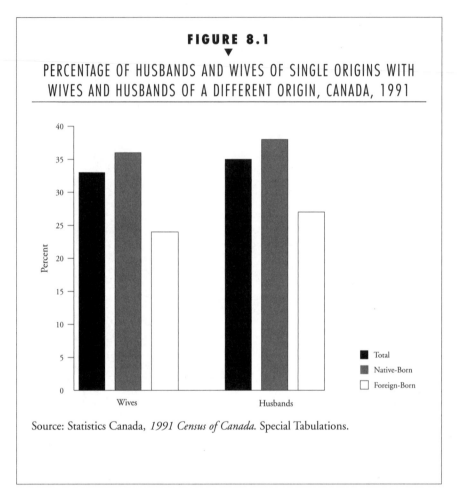

FIGURE 8.1

▼

PERCENTAGE OF HUSBANDS AND WIVES OF SINGLE ORIGINS WITH WIVES AND HUSBANDS OF A DIFFERENT ORIGIN, CANADA, 1991

Source: Statistics Canada, *1991 Census of Canada*. Special Tabulations.

Figures 8.2 and 8.3 reveal the percentage of husbands and wives of English, French, German, Italian, East Indian, Chinese, and Black/Caribbean origins who are married to spouses of different ethnic origins at the time of the 1991 census. As expected, native-born husbands and wives have higher proportions of ethnic exogamy than their foreign-born counterparts, and, in general, husbands are more exogamous than wives. Germans exhibit the highest rates of ethnic exogamy, followed by Blacks/Caribbeans and Italians. The more recent immigrant groups, that is, East Indian and Chinese, have the lowest rates of ethnic exogamy. Charter-group husbands and wives have relatively low levels of ethnic exogamy compared with most of the other groups because they are dominant numerically and culturally, and so do not have a shortage of potential mates to choose from.

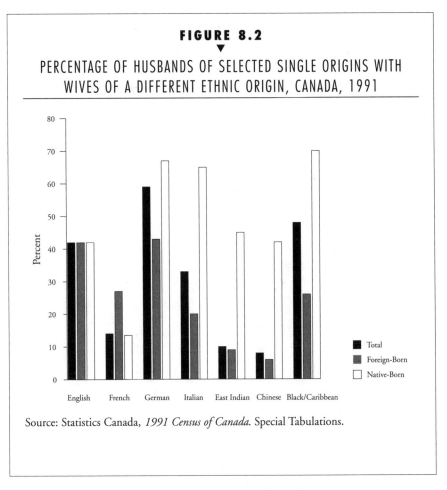

FIGURE 8.2
▼
PERCENTAGE OF HUSBANDS OF SELECTED SINGLE ORIGINS WITH
WIVES OF A DIFFERENT ETHNIC ORIGIN, CANADA, 1991

Source: Statistics Canada, *1991 Census of Canada.* Special Tabulations.

WHO MARRIED WHOM
▼

Hurd underlined the importance of intermarriage between ethnic minorities and the dominant British and French groups as a means of facilitating assimilation into Canadian society. He was able to show that British- and French-origin individuals were the most popular choices for a marriage mate (Richard, 1991). Richard's work confirmed this finding for 1871 and 1971. Analysis of the 1991 census data indicates that this is still the case. Further analysis of the data also indicates that wives selected mates who were British or French, followed by individuals of other European groups, such as Italian, Ukrainian, Dutch, and Polish, if they did not marry someone of the same ethnic or cultural origin as themselves. Chinese, East Indian, Arab, Latin/Cen-

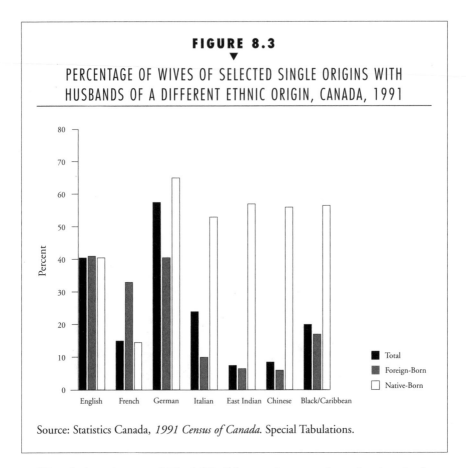

FIGURE 8.3
▼
PERCENTAGE OF WIVES OF SELECTED SINGLE ORIGINS WITH
HUSBANDS OF A DIFFERENT ETHNIC ORIGIN, CANADA, 1991

Source: Statistics Canada, *1991 Census of Canada.* Special Tabulations.

tral/South American, and Black/Caribbean wives, on the other hand, chose other visible minorities, such as Filipinos, West Asians, or Indo-Pakistanis as marriage mates. Similar patterns were exhibited by husbands who were ethnically intermarried at the time of the 1991 census.

CONCLUSION
▼

It appears as though ethnic intermarriage has been increasing in Canadian society since 1871 both overall and for specific ethnic-origin groups. In terms of ethnic mixing and assimilation through marriage in Canada, those of Northern, Western, and Eastern European origins tend to exhibit the highest proportions of ethnic exogamy, followed by the more recent immigrant groups such as the Greeks, Italians, and Portuguese. Latin/Central/South Americans, Blacks/Caribbeans, and

Arabs exhibit about the same levels as the more recent European ethnic groups, while Asians, the most recent immigrant groups in Canada, exhibit the lowest proportions of ethnic exogamy (Statistics Canada, 1998).

Husbands tended to ethnically out-marry to a greater extent than wives at the time of the 1991 census. Increases in immigration for any ethnic group, for example, Poles and Italians, can cause declines in the prevalence of ethnic exogamy because most of the husbands and wives who were married before emigrating to Canada married spouses of the same ethnic origin as themselves. In addition, it is clear that native-born husbands and wives exhibited higher levels of ethnic exogamy than their foreign-born counterparts at the time of the 1991 census.

Greater proportions of husbands and wives who married exogamously married husbands of British origins, followed by French and German. This supports Richard's (1991) findings for 1871 and 1971. In spite of the decline in the proportion of British and French of single origin in Canada's population at the time of the 1991 census, research indicates that the charter groups still form the main bases of Canadian society since the vast majority of those respondents claiming more than one origin are British and/or French multiples (see Chapters 5 and 12 in this volume).

While ethnic intermarriage has progressed in Canadian society over the twentieth century, it is not known whether the sons and daughters of husbands and wives in Canada who chose to ethnically intermarry will be influenced by either parent's ethnocultural identity. Lieberson and Waters (1988) indicate that, in some cases, offspring of intermarriages in the United States were indeed influenced by their parents' cultural identities in that ethnicity remained salient in their lives. One of the results of increasing ethnic intermarriage is larger proportions of the population who are of mixed origins. This suggests new questions for researchers of the future.

NOTES
▼

1. Data from the 1991 census was funded, in part, by Heritage Canada and the Prairie Centre of Excellence for Research on Immigrants and Integration.

REFERENCES
▼

Campbell, Douglas F., & Neice, David C. (1979). *Ties that bind: Structure and marriage in Nova Scotia.* Port Credit, ON: Scribbler's Press.

Drachsler, Julius. (1920). *Democracy and assimilation: The blending of immigrant heritages in America.* New York: Macmillan.

———. (1921). *Intermarriage in New York City.* New York: Columbia University Press.

Hurd, Burton W. (1929). *Origin, birthplace, nationality and language of the Canadian people.* 1921 Census Monograph. Dominion Bureau of Statistics. Ottawa: King's Printer.

———. (1942). *Racial origins and nativity of the Canadian people.* 1931 Census Monograph. Dominion Bureau of Statistics. Ottawa: King's Printer.

———. (1964). *Ethnic origin and nativity of the Canadian people.* 1941 Census Monograph. Dominion Bureau of Statistics. Ottawa: Queen's Printer.

Jansen, Clifford. (1982). Inter-ethnic marriages. *International Journal of Comparative Sociology, 23,* 225–235.

Kalbach, Warren E. (1970). *The impact of immigration on Canada's population.* Ottawa: Information Canada.

———. (1975). The demography of marriage. In S. Parvez Wakil (Ed.), *Marriage, family and society* (pp. 59–84). Scarborough: Butterworth's.

———. (1983). Propensities for intermarriage in Canada, as reflected in the ethnic origins of husbands and their wives: 1961–1971. In K. Ishwaran (Ed.), *Marriage and divorce in Canada* (pp. 196–212). Toronto: Methuen.

Lieberson, Stanley, & Waters, Mary. (1985). Recent social trends, ethnic mixtures in the United States. *Sociology and Social Research, 70*(1), 43–52.

———. (1988). *From many strands.* New York: Russell Sage Foundation.

Nelson, Lowry. (1943). Intermarriage among nationality groups in a rural area of Minnesota. *American Journal of Sociology, 48*(5), 585–592.

Richard, Madeline A. (1991). *Ethnic groups and marital choices.* Vancouver: University of British Columbia Press.

Statistics Canada. (1998). *1996 Census of Canada.* Ottawa: Special Tabulations.

RESIDENTIAL SEGREGATION AND CANADA'S ETHNIC GROUPS

T.R. BALAKRISHNAN

INTRODUCTION
▼

The study of residential segregation of ethnic and racial groups has been a long-standing interest of urban sociologists. Segregation, the tendency for members of a group to live together in a specific area apart from others, was studied in Chicago by Park and others as long ago as the 1910s (Park & Burgess, 1916). Since then, investigations of segregation have been done in cities all over the world. The availability of small-area statistics such as at the census-tract or enumeration-area level, and various methodological developments and high-speed computers, have facilitated research in this area. In Canada, many studies on ethnic residential segregation have been done in the last three decades (see Balakrishnan, 1976, 1982, 1990, 1995; Kalbach, 1990; Driedger, 1982; Driedger & Church, 1974; Darroch & Marston, 1971). These studies have looked at trends and changes in residential segregation. The focus has been on their causes and consequences, often through in-depth studies of ethnic neighbourhoods.

WHY STUDY RESIDENTIAL SEGREGATION?
▼

Apart from understanding the settlement patterns of specific ethnic groups, the reasons for studying residential segregation have a broad sociological significance. Residential segregation is often associated with segregation along religious, ethnic, occupational, and racial lines. Thus, we hear of Chinatowns; Little Italys; and Portuguese, Greek, or Black neighbourhoods. In U.S. cities, Blacks and Hispanics are often found to be highly segregated, a cause of concern for policy-makers. Apart from ethnicity and race, we also find segregation on the basis of other factors such as social class. One of the reasons for the interest in residential segregation is that it is often seen as a measure of how well or how poorly a group has integrated into the society at large. The assumption is that a group isolated in a particular area is probably not participating in the housing and labour markets to the fullest extent. It is argued further that living in close proximity to others of the same ethnic or racial background, while increasing interaction within the group, reduces interaction outside the group. Thus, while residential segregation maintains ethnic identity, it reduces assimilation into the wider society. On the other hand, a group that is widely settled in a community is also likely to be well represented in the various social and economic spheres in that area.

THEORETICAL BASIS FOR RESIDENTIAL SEGREGATION
▼

Why do we see trends and changes in segregation? Three hypotheses have been advanced and tested in various studies. The first can be called "the social-class hypothesis." According to this hypothesis, ethnic segregation is largely a reflection of social-class differences among the ethnic groups. Ethnic groups in Canada differ by their period of immigration, socio-economic background, language proficiency, and occupational skills, among other factors. Many ethnic groups are in a lower socio-economic class, which may force them to settle in certain areas of the city only, usually in the poorer sections, near the city centre. As their social position improves, they are able to disperse to more desirable neighbourhoods. According to this hypothesis, ethnic segregation is essentially social-class segregation and should decrease with the social mobility of the group. With increased assimilation in the country's occupational and industrial structure, ethnic residential segregation should decrease. This is basically a human ecological perspective that emphasizes the economic dimensions and puts less importance on the cultural factors in settlement patterns. That social class alone cannot explain all the ethnic and racial segregation is well documented (Darroch & Marston, 1971; Balakrishnan & Kralt, 1987). The high segregation of Blacks in the United States in spite of their socio-economic advancement over the decades is a striking example.

A second hypothesis states that ethnic residential segregation is due to the social distances among the ethnic groups. Social distance is basically a measure of cultural affinity. It has been measured by responses to questions such as accepting a member of a particular ethnic group as a work colleague, neighbour, close friend, or spouse. Greater social distance should be reflected in higher levels of residential segregation. Many studies have found a parallel between social distance and residential segregation (Balakrishnan, 1982; Lieberson, 1970; Lieberson & Waters, 1988; Kalbach, 1990). This is especially true of the segregation of African Americans in the United States (Massey & Denton, 1993).

A third hypothesis to explain ethnic residential segregation may be called "the ethnic-identity hypothesis." This is fundamentally different from the earlier two hypotheses. They were based on the premise that residential segregation is due to involuntary causes. One's social class or social distance determined the residential choices. In contrast, this hypothesis postulates that persons of the same ethnic ancestry choose to live in close proximity so that social interaction can be maximized, and group norms and values can be maintained (Driedger & Church, 1974; Balakrishnan & Selvanathan, 1990). Size and concentration may provide some advantages. Ethnic clubs, churches, language newspapers, and speciality stores require a threshold population. This voluntary residential segregation has certain merits, whether or not it is perceived as such by an ethnic group. According to this hypothesis, the greater the self-identity of an ethnic group, the more likely they will be residentially segregated. Self-identity may vary for several reasons. Apart from historical and political causes, it could be due to the strength of commonly held beliefs and values, kinship networks, in-group relations, and feelings of solidarity (Driedger & Peters, 1977). High Jewish residential segregation in North American communities is a classic example of the strength of self-identity in this group.

IS RESIDENTIAL SEGREGATION GOOD OR BAD?
▼

Whether residential segregation is good or bad depends on its actual and perceived consequences, not only for the group concerned, but for the society as a whole. In the United States, the conventional wisdom has been that residential segregation has more negative consequences than positive ones. It is believed to promote segregation in other social institutions, leading to various forms of discrimination. Residential segregation can affect a group's ability to speak English, and restrict its occupational mobility and the early acquisition of citizenship. In U.S. cities, residential segregation is often associated with unequal school facilities and budget allocations, school segregation, and increased drop-out rates. It has been suggested that segregation in the United States leads to the concentration of low-achieving students (Massey & Denton, 1993). Because residential segregation increases the visibility of a racial group or an ethnic group, it can sharpen prejudices and discrimination by the dominant group.

In contrast to the U.S. studies, research studies in Canada have focussed less on the negative aspects of residential segregation, but more on its positive aspects, mainly in maintaining cultural pluralism. It has been argued that segregation is necessary for the maintenance of the French language in Canada (Lieberson, 1970; Joy, 1972). French Canadians living in areas surrounding Quebec are able to maintain their French language because they benefit from the support of the religious, educational, and political institutions in Quebec. Residential segregation is important in the maintenance of institutional completeness. Many religious, educational, and welfare institutions that are crucial to a minority need a spatially concentrated population base.

The U.S. government has recognized the negative effects of residential segregation and passed various pieces of legislation to prevent discrimination in housing. Although the effects of these laws and other efforts to reduce residential segregation, especially of African Americans, have been questioned (Massey & Denton, 1993), it is clear that the intent of the policies has been to reduce segregation. There is no clear parallel to these policies in Canada. Though there is legislation to prevent discrimination in housing on the basis of such factors as colour, race, and national origin, it is not driven by any particular agenda to prevent residential segregation of specific ethnic or racial groups. In contrast to the "melting pot" concept of integration in the United States, the Canadian emphasis is on "multiculturalism." The idea here is that the best way of integrating immigrant groups into the Canadian social system is to preserve and enhance the multicultural heritage of Canadians while working to achieve the equality of all Canadians in the country's economic, social, cultural, and political life. It may even be argued that the Canadian policy of multiculturalism may sustain higher levels of residential segregation.

IMMIGRATION AND ETHNIC RESIDENTIAL SEGREGATION
▼

In Canada, at the present time, immigration is as important as natural increase for population growth. Immigration patterns have changed, not only in numbers, but also in composition. While immigrants from Western Europe predominated before the 1960s, in the 1960s and 1970s most immigrants were primarily from southern Europe. Since then, however, people from the third-world countries have formed the majority of immigrants. Thus, more than one-half of the immigrants in the 1980s were the so-called visible minority groups of Blacks, South Asians, Chinese, and many Latin and Central Americans. In 1991, 68.0 percent of new arrivals to Canada were visible-minority immigrants, about two thirds of whom were Blacks, Chinese, and South Asians (Dai & George, 1996). Further, of late, following the political developments in Russia and Eastern Europe, immigration from these countries to Canada has increased. We still do not know what the residential patterns of these immigrants in Canada will be.

Unlike the earlier immigrants from Western Europe, the new immigrants are more selective about their places of destination in Canada. Larger metropolitan areas attract a disproportionately greater share of recent immigrants. For example, during 1981–91, the percentages of Black immigrants who went to Montreal, Toronto, and Vancouver were 20.4, 58.1, and 1.8, respectively. The corresponding percentages for South Asians were 6.5, 52.7, and 16.7, and for Chinese, 6.8, 43.3, and 28.8, respectively. Selectivity in the choice of residential space on the part of the ethnic groups can be noticed not only at the regional and city levels, but within cities as well, in the form of distinct neighbourhoods.

Rapid growth of ethnic and racial minorities through migration may increase their concentration and their segregation from the major groups who have been settled for some time. Lack of language facility and social networks, occupational skills, and economic resources may all make immigrants settle in ethnic enclaves, which are often found in the poorer sections of the city. Discrimination against immigrant groups in housing and labour markets may also force them into certain areas of the city, and thus increase their spatial concentration and their segregation from specific groups, such as the British- or other European-origin groups in Canada. The interesting question is whether the levels of concentration decrease with length of stay in Canada and with increased social mobility.

ETHNIC CONCENTRATION WITHIN
THE METROPOLITAN AREAS
▼

We have commented earlier on why we find concentrations of ethnic groups in urban areas. Urban studies have also shown that, while some ethnic neighbourhoods persist over time, many others disappear due to ecological forces, such as gentrification of older areas by returning well-to-do suburbanites and by urban development. Ecological forces such as invasion and succession can change the nature of various sections of a city, especially near the city core. Apart from ecological forces, such factors as ethnic cohesion, language, and duration of stay will influence the continuation of an ethnic neighbourhood. While the assimilation of older immigrants will reduce the chances of maintenance of an ethnic enclave, new sustained immigration may increase its salience. Using census tracts as units of analysis, we will examine the relative concentration of ethnic groups in Canadian metropolitan areas.

One simple way of assessing the extent of concentration is by seeing whether a particular ethnic group is over- or underrepresented in an area. As the census tracts are supposed to be fairly comparable in overall population size, an idea of concentration can be had by comparing the cumulative proportion of census tracts with the cumulative proportion of the ethnic population in those tracts. Census tracts in each of the metropolitan areas were arranged in decreasing order of ethnic population in 1996, and the cumulative proportions of the population calculated. Tables 9.1 and 9.2 show the extent of concentration, by examining the proportion of tracts in which 50 and 90 percent of an ethnic-group population is found.

The cities show very little concentration of persons of British origin. This result is to be expected given that the British are the largest ethnic group in most cities, and are therefore more likely to be dispersed. When the census tracts are arranged in order of decreasing British population size, about a third of the tracts have to be covered to account for half of the British origin population and almost three fourths to account for 90 percent of the population. The only census metropolitan area (CMA) where they are concentrated to any noticeable degree is Montreal, where half of the British population can be found in 10 percent of the census tracts, and 90 percent in 46 percent of the tracts. Although the French are a much smaller group, they also show small concentrations and are quite similar in their distributions to the British. Almost 70 percent of the tracts need to be covered before 90 percent of the French population is included. Concentration is also low for the Northwestern European groups of Germans, Scandinavians, and Dutch. The only CMA where the concentration is significant is in Montreal, probably because of the importance of language.

The most residentially concentrated minority group in Canada are the Jews. In 1996, half the Jewish population is Montreal lived in 1.8 percent of the census tracts, and 90 percent in 7 percent of the tracts. Their concentration has actually increased in the period 1991–1996. In 1991, the corresponding figures were 2 percent and 9 percent, respectively (Balakrishnan & Hou, 1995). They are also heavily concentrated in all the other CMAs as well. Fifty percent of the Jewish population is found in 2.9 percent of the tracts in Toronto, and 90 percent in 13.9 percent of the tracts. It is also interesting to note that the two CMAs where about two thirds of all Jews in Canada live are also where they are most concentrated. It seems that size has a positive effect on concentration for the Jews, even though they are not recent immigrants, nor in the lower socioeconomic class. Italians and Poles are somewhat more concentrated than the Western European groups, but much less so than the visible minorities.

TABLE 9.1

▼

PERCENTAGE OF CENSUS TRACTS IN WHICH 50 PERCENT OF
ETHNIC-GROUP POPULATIONS ARE CONCENTRATED, 1996

	French	English	Italian	German	American Indian	Ukrainian	Dutch	Polish	Jewish	Scandinavian	Black	South Asian	Chinese
Halifax	28.0	35.0	14.6	28.0	12.0	14.6	25.3	13.3	7.9	14.6	10.6	13.3	13.3
Montreal	23.4	10.7	8.3	14.8	10.0	12.4	6.0	11.6	1.8	4.3	12.4	4.8	8.4
Ottawa–Hull	17.2	25.2	12.6	23.3	14.9	16.8	14.4	18.2	7.0	14.9	12.1	13.5	14.4
Toronto	22.3	26.6	10.6	24.7	7.9	12.6	13.8	11.0	2.9	3.4	14.4	12.0	8.8
Hamilton	24.8	28.5	19.8	25.4	9.9	23.6	13.6	22.9	3.2	14.9	18.0	13.04	16.1
St. Catharines–Niagara	21.6	32.5	19.2	22.8	9.9	25.3	12.0	22.8	6.0	16.8	16.8	12.04	15.0
Kitchener	27.1	30.8	18.5	25.9	9.8	20.9	23.4	22.2	8.0	17.5	20.3	17.5	14.2
London	27.5	32.1	18.3	25.3	13.7	20.6	21.8	20.5	4.5	19.5	19.3	12.8	13.7
Windsor	25.4	33.0	20.3	30.0	13.5	26.3	18.6	22.2	7.6	15.6	18.6	14.6	14.2
Winnipeg	13.2	28.6	15.0	25.4	8.0	23.5	23.0	21.0	2.6	19.1	19.2	8.2	10.4
Calgary	30.0	34.6	17.6	32.0	14.7	30.7	26.7	23.7	5.7	31.4	18.3	8.4	14.3
Edmonton	26.0	31.3	10.1	26.9	8.3	28.3	22.0	25.1	3.8	27.8	19.0	9.5	14.4
Vancouver	24.0	30.3	13.9	28.3	7.8	25.9	18.9	20.6	9.2	25.5	19.0	8.1	16.3
Victoria	25.3	31.2	22.1	31.0	9.3	28.0	23.7	22.0	17.6	28.4	22.7	15.65	17.4

Note: Based on single responses only.

Source: Statistics Canada, *1996 Census of Canada.* Special Tabulations.

TABLE 9.2
▼
PERCENTAGE OF CENSUS TRACTS IN WHICH 90 PERCENT OF ETHNIC-GROUP POPULATIONS ARE CONCENTRATED, 1996

	French	English	Italian	German	American Indian	Ukrainian	Dutch	Polish	Jewish	Scandinavian	Black	South Asian	Chinese
Halifax	70.0	78.0	44.0	70.6	36.0	38.6	62.6	44.0	29.3	40.0	52.0	45.3	46.6
Montreal	68.0	46.0	41.6	48.8	32.0	44.5	20.5	40.2	8.0	12.6	47.0	27.6	39.9
Ottawa–Hull	59.3	62.6	47.6	65.4	44.8	49.5	52.8	53.2	31.7	42.9	48.1	45.3	48.1
Toronto	64.6	70.7	50.4	67.4	26.7	53.3	52.4	49.2	13.9	27.8	51.3	47.1	44.2
Hamilton	66.4	74.5	62.1	69.5	36.0	63.9	52.17	67.0	15.5	40.3	51.5	47.8	50.9
St. Catharines—Niagara	69.8	75.9	62.6	69.8	43.3	68.7	57.8	62.6	25.2	50.6	56.6	36.1	44.5
Kitchener	72.8	74.0	58.0	67.9	29.6	58.0	70.3	62.9	22.2	48.1	62.9	55.5	49.3
London	72.4	78.1	60.9	72.4	45.9	63.2	71.2	64.3	19.5	55.1	57.4	47.1	50.5
Windsor	69.4	74.5	61.0	71.1	42.2	69.4	57.6	64.4	30.5	44.0	61.0	49.1	50.8
Winnipeg	62.4	71.9	52.8	70.7	39.4	70.0	61.7	61.7	19.1	56.0	61.0	37.5	43.9
Calgary	75.1	81.0	59.0	79.0	49.6	77.0	73.1	68.0	31.3	75.4	58.1	45.7	55.0
Edmonton	72.3	76.8	50.2	74.1	42.5	74.3	68.4	69.0	19.0	73.3	58.2	41.1	52.4
Vancouver	68.5	75.0	30.0	73.4	43.2	70.4	63.7	62.4	33.8	68.0	60.7	49.5	49.3
Victoria	69.0	81.0	65.0	75.0	44.5	70.8	70.1	61.5	45.7	73.4	61.2	54.1	59.0

Note: Based on single responses only.

Source: Statistics Canada, *1996 Census of Canada.* Special Tabulations.

After the Jewish population, visible minorities are the most concentrated groups in Canada. In Montreal, where the concentrations are highest for every group, half the South Asians live in 4.8 percent of the census tracts; the corresponding figures for the Chinese and Blacks are 8.4 and 12.4, percent respectively. In Toronto, where most of the visible minorities live, their concentrations are still noticeable, in spite of their large numbers. Half the Chinese live in 8.8 percent of the tracts. Blacks and South Asians also show high concentrations, with the corresponding figures being 14.4 and 12 percent, respectively. South Asians are even more concentrated than Blacks or the Chinese in the Western Canadian cities. In Winnipeg, Calgary, Edmonton, and Vancouver, half the South Asians live in about 8 percent of the census tracts.

A summary measure, the "Gini index," was constructed to investigate the extent of concentration of a minority group in a city. It is derived from concentration curves, also known as "Lorenz curves." Space dictates that only a few curves for the largest CMAs can be shown here (see Figures 9.1, 9.2, and 9.3). The vertical axis shows the cumulative percentage of the population in a particular ethnic group, and the horizontal axis shows the census tracts arranged in decreasing order of the ethnic population. A curve that coincides with the diagonal line indicates that the ethnic population is distributed equally among the census tracts, implying no spatial concentration. The farther the curve is from the diagonal, the greater the concentration. The Gini index is the ratio of the area between the curve and the diagonal to the area of the triangle above the diagonal line. Thus the range is from 0 to 1, where 0 indicates no concentration and 1 indicates complete concentration.

The Gini indices for selected ethnic groups in the major metropolitan areas, for the 1996 census year, are shown in Table 9.3. The indices are highest for the Jewish population, reaching values around .900 in the largest cities, Montreal and Toronto. There is also no evidence of a change in the decade 1986–96. The "visible minorities" of Blacks, Chinese, and South Asians have indices around .600. The European groups have somewhat lower indices.

The period of 1986–96 was one of heavy immigration of visible minorities. In spite of this heavy influx, there does not seem to be an increase in their concentration. In the case of Blacks, the indices show a decline in all the fourteen metropolitan areas. With a very few exceptions, this is also true of the Chinese and South Asians. There does not seem to be a case for rapid immigration resulting in greater segregation. One reason may be that many newer immigrants belong to higher socio-economic classes than the earlier immigrants and, consequently, may have more options as to which neighbourhoods they can settle in.

FIGURE 9.1
▼
LORENZ CURVES FOR SELECTED ETHNIC GROUPS, TORONTO, 1996

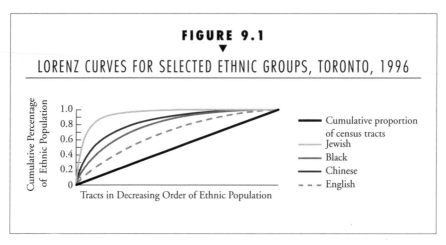

FIGURE 9.2
▼
LORENZ CURVES FOR SELECTED ETHNIC GROUPS, MONTREAL, 1996

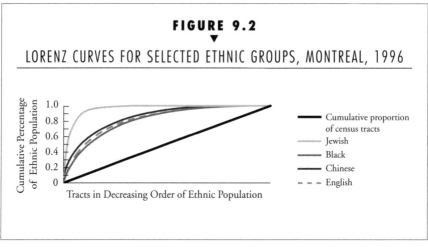

FIGURE 9.3
▼
LORENZ CURVES FOR SELECTED ETHNIC GROUPS, VANCOUVER, 1996

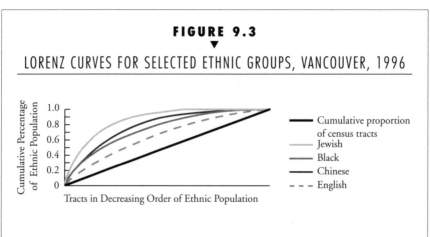

TABLE 9.3

▼

GINI INDICES OF CONCENTRATION BY ETHNIC GROUP FOR CANADA'S MAJOR CMAs, 1996

	French	English	Italian	German	American Indian	Ukrainian	Dutch	Polish	Jewish	Scandinavian	Black	South Asian	Chinese
Halifax	0.3415	0.2427	0.6230	0.3509	0.6996	0.6437	0.4190	0.6446	0.7735	0.6408	0.6167	0.6197	0.6225
Montreal	0.4042	0.6497	0.6912	0.5963	0.7540	0.6407	0.8315	0.6741	0.9267	0.8913	0.6245	0.8034	0.7040
Ottawa–Hull	0.5164	0.4130	0.6241	0.4204	0.6186	0.5760	0.5815	0.5314	0.7640	0.6297	0.6206	0.6228	0.6030
Toronto	0.4330	0.3574	0.6252	0.3925	0.7841	0.5924	0.5868	0.6300	0.8869	0.8141	0.5808	0.6235	0.6765
Hamilton	0.4085	0.3169	0.4777	0.3767	0.7159	0.4285	0.5879	0.4258	0.8861	0.6476	0.5451	0.6230	0.5669
St. Catharines-Niagara	0.4320	0.2740	0.4805	0.4106	0.6696	0.3780	0.5796	0.4395	0.8120	0.5731	0.5385	0.6776	0.6209
Kitchener	0.3505	0.3023	0.5041	0.3830	0.7541	0.4878	0.3921	0.4417	0.8070	0.5763	0.4659	0.5318	0.5911
London	0.3419	0.2609	0.5002	0.3579	0.6195	0.4555	0.4106	0.4483	0.8557	0.5224	0.4990	0.6241	0.5921
Windsor	0.3735	0.2617	0.4714	0.3302	0.6467	0.3715	0.5104	0.4336	0.7650	0.6157	0.4889	0.5995	0.5767
Winnipeg	0.5358	0.3291	0.5654	0.3687	0.7046	0.3936	0.4677	0.4590	0.8663	0.5138	0.4854	0.7167	0.6672
Calgary	0.2969	0.2210	0.5139	0.2638	0.5942	0.2841	0.3479	0.4008	0.7841	0.2836	0.5142	0.6658	0.5658
Edmonton	0.3590	0.2899	0.6321	0.3432	0.6921	0.3252	0.4184	0.3849	0.8615	0.3296	0.4992	0.6822	0.5781
Vancouver	0.3998	0.2992	0.5465	0.3275	0.6920	0.3668	0.4778	0.4601	0.7246	0.3832	0.4881	0.6533	0.5644
Victoria	0.3805	0.2116	0.4368	0.2775	0.6656	0.3394	0.3900	0.4549	0.5885	0.3268	0.4504	0.5488	0.5156

Note: Based on single responses only.

Source: Statistics Canada, *1996 Census of Canada*. Special Tabulations.

SEGREGATION OF ETHNIC GROUPS
▼

In the previous section, we calculated Gini indices, which measured the spatial concentration of a minority group. The indices would be high if the minority group lived in a small share of the total area of the city. In contrast, when the group is distributed widely in a city, the indices would be low. Segregation, on the other hand, measures the degree to which two or more groups live separately from one another. Thus, conceptually and methodologically, the two measures are different. However, they are often found to be highly correlated. Where a minority group is concentrated in space, it is also more likely to be segregated from other groups. In this section, instead of focussing on concentration, we will look at the extent of segregation between various ethnic groups, from the majority groups of British origin outside Quebec and French origin inside Quebec. The measure of segregation we selected is "the index of dissimilarity," which measures the differential distribution of two groups. It is the sum of either the positive or the negative differences between the proportional distributions of two populations.

The indices of dissimilarity for the three groups of Chinese, Blacks, and South Asians from the British in the various CMAs are very similar, ranging from .4 to .6 (Balakrishnan & Hou, 1995). In most CMAs, they increased slightly during 1986–91, probably due to the heavy immigration of these groups during this five-year period. The European groups, especially those from Western Europe who came to Canada mostly before 1961, had much lower indices of dissimilarity from the British, ranging from .150 to about .300. The other European groups such as the Italians, Poles, and Ukrainians had values in-between the Western Europeans and the visible minorities. While the British–French segregation was high in Montreal, it was lower in the CMAs outside of Quebec. The Aboriginal or First Nations population, though all are native born, had dissimilarity indices as high as those for recent visible-minority immigrants, an indication of their continued subordinate position in the Canadian social structure.

ETHNIC CONCENTRATION AND SOCIAL STATUS OF NEIGHBOURHOODS
▼

One may expect that the recent immigrants are more likely to be concentrated in the poorer neighbourhoods, which are often found near the city centre. They may not have the resources and, consequently, the option to choose among a number of preferred residential areas in a city. As this group improves its status and becomes more assimilated into Canadian society, we expect that it will have a greater opportunity for residential choice. With census data, one cannot examine in detail the relative importance of class and ethnicity in selecting a place of residence. However, one can still look at the overall status of neighbourhoods in which a particular ethnic minority is overrepresented. Balakrishnan and Hou (1995) constructed a socio-economic status (SES) index for each census tract by combining variables on education, income, and occupation, and related this to ethnic concentrations using 1991 census data. They found that the British reside in higher-than-average SES areas in nine of the fourteen CMAs, but below average in the others. The French are overrepresented in the poorer sections of all the CMAs except Toronto, where the average SES of the areas in which they are concentrated is only slightly over the city average.

The Aborginal and Native population is concentrated in the low SES areas in all the CMAs. Blacks are also concentrated in the lower SES areas in almost all the CMAs. In Toronto, where the largest number of Blacks live, the mean SES of the census tracts where they are overrepresented is the lowest for any group, the same being true in Halifax. In contrast, the Chinese are more likely to reside in areas with higher-than-average SES levels in almost all the CMAs, even though they are generally recent immigrants. South Asians, on the other hand, present an interesting case. In the two cities where the majority of them live, Toronto and Vancouver, they are concentrated in the poorer sections of the city. In the other CMAs, they live in above-average SES areas. Jews live in areas with the highest SES indices. Though they themselves contribute to the high values, they are only a minority in these tracts.

This short analysis does not do justice to the examination of the relationship among social class, ethnicity, and concentration. Individual, rather than aggregate level data are needed to make firm conclusions.

RESIDENTIAL SEGREGATION AND
SOCIO-ECONOMIC INTEGRATION
▼

We started this chapter with the statement that one of the reasons for the interest in the study of residential patterns of ethnic groups is that it may reflect their level of socio-economic integration. One way of looking at this is to see the occupational structure of a minority group in relation to the total population. If they are similar, we may conclude that they are economically integrated. Therefore, we could construct indices of dissimilarity for occupation and see whether they are related to indices of dissimilarity for residence. In other words, we could compare residential segregation with occupational segregation. Balakrishnan and Hou did this for the three years 1981, 1986, and 1991, using census data (Balakrishnan & Hou, 1999). They found that, while the residential segregation remained about the same during the decade 1981–91 for almost all the ethnic groups, occupational segregation decreased significantly. The immigrant minority groups, especially the visible minorities, are still underrepresented in the higher-status occupations, but their situation improved noticeably during 1981–91. One factor may be their selectivity in terms of higher education and job skills at the time of immigration.

It is clear that the association between occupational and residential segregation is weakening in Canada. One reason may be that closeness to place of work is less important in the selection of the place of residence than in the past. Though the journey to work has been increasing, improvements in transportation in the form of intracity highways and communication has meant that many can afford to live in a neighbourhood of choice and be able to commute to work economically and within a reasonable time. The different magnitudes and persistence of residential segregation among the various ethnic groups mean that, in spite of their occupational mobility, and hence the ability for a wider residential choice, many may prefer to live in close proximity to others of the same ethnic background to retain their ethnic identity and maintain ethnic connectedness.

CONCLUSION
▼

The ethnic diversity of Canadian cities has increased significantly as a result of recent immigration patterns. Canadian cities have truly become ethnic mosaics, with people from all over the world. In most areas, ethnic diversity has extended to areas within the cities as well, avoiding the high levels of segregation such as those faced by African Americans in the United States. Though there are moderate levels of segregation in many eastern Canadian cities, cities in the West, such as Calgary and Edmonton, show remarkably low levels of ethnic segregation. This implies that greater ethnic diversity need not necessarily lead to greater concentration.

Concentration of ethnic groups in cities varies by ethnicity as well as by city. It is also possible to have more than one ethnic enclave in a city. After the Jews, the "visible minorities" have the highest residential concentrations. However, the high levels of recent immigration among these groups have not increased their spatial concentrations. Some groups show a slight decline in selected CMAs. This may be because of selectivity that favours higher-status immigrants, and/or because of the heterogeneous character of the visible-minority immigrants. For example, Black immigrants to Canada come from the British, French, and Spanish Caribbean islands, and from Africa. Consequently, they have different language, educational, and occupational skills. Their cultural backgrounds differ, and they need not possess a common ethnic identity. The same may be true of the South Asian groups. Moreover, unlike the situation in many U.S. cities, urban public housing in Canada is less concentrated in the centre of the cities, contributing to lower levels of ethnic residential concentrations.

In the past, some of the residential segregation among Canada's ethnic groups was due to occupational segregation. There is abundant evidence that occupational differences by ethnicity are narrowing. With increased economic assimilation, one would expect residential segregation to decline in the future, though some level of segregation will remain, if only because of discrimination and prejudice toward certain minority groups, and the desire for some ethnic groups to live in proximity.

The future of ethnic residential segregation studies will depend on a number of factors. The nature of "ethnicity" itself is changing in Canada. Because of intermarriage, a majority of white European groups already report more than one ancestry. Though it will do so much slower, the situation will also change for recent immigrants. Though the Canadian government's policies of multiculturalism may help preserve ethnic identity, time will take its toll. Many immigrant groups lose their mother tongue in one generation, adopting English or French as their home language. The addition of the category "Canadian" in the recent censuses has also reduced the relevance of the ethnicity variable for social science research. Residential segregation will always be present in cities because of differences in social class. As the social mobility of minority groups increases, whether additional segregation will exist beyond that explained by their differences in social class is a difficult question to answer. It will depend on the extent of discrimination, and the need for a separate cultural identity. These trends are hard to predict.

REFERENCES
▼

Balakrishnan T.R. (1976.) Ethnic residential segregation in the metropolitan areas of Canada. *Canadian Journal of Sociology, 1*(4), 481–498.

———. (1982.) Changing patterns of ethnic residential segregation in the metropolitan areas of Canada. *Canadian Review of Sociology and Anthropology, 19*(1), 92–110.

Balakrishnan T.R., & Hou, Feng. (1995.) The changing patterns of spatial concentration and residential segregation of ethnic groups in Canada's major metropolitan areas 1981–91. Paper presented at the 1995 Population Association of America meetings, San Francisco.

———. (1999). Socioeconomic integration and spatial residential patterns of immigrant groups in Canada. *Population Research and Policy Review, 18*(6).

Balakrishnan T.R., & Kralt, John. (1987). Segregation of visible minorities in Montreal, Toronto and Vancouver. In Leo Driedger (Ed.), *Ethnic Canada: Identities and inequalities* (pp. 138–157). Toronto: Copp Clark Pitman.

Balakrishnan T.R., & Selvanathan, K. (1990.) Ethnic residential segregation in metropolitan Canada. In Shiva S. Halli, Frank Trovato, & Leo Driedger (Eds.). *Ethnic demography* (pp. 399–413). Ottawa: Carleton University Press.

Dai, S.Y., & George, M.V. (1996). *Projections of visible minority population groups, Canada, provinces and regions, 1991–2016.* Product 91-541-XPE. Ottawa: Statistics Canada.

Darroch A.G., & Marston, W.G. (1971). The social class basis of ethnic residential segregation: The Canadian case. *American Journal of Sociology, 77,* 491–510.

Dreidger, Leo. (1982). Ethnic boundaries: A comparison of two urban neighbourhoods. In George A. Theodorson (Ed.). *Urban patterns: Studies in human ecology* (pp. 207–217). University Park, PA. Pennsylvania State University Press.

Driedger, Leo, & Church, Glenn. (1974). Residential segregation and institutional completeness: A comparison of ethnic minorities. *Canadian Review of Sociology and Anthropology, 11,* 30–52.

Driedger, Leo, & Peters, Jacob. (1977). Identity and social distance: Towards Simmel's "The Stranger." *Canadian Review of Sociology and Anthropology, 14,* 158–173.

Joy, Richard. (1972). *Languages in conflict.* Toronto: McClelland & Stewart.

Kalbach, Warren E. (1990). Ethnic residential segregation and its significance for the individual in an urban setting. In Raymond Breton, Wsevolod Isajiw, Warren Kalbach, & Jeffrey G. Reitz (Eds.), *Ethnic identity and equality: Varieties of experience in a Canadian city* (pp. 92–134). Toronto: University of Toronto Press.

Lieberson, Stanley. (1970). *Language and ethnic relations in Canada.* New York: John Wiley and Sons.

Lieberson, Stanley, & Waters, Mary C. (1988). *From many strands.* New York: Russell Sage Foundation.

Massey, Douglas S., & Denton, Nancy. (1993). *American Apartheid.* Cambridge, MA: Harvard University Press.

Park, Robert E. & Burgess, Ernest (Eds.). (1916). *The city.* Chicago: University of Chicago Press.

ETHNICITY AND IMMIGRANT OFFSPRING[1]

MONICA BOYD

INTRODUCTION

To date, few Canadian studies on immigrant offspring exist, despite the number of foreign-born and the substantial shifts in their ethnic origins during the past 50 years. What do we mean by the term "immigrant offspring," and why the neglect? Immigrant offspring usually are called either "the 1.5 generation" or "the second generation." Since foreign-born adults are considered to be the "first generation" to arrive in a new country, Canadian-born offspring of this "first" generation are called the "second" generation. Those foreign-born who immigrated as children, and who thus are neither the first nor the second generation, are "the 1.5 generation." Research has generally neglected the 1.5 and second generations because many censuses and surveys do not ask questions about the birthplace of parents or the age at immigration. For example, the 1971 census of population was the last to ask respondents about the birthplace of their parents. This question is necessary in order to distinguish between those Canadian-born who are offspring of foreign-born parents (the second generation) and those who are born to parents who are also Canadian-born (the third-plus generation). As a result, few studies of the 1.5 or the second generation exist in Canada (Boyd & Grieco, 1998).

Despite data gaps that dampened research on immigrant offspring, interest in the topic revived during the 1990s. This revival has three important characteristics. First, the earlier theory on the likely successes of these offspring has been revised. This revision explicitly acknowledges the roles played by ethnicity in shaping the variegated experiences of immigrant offspring. Second, the accompanying empirical studies redirect attention away from the experiences of adults to those youth who are still living with parents, particular those under age 18 or still in school. Third, scholars in the United States have dominated new approaches to theory and research on immigrant offspring. However, countries vary in their histories of race relations; in their approaches to multiculturalism; and in their policies and practices concerning immigration flows, labour markets, educational systems, and social welfare (see Reitz, 1998). Such differences generate two possibilities: (1) United States–based theoretical revisions may not fully apply to immigrant youth in Canada and in other countries; and (2) empirical conclusions on immigrant offspring in the United States may not be replicated elsewhere.

The objectives of this chapter derive from these three characteristics. First, we review the approaches to the study of North America's immigrant offspring, highlighting new developments that emphasize the roles played by ethnic identity and socio-economic resources. Second, we place these recent developments in the Canadian context. Data from the 1991 census show that the living situations of young immigrant offspring vary substantially according to their ethnic origins. The patterns of advantage and disadvantage caution us against constructing a homogeneous script about the experiences of immigrant offspring.

UNILATERAL SUCCESS OR SEGMENTED ASSIMILATION?
▼

How has research related to immigrant offspring been conceptually recast in recent years? Prior to the 1990s, the orthodox approach stressed an optimistic scenario for immigrant offspring. According to the earlier linear (or "straight-line") theory, with increasing length of time spent by immigrants in the host society, or with each generation further removed from foreign-born predecessors, the socio-economic situations of "newcomer" groups would become similar to those of the North American–born (who were often of British ancestry). Such increasing similarities imply that any disadvantages faced by immigrants are overcome by subsequent generations.

The straight-line scenario is firmly embedded in the "classical" model of acculturation and assimilation, articulated first by writers in the Chicago School, headquartered at the University of Chicago during the early 1900s. This model was embellished by successive generations of U.S. scholars (for reviews, see Alba & Nee, 1997; Driedger, 1996: 23–37; Gans, 1992; Kallen, 1995: 162–187). Referring to newcomers' adoption of behaviours, rules, values, and norms of the host society, acculturation was almost always a faster process than assimilation, which includes the movement of groups out of the ethnic-based associations and other institutions into non-ethnic primary groups and institutions (Gans, 1997: 877). Yet both were seen as occurring in tandem, and as desired by social scientists and the public at large.

In recent years, this classical model has been extensively criticized, not only because of the normative element that views acculturation and assimilation as optimal and desirable, but also because of what it omits. At best a sociocultural theory (Gans, 1992), the straight-line, or linear, model pays little or no attention to influences coming from the following: shifts from an industrial to a service-based economy; economic booms and busts; changing residential patterns in the context of post–World War II metropolitan growth and suburbanization; the cessation of immigration flows between World Wars I and II that, in turn, alter the context within which integration occurs; and structural impediments arising from ethnic and racial discrimination (Alba & Nee, 1997; Gans, 1992; Massey, 1995; Zhou, 1997a, 1997b). Furthermore, it ignores dimensions of ethnicity that influence the experiences of the immigrant offspring, notably ethnic identity and ethnic-based communities.

Although it has many components and is expressed in many forms, ethnic identity generally describes the psychological and social attachments of individuals to groups on the basis of shared ancestry and/or social and cultural attributes (Driedger, 1996: Ch. 6; Isajiw, 1990). Ethnic identity can be modified over time, or maintained in two ways. The actions of other groups can create externally imposed boundaries on any given ethnic group. This typically occurs when the majority group discriminates against a particular group or defines it as racially distinct. Boundaries also can be created or enhanced by the existence of institutionally complete ethnic communities, often depicted by labels such as "Little Italy" or "Chinatown" (Breton, 1964). Constituted from social interaction based on common ties, ethnic communities often provide social and economic resources to members. In such communities, the monitoring actions of members can reinforce parental efforts at communicating values, norms, and expectations to young children (Zhou & Bankston, 1994, 1998). Although traditionally viewed as geographically delimited (e.g., Little Italy or Chinatown), ethnic communities need not be spatially grounded (Goldenberg & Haines, 1992). Non-local ties can reinforce ethnic identity by supplying needed resources (e.g., marriage partners, jobs, loans, financial backers).

Recent models modify the optimistic view of integration and acculturation implied by linear assimilation theory. Two U.S. sociologists (Portes, 1995; Portes & Zhou, 1993; Zhou, 1997a, 1997b) have articulated three distinctive forms of integration for the 1.5 and second generations in the United States. The first assumes the orthodox success story. Over time, acculturation occurs alongside the integration of the (white) immigrant offspring into (white) mainstream economic and social life. However, this experience does not necessarily hold for all immigrant offspring. Rather, the pattern can be one of segmented assimilation incorporating two additional scenarios. One depicts offspring rejection of parental values emphasizing education and hard work as mechanisms of mobility in the host society. Instead, immigrant offspring undergo acculturation and integration, and shift their identities into a primarily Black inner-city underclass, where outcomes are those of poverty and irregular employment. According to Portes and Zhou (1993), Caribbean youths are examples of this segmented, or truncated, assimilation. The other scenario emphasizes economic advancement, but with deliberate preservation of ethnic membership and values, and with continued economic attachment to ethnic communities. U.S. offspring most likely to display this pattern are members of immigrant groups that have well-developed ethnic-based economies such as the Chinese- or Cuban-origin groups (Portes, 1995; Portes & Zhou, 1993; see also Hirschman, 1994; Waters, 1994, 1997).

As developed most fully in the writings of Portes and Zhou, the new sociological perspectives of the 1990s offer conditional scripts. Which pathway is followed by an immigrant offspring group is heavily influenced by two sets of social relations: those that exist between parents and offspring, and convey norms, values, and expectations; and those that link parents and children to others. In the segmented-assimilation approach, ethnic-community ties and social networks are important mechanisms for accessing resources, particularly when parents lack the human capital (such as education, labour-market experience, or language skills) to sustain desired consumption patterns and to socialize offspring for life in the host society. In the absence of human capital, and in the face of racial barriers and inner-city residential nearness to the Black underclass, social capital is the key to thwarting the segmented-assimilation pattern of downward mobility into an underclass culture. Social capital is defined as the ability to command scarce resources by virtue of membership in networks, associations, or other social institutions. In an ethnic community, social capital allows parents to call on co-ethnics to reinforce normative expectations and to monitor the behaviours of offspring (see Zhou & Bankston, 1994, 1998). Resources outside the immediate family, such as educational loans or jobs for immigrant offspring, also may be obtained through networks (Portes, 1995; Portes & Zhou, 1993). In such circumstances, immigrant offspring are as likely as adults to assimilate into the larger society or to remain socially and economically active within an ethnic community.

Without social capital intimately associated with ethnic bonds, four other factors can determine the pathway of immigrant offspring. According to Portes and Zhou, in the absence of strong community ties, parental authority is most likely to be undermined under conditions of poverty and/or in settings where only one adult is present or when employment demands frequently make both parents absent. The absence of a strong parental influence on normatively set goals is most likely to be converted into that of downward mobility and oppositional behaviours when three additional conditions hold: geographical residence in poor inner-city areas of the United States; historically rooted racial barriers that over time have created an underclass culture; and the existence of institutions such as schools that provide settings in which underclass norms and oppositional cultures are communicated. Depressed economic opportunities due either to economic restructuring or to pre-existing racial/ethnic barriers contribute further to the likelihood of assimilation into an underclass culture and to downward mobility, when the circumstances of immigrant offspring are compared with those of the parental generation or the mainstream groups.

In sum, scholars now outline three possible outcomes for immigrant children: (1) assimilation to the mainstream society, with economic success being a major indicator; (2) a continued emphasis on ethnic identity accompanied by integration into ethnic enclaves; and (3) the assumption of underclass identities along with marginal labour-market integration. Class and ethnicity influence the likelihood of each scenario. Groups that immigrate with high economic resources appear to be the most likely to follow the first pathway. Lower resources and strong ethnic fault lines increase the likelihood of the second or third pathway. Often such fault lines have originated historically through the actions of the majority against a particular group, resting on a "we–they" conceptualization. This process of racialization (Miles, 1989) is not solely based on colour, as shown by the nineteenth-century experiences of the Irish and Eastern European groups in the United States and in Canada. However, by themselves, low resources and ethnic boundaries do not elicit one outcome over another for immigrant offspring. Whether the second or third scenario holds is conditional on exposure to alternative ethnic identities, and on the presence or absence of ethnic communities with economic and social resources that can be accessed by parents and offspring.

These revisionist approaches to the fates of immigrant offspring largely rest on U.S. scholarship. It thus is appropriate to ask what the implications are for a Canadian audience. Two exist. First, the new theories provide new agendas for research on ethnic identity. Previous sociological studies in both Canada and the United States have emphasized ethnic-identity retention or loss between the first and second and third-plus generations (see Isajiw, 1990). Implicit in many of these studies is the assumption that loss of ethnic identity means the acquisition of an identity that represents either the dominant ethnic majority or a regional or national identity (Boyd, 1997; Kalin & Berry, 1995). However, the segmented-assimilation model describes an additional outcome: acquiring a new ethnic identity that is accompanied by negative so-cial and economic consequences. Whether or not, and under what conditions, persons acquire non-mainstream ethnic identities is a new question supple-menting current Canadian research on retention and loss. Answering this question also is integral to the second issue arising from the U.S. discourse on immigrant offspring — notably, the need for an assessment of how well or how badly the new integration scenarios describe the situation in Canada. At the moment, there is no clear conclusion due to the lack of data on the 1.5 and second generations in Canada. However, as shown in the next section, both differences and similarities are likely to be observed in future studies.

THE CANADIAN CONTEXT
▼

A central question arising from the new approaches to immigrant offspring is: which model holds for what ethnic/racial groups in Canada? Analysis of a 1994 survey on the educational and occupational achievements of second-generation adults supports the "straight line" upward-mobility scenario for a population whose parents are primarily born in the United States, the United Kingdom, or European countries (Boyd & Grieco, 1998). Earlier studies also find intergenerational mobility for immigrant offspring belonging to various ethnic-origin groups (see Isajiw, Sev'er, & Driedger, 1993; Kalbach et al., 1983; Richmond, 1986).

So far, little is known about the situation of immigrant offspring from areas such as Asia, South America and the Caribbean, and Africa. Immigrants from these areas began arriving in large numbers only after the removal of na-tionality as a criterion of admissibility in 1962 and 1967, and most second-generation adults are still young, having been born in the 1970s and 1980s. As a result, second-generation adults from non-European ethnic origins are not found in surveys in numbers sufficient for analysis. At the moment, one can only speculate about possible outcomes. Many of the non-European eth-nic-origin groups in Canada appear to have well-developed ethnic economies, where members are self-employed, and/or own businesses that both service and employ co-ethnics. For the largest of these groups, the Chinese, the model of ethnic-enclave assimilation may characterize immigrant offspring. Howev-er, the extent to which this route is followed, and by what ethnic groups, re-mains to be explored. In their critique of the ethnic-enclave concept, Alba and Nee (1997) suggest that ethnic economies have not been large enough to offer much employment for subsequent generations. They note that most immi-grants and their offspring work in the "open" or non-ethnic economy.

In the Canadian context, the scenario that emphasizes the absorption of (Black) immigrant offspring into the inner-city underclass remains the scenario least likely to be successfully transposed from U.S. research. This motif emphasizes not merely the movement of youth into a world of poverty, marginal employment, and crime, but its subsequent persistence for later generations. Two factors make this "underclass" scenario less of a possibility for immigrant offspring in Canada. First and foremost, Canada never developed the pervasive and pernicious Black/white fault line of race relations and stratification that has so powerfully shaped U.S. history, politics, and policy. Although discrimination along colour lines existed and continues into the present day (Henry et al., 1995), slavery was outlawed in Britain and in the dominions in the 1830s. Canada did not experience a war of secession over slavery or the Jim Crow practices that effectively disenfranchised a Black population. As well, historically, Canada's Black population was small in contrast to a larger U.S. Black population heavily concentrated in the South. The particular configuration of forces shaping race relations in the United States — the institution of slavery; large numbers of Blacks; high regional concentration but over a large geographical area, primarily in the South; a civil war; and subsequent actions by the white majority to maintain power over Blacks in the South — were not replicated in Canada.

Second, in Canada, the 1759 British victory over the French on the Plains of Abraham in Quebec City left a legacy that emphasized language and culture rather than race. Unlike the United States, Canada has an explicit multiculturalism policy, first adopted in 1971, and reaffirmed with the 1988 passage of the Canadian Multiculturalism Act. The minimal impact of such policy is twofold: (1) it emphasizes the symbolic importance of diversity in Canadian society; and (2) it contributes to the emergence of specific ethnic associations and to the existence of umbrella ethnocultural organizations that lobby and interact with municipal, provincial, and federal government departments. By shaping the context in which race and ethnicity are viewed, and the discourse where ethnic and race relations are discussed, multiculturalism policy has the potential to influence indirectly the experiences of immigrant offspring.

These factors suggest that segmented assimilation into the underclass may be less likely in Canada. Whether the underclass scenario is less viable in Canada, however, awaits future research on groups of immigrant offspring that are most vulnerable. This includes those who are members of visible minorities, where parental resources are low and where ethnic-based communities are non-existent or lacking in resources. As well, the underclass model assumes that such immigrant offspring live near and attend school with members of indigenous groups that have developed cultures and economic strategies to deal with decades and centuries of deprivation and discrimination. In the United States, the inner-city impoverished Black population is considered to be such an indigenous group. It is not clear that Canada has a comparable underclass residing in its large cities. The Black population in Canada is diverse in history, in origins, and in socio-economic circumstances. Some arrived in Canada in the 1800s, via the United States, while others are relative newcomers, having immigrated since the 1960s from Caribbean, Latin American, and African countries. Aboriginal youth also appear to have a low potential for influencing immigrant youth. Although the Aboriginal population does concentrate in areas of Canada's cities characterized by high poverty (Balakrishnan & Hou, 1999; Kazemipur & Halli, 1997), other conditions mitigate their selection as a reference population: numbers are relatively small; many migrate from reserves to cities as older adolescents or as adults; they thus are not attending elementary or secondary schools; and the geographical space occupied is not as extensive as found in many inner-city ghettos in the United States. Overall, one task in any future Canadian depictions of underclass assimilation will be to identify the underclass reference-group population(s) for immigrant youth.

SOCIO-ECONOMIC CIRCUMSTANCES OF IMMIGRANT OFFSPRING IN CANADA
▼

Although the "jury is still out" on the fate of immigrant offspring of non-European ethnic origin, the experiences of growing up in Canada and earning a living in adulthood without a doubt will vary by ethnic origins. This assertion rests on the fact that countries vary internationally in their educational systems, in economic structures, in family structures and living arrangements, and in norms and practices concerning social and economic exchanges. Immigrants bring with them the imprint of their societies, and in doing so vary in the resources they can individually and collectively offer their children. Hints of this likely variability are evident from 1991 census data for youth under the age of 15, living in Montreal, Toronto, and Vancouver. These cities were chosen because they attract most of the post-1960s immigrants, and it is here that 61 percent of the 1.5 generation (i.e., foreign-born children) resided in 1991 (compared with 27 percent of Canadian-born children).

Census data from the Public Use Microdata Files are not perfect for this task of examining the current situation of immigrant offspring. The absence of a census question on birthplace of parents means that the second generation cannot be separated from the third-plus generation. (For many recently arrived ethnic groups, the former probably predominates in the Canadian-born category.) Because records on parents and children cannot be linked in the Public Use Microdata File (PUMF) of individuals, the human capital and resources of parents cannot be determined.[2] However, indirect information can be obtained by examining the household and housing situation, the living arrangements, and the economic characteristics of the units in which children reside. This is done for those ethnic-origin groups[3] that had at least 100 foreign-born respondents in the PUMF of individuals who were less than 15 years old and who were living in Montreal, Toronto, or Vancouver. Because the microdata file of individuals is a 3 percent sample of the Canadian population, 100 children represent approximately 3333 persons.

Reflecting the legacy of over 300 years of immigration, most children under age 15 in Canada are Canadian-born, and the British (English, Irish, Scottish, and Welsh) and French ethnic-origin groups are the largest. Not surprisingly, fewer than 10 percent of children living in Canada's three largest cities are foreign-born, with 2 percent and 1 percent, respectively, for British and French ethnic-origin groups (see Table 10.1). However, the 1.5 generation occupies a larger share of the under-15 youth for other ethnic-origin groups, ranging from 10 percent for those of Jewish ethnic origin to over 40 percent for West Asian youth. With the exception of the Vietnamese, over half of these children were age 5 or older when they arrived, implying that in many instances new languages must be acquired simultaneously with insertion into provincial educational systems. Many also are recent arrivals, possibly still grappling with Canadian customs and institutions, and mass culture.

The new models of assimilation emphasize the importance of resources in shaping the experiences of immigrant offspring. U.S. studies show that some Hispanic, Asian, and Caribbean immigrant youth live in crowded conditions, in lone-parent families and in households with low incomes, implying that these groups with low resources may be at risk for segmented assimilation paths (Jensen & Chitose, 1994; Landale & Oropesa, 1995; Oropesa & Landale, 1997). In Canada, substantial ethnic variation exists in such indicators (see Table 10.2), and at least two patterns are discernible for Canadian-born and foreign-born youth under age 15. First, when the fourteen ethnic-origin groups are arranged in order for foreign-born offspring (see Table 10.2), a pattern is evident in which the more disadvantaged are usually immigrant offspring whose ethnic origins are non-European. This pattern describes foreign-born offspring living in households where: (a) density is one person or more per room; and (b) economic indicators show low levels of economic re-

TABLE 10.1

▼

SAMPLE NUMBERS, PERCENT CANADIAN- AND FOREIGN-BORN, AND AGE AT IMMIGRATION AND AVERAGE YEARS IN CANADA FOR THE FOREIGN-BORN, CHILDREN, AGE 14 AND LESS, FOR SELECT ETHNIC-ORIGIN GROUPS, LIVING IN MONTREAL, TORONTO, AND VANCOUVER, 1991

	Sample Numbers		Percent of Ethnic Groups that are		Foreign-Born Only	
	Canadian-Born	Foreign-Born	Canadian-Born	Foreign-Born	Percent Immigrating at Age 5+	Average Years in Canada
Total, Select Groups[a]	37 232	3 757	91	9	54	3.8
British	16 097	327	98	2	40	5.2
French	14 483	112	99	1	43	4.9
Polish	1 256	234	84	16	58	4.1
Portuguese	1 198	180	87	13	56	3.9
Spanish	516	173	75	25	64	3.7
Jewish	1 572	175	90	10	49	3.9
Chinese	2 032	887	70	30	59	3.5
Filipino	542	166	77	23	52	3.5
Vietnamese	245	148	62	38	35	5.8
Black/Caribbean	2 399	396	86	14	54	4.2
Arab	567	314	64	36	54	2.4
West Asian	268	190	59	42	60	3.3
South Asian	2 100	470	82	18	53	3.6
Latin/Central/ South American	363	244	60	40	55	3.5

[a] Refers only to those ethnic-origin groups listed in the table. Multiple ethnic-origin responses exist, and an individual may be in one or more of the listed ethnic groups.

Source: Produced by the author from records on individual respondents, Statistics Canada, *1991 Census of Population*, Public Use Microdata File, Individuals.

TABLE 10.2
▼
SELECTED CHARACTERISTICS OF CHILDREN, AGE 14 AND LESS, FOR SELECT ETHNIC-ORIGIN GROUPS, CANADIAN- AND FOREIGN-BORN POPULATION, LIVING IN MONTREAL, TORONTO, AND VANCOUVER, 1991

| | Percentages | | Rank Order | | Ratio (1)/(2) |
	Foreign-Born (1)	Canadian-Born (2)	Foreign-Born (3)	Canadian-Born (4)	Foreign- to Canadian-Born (5)
PERCENT WITH 1+ PERSON PER ROOM					
Total, Select Group[a]	40.6	13.7	–	–	2.97
British	15.0	7.8	1	1	1.93
French	15.2	10.9	2	4	1.39
Jewish	25.1	8.0	3	2	3.14
Chinese	27.8	21.3	4	6	1.31
Portuguese	40.6	18.6	5	5	2.18
Polish	41.5	9.3	6	3	4.45
South Asian	43.4	25.1	7	7	1.73
Black/Caribbean	44.2	27.7	8	9	1.60
Latin/Central/ South American	53.3	31.4	9	13	1.70
Vietnamese	55.4	46.1	10	14	1.20
Filipino	56.0	29.7	11	12	1.89
West Asian	56.3	27.2	12	8	2.07
Spanish	57.8	29.3	13	11	1.98
Arab	59.2	27.9	14	10	2.13
PERCENT IN LONE-PARENT FAMILIES					
Total, Select Group[a]	11.7	14.6	–	–	0.80
Portuguese	4.4	8.4	1	4	0.53
Chinese	4.8	6.0	2	2	0.81
Jewish	5.7	9.4	3	6	0.61
Arab	5.7	8.1	4	3	0.71
South Asian	6.4	4.7	5	1	1.37
Filipino	8.4	9.4	6	7	0.90
Polish	8.5	11.1	7	8	0.77
West Asian	11.6	9.0	8	5	1.29
French	15.2	15.6	9	10	0.98
British	16.8	14.0	10	9	1.20
Latin/Central/ South American	18.0	18.7	11	13	0.96
Vietnamese	20.9	18.0	12	12	1.17
Spanish	22.5	17.2	13	11	1.31
Black/Caribbean	34.1	36.0	14	14	0.95

(continued)

(Table 10.2 continued)

| | Percentages | | Rank Order | | Ratio (1)/(2) |
	Foreign-Born (1)	Canadian-Born (2)	Foreign-Born (3)	Canadian-Born (4)	Foreign- to Canadian-Born (5)
PERCENT LIVING IN FAMILIES BELOW LOW-INCOME CUTOFFS[b]					
Total, Select Group[a]	17.8	28.7	–	–	0.62
Filipino	7.8	13.7	1	3	0.57
Portuguese	12.1	16.1	2	7	0.75
Jewish	13.1	11.9	3	1	1.10
British	13.7	13.9	4	4	0.99
Polish	16.7	12.9	5	2	1.29
French	23.0	17.5	6	8	1.31
Chinese	26.7	14.6	7	5	1.83
South Asian	28.1	15.5	8	6	1.81
Black/Caribbean	36.6	37.5	9	12	0.98
West Asian	39.4	26.1	10	9	1.51
Spanish	40.0	30.7	11	11	1.30
Latin/Central/ South American	47.7	38.1	12	13	1.25
Vietnamese	49.1	40.2	13	14	1.22
Arab	50.5	26.3	14	10	1.92
PERCENT LIVING IN FAMILIES WHERE GOVERNMENT TRANSFER PAYMENTS ARE THE MAIN SOURCE OF 1990 INCOME[b]					
Total, Select Group[a]	9.5	12.5	–	–	0.76
Filipino	1.1	6.7	1	5	0.17
Portuguese	3.0	7.1	2	6	0.43
British	6.9	7.7	3	7	0.90
Chinese	7.0	5.4	4	2	1.30
South Asian	7.1	6.4	5	4	1.11
Polish	9.2	5.5	6	3	1.65
Jewish	12.1	4.6	7	1	2.62
French	12.3	10.1	8	9	1.22
Spanish	18.8	15.5	9	11	1.21
Arab	19.2	9.5	10	8	2.02
Black/Caribbean	19.3	21.5	11	13	0.90
Latin/Central/ South American	21.5	16.7	12	12	1.29
West Asian	25.0	10.2	13	10	2.44
Vietnamese	37.5	28.1	14	14	1.33

(continued)

(Table 10.2 continued)

| | Income | | Rank Order | | Ratio (1)/(2) |
	Foreign-Born (1)	Canadian-Born (2)	Foreign-Born (3)	Canadian-Born (4)	Foreign- to Canadian-Born (5)
PER CAPITA 1990 HOUSEHOLD INCOME[b]					
Total, Select Group[a]	10 742	13 645	–	–	0.79
British	14 346	14 982	1	3	0.96
French	13 329	13 495	2	5	0.99
Jewish	13 288	16 841	3	1	0.79
Polish	12 749	15 150	4	2	0.84
Filipino	12 712	13 111	5	6	0.97
Portuguese	11 942	11 849	6	10	1.01
South Asian	10 763	11 995	7	8	0.90
Chinese	10 574	13 553	8	4	0.78
West Asian	10 512	11 989	9	9	0.88
Black/Caribbean	8 926	9 965	10	12	0.90
Latin/Central/ South American	8 782	9 584	11	14	0.92
Spanish	8 169	10 913	12	11	0.75
Arab	7 519	12 036	13	7	0.62
Vietnamese	7 006	9 670	14	13	0.72

[a] Refers only to those ethnic-origin groups listed in the table. Multiple-ethnic-origin responses exist, and an individual may be in one or more of the listed ethnic groups.
[b] Calculated only for children arriving before 1990. Income data are assigned a value of zero for immigrants arriving in 1991. For immigrants arriving in 1990, most income data refer to Canadian income, and the magnitude of total income thus is sensitive to when in 1990 individuals, families, or households arrived.

Source: Produced by the author from records on individual respondents, Statistics Canada, *1991 Census of Population*, Public Use Microdata File, Individuals.

sources. These indicators are low per-capita household incomes, higher percentages with family income below the Statistics Canada measure of low-income cutoffs, and where government transfer payments are the major source of 1990 income. Living in households or families with poor economic resources is particularly likely for immigrant offspring whose ethnic origins are Arab, Black/Caribbean, Latin/Central/South American, Spanish (which, among the foreign-born, includes primarily persons born in the Americas, including the United States), Vietnamese, and West Asian. The pattern for immigrant offspring in lone-parent families does not completely fit the more general findings for density and economic indicators, in part because relatively high percentages of immigrant children of British or French origins are likely to be in lone-parent families. Offspring of other non-European ethnic-origin groups are less likely to be in lone-parent families, perhaps because of the emphasis on familism in these groups (Boyd, 1998) and strong sanctions again divorce.

A second pattern is the similar rankings of indicators for both foreign-born and Canadian-born children of the same ethnic-origin groups.[4] This second pattern indicates that ethnic stratification exists. Regardless of birthplace, children in some groups are more likely than those in other groups to be in households characterized by higher density, to be in lone-parent families, and to experience low economic status. However, as indicated by ratios calculated by dividing percentages for the foreign-born by those for Canadian-born youth (see Table 10.2, column 5), foreign-born offspring usually are more likely than Canadian-born offspring to live in such circumstances. Again, the one exception to this is the indicator of living in lone-parent families. Other than those of British, Latin American, Spanish, South Asian, Vietnamese, and West Asian ethnic origins, immigrant children have lower percentages living in lone-parent families than do corresponding Canadian-born children. Why this is so cannot be determined from available census data.

CONCLUSION
▼

The model of linear, or straight-line, assimilation depicts a scenario in which later generations of offspring will steadily move up socially and economically. In the process, these offspring will surpass the achievements of the foreign-born generation and achieve — or exceed — the standing of the majority population. This script has been rewritten in the past ten years by scholars in the United States, who argue that pathways to assimilation also can include assimilation into the ethnic enclave or absorption into the underclass. Ethnic identities and social capital found in ethnic communities are key determinants of which groups will follow which path.

Left uncharted are the trails to be travelled by the offspring of the post-1960s immigrant groups in Canada. The ambiguity is caused partly by the fact that many of these offspring are still young and, at best, in early adulthood. Data gaps also exist, with no census and few surveys asking respondents where their parents were born. Part of the ambiguity arises as well from the differences that exist between Canada and the United States in their histories and in their emphases on multiculturalism, suggesting that what is observed in the United States may not occur in Canada. A final uncertainty comes from the fact that situations do change over time, and the circumstances today for young immigrant offspring may not describe their experiences in adulthood (Alba & Nee, 1997).

It is true that immigrant youth whose ethnic origins are Arab, Black/Caribbean, Latin/Central/South American, Spanish, Vietnamese, or West Asian are, in varying degrees, growing up in settings of high density, with a single parent, and in reduced economic circumstances. Sociologists have documented that, in general, children growing up in single-parent families and/or in impoverished circumstances are themselves likely to leave home and school early, and to thus be at a disadvantage in the labour market. Such conditions also can be precursors of segmented, rather than linear, assimilation of immigrant offspring. However, low resources indicate a potential for, rather than a prediction of, segmented assimilation either into an ethnic enclave or accompanied by downward mobility. For some offspring, low resources in childhood — although real — may be temporary to the extent that they reflect how recently immigration was (see Table 10.1). Ties and social networks within a larger ethnic community also may provide access to needed resources, thus offsetting low levels existing within the immediate family. In short, the revisionist scripts that carry us into the twenty-first century caution us against anticipating a homogeneous outcome, pointing instead to the importance of ethnic identity, resources, and ethnic communities in shaping the futures of Canada's immigrant offspring.

NOTES
▼

1. The author thanks Elizabeth Grieco for editorial suggestions on an earlier draft.
2. Statistics Canada also produces family and household public-use files. However, birthplace and ethnic origins categories are very collapsed on these files, thereby preventing a meaningful analysis of the socio-economic circumstances of immigrant offspring by ethnic origins.
3. Ethnic-origin groups are constructed by Statistics Canada from answers obtained from the following quesion on the 1991 census questionnaire: "To which ethnic or cultural group(s) did this person's ancestors belong?"
4. Foreign- and Canadian-born similarities in rankings also are evident from high and positive Spearman rank-order correlations of .807 for one or more persons per room, .877 for lone-parent families, .798 for 1990 per-capita household income; .767 for families below low-income cutoffs, and .820 for families where government transfer payments are the main income source. The Spearman rank-order correlation has a value of 0 where no association between rankings exists, a value of −1 when two rankings are completely opposite, and a value of +1 when two rankings are identical.

REFERENCES
▼

Alba, Richard, & Nee, Victor. (1997). Rethinking assimilation theory for a new era of immigration. *International Migration Review, 31* (Winter), 826–875.

Balakrishnan, T.R., & Hou, Feng. (1999). Residential patterns in cities. In Leo Driedger & Shiva Halli (Eds.), *Immigrant Canada* (pp. 116–147). Toronto: University of Toronto Press.

Boyd, Monica. (1997). Offspring-parent shifts in ancestry: Ethnic bedrock or ethnic quicksand? Working Paper Series 97-138. Tallahassee: Center for the Study of Population and Demography, Florida State University.

———. (1998). Birds of a feather …: Ethnic variations in young adults living with parents. Working Paper Series 98-140. Tallahassee: Center for the Study of Population, Florida State University.

Boyd, Monica, and Grieco, Elizabeth. (1998). Triumphant transitions: Socioeconomic achievements of the second generation in Canada. *International Migration Review, 32* (Winter), 857–876.

Breton, Raymond. (1964). Institutional completeness of ethnic communities and the personal relations of immigrants. *American Journal of Sociology, 70*(2), 193–205.

Driedger, Leo. (1996). *Multi-ethnic Canada: Identities and inequalities.* Toronto: Oxford University Press.

Gans, Herbert. (1992). Second generation decline: Scenarios for the economic and ethnic futures of the post-1965 American immigrants. *Ethnic and Racial Studies, 15* (April), 173–191.

———. (1997). Toward a reconsideration of "assimilation" and "pluralism": The interplay of acculturation and ethnic retention. *International Migration Review, 31* (Winter), 875–892.

Goldenberg, Sheldon, & Haines, Valerie A. (1992). Social networks and institutional completeness: From territories to ties. *Canadian Journal of Sociology, 17*(3), 301–312.

Henry, Frances, Tator, Carol, Mattis, Winston, & Rees, Tim. (1995). *The colour of democracy: Racism in Canadian society.* Toronto: Harcourt Brace Canada.

Hirschman, Charles. (1994). Problems and prospects of studying immigrant adaptation from the 1990 population census: From generational comparisons to the process of "becoming American." *International Migration Review, 28* (Winter), 690–713.

Isajiw, Wsevolod W. (1990). Ethnic identity retention. In Raymond Breton, Wsevolod W. Isajiw, Warren E. Kalbach, & Jeffrey G. Reitz, *Ethnic identity and equality: Varieties of experience in a Canadian city* (pp. 34–91). Toronto: University of Toronto Press.

Isajiw, Wsevolod W., Sev'er, Aysan, & Driedger, Leo. (1993). Ethnic identity and social mobility: A test of the "drawback" model. *Canadian Journal of Sociology, 18*(2), 177–198.

Jensen, Leif, & Chitose, Yoshimi. (1994). Today's second generation: Evidence from the 1990 census. *International Migration Review, 28* (Winter), 714–735.

Kalbach, Warren, Lanphier, Michael, Rhyne, Don, & Richmond, Anthony H. (1983). *Ethnogenerational factors in socio-economic achievement in Toronto: The second generation during the 1970s.* Toronto: Institute for Behavioural Research, York University.

Kalin, Rudolf, & Berry, J.W. (1995). Ethnic and civic self-identity in Canada: Analyses of 1974 and 1991 national surveys. *Canadian Ethnic Studies, 27*(2), 1–15.

Kallen, Evelyn. (1995). *Ethnicity and human rights in Canada* (2nd ed.). Toronto: Oxford University Press.

Kazemipur, Abdolmohammad, & Halli, Shiva. (1997). Plight of immigrants: The spatial concentration of poverty in Canada. *Canadian Journal of Regional Science, 20* (Spring/Summer), 11–28.

Landale, Nancy, & Oropesa, R.S. (1995). Immigrant children and children of immigrants: Inter-and intra-ethnic group differences in the United States. Population Research Group Research Paper 95-02. University Park: Department of Sociology and Population Research Institute, Pennsylvania State University.

Massey, Douglas. (1995). The new immigration and ethnicity in the United States. *Population and Development Review, 21* (September), 631–652.

Miles, Robert. (1989). *Racism.* London: Routledge.

Oropesa, R.S., & Landale, Nancy S. (1997). Immigrant legacies: Ethnicity, generation and children's familial and economic lives. *Social Science Quarterly, 78* (June), 399–416.

Portes, Alejandro. (1995). Children of immigrants: Segmented assimilation and its determinants. In Alejandro Portes (Ed.), *The economic sociology of immigration: Essays on networks, ethnicity and entrepreneurship* (pp. 248–279). New York: Russell Sage Foundation.

Portes, Alejandro, & Zhou, Min. (1993). The new second generation: Segmented assimilation and its variants. *Annals of the American Academy of Political and Social Science, 530* (November), 74–96.

Reitz, Jeffrey G. (1998). *Warmth of welcome: The social causes of economic success for immigrants in different nations and cities.* Boulder, CO: Westview.

Richmond, Anthony. (1986). Ethnocultural variation in educational achievement. *Canadian Ethnic Studies, 18*(3), 75–89.

Waters, Mary. (1994). Ethnic and racial identities of second-generation Black immigrants in New York City. *International Migration Review, 28* (Winter), 795–820.

———. (1997). Immigrant families at risk: Factors that undermine chances for success. In Alan Booth, Ann C. Crouter, & Nancy Landale (Eds.), *Immigration and the family: Research and policy on U.S. immigrants* (pp. 79–87). Mahwah, NJ: Lawrence Erlbaum Associates.

Zhou, Min. (1997a). Growing up American: The challenge confronting immigrant children and children of immigrants. *Annual Review of Sociology, 23*, 63–95.

————. (1997b). Segmented assimilation: Issues, controversies, and recent research on the new second generation. *International Migration Review, 31* (Winter), 975–1008.

Zhou, Min, & Bankston III, Carl L. (1994). Social capital and the adaptation of the second generation: The case of the Vietnamese youth in New Orleans. *International Migration Review, 28* (Winter), 821–845.

————. (1998). *Growing up American: How Vietnamese children adapt to life in the United States.* New York: Russell Sage Foundation.

11

▼

OWNERSHIP AND MANAGEMENT POSITION OF CANADIAN ETHNIC GROUPS IN 1973 AND 1989[1]

M. REZA NAKHAIE

INTRODUCTION
▼

The relationship between ethnicity and class position continues to be a commanding subject for scholarly research and debate. Little of the research on this relationship, however, has focussed on access to the ownership of means of production or to control over the labour process (see Li, 1988). Moreover, the patterns of change in ethnic groups' access to ownership and authority, and the confounding influence of education, sex, age, and nativity (Canadian-born versus immigrants) on this process of change, have been ignored.

PREVIOUS RESEARCH
▼

Porter's *Vertical Mosaic* (1965) stands as one of the most influential and, at times, controversial books on social inequality in Canada. Porter pointed to the existence of a hierarchy of stratified social positions, such that each ethnic group has differential access to opportunities, resources, and rewards. Moreover, he argued and empirically substantiated that these inequalities have persisted over time. In 1931 census data, there was little difference among the three British groups (English, Irish, and Scottish), and they and the Jews ranked high among the occupational classes. The French, Germans, and Dutch ranked next, "followed by Scandinavian, East European, Italian, Japanese, 'Other Central Europeans,' Chinese, and native Indians" (1965: 81). By the 1961 census, "the relative positions of the various groups had changed very little" (1965: 86). In fact, French, Italian, and Native people became increasingly underrepresented in professional and financial positions, while the British and other groups improved their representation in these occupational categories.

Porter attributed the blocked mobility of Canadian non-British ethnic groups to early immigration policies that placed British and northern Europeans in privileged positions and to ethnic groups' differences in achievement orientation, educational attainments, and immigration history. "Non-British immigrants went into low status occupations because there was a fairly high rate of illiteracy among them.... Cultural barriers at the time of entry harden into a set of historical relations tending to perpetuate entrance status" (1965: 69). However, Porter later argued that over time the relationship between ethnicity and class structure may become unimportant because of the assimilation and integration of "entrance groups." In fact, Pineo and Porter's (1985) analysis of the 1973 Canadian Mobility Study concluded that "the vertical mosaic may have been only a period in Canadian history — a sharpening of the effects of ethnicity during the decades of great immigration" (390–91).

Following Porter, many scholars continued research on ethnic occupational inequality.[2] Many of the new researchers came to question the conventional blocked-ethnic-mobility thesis by concluding that, empirically, ethnicity did not significantly block occupational mobility either in 1871 (Darroch & Ornstein, 1980) or more recently (Darroch, 1979; Herberg, 1990). More specifically, this new research revealed that ethnic occupational inequalities still exist but have declined over time, that they are specific to a few ethnic groups, and that the British are not at the pinnacle of the class structure. Basing his study on census data from 1931 to 1971, Darroch (1979) showed that the mean index of occupational dissimilarity has decreased from 27.23 in 1931 to 14.32 in 1961 for eleven ethnic groups; and then to 13.9 in 1971, once thirteen ethnic groups are included in the analysis. Lautard and Loree (1984) considered the same time span, but for males and females separately, and showed that the mean index of ethnic occupational dissimilarity declined from 37 to 24 for males, and from 37 to 21 for females, among the twelve ethnic groups considered. Lautard and Guppy (1990) extended the number of ethnic groups to seventeen, and showed that the mean index of ethnic occupational dissimilarity declined from 30 in 1971 to 26 in 1986 for males, and from 27 to 21 for females, in the same period.[3]

Furthermore, the new research showed that, for example, in 1981, Jews, East Indians, Filipinos, and Blacks possessed more secondary and post-secondary education than the British; that Jews, Chinese, Blacks, and Filipinos were more likely to be in administrative and professional jobs than the British; and that Jews, Scandinavians, Ukrainians, Germans, Poles, and Dutch individuals ranked higher in income attainment than the British (see Winn, 1985a: 690; Herberg, 1990: 212, 217; Reitz, 1990). The new research concluded that the prevailing views on ethnic inequality (including Porter's) are exaggerated. In fact, Isajiw, Sev'er, and Driedger (1993), in a stringent test of Porter's thesis in a Toronto sample, could not find support, with two exceptions out of sixteen tests, for the thesis that ethnic-identity retention is a drawback to educational and occupational mobility. In contrast, they found substantial support for the hypothesis that there is no relationship between ethnic identity and mobility.

The blocked-ethnic-mobility thesis has also been questioned in terms of access to the positions of power. Porter's study of economic elites in 1951 revealed that "economic power belongs almost exclusively to those of British origin" (1965: 286). This conclusion was further substantiated by Clement (1975a, 1975b), who showed that there is little "ethnic" representation among elites. French Canadians, though constituting approximately one third of the Canadian population, made up only 8.4 percent of the elites in 1972. The "other" ethnic groups, about a quarter of the Canadian population, constituted 5.4 percent of the elite. English Canadians constituted about 45 percent of the population and possessed over 86 percent of the elite positions in 1972. Furthermore, he revealed that, despite a proportional decline in the English population, their index of representation in the economic elite remained virtually the same from 1951 to 1972 (Clement, 1975a: 234, 1975b: 46; Porter, 1955, 1965, 1975; see also Kelner, 1970; Presthus, 1973, 1974; Newman, 1975; Olsen, 1980; Niosi, 1981; Francis, 1986).

As with ethnic occupational inequality, new research on ethnic representation among the elites also questioned the conclusion of Porter, Clement, and others. Brym's review of the literature allowed him to conclude that at "the level of elites ... members of 'other' groups have registered gains since the Second War" (Brym & Fox, 1989: 112; Hunter, 1986; Berkowitz, 1984: 252; Rich, 1991: 419). Ogmundson's (1990, 1992, 1993) research also pointed to a similar conclusion. He questioned, both methodologically and empirically, the conventional image of Canadian elites as being dominated by a homogeneous group of white male Protestants of British ancestry: he concluded that Canadian elites have become less exclusive in class and ethnic origin (Hunter, 1986; Berkowitz, 1984; Rich, 1991; but see Clement, 1990b). In two subsequent articles, Ogmundson and McLaughlin (1992, 1994) showed that the proportion of British in every category of elites has continually declined, and the proportions of French and the "third force" have increased. Ogmundson

(1993: 389) concluded that the vertical-mosaic imagery should be "abandoned." This conclusion was also reached earlier by Tepperman (1975: 156), who saw the traditional view of blocked ethnic mobility as "patently false" and by Rich who called the vertical-mosaic imagery a "caricature" (1976: 15) of Canadian society and a "myth" (1991: 419).

A conclusive rejection of the blocked-ethnic-mobility thesis, however, requires an exploration of the relationship between ethnicity and class positions with respect to all dimensions of inequality. Previous researchers have studied occupational and power differences among, and educational and income attainment of, the ethnic groups. They have paid little attention to the class positions of ethnic groups as defined by an individual's relationship to the organization of production; that is, relations of ownership and authority. Li (1988: 71) warns against premature conclusions about the relationship between ethnicity and class. He reminds us that the debate surrounding the vertical mosaic has been clouded by different ways of measuring the class concept. "What is referred to as social class in the literature frequently is not based on a relational construct of class in the Marxian sense." His subsequent analysis of ethnic groups' access to the ownership of the means of production and control over the labour process, however, revealed that the British position in the class structure is most similar to that of the entire labour force in Canada. The French, on the other hand, are overrepresented in the working class and underrepresented in the managerial class, compared to the British. Among the non-charter groups, those of Jewish origin are overrepresented as employers, managers, professionals, and petty bourgeoisie, while the remaining West Europeans are underrepresented as managers and professionals, and overrepresented as employers and petty bourgeoisie. In contrast, South Europeans are overrepresented as workers and underrepresented as managers and professionals. Finally, non-whites (Chinese and Blacks) are overrepresented in the professional class, and Chinese among employers. Li concludes: "it is misleading that there is a strong relationship between ethnicity and class, as implied in the vertical mosaic thesis" (1988: 93). However, his study is based on the 1981 census and, as such, does not evaluate changes in class position across time, nor does he control for the effects of education, nativity, sex, and age differences among ethnic groups. A conclusive justification of the blocked-mobility thesis requires establishing not only that the British command greater power and privilege than other ethnic groups, but also that ethnic inequality is stable over time and, further, that ethnic inequality persists even after "non-ethnic" forces are taken into account. This paper utilizes two large sets of survey data to evaluate the above-mentioned assumptions with respect to the Marxian class categories.

DATA
▼

In estimating the class position of various ethnic groups at two different times, data from the 1973 Canadian Mobility Survey (CMS: see Boyd et al., 1985) and the General Social Survey of 1989 (GSS) are utilized. Both data sets are multistage stratified probability samples and are weighted for region, age, and sex. We selected 17 225 employed individuals between the ages of 20 and 65 from the CMS, and 5837 from the GSS. The two samples are pooled for the purpose of this analysis. Although survey samples are not typically used for trend studies, the large sample size of these surveys, and their comparable designs and purposes, may help to provide some evidence of trends in the class structure of Canadian ethnic groups. Moreover, survey samples have an advantage over census data in that surveys enable us to perform multivariate analyses and thus probe more deeply into the causes of ethnic variations in class positions.

MEASUREMENT
▼

The GSS asked the respondents: "To which ethnic or cultural group do you or did your ancestors belong?" These groups were reclassified into English, Scottish, Irish, French, German, Ukrainian, Italian, "Others," Canadian, and "Don't know." If respondents placed themselves into the "Canadian" category, they were probed further and were placed among one of the above-mentioned categories. In addition, the Jewish category was identified by a religious-denomination variable. The CMS contained two questions pertaining to ethnic self-placement: "To which ethnic or cultural group did you or your ancestor (on the male side) belong on coming to this continent? (check one)" and "To which ethnic or cultural group do you feel that you now belong? (check one)." In order to make the ethnic groups comparable across the two samples, respondents who identified with the same ethnic group on both questions in 1973 were first selected. Respondents who said they are Canadian on the second question but placed themselves in an ethnic group in the first question were then added to the first selected groups.[4] We excluded "No response" and "Don't know" categories from both surveys.[5] These ethnic groups were then coded into nine groups, with the English category as the reference group. We selected the English group as the reference category because research on ethnic blocked mobility originated with an understanding that the English ethnic group in Canada commanded greater power, wealth, and status than any other group (Porter, 1965; Hunter, 1986; Herberg, 1990; Agocs

& Boyd, 1993). Thus, it is useful to compare the power and privilege of other ethnic groups to that of the traditionally dominant category. Other ethnic groups included in the analysis are: French, Irish, Scottish, Germans, Italians, Ukrainians, Jews, and "Others."

For this paper, social class is defined in terms of the individual's relationship to the organization of production. However, there is a good deal of disagreement among Marxists about the determination of class structure in advanced capitalist societies (for a discussion of Marxian class categories, see Poulantzas, 1975; Wright, 1976, 1985, 1989; Carchedi, 1977; and in Canada see Johnston & Ornstein, 1985). Wright, for example, responding to criticism of his conceptualization of class, reinstated the concept of exploitation rather than domination as the basis for the assignment of agents to class position. Moreover, the operationalization of class categories has been cumbersome and has not often strictly complied with Marx's notion of class concept, particularly for the capitalist class. Wright (1978: 80) suggests that "there is no a priori basis for deciding how many employees are necessary to become a small capitalist." However, since there exists a qualitative distinction between having and not having any employees (i.e., problematic of exploitation), any arbitrary differentiation of class position by the number of employees would be misleading. Therefore, it is appropriate to distinguish between the self-employed who does not purchase the labour-power of others and the self-employed who exploits workers by virtue of employing their labour-power. Furthermore, Marx (1967: 330) has argued that a minimum number of employees are required "to liberate the employer himself from manual labour, to convert him from a small master into a capitalist...." In this paper, the employer who hires more than five employees is classified as bourgeoisie, otherwise he or she is considered as petty bourgeoisie. Finally, we have made a distinction between middle and small managers based on the number of people they supervise. It would have been appropriate to distinguish between, for example, the top executive of the Bank of Canada and the lower-level managers in any corporation. But the data do not allow us to make such a refinement other than a distinction based on the number of employees. Nevertheless, as can be seen, our conceptualization is faithful to Wright and Perrone (1977), Wright (1985, 1989), and Poulantzas (1975), who distinguished between ownership and control — and the degree of ownership and control — as well as conceptualizing classes as conflict groups with incompatible interests.

The CMS asked respondents if they work: (a) for others for wages, a salary, or a commission; or (b) in their own business, farm, or professional practice. Furthermore, it asked, "If, in this job, you own a business or farm, or are a manager or supervisor ... how many personnel do you employ or have working under you?" The GSS asked respondents, during 1988, "Were you mainly (a) an employee working for someone else? or (b) self-employed?" Moreover, they were asked if they had "any paid employees" and "how many paid employees?"

Based on these questions, the following class categories were identified: (a) employers with more than five employees (designated as bourgeoisie);[6] (b) employers with up to five employees (defined as petty bourgeoisie); (c) self-employed with no employees; (d) supervisors with more than five employees (delineated as middle managers); (e) supervisors with fewer than five employees (called small managers); and (f) workers with no subordinates or ownership.

Table 11.1 presents the frequency distribution of ethnic groups and class categories. This table shows a close similarity in the proportion of ethnic and class categories based on the survey and census samples. For example, the proportion of individuals from the British Isles (English, Scots, and Irish) declined from 48.3 to 41.1 percent in the survey samples from 1973 to 1989. These proportions and the decline are almost identical to the census samples. However, the estimates for the French population in the two surveys seem to be lower, and those of the "entrance" groups higher, than those reported by the censuses (see also Kalbach, 1987: 87–88 for the distribution of ethnic groups in 1971 and 1981 censuses).

Similarly, the surveys show a lower proportion of the working class, and a higher proportion of the ownership class, as compared with the census samples. The differences between surveys and censuses are, however, due to technical change in the classification of the ownership class by Statistics Canada. Since 1971, Statistics Canada has reclassified the incorporated self-employed (both employer and own-account) as wage and salary workers. This change resulted in an increase in the proportion of the working class and a decrease in that of the bourgeoisie and petty bourgeoisie from 1971 onwards (see Cuneo, 1985: 471; Carroll, 1987: 572). The survey estimates presented here thus diverge from the census estimates but are similar to those shown by Clement (1990a) and Ornstein (1988) based on survey data. Moreover, the changes in class structure in the two surveys are consistent with our expectations. The three ownership-class categories (bourgeoise, petty bourgeoisie, and self-employed) slightly declined, from 15.8 to 14.3 percent from 1973 to 1989, as did the proportion of the working class (from 72.8 to 62.8 percent). These reductions were absorbed by the expanding managerial-class categories (from 11.4 to 22.9 percent). Overall, these findings increase our confidence in the comparability of these two sample surveys with respect to these two important variables.

TABLE 11.1
▼
FREQUENCY DISTRIBUTION OF ETHNIC AND CLASS CATEGORIES, BY YEAR, EMPLOYED, 20–65 YEARS OF AGE

	Survey Sample				Census Sample	
	1973[a]		1989[b]		1971[c]	1986[d]
Ethnic Categories						
English	29.5		18.9			
Irish	8.7		8.8			
Scottish	10.1	(48.3)	13.4	(41.4)	47.6	40.5
French	20.8	(20.8)	21.1	(21.2)	26.1	27.5
German	7.1		8.4			
Italian	3.0		2.4			
Ukrainian	3.3		3.7			
Jewish	1.0		0.9			
Other	16.5	(30.9)	22.3	(37.7)	26.3	32.1
Total (%)	100.0	100.0	100.0	100.0	100.0	100.0
Class Categories						
Bourgeoisie	1.7		2.2			
Petty bourgeoisie	4.8		4.7			
Self-employed	9.3	(15.8)	7.4	(14.3)	8.2	10.8
Middle managers	6.5		9.6			
Small managers	4.9		13.3			
Workers	72.8	(84.2)	62.8	(85.7)	91.2	89.2
Total (%)	100.0	100.0	100.0	100.0	100.0	100.0
Total Number	17 225		5 837		65 650	172 852

Bourgeoisie = employers with more than five employees.
Petty bourgeoisie = employers with one to five employees.
Self-employed = self-employed with no employees.
Middle manager = supervises more than five employees.
Small manager = supervises one to five employees.
Worker = without subordinates or ownership.

Sources:
[a] Canadian Mobility Study, 1973.
[b] General Social Survey, 1989.
[c] Census of Canada Public Use Sample Tapes, 1971 (based on 1% of the population of the area with a minimum of 250 000 persons).
[d] Census of Canada Public Use Microdata File, 1986 (based on 2% of the total population).

As we suggested earlier, the relationship between ethnicity and class position is often confounded with the role of education, nativity, and age differences between ethnic and class categories. Thus, it is important to control for these variables.

One would expect that those who are born in Canada have a better chance for the inheritance of ownership, a higher access to networks for occupational placement and mobility, and often a superior command of the official languages than immigrants (see for example, Porter, 1965: 79; Pineo & Porter, 1985: 376; Boyd, 1985: 441, 1990: 279; Winn, 1985a: 692–693; see also Beaujot & Rappak, 1990: 130). Both surveys indicated whether respondents were Canadian-born or were first-generation immigrants.

Another factor that may influence an individual's class position is age (Porter, 1965: 75; Darroch & Ornstein, 1980: 317–319). Age may be interpreted as a proxy of labour-market experience. Not only do older individuals have more experience, but they are also more likely to have more opportunities to save money, which might enable them to start their own businesses. Some firms are also more likely to place individuals in authority positions based on their seniority and experience. For the purpose of this study, age is coded in both surveys into three categories (20–34, 35–49, 50–65).

Porter (1965: 69) argued that the low socio-economic status of many non-British groups was due to a "fairly high rate of illiteracy among them ..." (see also Reitz, 1980; Boyd et al., 1980: 224). Based on the comparable information available in both surveys, a three-category educational credential is constructed. These categories included: elementary or less; some or completed secondary; some or completed post-secondary.

Finally, research has shown that males are more likely to be found in the upper-class categories and females are more likely to be proletarianized (see Porter, Ch. 3; Kalbach, 1970; Richmond & Kalbach, 1980; Lautard & Loree, 1984; Cuneo, 1985; Carroll, 1987). In fact, only 6 of the 946 persons in the elite in 1972 (Clement, 1975a: 266n) and 7 of the 1169 chief executive officers in the 1990 *Directory of Directors* were women (Clement, 1990b: 184n; also see Cachon & Carter, 1989: 25; Cromie & Hayes, 1988: 91; Belcourt, 1988; Goffee & Scase, 1983).

MODEL SELECTION
▼

The basic initial questions are: (a) whether ethnicity is related to the Marxian conceptualization of social-class position as defined here; and (b) whether the relationship between ethnicity and class position differs between 1973 and

1989. Answers to these questions are presented in Table 11.2, using multinomial logit models, for males and females separately. The decision to present separate analyses for males and females was based on: (a) the research literature cited above pointing to underrepresentation of women in ownership and managerial classes, and their overrepresentation in the working class; and (b) a preliminary loglinear analysis (see Goodman, 1972; Knoke & Burke, 1991) which revealed that, in combination, ethnicity and gender and year interact to produce an effect on class position beyond that of each variable alone. All two-way and three-way interaction effects involving ethnicity, year, and gender were significant. The three-way interaction of gender by ethnicity by year was highly significant ($G^2 = 79.2$; df = 40; p = 0.0001).[7]

In Table 11.2, G^2 is the value of the likelihood ratio model; this statistic summarizes the differences between observed frequencies and frequencies estimated under the given model, large values of G^2 indicating lack of fit of the

---

TABLE 11.2
▼
MULTINOMIAL LOGIT MODELS FOR THE EFFECT OF ETHNICITY (E) AND YEAR (Y) ON CLASS (C) (EMPLOYED, 20–65 YEARS OF AGE, 1973 AND 1989)

Models		G^2	df	P.	ΔG^2 for CE term (df: M=40; F=39)	ΔG^2 for CY term (df=5)	ΔG^2 for CEY term (df: M=40; F=39)
1-C	M	754.3	85	0.000			
	F	573.5	85	0.000			
2-C CE	M	353.1	45	0.000	401.2		
	F	418.6	44	0.000	154.9		
3-C CY	M	528.2	80	0.000		226.1	
	F	258.1	80	0.000		315.4	
4-C CE CY	M	109.9	40	0.000	418.3	243.2	
	F	99.9	39	0.000	158.2	318.7	
5-C CE CY CEY	M	0.000	0	1.000			109.9
	F	0.000	0	1.000			99.9

E = ethnicity, C = class, Y = year, M = male, F = female

G^2 measures the differences between observed frequencies and those expected under the model. The larger the G^2 values relative to the degrees of freedom, the greater the dissimilarities between observed and expected cell frequencies.

ΔG^2 measures the differences in goodness-of-fit between two models when a new term is added. The larger the value of ΔG^2, the more significant the added term.

model. The G^2 statistic is approximately chi square distributed with degree of freedom under the null hypothesis that the model fits the data (Knoke & Burke, 1991: 11, 30–31). The statistic ΔG^2 in Table 11.2 is the difference between two G^2 statistics, one for a model containing the model term in question and one not containing that model term; as such, it measures the significance of the model term in question (large values indicating greater significance). The ΔG^2 statistic is approximately chi square distributed with degrees of freedom given by the difference in degree of freedom between the two models.[8]

Table 11.2 identifies five logit models representing the effects of ethnicity and year on class position. Model 1 hypothesizes no effect of ethnicity or year on class position. This model is rejected for both males and females. Models 2 and 3 hypothesize that ethnicity and year, respectively, are not related to class position. The small value of P and the large values of G^2 suggest that the dissimilarity between the expected and the observed data is too large, which prevents us from concluding that the observed dissimilarities are due to the sampling error and/or chance. These models are rejected, too. Line 4 shows that our prediction can be improved by including terms for both ethnicity and year. The findings thus indicate that ethnicity matters and that the distribution of class positions has changed between 1973 and 1989.

To test the idea that the relationship between class position and ethnicity depends on year, we must compare a model that includes no interaction between ethnicity and year to a model that incorporates such an effect. Here, we compare the model that has no three-way effects (model 4) with the final, saturated model. The value of ΔG^2 in model 5 for EY is 109.9 for males and 99.9 for females [109.9 - 000.0 = 109.9; P = 0.0001 and 99.9 - 000.0 = 99.9; P = .00001, respectively]. Thus, we can conclude that the relationship between ethnicity and class position differs significantly from 1973 to 1989 for both men and women. These findings raise doubts about the position which holds that Canadian ethnic groups are categorized by class immobility. Another relevant question to ask is whether class positions of ethnic groups differ once the impact of control variables is taken into account. That is to say, can the underlying differences in education, nativity, and age account for the class differences of ethnic groups? Multinomial logit analysis allows us to include covariates in the model, which will enable us to answer this question. Two separate analyses for males and females revealed a significant two-way interaction between ethnicity and year for both males and females, despite the inclusion of covariates (ΔG^2 = 100.3, df = 37 for males, and ΔG^2 = 70.0, df = 36 for females).

Having established that: (a) ethnic differences in class positions are real; (b) there is significant ethnic mobility from 1973 to 1989 among social classes; and (c) education, nativity, and age differences among the ethnic groups can't eliminate the ethnic differences in class structure, we can now analyze the magnitudes of these differences.

INTERPRETATION OF PARAMETERS
▼

Tables 11.3 and 11.4 present parameter estimates for ethnicity and ethnicity-by-year interactions with and without covariates, for both males and females. These parameter estimates give the differences in the log odds of being in a class category compared to the working class for each ethnic group compared to the English reference category, with and without the covariates (see Aldrich & Nelson, 1984).

Since log odds have little intuitive meaning, we exponentiate them in our discussion of results. The exponential of a coefficient is the factor by which the unlogged odds on class position are multiplied for one unit change in the independent variable (e.g., ethnic category). Moreover, given the large sample size in the male subpopulation, we will discuss only the coefficients that are significant at the 0.01 level and better. Finally, the discussion of results will focus on the coefficients that included the covariates (numbers in the parentheses). The reader may wish to compare other coefficients.

A quick glance at Table 11.3 reveals that, in 1973, contrary to the traditional view on blocked ethnic mobility, there was no clear pattern of advantage for the English males as compared to the non-English males in the class structure. In fact, in 1973, the English were significantly under-represented among the bourgeoisie when compared to their Jewish counterparts and were statistically similar to other ethnic groups (with and without controls). They were also significantly underrepresented when compared to the Jews and Germans in the petty bourgeoisie and the self-employed class categories as well as compared to the Ukrainians in the small-employer class category. For example, when the effects of other variables is controlled, the odds of Jews being in the bourgeoisie as compared to the working class were over thirteen times higher than those for the English ($e^{2.57} = 13.06$). The Jewish odds were 4.75 times ($e^{1.56} = 4.75$), the German odds were just under two times ($e^{.68} = 1.97$), and Ukrainians had 1.7 times ($e^{.54} = 1.72$) greater odds of being in the petty bourgeoisie compared to the working class than the English. Moreover, Germans had a 48 percent ($e^{.39} = 1.48$) greater odds of being in the self-employed class than the English. Nevertheless, Ukrainians in the bourgeoisie ($n = 9$) and Italians in the self-employed class were in a disadvantageous position compared to the English.

TABLE 11.3
▼

LOG ODDS RATIOS OF ETHNICITY, BY YEAR AND CLASS POSITION, EMPLOYED MALES, 20–65 YEARS OF AGE, 1973 AND 1989

	Bourgeoisie	Petty Bourgeoisie	Self-Employed	Middle Manager	Small Manager
Ethnicity					
French	0.22	-0.03	-0.17	-0.44***	-0.84***
	(0.22)	(0.01)	(-0.09)	(-0.44***)	(-0.85***)
Irish	-0.41	0.28	-0.01	-0.01	-0.23
	(-0.45)	(0.29)	(0.06)	(-0.02)	(-0.24)
Scottish	-0.21	-0.19	-0.06	0.23*	0.01
	(-0.31)	(-0.16)	(-0.01)	(0.21)	(-0.01)
German	0.02	0.65***	0.33*	-0.09	-0.25
	(0.01)	(0.68***)	(0.39**)	(-0.10)	(-0.28)
Italian	0.09	-0.10	-0.59***	-0.74***	-1.01***
	(0.04)	(-0.06)	(-0.58*)	(-0.85***)	(-1.04***)
Ukrainian	-0.93	0.52*	-0.22	-0.03	-0.38
	(-9.44***)	(0.54**)	(-0.21)	(0.01)	(-0.35)
Jewish	2.36***	1.36***	1.07***	0.09	-0.02
	(2.57***)	(1.56***)	(1.09***)	(0.02)	(-0.16)
Others	0.01	0.25	0.15	-0.08	-0.38***
	(-0.05)	(0.28)	(0.22)	(-0.09)	(-0.39***)
Ethnicity–Year Interaction					
French* Year	0.65	0.03	-0.79***	0.55***	0.43*
	(0.68)	(0.09)	(-0.67***)	(0.53***)	(0.42)
Irish* Year	-0.92	0.01	-0.38	0.42	-0.11
	(-1.02)	(0.05)	(-0.25)	(0.42)	(-0.12)
Scottish* Year	-0.40	-0.44	-0.23	-0.03	-0.19
	(-0.60)	(-0.39)	(-0.06)	(-0.05)	(-0.19)
German* Year	0.38	-0.25	-0.97***	-0.61*	0.15
	(0.40)	(-0.18)	(-0.86***)	(-0.64*)	(0.18)
Italian* Year	0.03	1.08**	0.43	0.58	0.93*
	(0.05)	(1.08**)	(0.36)	(0.28)	(0.86*)
Ukrainian* Year	-2.08	0.52	-1.46***	0.12	0.08
	(-19.02)	(0.38)	(-1.47**)	(0.09)	(0.06)
Jewish* Year	0.35	-0.83	0.56	-0.09	-1.59
	(0.09)	(-0.89)	(0.75)	(-0.22)	(-1.86*)
Other* Year	0.18	0.32	-0.12	0.22	0.01
	(0.05)	(0.20)	(0.02)	(0.21)	(-0.14)
English* Year	0.20	0.14	-0.01	0.42***	0.88***
	(-1.78***)	(0.10)	(-0.05)	(0.37***)	(0.83***)

Numbers outside the parentheses are the parameter estimates from the multinomial logit model. Numbers in the parentheses are the parameter estimates from a similar model but including the covariates (age, education, and nativity).

The reference category for ethnic categories = English, for year = 1973, and for class position = working class.

*P < .05; **P < .01; ***P < .001

TABLE 11.4
▼

LOG ODDS RATIOS OF ETHNICITY, BY YEAR AND CLASS POSITION, EMPLOYED FEMALES, 20–65 YEARS OF AGE, 1973 AND 1989

	Bourgeoisie	Petty Bourgeoisie	Self-Employed	Middle Manager	Small Manager
Ethnicity					
French	0.74	-0.38	-0.21	-0.38*	-0.74***
	(0.80)	(-0.39)	(-0.22)	(-0.39*)	(-0.74***)
Irish	0.41	-0.53	-0.06	0.36	-0.09
	(0.29)	(-0.62)	(-0.12)	(0.35)	(-0.10)
Scottish	0.24	-0.71*	-0.44*	0.39*	0.04
	(0.15)	(-0.79*)	(-0.46*)	(0.36*)	(0.05)
German	0.85	0.14	0.41*	0.27	-0.08
	(0.81)	(0.12)	(0.42*)	(0.28)	(-0.07)
Italian	0.23	-2.18*	-0.78	-0.36	-1.99***
	(-9.25)	(-20.17)	(-1.05)	(-0.42)	(-10.49***)
Ukrainian	1.47*	0.17	0.82***	0.46	0.12
	(1.33)	(0.02)	(0.80***)	(0.41)	(0.10)
Jewish	2.55***	0.51	0.90***	-0.47	0.01
	(2.50***)	(-8.03***)	(0.72*)	(-9.54***)	(-0.12)
Others	0.35	-0.22	0.18	-0.07	-0.35***
	(0.40)	(-0.22)	(0.18)	(-0.08)	(-0.36**)
Ethnicity–Year Interaction					
French* Year	-1.46	-1.02*	-1.36***	-0.11	0.30
	(-1.52)	(-1.04*)	(-1.36***)	(-0.11)	(0.30)
Irish* Year	-1.46	0.35	-0.52	0.24	-0.37
	(-1.69)	(0.40)	(-0.65)	(0.24)	(-0.36)
Scottish* Year	-2.00	0.32	-0.14	-0.29	0.18
	(-2.26)	(0.40)	(-0.16)	(-0.22)	(0.19)
German* Year	-1.57	-0.73	-0.69	-0.16	0.31
	(-1.72)	(-0.74)	(-0.70)	(-0.14)	(0.34)
Italian* Year	0.53	-0.02	-2.22*	0.66	2.79
	(19.20)	(-0.03)	(-2.81*)	(0.65)	(19.74)
Ukrainian* Year	-1.30	0.50	-0.33	1.44**	0.17
	(-1.54)	(0.60)	(-0.37)	(1.53**)	(0.28)
Jewish* Year	-0.55	-3.23*	0.02	2.20	-1.53
	(-0.49)	(-20.24)	(0.25)	(20.18)	(-1.71)
Other* Year	-1.26	-0.15	-0.02	0.26	0.59*
	(-1.34)	(-0.15)	(-0.04)	(0.24)	(0.58*)
English* Year	1.10***	0.80**	0.40**	1.36***	1.47***
	(3.14)	(-1.07***)	(0.36)	(3.37***)	(3.33***)

Numbers outside the parentheses are the parameter estimates from the multinomial logit model. Numbers in the parentheses are the parameter estimates from a similar model but including the covariates (age, education, and nativity).

The reference category for ethnic categories = English, for year = 1973, and for class position = working class.

*P < .05; **P < .01; ***P < .001

Analysis of ethnic–year interaction effects for the ownership-class categories reveals that the English were not in an advantageous position in 1989, either. In order to estimate ethnic differences in 1989, we sum the ethnic coefficient with that for the interaction term. For example, the odds of Italians being in the petty bourgeoisie compared to the working class was about three times that of the English ($e^{-.06 + 1.08} = 2.27$). However, the French, German, and Ukrainians became more underrepresented in the self-employed class when compared to the English ($e^{-.09 + -.67} = .47$; $e^{.39 + (-.86)} = .62$; $e^{.21 + (-1.47)} = .19$, respectively).

An analysis of the managerial categories, however, points to a clearer English advantage as compared to other ethnic groups. In 1973, signs for the coefficients were all negative (the signs for the Scottish, Ukrainian, and Jewish groups for the middle managers were positive but the coefficients are close to zero), suggesting that the non-English ethnic categories were at a disadvantage. For example, the French odds of being in the middle-managerial-class category compared to being in the working class was about two-thirds ($e^{-.44} = .64$), and they had 43 percent lower odds ($e^{-.85} = .43$) of being in the small-managerial category than the English. Moreover, Italians had about a 43 percent ($e^{-.85} = .43$) lower odds of being in the middle-managerial class compared to the English. They had about a 35 percent ($e^{-1.04} = .35$) and the "Other" ethnic group a 68 percent ($e^{-.39} = .68$) lower odds of being in the small-managerial category when compared to the English.

Analysis of ethnic–year interaction shows that the French increased their representation in the middle-managerial-class category as compared to the English ($e^{-.44 + (.53)} = 1.09$). The Italians also increased their representation in the small-managerial category but only at $P = 0.05$.

Table 11.4 reproduces the parameter estimates from the multinomial logit model of ethnic by class by year for females. Many of these estimates are, however, based on the cells with a small number of cases, particularly, as can be expected, in the ownership-class categories (see Table 11.5). Therefore, we will discuss the ethnic–class relationships where the cells are equal or larger than 10 and where the $P < 0.05$.

Table 11.4 shows that the English females were not in an unequivocal dominant position compared to other ethnic groups in the class structure, either. In fact, the Jewish females in the bourgeoisie and with the Ukrainian and German females in the self-employed class were overrepresented compared to the English females in 1973. The only ethnic group that was underrepresented compared to the English was the Scots among the petty bourgeoisie and the self-employed categories. Moreover, the only interaction effects for the ownership-class categories were those of the French females, who became more underrepresented compared to their English counterparts among the

TABLE 11.5
▼
CLASS DISTRIBUTION OF CANADIAN ETHNIC CATEGORIES, BY YEAR, EMPLOYED, 20–65 YEARS OF AGE, 1973, 1989

	Bourgeoisie		Petty Bourgeoisie		Self-Employed		Middle Manager		Small Manager		Workers	
	'73	'89	'73	'89	'73	'89	'73	'89	'73	'89	'73	'89
Males												
English	2.5	3.1	5.1	4.7	7.6	8.5	11.2	12.4	8.4	17.3	65.2	53.9
French	2.5	6.0	5.4	5.3	10.5	5.5	6.1	12.0	3.2	10.4	72.3	60.9
Irish	2.7	1.2	6.7	6.5	9.1	7.2	9.0	15.7	7.1	13.3	65.6	58.2
Scottish	2.4	2.0	5.0	3.2	7.6	7.3	13.8	15.8	8.8	16.2	62.4	55.5
German	1.8	3.7	9.7	8.4	14.7	7.5	12.1	8.7	5.2	15.1	56.5	56.5
Italian	3.3	3.7	3.3	8.3	4.5	6.5	4.9	8.8	2.3	11.2	82.0	61.5
Ukrainian	2.6	—	6.9	10.1	12.0	3.1	10.3	14.5	5.5	13.8	62.6	58.5
Jewish	15.7	29.6	20.8	8.1	9.2	19.5	7.0	6.9	10.1	3.5	37.2	32.3
Others	2.4	3.5	6.2	6.8	9.5	9.6	9.5	13.1	5.9	11.9	66.6	55.0
Total	2.6	4.0	5.9	6.0	9.2	7.6	9.4	12.7	6.1	13.1	66.7	56.7
Females												
English	0.2	1.1	1.5	4.1	3.3	7.0	3.3	6.4	5.1	13.1	86.6	68.4
French	0.8	1.3	1.7	1.9	5.3	3.3	2.4	4.8	2.1	8.5	87.7	80.2
Irish	0.5	0.6	0.7	2.8	3.9	5.1	4.1	10.6	5.5	10.2	85.4	70.7
Scottish	0.5	0.4	0.6	2.3	2.2	4.1	5.6	8.3	4.8	15.3	86.3	69.6
German	0.8	1.0	2.3	3.1	6.8	7.2	4.5	7.5	3.7	13.8	82.2	67.4
Italian	—	1.8	—	—	4.8	0.7	1.6	7.0	—	8.3	93.6	82.2
Ukrainian	1.2	1.5	1.1	4.5	8.2	10.3	2.2	16.3	4.6	13.1	82.7	54.4
Jewish	2.0	2.1	10.2	—	6.3	14.9		2.9	8.8	4.4	72.7	61.6
Others	0.4	0.8	1.3	3.0	4.1	8.3	2.8	6.8	2.7	12.3	88.7	68.8
Total	0.5	1.1	1.4	2.7	4.3	6.0	3.3	7.1	3.8	11.6	86.8	71.4

Note: Underlined figures represent the categories where N is fewer than ten cases.

petty bourgeoisie and self-employed class categories in 1989 ($e^{-.39 + (-1.04)} = .24$; $e^{-.22 + (-1.36)} = .20$).

However, the English females were in a significant advantageous position compared to the French and Jewish females among the middle managers, and compared to the French, Italian, and "Other" ethnic females among the small managers, in 1973. On the other hand, the English females were in a significantly disadvantageous position compared to the Scots among the middle managers in 1973. The only significant year–ethnic interaction effects were those of the Ukrainian and "Other" ethnic females, suggesting that they increased their representation compared to the English females in the middle- and small-managerial class categories, respectively, in relation to the working class from 1973 to 1989.

Many other comparisons could be made for both males and females, but the basic findings are that the English ethnic group was not unequivocally in an advantageous class position in 1973 and that the English and other ethnic groups' differences in the ownership and managerial-class categories declined further by 1989. This decline was due more to a faster improvement in the position of other ethnic groups in the class structure than to a decline in the position of the English from 1973 to 1989. In fact, the English males had significantly lower odds of being among the bourgeoisie and higher odds of being in the middle- and small-managerial categories than in the working class in 1989 compared to 1973. English females also had higher odds of being among middle and small managers but lower odds of being in the petty bourgeoisie as compared to the working class in 1989 than in 1973 (see the year coefficients at the bottom of the Tables 11.3 and 11.4, which represent the English–year interaction coefficients). Finally, Table 11.5 presents the class distribution of the Canadian ethnic groups. If we were to ignore the magnitude of the differences in ownership positions and rank the groups, the English males in 1973 and 1989, respectively, would place fifth (tied with French) and sixth among the bourgeoisie, seventh and eighth among the petty bourgeoisie, and seventh (tied with Scots) and third among the self-employed. A rough estimate of ethnic hierarchy places the English third in 1973 and fifth in 1989 among the middle managers, and third and first, respectively, among the small managers. The English females in 1973 and 1989, respectively, were at eighth and fifth among the bourgeoisie, fourth and second among the petty bourgeoisie, eighth and fifth among the self-employed. They were fourth and eighth among middle managers, and third (tied with Ukrainians) among the small managers. The Italian and French (both males and females) ranked first and second in the working class, respectively.

The multinomial logit model does not present the parameter estimates for the covariates. Separate analyses using logistic regression revealed that the relationship between education and age with class positions was significant and generally in the expected direction. The older and more educated males and females had higher odds of being in the ownership and managerial class categories compared to their younger and less-educated counterparts. However, the foreign-born male and female immigrants were not significantly different from Canadian-born in the class structure. The only exception was the foreign-born females, who had 30 percent higher odds of being in the petty bourgeoisie than in the working class compared to their Canadian counterparts (P = 0.05; see Winn, 1985a: 693).[9]

Of possible interest, here, is the relationship between the timing of immigration and class position. The 1989 survey asked foreign-born respondents: "In what year did you first immigrate to Canada?" We compared the class positions of those who came to Canada prior to 1966 (just prior to the Immigration Act of 1967) and between 1966 and 1989 with those born in Canada. Males who immigrated prior to 1967 were significantly more overrepresented than the Canadian-born in the bourgeoisie compared to the working class. This pattern was observed also for the earlier female immigrants in the self-employed category ($e^{.72} = 2.05$; $e^{.95} = 2.58$, respectively).

The CMS did not measure the respondent's time of immigration. It did, however, ask about the period that the respondent's father immigrated to Canada. We compared the class positions of those whose fathers migrated before 1930 and those between 1930 and 1973 with those whose fathers were born in Canada. This comparison showed the advantageous class positions of those respondents whose fathers migrated prior to 1930 compared to those whose fathers were born in Canada among the male bourgeoisie ($e^{1.22} = 3.39$), petty bourgeoisie ($e^{.61} = 1.84$) and the self-employed ($e^{.47} = 1.60$) as well as among the female self-employed ($e^{.74} = 2.10$). In addition, females whose fathers migrated to Canada between 1931 and 1973 were also more likely to be found in the petty bourgeoisie than in the working class compared to those whose fathers were born in Canada ($e^{.90} = 2.46$).

The fact that the earlier immigrants in the 1989 survey and those whose fathers came to Canada prior to 1930 were more likely to be found in the ownership-class categories than in the working class in comparison to the Canadian-born could be due to many factors. Weiss (1994) reports on the wealthy position of the American Vietnamese who were evacuated from Saigon in 1975 and the near poverty position of the Vietnamese who have arrived since the late 1980s. He suggests that earlier immigrants arrived during a period of economic prosperity, while recent immigrants arrived during economic recession, when jobs are more scarce and there is a housing crisis, and when federal refugee assistance to the United States has dropped from 36 months' benefits in 1975 to only 8 months'. Nevertheless, Weiss (1994) also reported that earlier Vietnamese arrivals were from the North of Vietnam with a higher work ethic, contrasting with recent Southern arrivals. Moreover, recent arrivals experienced the horror of imprisonment, with negative psychological consequences such as depression and stagnation.

Beaujot and Rappak (1990: 111) argue that immigrants are at an initial disadvantage, perhaps due to culture shock, settlement problems, and/or recognition of credentials. However, after a period of settlement, perhaps due to self-selection for inner drive and achievement orientation, immigrants may acquire a relative advantage. The Beaujot–Rappak analysis of immigrants from Europe and the United States as compared to those from other parts of the world in the 1971, 1981, and 1986 Canadian censuses suggests that the timing of arrival is key to immigrants' subsequent economic progress. However, the timing of arrival is related to "the relative selectivity of immigrants and the receptivity of the host society" (1990: 139; see also Boyd, 1990: 279).

In sum, timing of the immigration, length of residency in the new country, and characteristics of the immigrants all seem to be intimately related to the class position of the newcomers. Future studies may do well to provide a detailed analysis of the effect of the economic timing of immigration on class position.

CONCLUSION
▼

The findings presented here reveal that: (a) the English are not overrepresented in the ownership class categories when compared to other ethnic groups;[10] (b) there are significant changes in the class positions of ethnic groups from 1979 to 1989; and (c) conclusions (a) and (b) above are confirmed for both males and females even after education, age, and nativity are taken into account. These findings support the recent evidence of a declining relationship between ethnicity and one's position in the system of inequality (see Darroch, 1979; Brym & Fox, 1989; Herberg, 1990; Rich, 1991; Ogmundson, 1990, 1993; Ogmundson & McLaughlin, 1992, 1994).

This analysis also shows that the English were overrepresented in the managerial categories in 1973 when compared to the French, Italians, and "Other" ethnic groups, for both males and females. It also shows, however, that ethnic differences in the managerial class categories declined from the 1973 to the 1989 samples, particularly for the French. Thus, although ethnicity may have played some part in influencing ethnic advancement in authority positions, it would seem to be less relevant in recent years. The decreasing importance of ethnicity for managerial positions may point to a less pronounced advancement in the educational credentials of the British compared to other ethnic groups (see Hunter, 1986; Herberg, 1990).

As is consistent with previous findings on ethnic inequality, the present study also shows that the Jews are significantly overrepresented when compared to the English in the ownership-class categories. French Canadians remain the junior charter group in the managerial class, and the Italians are at the bottom of this class. Both are significantly overrepresented in the working class (Li, 1988). These findings contrast with many recent studies of education, occupation, and income attainment, which have shown a close parity between the two charter groups (Winn, 1985a; Hunter, 1986; Herberg, 1990; Reitz, 1990).

In sum, although ethnicity still matters and has an independent effect on class position after controlling for education, age, and nativity, for both males and females, its influence seems to be declining. The relationship between ethnic origin and class position is in flux, and no ethnic group unequivocally dominates the Canadian class structure. Nevertheless, some elements of ethnic inequality reported by Porter still remain. The British ethnic group has some advantage among the business elites (Brym & Fox, 1989: 99; Ogmundson & McLaughlin, 1992) and perhaps among the managerial-class categories. But their advantage among the lower strata of the capitalist class, as shown here, and in the technical division of labour (Lautard & Loree, 1984; Lautard & Guppy, 1990) is substantially reduced. The traditional imagery of the *Vertical Mosaic* seems to be increasingly undermined by recent empirical realities. There is a need for a new generation of research on the relationship between ethnicity and class position to address the "myth" (Rich, 1991) of the *Vertical Mosaic* and to see whether the blocked-ethnic-mobility thesis should be "abandoned" (Ogmundson, 1993).

NOTES
▼

1. A short version of this paper was presented at the Learned Societies Conference, Canadian Sociology and Anthropology Association, 28th annual meeting.

   I gratefully acknowledge that the data presented here are drawn from the 1973 Mobility Study, which was collected by Professors M. Boyd, J. Goyer, F.E. Jones, H. McRoberts, P.C. Pineo, and J. Porter, and from the 1989 General Social Survey Cycle 4, Statistics Canada.

I am indebted to the reviewers and to Professors R. Arnold, B. McFarlane, M. Smith, and E. Zureik for their helpful and critical comments on an earlier draft of this paper.

2. See Richmond, 1965; Blishen, 1970; Forcese, 1975; Goldlust and Richmond, 1974; Pineo, 1976; Li, 1978; Darroch, 1979; Hartmann & Isajiw, 1980; Darroch & Ornstein, 1980; Reitz, 1980; Boyd et al., 1980; Kallen, 1982; Lautard & Loree, 1984; Pineo & Porter, 1985; Boyd, 1985; Winn, 1985a, 1985b; Denis, 1986; Hunter, 1986; Satzewich and Li, 1987; Lautard & Guppy, 1990; Agocs & Boyd, 1993; and Isajiw, Sev'er, & Driedger, 1993.

3. Critics have argued that the dissimilarity index is flawed in that it fluctuates with changes in the ethnic and occupational composition of employment or with changes in the marginal totals. Moreover, the value of the dissimilarity index is proportional to the number of ethnic or occupational categories used. Finally, the index may fail to take into account the inconsistency of the occupational or ethnic classification schemes over time (see Darroch, 1979: 12; Lautard & Guppy, 1990: 194; Blackburn et al., 1993: 336; Cherry & Mobilia, 1993: 102).

4. There is no clear consensus as to the definition of ethnicity (Isajiw, 1974; Anderson & Frideres, 1981). Even though most white Americans, for example, are at least third-generation immigrants, 89.4 percent mentioned a European country in response to the subjective ancestry question. And among these, about half named more than one country. Most of these self-identified ethnic groups are children of English, Irish, German, and Italian immigrants who arrived in the United States prior to 1920 (Hout & Goldstein, 1994: 64–65). Hout and Goldstein conclude that length of time in the United States, rate of fertility, intermarriage, and ethnic-identity preferences all account for the differences in the actual number of immigrants from these countries and the current size of the self-identified European-origin population. Not surprisingly, second- and third-generation Americans exercise a significant level of choice in defining ethnicity, leading to some unreliability in definition of ethnicity in survey and census question (Hout & Goldstein, 1994: 69, 79).

The unreliability and the lack of consensus in definition of ethnicity is also responsible for the considerable changes in the ethnic question in the Canadian surveys and censuses (White, 1992). Thus, whether one emphasizes the objective or subjective approach to the definition of ethnicity is a matter of research agenda. For these reasons, the classification of ethnic categories presented here is not necessarily a valid measure of ethnicity or of ethnic groups as outlined in the subjective definition. These categories are not ethnic-for-themselves, or ethnic groups, because ethnic members may not have a sense of belonging, share common values and traditions, and have an awareness of a common purpose. These ethnic categories comprised individuals who placed themselves in an ethnic group despite the real possibility that some have been in Canada for many generations, and as such are very likely to have been assimilated in Anglo- or French-Canadian culture (see Reitz, 1985; Isajiw, 1990; Breton et al., 1990). Nevertheless, many observers have agreed that "in spite of assimilation some percentage and some form of ethnic identity often remains in the second, third, and even later generations" (Isajiw, 1990: 45). Some call this "symbolic" (Gans, 1979; Roberts & Clifton, 1982) and others "fragmented" ethnicity (Breton, 1978). In this paper, ethnic "groups" and ethnic "categories" are used interchangeably.

5. We decided to take advantage of the distinctions made in the surveys and analyze the English, Scottish, and Irish groups separately because research shows important distinctions between them (see Porter, 1965: 63, 71, 80; Darroch & Ornstein, 1980: 318). Furthermore, it needs to be stressed that substantial effort has been made to make the ethnic groups comparable in 1973 and 1989. The reader should, nevertheless, note that the Jewish category in the GSS is measured by religious affiliation, while in the CMS it is identified by the ancestor's ethnic or cultural group. This should not produce a major problem for our purpose since the "Jews can be considered as a religious and/or an ethnic group" (Weinfeld, 1993: 220).

6. We are unable to generate a category representing large employers or the capitalist class *par excellence*. This information is not available in surveys. The small number of capitalists relative to the entire labour force limits the probability of this social group being selected in the samples, and even if selected they probably will not respond to the questionnaire. Even in censuses, large capitalists are collapsed with other class categories to protect individual confidentiality (Li, 1988: 91).

7. Reviewers asked for a separate analysis for men and women, too. We should ask the reader to exercise caution because the number of cases of women in ownership and managerial-class categories is often fewer than ten in each cell.

8. We employed the SPSS multinomial logit model using special contrasts. Reference categories are the English group for ethnicity, working class for class position, and 1973 for the sample year.

9. Reference categories are elementary and less for education, 20–34 for age, and Canadian-born for nativity.

10. There are few class differences between the Irish and Scottish ethnic groups as compared with the English (see Darroch & Ornstein, 1980: 314–15, 325; Porter, 1965: 63, 71, 80). The possible exceptions are overrepresentation of Scottish males and females among middle managers, along with the underrepresentation of the Scottish males in the petty bourgeoisie and self-employed class categories compared to their English counterparts. But notice that in all of these cases $P = 0.05$.

REFERENCES
▼

Agocs, Carol, & Boyd, Monica. (1993.) The Canadian ethnic mosaic recast for the 1990s. In James Curtis, Edward Grabb, & Neil Guppy (Eds.). *Social inequality in Canada: Patterns, problems, policies* (pp. 330–352). Scarborough, ON: Prentice-Hall.

Aldrich, John, & Nelson, Forrest D. (1984). *Linear probability, logit and probit models*. Beverly Hills, CA: Sage.

Anderson, Alan B., & Frideres, James. (1981). *Ethnicity in Canada: Theoretical perspectives*. Toronto: Butterworths.

Beaujot, Roderic, & Rappak, J. Peter. (1990). The evolution of immigrant cohorts. In S.S. Halli, F. Trovato, & L. Driedger (Eds.). *Ethnic demography* (pp. 111–140). Ottawa: Carleton University Press.

Belcourt, Monica. (1988). The family incubator model of female entrepreneurship. *Journal of Small Business & Entrepreneurship, 5*(3), 34–44.

Berkowitz, S.D. (1984). Corporate structure, corporate control, and Canadian elites. In S.D. Berkowitz (Ed.). *Models & myths in Canadian sociology* (pp. 233–262). Toronto: Butterworths.

Blackburn, Robert M., Jarman, Jennifer, & Siltanen, Janet. (1993). The analysis of occupational gender segregation over time and place: Considerations of measurement and some new evidence." *Work, Employment & Society, 7*(3), 335–362.

Blishen, Bernard R. (1970). Social class and opportunity in Canada. *Canadian Review of Sociology and Anthropology, 7*(2), 110–127.

Boyd, Monica. (1985). Immigration and occupational attainments of native-born Canadian men and women. In Monica Boyd, John Goyer, Frank E. Jones, Hugh A. McRoberts, Peter C. Pineo, & John Porter (Eds.) *Ascription and achievement: Studies in mobility and status attainment in Canada* (pp. 393–446. Ottawa: Carleton University Press.

———. (1990). Immigrant women, language, and socioeconomic inequalities and policy issues. In S.S. Halli, F. Trovato, & L. Driedger (Eds.). *Ethnic demography* (pp. 275–296). Ottawa: Carleton University Press.

Boyd, M., Featherman, D.L., & Matras, J. (1980). Status attainment of immigrant and immigrant origin categories in the United States, Canada, and Israel. *Comparative Social Research, 3*, 199–228.

Boyd, M., Goyer, J., Jones, F., McRoberts, H.A., Pineo, P.C., & Porter, J. (1985). The Canadian mobility study. In Monica Boyd, John Goyer, Frank E. Jones, Hugh A. McRoberts, Peter C. Pineo, & John Porter (Eds.). *Ascription and achievement: Studies in mobility and status attainment in Canada* (pp. 1–28). Ottawa: Carleton University Press.

Breton, Raymond. (1978). The structure of relationships between ethnic collectivities. In L. Driedger (Ed.). *The Canadian ethnic mosaic* (pp. 60–61). Toronto: McClelland & Stewart.

Breton, R., Isajiw, W.W., Kalbach, W.E., & Reitz, J.G. (1990). *Ethnic identity and equality: Varieties of experience in a Canadian city*. Toronto: University of Toronto Press.

Brym, Robert J., & Fox, Bonnie J. (1989). *From culture to power: The sociology of English Canada*. Toronto: Oxford University Press.

Brym, Robert J., Shaffir, William, & Weinfield, Morton. (1993). *The Jews in Canada*. Toronto: Oxford University Press.

Cachon, J.C., & Carter, S. (1989). "Self-employed females and the workforce: Some common issues across the Atlantic. *Journal of Small Business and Entrepreneurship, 6*(4), 20–31.

Carchedi, Guglielmo. (1977). *On the economic identification of social classes.* London: Routledge & Kegan Paul.

Carroll, William K. (1987). Which women are more proletarianised? Gender, class and occupation in Canada. *Canadian Review of Sociology and Anthropology, 24*(4), 571–85.

Cherry, R., & Mobilia, P. (1993). Trends in various dissimilarity indexes. *Review of Radical Political Economics, 25*(3), 93–103.

Chiswick, B.R. (1983). The earnings and human capital of American Jews." *Journal of Human Resources, 18*(3), 313–336.

Clement, Wallace. (1975a). *The Canadian corporate elite: An analysis of economic power.* Toronto: McClelland & Stewart.

———. (1975b). Inequality of access: Characteristics of the Canadian corporate elite. *The Canadian Review of Sociology and Anthropology, 12*(1), 33–52.

———. 1990a. Comparative class analysis: Locating Canada in a North American and Nordic context. *Canadian Review of Sociology and Anthropology, 27*(4), 462–486.

———. (1990b). A critical response to "Perspective on the Class and Ethnic Origins of Canadian Elites." *The Canadian Journal of Sociology, 15*(2), 179–185.

Cromie, S., & Hayes, J. (1988). Towards a typology of female entrepreneurs. *The Sociological Review, 36*, 87–113.

Cuneo, Carl J. (1985). Have women become more protetarianised than men?" *Canadian Review of Sociology and Anthropology, 22*(3), 465–495.

Darroch, A. Gordon. (1979). Another look at ethnicity, stratification, and social mobility in Canada. *The Canadian Journal of Sociology, 4*(1), 1–25.

Darroch, A. Gordon, & Ornstein, Michael D. (1980). Ethnicity and occupational structures in Canada in 1871: The vertical mosaic in historical perspective. *Canadian Historical Review, 61*(3), 305–332.

Denis, Ann. (1986). Adaptation to multiple subordination? Women in the vertical mosaic. *Canadian Ethnic Studies, 18*(3), 61–74.

Forcese, Dennis. (1975). *The Canadian class structure.* Toronto: McGraw-Hill Ryerson.

Francis, Diane. (1986). *Controlling interest: Who owns Canada?* Toronto: Macmillan.

Gans, H. (1979). Symbolic ethnicity: The future of ethnic groups and cultures. *Racial and Ethnic Studies, 16*, 33–60.

Goffee, R., & Scase, R. (1983). Business ownership and women's subordination: A preliminary study of female proprietors. *The Sociological Review*, new series (November), 625–648.

Goldlust, J., & Richmond, Anthony H. (1974). A multivariate analysis of the economic adaptation of immigrants in Toronto." *International Migration Review, 8*, 193–225.

Goodman, Leo A. (1972). A general model for the analysis of surveys. *American Journal of Sociology, 77*(6), 1035–1086.

Hartmann, N., & Isajiw, W.W. (1980). Ethnicity and occupation: An assessment of the occupational structure of Ukrainian Canadians in the 1960s. *Canadian Ethnic Studies, 12*(2), 55–73.

Herberg, Edward N. (1990). The ethno-racial socioeconomic hierarchy and analysis of the new vertical mosaic. *International Journal of Comparative Sociology, 31*(3/4), 206–221.

Hout, Michael, & Goldstein, Joshua R. (1994). How 4.5 million Irish immigrants became 40 million Irish Americans: Demographic and subjective aspects of the ethnic composition of white Americans. *American Sociological Review, 59,* 64–82.

Hunter, Alfred A. (1986). *Class tells: On social inequality in Canada.* Toronto: Butterworths.

Isajiw, Wsevolod W. (1974). Definitions of Ethnicity. *Ethnicity, 1*(2), 111–124.

———. (1990). Ethnic-identity retention. In Raymond Breton, Wsevolod Isajiw, Warren Kalbach, & Jeffrey G. Reitz (Eds.), *Ethnic identity and equality: Varieties of experience in a Canadian city* (pp. 34–91). Toronto: University of Toronto Press.

Isajiw, Wsevolod W., Sev'er, Aysan, & Driedger, Leo. (1993). Ethnic identity and social mobility: A test of the "drawback model." *Canadian Journal of Sociology, 18*(2), 179–198.

Johnston, William, & Ornstein, Michael. (1985). Social class and political ideology in Canada. *Canadian Review of Sociology and Anthropology, 22*(3), 369–393.

Kalbach, Warren E. (1970). *The impact of immigration on Canada's population.* Ottawa: Dominion Bureau of Statistics.

———. (1987). Growth and distribution of Canada's ethnic population, 1871–1981. In Leo Driedger (Ed.), *Ethnic Canada: Identities and inequalities* (pp. 82–110). Toronto: Copp Clark Pitman.

Kallen, E. (1982). *Ethnicity and human rights in Canada.* Toronto: Gage.

Kelner, Merrijoy. (1970). Ethnic penetration into Toronto's elite structure. *Canadian Review of Sociology and Anthropology, 7*(2), 128–137.

Knoke, David, & Burke, P.J. (1991). *Log-linear models.* Newbury Park, CA: Sage.

Lautard, E. Hugh, & Guppy, Neil. (1990). The vertical mosaic revisited: Occupational differentials among Canadian ethnic groups. In P.S. Li (Ed.), *Race and ethnic relations in Canada,* (pp. 189–208). Toronto: Oxford University Press.

Lautard, E. Hugh, & Loree, Donal J. (1984). Ethnic stratification in Canada. *Canadian Journal of Sociology, 9*(3), 333–344.

Li, Peter S. (1978). The stratification of ethnic immigrants: The case of Toronto. *Canadian Review of Sociology and Anthropology, 15*(1), 31–40.

———. (1988). *Ethnic inequality in a class society.* Toronto: Thompson Educational.

Marx, Karl. (1967). *Capital: A critical analysis of capitalist production,* vol. 1 (Ed. by Frederick Engels). New York: International.

Newman, Peter. (1975). *The Canadian establishment,* vol. I. Toronto: McClelland & Stewart.

Niosi, Jorge. (1981). *Canadian capitalism.* Toronto: James Lorimer.

Ogmundson, Richard. (1990). Perspectives on the class and ethnic origins of Canadian elites: A methodological critique of the Porter/Clement/Olson tradition. *Canadian Journal of Sociology, 15*(2), 165–177.

———. (1992). Commentary and debate. *Canadian Journal of Sociology, 17*(3), 313–325.

———. (1993). At the top of the mosaic: Doubts about the data. *American Review of Canadian Studies, 23* (Autumn), 373–386.

Ogmundson, Richard, & McLaughlin, James. (1992). Trends in the ethnic origins of Canadian elites: The decline of the Brits? *Canadian Review of Sociology and Anthropology, 29*(2), 227–242.

———. (1994). Changes in an intellectual elite, 1960–1990: The Royal Society revisited. *Canadian Review of Sociology and Anthropology, 31*(1), 1–13.

Olsen, Dennis. (1980). *The state elite.* Toronto: McClelland & Stewart.

Ornstein, Michael. (1988). Social class and economic inequality. In J. Curtis & L. Tepperman (Eds.), *Understanding Canadian society* (pp. 185–221). Toronto: McGraw-Hill Ryerson.

Pineo, Peter C. (1976). Social mobility in Canada: The current picture. *Sociological Focus, 9,* 109–123.

Pineo, Peter C., & Porter, John. (1985). Ethnic origin and occupational attainment in Canada. In Monica Boyd, John Goyer, Frank E. Jones, Hugh A. McRoberts, Peter C. Pineo, & John Porter (Eds.), *Ascription and achievement: Studies in mobility and status attainment in Canada* (pp. 357–392). Ottawa: Carleton University Press.

Poulantzas, Nicos. (1975). *Classes in contemporary capitalism.* London: New Left.

Porter, John. (1955). Elite groups: A scheme for the study of power in Canada. *Canadian Journal of Economics and Political Science, 21*(4), 498–512.

———. (1965). *The vertical mosaic: An analysis of social class and power in Canada.* Toronto: University of Toronto Press.

———. (1975). Foreword. In W. Clement, *The Canadian corporate elite: An analysis of economic power* (pp. ix–xv). Toronto: McClelland & Stewart.

Presthus, Robert. (1973). *Elite accommodation in Canadian politics.* Toronto: Macmillan.

———. (1974). *Elites in the policy process.* London: Cambridge University Press.

Reitz, Jeffrey. (1980). *The survival of ethnic groups.* Toronto: McGraw-Hill Ryerson.

———. (1985). Language and ethnic community survival. In R.M. Bienvenue & J.E. Goldstein (Eds.), *Ethnicity and ethnic relations in Canada* (pp. 105–123). Toronto: Butterworths.

———. (1990). Ethnic concentration in labour markets and their implications for ethnic inequality. In Raymond Breton, Wsevolod Isajiw, Warren Kalbach, & Jeffrey G. Reitz (Eds.), *Ethnic identity and equality: Varieties of experience in a Canadian city* (pp. 135–95). Toronto: University of Toronto Press.

Rich, Harvey. (1976). The vertical mosaic revisited. *Journal of Canadian Studies, 11,* 14–31.

————. (1991). Observations on "class and ethnic origins of Canadian elites" by Richard Ogmundson. *Canadian Journal of Sociology, 16*(4), 419–423.

Richmond, Anthony H. (1965). Social mobility of immigrants in Canada. *Population Studies: A Journal of Demography, 18*(1), 53–69.

Richmond, Anthony H., & Kalbach, Warren E. (1980). *Factors in the adjustment of immigrants and their descendants.* Ottawa: Ministry of Supply and Services.

Roberts, Lance W., & Clifton, Rodney A. (1982). Explaining the ideology of Canadian multiculturalism. *Canadian Public Policy, 8,* 88–94.

Satzewich, Vic, & Li, Peter S. (1987). Immigrant labour in Canada: The cost and benefit of ethnic origin in the job market. *Canadian Journal of Sociology, 12*(3), 229–241.

Tepperman, Lorne. (1975). *Social mobility in Canada.* Toronto: McGraw-Hill Ryerson.

Weinfeld, Morton. (1993). The ethnic sub-economy: Explication and analysis of a case study of the Jews of Montreal. In R. Brym, W. Shaffir, & M. Weinfeld (Eds.), *The Jews in Canada* (pp. 218–237). Toronto: Oxford University Press.

Weiss, L. (1994). Timing is everything. *The Atlantic Monthly Review, 273*(1), 32–45.

White, P. (1992). Challenges in measuring Canada's ethnic diversity. In S. Hryniuk (Ed.), *Twenty years of multiculturalism* (pp. 163–182). Winnipeg, MB: St. John's College Press.

Winn, Conrad. (1985a). Affirmative action and visible minorities: Eight premises in quest of evidence. *Canadian Public Policy, 11*(4), 684–700.

————. (1985b). Affirmative action for women: More than a case of simple justice. *Canadian Public Administration, 28*(1), 24–46.

Wright, Erik O. (1976). Class boundaries in advanced capitalist societies. *New Left Review, 98,* 3–41.

————. (1978). *Class, crisis and the state.* London: New Left.

————. (1985). *Classes.* London: Verso.

————. (1989). *The debate on classes.* London: Verso.

Wright, Erik O., & Perrone, L. (1977). Marxist class categories and income inequality. *American Sociological Review, 42*(1), 32–55.

THE IMPORTANCE OF
ETHNIC-CONNECTEDNESS FOR
CANADA'S POSTWAR IMMIGRANTS
MADELINE A. KALBACH AND WARREN E. KALBACH

INTRODUCTION
▼

Canada's official multicultural policy "had as much to do with removing barriers to full participation in Canadian society and with inter-cultural activity, and therefore assimilation, as it did with the preservation of ethnic heritage" (Richard, 1991: 3). Given this fact, it becomes increasingly important to determine the extent to which social reality diverges from Canada's multicultural policy. A persistent question in immigration research in Canada concerns the significance of the immigrant's ethnic and cultural origins for successful acculturation and integration into Canadian society. More specifically, the question is, "To what extent does the individual's ethnic identity or degree of ethnic-connectedness serve to facilitate or impede the individual's degree of social mobility?" Classical assimilation theory and previous research suggest that assimilation can also occur within generations (Kalbach & Richard, 1980, 1985a, 1988, 1990, 1991a, 1991b). Such research has used a multidimensional definition of ethnicity, an approach to which much of previous ethnic social-mobility research using census data has been relatively insensitive. An additional question that often arises is whether age at immigration has any effect on an immigrant's social and economic mobility in Canada (Kalbach & Richard, 1985b).

Regardless of the postwar emphasis on multiculturalism, it would not be unrealistic to assume that a fairly high proportion of the culturally dominant populations of British and French origins continue to expect immigrants to "fit in" and to become less ethnic and more Canadian (Economic Council of Canada, 1991). Cultural anthropology and the sociological and psychological principles of group and individual behaviour still lead social scientists to expect significant differences between Canada's minority ethnic groups and that these differences between interacting groups will tend to diminish over time. However, they have not been very successful in establishing the significance of ethnicity as a differentiating variable or in developing more precise explanations as to the extent and nature of changes to be expected within both immigrant and culturally dominant populations, or in interpreting their significance with respect to the processes of acculturation and socio-economic integration.

The purpose of this article is to examine differentials in language assimilation and social and economic status for Germans, Ukrainians, Portuguese, Middle Eastern/Arab/Asians, Indo-Pakistanis, Chinese, and Indo-Chinese immigrants to Canada at the time of the 1981 census, using a multidimensional definition of ethnicity to see to what extent age at immigration is a factor in social and economic mobility.[1] The importance of this research is that it uses census data to examine the importance of ethnic-connectedness for recent immigrants belonging to specific groups. Furthermore, it examines, for the first time, the extent to which age at immigration is a factor in their social and economic mobility.

LITERATURE REVIEW
▼

Earlier research that used census data has demonstrated the utility of employing a multidimensional definition of ethnicity (Richard, 1991; Kalbach & Richard, 1980, 1985a, 1985b, 1988, 1990, 1991a, 1991b). These studies took into account the basic multidimensional nature of ethnocultural groups and variations in religious heterogeneity by identifying and disaggregating their ethnoreligious components for separate analysis. Kalbach and Richard, for example, investigated the relationship between ethnoreligious identity and socio-economic attainment of selected minority groups in Canada (Kalbach & Richard, 1980, 1985a, 1985b, 1988, 1990, 1991a, 1991b). Data from the 1971 and 1981 censuses indicated that many non-British European groups such as Germans and Ukrainians, who relinquished their identification with their traditional ethnoreligious group by affiliating with the dominant Anglican and United Canadian churches, exhibited greater assimilation and higher socio-economic status than those who remained connected to their ethnic church. Furthermore, those who indicated no religious preference exhibited an even higher level of socio-economic achievement. These results suggest that, of the three pathways to assimilation, the ethnic church is the greatest inhibitor of social and economic mobility, while the secular pathway is the best resource for mobility. An examination of the data for both foreign- and native-born individuals revealed that these results tended to be significant only for the foreign-born.

Similar results were found for non-European ethnoreligious groups as a whole (Kalbach & Richard, 1988, 1990). Analyses of the Chinese, Black and Caribbean, Indo-Pakistani, and Middle Eastern/Arab/Asian groups, using data from the 1981 census, revealed that only Black and Caribbean immigrants exhibited the same mobility pattern as the non-British European groups. Affiliation with the ethnic church appeared to provide the least opportunity for upward mobility for the foreign-born of all four immigrant groups, while the Canadian church provided the greatest opportunity for the Chinese, Indo-Pakistanis, and Middle Eastern/Arab/Asians.

Age at immigration has been shown to exert both a strong effect on social and economic mobility (Kalbach & Richard, 1985b; Boyd et al., 1985; Inbar, 1977) and a negligible effect (Jones, 1987). Boyd's analysis, for example, revealed that foreign-born males who came to Canada prior to the age of 17 exhibited an educational and occupational advantage over those who were older when they emigrated to Canada. Similar results were found by Kalbach and Richard (1985b) in terms of education and income. Jones's research (1987), on the other hand, indicated that, when age at immigration was added to the status attainment model, it added little to the explained variation in occupational mobility.

Research by Kalbach and Richard (1985b) showed that a negative relationship between age at immigration and the use of English or French in the home held for all periods of immigration at the time of the 1981 census for non-British and non-French European ethnic groups. In addition, it was shown that the proportions using English as a home language increased consistently for each age at immigration category as length of residence (reflected in period of immigration) increased. Those who came as children, and had been in Canada the longest, had the highest percentage using English as their home language; those who were older when they arrived and had lived here for the shortest period of time (five years or less) were the least acculturated with respect to their language behaviour.

In spite of the variation in the effects of age at immigration on social and economic mobility as indicated by previous research, there is general agreement in the literature that the younger a child was when he or she emigrated, the better his or her chances of mobility would be (Inbar, 1977). While this theory has been applied to linguistic groups and immigrants as a whole, it has not generally been applied to specific ethnic- or cultural-origin groups. Nevertheless, immigrants who emigrate at younger ages than others, for example, would have significantly greater exposure to the socialization experiences of the Canadian school system and peer networks. Therefore, it is likely that age at immigration would exert some effect on specific ethnoreligious groups as well as on immigrants as a whole.

Educational and economic achievement profiles of the second generation, revealed in analyses by Richmond and Kalbach (1980), raised questions regarding the related performance and achievement levels of the first-generation foreign-born who had arrived in Canada as children. The question on birthplace of parents asked in the 1971 Census of Canada was dropped from the 1981 census, making it impossible to disaggregate the second generation from subsequent generations of the native born. However, its loss was partially compensated for by the new variable "age at immigration." As previously indicated, one would expect that those who had experienced the socialization effects of formal education and peer-group pressures in Canada as children would become much more like their native-born counterparts than the older members of their own particular ethnic-origin immigrant group, with whom they have always been grouped for analysis. Furthermore, the logic of the classic assimilation model suggests that adults who had arrived in Canada as young children would be more like their native-born counterparts than the foreign-born, with respect to their educational attainment and economic status.

DATA SOURCE AND VARIABLE DEFINITIONS
▼

Special tabulations from the 1981 federal Census of Canada for the population 15 years of age and over are used in this analysis. The specific variables and their definitions follow, as given in the 1981 *Census Dictionary* (Statistics Canada, 1982).

1. *Ethnic Origin:* Refers to the ethnic or cultural group to which the respondent or the respondent's ancestors belonged on coming to this continent. Previous censuses asked only for paternal ancestry. The 1981 census removed this restriction, resulting in the possibility that an individual may have more than one ancestry.
2. *Religion:* Refers to the specific groups or bodies, denominations, sects, cults, or religious community of which the individual is a member or favours or adheres to.
3. *Generation:* Refers to whether a person was born in or outside of Canada, that is, is native- or foreign-born.

4. *Age at Immigration:* Refers to age at which the respondent first immigrated to Canada. This is a new variable constructed from the information on year of immigration and date of birth.
5. *Home Language:* Refers to the specific language spoken at home by the respondent at the time of the census. It is used as an index of acculturation and as an index of ethnic-connectedness.
6. *Education:* Refers to the highest grade or year of schooling completed. The attainment of some university or university degree is employed as an indicator of socio-economic status.
7. *Income:* Refers to total census family income. Family income of $50 000 or more is used as an indicator of socio-economic status.

CONCEPTUAL FRAMEWORK AND METHODOLOGY
▼

Previous research on the significance of ethnic origin for assimilation has been handicapped to a great extent because of the ambiguity surrounding the definition and meaning of such terms as ethnic identity, ethnic origin, and nationality (Ryder, 1955). Additional problems have arisen due to the difficulty of employing such concepts in a manner consistent with their theoretical conceptualization as a multidimensional phenomenon. Gordon's definition of ethnicity as a multidimensional phenomenon has been accepted for some time (Darroch & Marston, 1969; Yinger, 1985; Richard, 1991). Moreover, it has been argued convincingly that it is pointless to treat ethnicity and religion as separate, independent variables when in fact they are inseparable and intertwined (Porter, 1965: 100; Greeley, 1971; Kornacker, 1971: 152; Richard, 1991). Hence, this research uses a multidimensional definition of ethnicity as an index of ethnic-connectedness.

It is hypothesized that traditional ethnic-church affiliation will tend to be associated with greater ethnic-connectedness on the part of the individual than is the case for either Canadian church affiliation or no expressed religious preference. An individual's statement of an ethnic-church affiliation is taken as evidence of a greater commitment to his or her ethnic group compared to those who indicate an affiliation with a Canadian church or those who expressed no religious preference. Evidence of this greater ethnic-connectedness can be found in the use of non-official (neither English nor French) languages in the home. Thus, the strength of ethnic identity or ethnic-connectedness that may be said to characterize a particular ethnoreligious group can be measured in terms of the proportions of ethnoreligious groups reporting the use of ethnic languages in the home.

It is also hypothesized that the younger the foreign-born population was at the time of their immigration to Canada, the greater the congruence of their characteristics with those of their native-born counterparts. The youngest immigrants, youth (that is, those 12 years of age and under), at the time of arrival will have experienced greater acculturation and economic integration than those who arrived in Canada as teenagers, because of their longer exposure to school and peer groups. Given the generally shorter exposure of teenage immigrants to the same socialization influences, they would likely be further impaired by the earlier entry into the labour force generally required by immigrant families to provide additional support during the initial and often difficult period of settlement.

The migration process would appear to be more disruptive for teenage immigrants than for younger children. As a consequence, one would expect to see evidence of greater acculturation with respect to language use among the youngest immigrants, as well as evidence of a more successful social and economic integration over the long term. On the other hand, teenage immigrants would experience more rapid economic integration but suffer some competition disadvantage in the long run because of their somewhat lower levels of acculturation, as are reflected in their language skills, and possible disruption or termination of their formal education.

The following analysis explores the variations in ethnic-connectedness between ethnoreligious groups using language in the home as a measure of ethnic-group identity to demonstrate the greater ethnic commitment of those with ethnic-church affiliations. The analysis also examines the relationship between age at immigration, acculturation in terms of declining ethnic commitment, and social and economic status achievement.

ANALYSIS
▼

ETHNIC CHURCH AND ETHNIC-CONNECTEDNESS

The data in Table 12.1 are consistent with the hypothesis of a greater ethnic commitment on the part of those identifying with the more traditional ethnic religions. For the seven groups shown, the proportion of traditional ethnoreligious groups using an ethnic language in the home exceeded that for any of those reporting non-traditional religions. Twenty-one percent of German Lutherans, Mennonites, and Hutterites combined, for example, reported the use of non-official languages in the home, compared to only 1.7 percent of those identifying with the major Protestant churches in Canada and 5.8 percent of those reporting no religious preference.

TABLE 12.1
▼

PERCENT OF THE POPULATION WITH NON-OFFICIAL LANGUAGES SPOKEN IN THE HOME, FOR SELECTED ETHNORELIGIOUS GROUPS, BY NATIVITY AND AGE AT IMMIGRATION, FOR THE FOREIGN-BORN, CANADA, 1981

Ethnoreligious Group	Total Population	Native Born	Foreign-Born				Total Number
			Total	Age at Immigration			
				0–12	13–19	20+	
German	11.6	5.3	30.9	12.8	22.9	41.7	1 142 375
Lutheran/Mennonite/ Hutterite	21.0	13.2	38.3	20.1	29.7	48.1	413 255
Roman Catholic	8.8	1.6	29.6	9.7	18.0	39.8	282 805
Major Protestant	1.7	0.4	11.6	3.5	9.3	20.3	210 280
No Religious Preference	5.8	1.6	18.5	7.8	10.7	27.4	91 420
Ukrainian	16.7	9.2	61.1	31.1	58.5	79.0	529 605
Ukrainian Catholic	30.0	17.4	72.1	42.6	66.8	84.8	159 170
Eastern Orthodox	26.8	16.9	64.2	38.9	59.7	78.6	98 690
Roman Catholic	5.8	3.1	37.7	14.9	38.9	59.2	88 910
Major Protestant	2.8	1.8	25.0	7.0	40.6	56.1	96 130
No Religious Preference	5.1	2.5	35.9	10.9	59.2	60.6	41 860
Portuguese	67.3	48.1	73.6	54.1	68.2	84.4	188 080
Roman Catholic	68.1	49.2	74.2	54.9	69.0	85.0	181 075
Other Protestant	54.1	34.0	62.2	35.7	51.7	75.7	3 375
No Religious Preference	44.0	29.3	50.0	38.4	41.2	60.8	2 135
Middle Eastern/ Arab/Asian	45.5	22.3	55.1	41.6	58.0	58.7	101 595
Eastern Non- Christian	46.8	31.9	51.3	38.8	61.6	53.0	30 755
Eastern Orthodox	57.6	26.5	67.8	54.8	65.1	72.2	26 385
Roman Catholic	34.0	14.3	45.0	33.5	46.7	48.7	28 370
Major Protestant	20.8	5.6	44.4	27.2	44.0	50.9	4 420
No Religious Preference	15.4	2.6	24.6	25.0	31.9	22.3	2 300
Indo-Pakistani	44.7	32.8	48.2	30.6	51.8	53.5	196 390
Eastern Non- Christian	52.4	39.8	56.1	36.9	59.9	61.7	160 390
Roman Catholic	5.6	4.7	5.9	1.8	5.0	7.6	16 995

(continued)

(Table 12.1 continued)

Ethnoreligious Group	Total Population	Native Born	Foreign-Born				Total Number
			Total	Age at Immigration			
				0–12	13–19	20+	
Other Protestant	16.2	5.0	20.3	8.5	18.2	25.7	4 895
Major Protestant	8.6	1.5	11.1	3.6	9.5	13.9	6 555
No Religious Preference	18.8	10.8	23.5	15.0	17.1	29.2	6 000
Chinese	65.2	34.4	75.7	55.1	74.9	82.4	289 255
Eastern Non-Christian	82.0	51.4	84.9	73.3	84.3	88.3	18 245
Roman Catholic	49.5	29.0	54.5	32.9	53.7	61.7	42 810
Other Protestant	65.8	35.1	75.5	53.7	72.5	82.7	25 255
Major Protestant	42.3	16.9	61.6	37.5	59.7	70.4	35 285
No Religious Preference	72.3	41.5	82.6	62.4	82.0	89.3	164 315
Indo-Chinese	73.3	36.8	76.8	72.5	79.5	77.9	54 730
Eastern Non-Christian	75.9	46.7	77.9	73.5	80.3	79.2	25 390
Roman Catholic	61.1	24.3	66.5	62.3	74.3	66.5	11 995
Other Protestant	70.0	25.0	74.7	71.2	69.6	78.0	2 525
Major Protestant	59.7	11.9	68.4	66.7	78.1	68.0	1 925
No Religious Preference	82.8	49.2	85.7	82.4	83.2	88.2	11 915

Source: Statistics Canada, *1981 Census of Canada.* Special Tabulations.

The older immigrant groups, that is, Germans and Ukrainians, show considerably lower levels of ethnic language use in the home at the time of the 1981 census compared to the other, more recent immigrant groups. In all but one case, however, the more traditional ethnoreligious groups reported higher proportions using ethnic languages in the home, but the differences between the traditional ethnoreligious groups and those identifying with the more Canadian churches, or reporting no religious preference, tended to be somewhat less for the more recent arrivals than for the older and more established groups such as the Germans and Ukrainians. The Indo-Chinese were the only exception to the hypothesized relationship between traditional ethnic-church identity and use of ethnic languages in the home in that the proportion reporting Eastern non-Christian religions was lower (75.9 percent) compared to the proportion reporting no religious preference (82.8 percent).

Previous research indicates that those claiming no religious preference would be the most secularized and least ethnically connected, regardless of their stated origins (Kalbach & Richard, 1985b). However, as may be seen in Table 12.1, this is true only for the Portuguese and Middle Eastern/Arab/Asian groups. It would appear that, for some non–European-origin groups, those reporting no religious preference tend to be in an intermediate position between their traditional religions and Canadian church counterparts with respect to their degree of ethnic-connectedness rather than in an even more secularized position than that represented by the major Canadian Protestant churches. Clearly there may be some cultural ambiguity in the meaning of the "no religious preference" response for those of different cultural origins which muddies the interpretation of these data.

Comparisons between the native- and foreign-born generations of the ethnoreligious populations, also shown in Table 12.1, indicate that the older and more settled immigrant groups show the greatest generational decline in the use of their ethnic languages in the home. Germans and Ukrainians, for example, exhibited declines of 83 and 85 percent, respectively, compared to only 35 percent for the Portuguese and variations of between 32 and 60 percent for the other, more recent ethnic groups.

The decline in ethnic-language use in the home for the native-born compared to the foreign-born tended to be lower for the more ethnically connected groups than for those who were less ethnically connected by religion. For example, the most ethnically connected Germans, that is, German Lutherans, Mennonites, and Hutterites, exhibited a generational decline of 66 percent in the use of an ethnic language in the home, while less ethnically connected Germans exhibited declines ranging from 91 to 97 percent. The generational percentage decline for the most ethnically connected Ukrainian groups was slightly higher than for Germans belonging to the ethnic church, at about 75 percent. Generational declines in the use of ethnic languages at home for the remaining five groups ranged from a low of 29 percent for Eastern non-Christian Indo-Pakistanis to a high of about 40 percent for the Chinese and Indo-Chinese Eastern non-Christians.

To summarize, the native born and foreign-born who identify with the more traditional ethnic churches within any ethnic origin group show higher ethnic-language retention and suffer less generational language loss and weakening of their ethnic-connectedness than those who identify with the more Canadian churches or no church.

AGE AT IMMIGRATION AND ACCULTURATION
▼

The central role played by language in the socialization process and in the transmission of cultural values makes it a particularly sensitive indicator of acculturation and assimilation. Analysis of the 1981 data shows that age at immigration also has an effect on the use of non-official languages in the home, independent of the ethnoreligious identity of the immigrant. In that of the 32 ethnoreligious groups shown in Table 12.1, only six failed to show a consistent positive relationship between age at immigration and use of ethnic languages in the home. Four of these were Indo-Chinese and two were Middle-Eastern/Arab in origin; however, among these, five of the relationships were positive for ages at immigration of under twenty years. The exceptions, in every case, were the lower-than-expected proportions of adult immigrants (arriving in Canada over twenty years of age) indicating that they did not use an ethnic language in the home. Part of the explanation for these particular exceptions may lie in the fact that adult immigrants of Asian origins have tended to be highly selected on the basis of their educational attainment and proficiency in their use of either English or French. In other words, Canada's criteria for selecting immigrants from non-European countries would appear to have favoured those immigrants showing evidence of prior acculturation in terms of their education and language skills.

For most, it is clear that the younger the age at immigration the longer the period of exposure to acculturative forces and the greater the likelihood of a weakening of the pre-existing cultural ties, that is, the ethnic connection, insofar as the use of ethnic language in the home is concerned. None of these age-at-immigration groups appears to be completely immune to the effects of acculturation and assimilation. But regardless of nativity and age at immigration, those with the more traditional ethnic-church or religious identity tend to be more resistant to the processes of acculturation and assimilation, insofar as their language behaviour is concerned. Their higher proportions of using languages other than English or French in the home suggest that they are generally more ethnic or ethnically connected than those reporting the use of one of the two official languages. While the seven ethnic-origin groups included in this analysis are not a representative sample of Canada's ethnic populations, they do represent a range of groups from the old and new European immigrations as well as the more recent Asian immigration to Canada. If the use of ethnic language in the home is taken as an index of cultural commitment or ethnic-connectedness, the degree of variability observed between ethnoreligious groups suggests that these subgroups would be the more appropriate units for the analysis of the significance of the ethnic cultural factor, or ethnic connectedness, for intergroup differences in socio-economic behaviour.

DIFFERENCES IN EDUCATIONAL ATTAINMENT AND
SOCIO-ECONOMIC ACHIEVEMENT
▼

In the early settlement of North America, the requisite for success was hard, physical, manual work needed for clearing land, building shelter, and working the soil. Canada sought out the landless peasants of Europe to help it settle the West. However, with increasing industrialization and urbanization, skills in English (or French) and education have become increasingly important for socio-economic achievement and social integration. That there were opportunities to do so can be attested to by virtue of the fact that the population of 5–19-year-olds attending school in Canada increased from slightly more than 50 percent to over 78 percent in a period of almost 60 years, from 1901 to 1961. Even so, by 1961 fewer than half of those who had finished their schooling had not completed more than an elementary school education (Kalbach, 1970). Higher incomes in an industrializing and technological society were increasingly tied to longer periods of training and higher attainment levels.

Between 1960 and 1986, the proportion of the population with less than Grade 9 schooling declined from 44 to just 18 percent. This, of course, reflects not only the rising levels of educational attainment of the general native-born population, including the children of immigrants, but also the generally rising education levels throughout the world as well as the greater selectivity in admitting immigrants since 1961, with respect to their educational qualifications. In this analysis, interest is focussed on variations in educational attainment levels as an index of socio-economic status differentiation not only for the more general and ethnically heterogeneous origin categories, but also for the more significantly ethnoreligious subgroups that comprise them. More specifically, the focus is directed to the "within" ethnic group variation in ethnic-connectedness and its relationship to educational and economic status for a number of older European and more recent non-European-origin immigrant groups.

ETHNIC-CONNECTEDNESS AND EDUCATIONAL ACHIEVEMENT LEVELS

Before examining variations in educational achievement levels between ethnoreligious subgroups of the major ethnic-origin categories, it is interesting to note the differences between the seven ethnic origin populations included in this analysis. For the older and more established German and Ukrainian populations, 14 and 15 percent, respectively, had achieved some university education or a degree by the time of the 1981 census. In contrast, only 4 percent of the more recent European immigrants of Portuguese origin had reported achieving similar educational levels. For the other four newer non-European immigrant groups, educational achievement levels were significantly higher and in contrast to the historical pattern in which the more recent ethnic-minority immigrants usually exhibited lower levels of educational achievement than the established population. However, since these unusually high educational-attainment levels are clearly the consequence of a highly selective immigration policy based on educational, occupational, and language-skill criteria, direct comparisons between ethnic origin groups, per se, are not useful for testing hypotheses concerning the significance of the ethnic factor vis-à-vis the achievement of socio-economic status in Canada. In the case at hand, the more valid comparisons would be those between the various ethnoreligious groups within each of the major ethnic groupings while controlling for nativity and age at immigration effects.

Given the assumption that individual ethnic identity or degree of ethnic-connectedness varies according to identity with a traditional ethnic church, Canadian church, or no church, the data in Table 12.2 provide evidence of a generally negative relationship between ethnic-connectedness and social status in terms of educational attainment for most of the ethnoreligious groups included in this analysis. The most consistent evidence for a negative relationship is provided by Germans, Indo-Pakistanis, and to a slightly lesser extent by the Portuguese-origin population. For the Ukrainian and Middle Eastern/Arab/Asian origins, a simple negative pattern appears to hold if the degree of ethnic-connectedness is dichotomized between any religious preference and none at all; while, for the Chinese, the negative pattern appears when comparing the more traditional Eastern non-Christian ethnics with all other religious and non-church preferences combined. Only the Indo-Chinese ethnoreligious groups fail to provide consistent evidence. But, the Roman Catholic Indo-Chinese do exhibit a somewhat higher proportion with some university education or a degree than the Eastern non-Christian (36 percent vs. 31 percent). This effect is produced by the foreign-born, especially those who had immigrated before they were 12 years of age (18 percent vs. 11 percent) and those who had been 20 years of age or older (42 percent vs. 34 percent). In this case, insufficient numbers in the Protestant religious categories make it difficult to generalize about the nature of this relationship with any degree of confidence.

ETHNIC-CONNECTEDNESS AND ECONOMIC STATUS

Of the several available indexes of economic status, average total family incomes are used in this analysis of the relationship between the degree of ethnic-connectedness and economic-status achievement of the native- and foreign-born components of seven selected ethnic-origin populations. While income in-

TABLE 12.2
▼
PERCENT OF THE POPULATION WITH SOME UNIVERSITY OR DEGREE, FOR SELECTED ETHNORELIGIOUS GROUPS, BY NATIVITY AND AGE AT IMMIGRATION, FOR THE FOREIGN-BORN, CANADA, 1981

Ethnoreligious Group	Total Population	Native Born	Foreign-Born Total	Age at Immigration 0–12	13–19	20+	Total Number
German	13.9	13.6	14.6	18.4	10.5	13.9	957 460
Lutheran/Mennonite/ Hutterite	12.0	12.3	11.5	16.0	8.1	10.6	342 760
Roman Catholic	13.4	13.6	12.9	18.6	9.9	11.5	240 740
Major Protestant	14.8	13.8	21.3	18.2	15.4	26.1	179 555
No Religious Preference	22.8	19.3	31.1	33.3	23.8	31.4	75 225
Ukrainian	15.3	16.3	10.6	17.4	5.6	7.9	459 525
Ukrainian Catholic	15.3	16.5	12.1	23.5	7.0	8.5	138 915
Eastern Orthodox	13.7	15.3	8.5	15.3	4.5	6.1	88 540
Roman Catholic	14.1	14.7	7.7	9.4	4.4	7.2	75 855
Major Protestant	15.6	15.9	9.1	10.8	3.6	8.7	82 125
No Religious Preference	22.3	22.8	17.0	22.8	7.2	12.8	36 535
Portuguese	4.4	7.6	4.2	8.1	4.8	2.8	135 505
Roman Catholic	4.1	6.8	3.9	7.7	4.4	2.6	130 275
Other Protestant	5.2	5.1	5.3	10.6	8.3	2.7	2 480
No Religious Preference	19.6	21.7	19.3	24.1	20.6	16.5	1 630
Middle Eastern/ Arab/Asian	31.7	24.6	33.2	27.4	27.2	35.5	77 860
Eastern Non- Christian	37.2	12.6	38.4	18.4	24.3	43.7	21 580
Eastern Orthodox	28.0	22.7	28.8	24.7	25.6	30.1	21 070
Roman Catholic	30.9	27.0	32.2	31.2	30.2	33.0	22 105
Major Protestant	26.5	21.6	33.1	33.9	21.6	35.6	3 830
No Religious Preference	56.0	42.4	62.9	56.6	50.0	69.6	1 865
Indo-Pakistani	36.8	20.5	37.4	21.4	24.8	42.1	136 120
Eastern Non- Christian	35.9	21.8	36.3	18.4	22.7	41.3	110 565
Roman Catholic	37.2	13.2	38.3	28.5	31.9	41.4	12 265

(continued)

(Table 12.2 continued)

Ethnoreligious Group	Total Population	Native Born	Foreign-Born				Total Number
			Total	Age at Immigration			
				0–12	13–19	20+	
Other Protestant	39.9	15.0	42.4	24.7	31.0	48.3	3 380
Major Protestant	42.1	14.0	45.1	30.3	40.6	48.2	4 755
No Religious Preference	48.3	29.5	52.4	42.1	47.4	56.5	4 070
Chinese	28.2	33.1	27.4	31.6	31.5	25.6	222 080
Eastern Non-Christian	16.7	30.0	16.2	16.7	16.7	16.0	14 750
Roman Catholic	38.3	30.2	38.3	29.3	50.7	37.2	32 480
Other Protestant	38.8	32.3	39.7	34.5	47.8	37.9	20 040
Major Protestant	31.7	36.4	29.2	35.2	31.2	27.1	28 365
No Religious Preference	24.3	31.6	23.3	32.3	25.8	21.3	123 790
Indo-Chinese	29.2	19.4	29.4	13.8	20.9	32.6	38 100
Eastern Non-Christian	30.6	30.8	30.6	11.1	22.9	33.8	18 075
Roman Catholic	36.1	22.0	36.8	17.6	21.7	42.1	8 265
Other Protestant	22.0	0.0	22.9	0.0	11.1	26.9	1 615
Major Protestant	25.6	17.1	27.0	0.0	11.5	29.9	1 230
No Religious Preference	22.3	23.1	22.3	11.8	20.3	23.2	8 290

Source: Statistics Canada, *1981 Census of Canada.* Special Tabulations.

dexes are generally less biased than educational-attainment measures by Canada's selective immigration policies, there is still some bias introduced by the preferential selection and admission of entrepreneurial types and investors, but their numbers have been relatively small in comparison to the total immigrant admissions under the independent-worker and family-class categories. Furthermore, numerous studies have suggested that economic-status achievement indexes based on income are particularly sensitive to the ethnic factor with respect to the types of work available and wages and salaries, etc. (Li, 1988; Driedger, 1989; Anderson & Frideres, 1981).

The relationship between ethnic-connectedness, age at immigration, and socio-economic achievement are shown in Table 12.3. The data support a general negative relationship between the degree of ethnic-connectedness and family income for all of the groups except the Indo-Chinese. Generally speaking, the proportions of families earning $50 000+ for the more traditional ethnoreligious groups tend to be consistently less than for those pro-

TABLE 12.3
▼

PERCENT OF THE POPULATION WITH FAMILY INCOMES OF $50 000+, FOR SELECTED ETHNORELIGIOUS GROUPS, BY NATIVITY AND AGE AT IMMIGRATION, FOR THE FOREIGN-BORN, CANADA, 1981

Ethnoreligious Group	Total Population	Native Born	Foreign-Born				Total Number
			Total	Age at Immigration			
				0–12	13–19	20+	
German	10.6	10.9	8.4	12.4	7.2	6.0	784 575
Lutheran/Mennonite/ Hutterite	10.0	10.7	6.6	10.1	5.9	4.8	280 520
Roman Catholic	11.9	12.2	9.4	15.3	7.1	6.4	197 535
Major Protestant	10.8	10.8	11.6	14.2	13.1	7.8	150 395
No Religious Preference	11.2	10.9	13.0	15.0	9.2	12.3	57 325
Ukrainian	10.6	11.1	4.8	8.2	6.1	2.3	364 885
Ukrainian Catholic	9.6	10.4	4.2	8.5	6.9	1.8	109 280
Eastern Orthodox	9.9	10.7	4.6	9.4	3.0	2.2	68 295
Roman Catholic	10.6	10.7	7.3	9.5	5.6	5.3	60 375
Major Protestant	12.9	13.0	7.1	8.1	9.3	4.3	69 155
No Religious Preference	12.6	12.8	9.4	9.8	13.5	7.7	27 195
Portuguese	4.4	4.5	4.3	5.8	3.2	1.1	123 330
Roman Catholic	4.4	4.4	4.4	5.8	3.2	1.1	118 775
Other Protestant	2.4	2.7	1.9	2.0	0	0	2 260
No Religious Preference	6.8	6.7	6.9	9.2	0	0	1 330
Middle Eastern/ Arab/Asian	10.7	12.2	8.8	11.6	5.2	5.8	63 295
Eastern Non- Christian	6.4	6.4	6.3	6.9	5.2	5.9	17 770
Eastern Orthodox	11.0	14.5	7.8	10.2	6.6	5.3	16 980
Roman Catholic	14.4	15.8	12.3	16.8	6.7	7.0	18 085
Major Protestant	13.7	13.7	13.8	22.2	0	5.6	3 130
No Religious Preference	14.2	13.6	15.6	16.7	0	17.4	1 195
Indo-Pakistani	8.3	7.8	8.8	11.8	6.5	4.3	117 735
Eastern Non- Christian	7.6	7.2	7.9	10.7	6.1	3.9	96 590
Roman Catholic	10.9	10.1	11.5	13.7	8.2	7.4	10 330

(continued)

(Table 12.3 continued)

Ethnoreligious Group	Total Population	Native Born	Foreign-Born				Total Number
			Total	Age at Immigration			
				0–12	13–19	20+	
Major Protestant	14.1	13.8	14.6	20.0	0	6.2	3 960
No Religious Preference	15.8	14.5	17.9	24.4	12.0	9.3	3 075
Chinese	11.4	14.3	8.8	11.8	8.5	4.7	179 695
Eastern Non-Christian	6.1	8.7	4.9	8.0	1.4	2.2	10 880
Roman Catholic	13.3	13.5	13.3	18.8	10.2	6.4	27 440
Other Protestant	12.0	14.7	9.6	10.8	12.3	6.7	16 340
Major Protestant	16.5	18.8	11.7	17.5	4.5	7.0	23 575
No Religious Preference	10.2	13.3	7.5	9.5	8.7	3.8	99 355
Indo-Chinese	6.2	9.6	4.9	5.3	4.6	3.3	26 210
Eastern Non-Christian	6.8	10.6	5.6	6.5	7.0	1.7	12 850
Roman Catholic	7.6	11.0	5.7	6.0	3.6	7.0	5 840
Other Protestant	2.9	0	3.9	5.1	0	0	1 195
Major Protestant	7.3	10.6	5.3	3.8	0	0	895
No Religious Preference	3.4	7.9	2.1	1.9	1.6	3.4	4 940

Source: Statistics Canada, *1981 Census of Canada*. Special Tabulations.

fessing either a preference for the more Canadian churches or none at all. The most consistent patterns are exhibited by the Germans, Ukrainians, and Indo-Pakistanis, with the differences tending to be greater among the foreign-born components than for the native-born.

The Portuguese, Middle Eastern/Arab/Asians, and the Chinese show a similar relationship if the comparisons are based on a dichotomized ethnic-connectedness variable, for example, the more traditional Eastern non-Christian versus all others. The Indo-Chinese show a slight advantage for both the native- and foreign-born Roman Catholics as opposed to Eastern to non-Christians, but not for the Canadian Protestant churches or those preferring no religion. Again, small numbers tend to make estimates for this group unreliable.

ETHNIC-CONNECTEDNESS IN 1991

The only readily available data source for an analysis of the 1991 data is the Public Use Microdata File (Individual File). This source, however, does not provide comparability for analyses of Canada's ethnic populations. Strictly speaking, historical analyses of Canada's ethnic-origin populations ended with the 1981 census because of the major change in the ethnic-origin question in the 1991 census.[2] There are also other problems with these data. The categorization of two of the major variables, that is, age at immigration and ethnic origin, in the 1991 Public Use Microdata File are cases in point.[3] Hence, a replication of the 1981 analyses was not possible. In spite of the incongruence of the 1991 data, they do seem to indicate a continuation of the trends discerned in the 1981 analysis. Table 12.4, for example, reveals a generally negative relationship between ethnic-connectedness and social status in terms of educational attainment for most of the ethnoreligious groups included in the analysis. In fact, in most instances the data reveal similar findings to those found in Table 12.2. Language loss and high levels of income also revealed similar patterns in 1991 to those exhibited at the time of the 1981 census. In the case of the latter, using total family income of $75 000 or more as the cut-off point and dichotomizing ethnic-connectedness (for the more recent Portuguese and the non-European groups) into Eastern non-Christian and all other, the same general pattern of differences between the more and less ethically connected groups are still quite apparent for the native-born and foreign-born groups alike. Where the results were less consistent using 1991 data, particularly in the case of the Germans and Ukrainians, there is reason to believe that the obfuscation and weakening of the relationship were in part a consequence of the changes made in the categorization of census variables, for example, age at immigration and acceptance of multiple origins as a valid category for the ethnic origin variable.

Although the analysis of the 1991 census data is not directly comparable to the 1981 analysis, the findings from the former provide a rough idea of the situation at that time. Hence, it would appear that if an exact replication of the 1981 analysis were possible, the hypothesized relationships would be stronger and more consistent for the most recent ethnoreligious groups included in this analysis in 1991 than they were at the time of the 1981 census.

CONCLUSION
▼

With minor exceptions, the general pattern of relationships between ethnic-connectedness and economic status in terms of average total family income are much the same as for educational status. Individuals in the more traditional ethnoreligious groups, who exhibit their greater ethnic commitment or connectedness through greater use of their ethnic language in the home, tend to report lower levels of educational and economic-status attainment than those

TABLE 12.4
▼

PERCENT OF THE POPULATION WITH SOME UNIVERSITY OR DEGREE, FOR SELECTED ETHNORELIGIOUS GROUPS, BY NATIVITY AND AGE AT IMMIGRATION, FOR THE FOREIGN-BORN, CANADA, 1991

Ethnoreligious Group	Total Population	Native Born	Foreign-Born Total	Age at Immigration 0–12	13–19	20+	Total Number
German	16.6	16.7	16.3	22.8	10.8	14.4	133 967
Lutheran/Mennonite/ Hutterite	15.4	16.3	13.8	20.7	10.4	11.9	42 667
Roman Catholic	16.2	17.1	14.3	23.4	6.7	12.6	31 333
Major Protestant	15.8	14.4	20.2	25.4	14.6	19.0	17 267
No Religious Preference	20.3	18.9	23.8	31.8	21.8	19.6	19 367
Ukrainian	18.6	18.9	16.5	23.9	15.8	12.3	69 700
Ukrainian Catholic	22.0	23.0	19.0	37.8	26.0	11.8	18 600
Eastern Orthodox	17.7	18.3	15.1	20.4	10.8	12.3	13 100
Roman Catholic	17.0	17.5	12.9	17.7	4.3	10.9	13 200
Major Protestant	16.6	16.7	13.6	13.5	—	16.7	9 300
No Religious Preference	10.6	19.5	22.0	22.9	15.4	23.3	8 733
Portuguese	7.2	13.9	5.8	13.6	3.9	2.9	13 800
Roman Catholic	8.5	15.0	7.4	14.7	—	4.8	400
Other Protestant	5.2	5.1	5.3	10.6	8.3	2.7	2 480
No Religious Preference	20.0	28.1	17.2	34.4	—	9.8	833
Middle Eastern/ Arab/Asian	37.6	25.0	39.0	33.3	33.3	40.5	63 800
Eastern Non- Christian	39.4	19.4	40.3	21.5	30.3	43.3	27 100
Eastern Orthodox	31.9	27.3	32.5	33.9	32.0	32.4	11 033
Roman Catholic	35.7	25.7	37.6	41.0	29.8	38.2	12 300
Major Protestant	33.8	23.3	47.1	60.0	—	46.4	867
No Religious Preference	58.1	21.7	62.3	31.8	64.3	66.1	4 400
Indo-Pakistani	32.3	24.2	32.9	38.5	23.5	33.1	101 467
Eastern Non- Christian	30.9	21.4	31.5	36.5	21.7	32.1	79 467
Roman Catholic	38.6	32.8	39.1	44.2	42.6	37.4	9 467

(continued)

(Table 12.4 continued)

Ethnoreligious Group	Total Population	Native Born	Foreign-Born				Total Number
			Total	Age at Immigration			
				0–12	13–19	20+	
Other Protestant	27.8	23.8	28.3	39.7	13.0	27.0	3 333
Major Protestant	41.5	32.4	42.9	54.2	29.4	42.7	3 400
No Religious Preference	39.0	37.0	39.6	48.2	32.1	36.7	2 967
Chinese	33.5	44.6	32.1	39.4	33.6	30.5	154 200
Eastern Non-Christian	15.7	18.6	15.6	21.5	17.5	14.4	9 133
Roman Catholic	41.6	39.2	41.9	46.7	55.2	39.2	25 200
Other Protestant	50.8	54.2	50.4	57.5	55.4	48.3	24 333
Major Protestant	47.7	52.9	45.0	54.7	40.0	43.0	10 533
No Religious Preference	31.3	43.2	29.6	36.8	28.5	28.4	81 267
Indo-Chinese	31.3	32.8	30.9	28.4	22.1	32.8	52 800
Eastern Non-Christian	22.9	19.9	23.3	21.9	17.0	24.7	13 967
Roman Catholic	32.6	34.7	32.5	24.0	25.8	35.6	8 667
Other Protestant	38.2	31.2	39.6	32.8	20.0	43.4	6 233
Major Protestant	43.1	34.4	52.6	52.1	58.1	52.0	9 733
No Religious Preference	33.2	41.4	31.1	28.9	18.3	33.5	13 467

Source: Statistics Canada, *1991 Census of Canada.* Public Use Microdata File, Individuals.

who are less ethnically connected by virtue of their identity with the more Canadian churches or no church at all. In addition, the cross-tabular analysis has shown the significance of age at immigration, which tends to favour those who were under 13 years of age, for the attainment of educational and economic status for the foreign-born of both European and non-European origins.

The analysis of the relationship between ethnic-group membership (ethnic-connectedness) and socio-economic-status attainment appears to be somewhat obfuscated by the difficulties in differentiating between "traditional ethnic" and "Canadian" churches, as well as confounded by what appears to be the results of a more selective application of educational and occupational criteria in determining admissibility of the more visible-minority immigrant groups under Canada's current immigration policy. Though census-based measures of ethnic connectedness are indirect and lacking in precision, and the analysis exploratory and descriptive, the results would appear to be sufficiently consistent with the general working hypothesis to warrant further research on the significance of ethnic-group membership (or connectedness) for access to and full participation in the educational and opportunity structures in an officially multicultural society such as Canada. In a society that has officially proclaimed itself to be multicultural, the retention of distinctive ethnic traits and cultural patterns would not be expected to unduly deny any individual access to society's social and economic opportunity structure. However, the evidence to date still suggests that being more ethnic, regardless of origin, presents more obstacles to educational and socio-economic-status achievement than being less ethnically oriented or committed.

NOTES
▼

1. Findings from the 1991 census will also be discussed, but briefly, since the 1991 census data are not totally comparable to the 1981 census data.
2. The ethnic-origin question in the 1981 census referred to the ethnic or cultural group to which the respondent or the respondent's ancestors belonged on coming to this continent. In 1991 the question asked was the same but with the additional instruction: "Mark as many as apply." The outcome was that the proportion of multiple-origin responses increased to about 29 percent in 1991 from about 7 percent in 1981.
3. It has been demonstrated in previous research that the crucial age-at-immigration categories are 0–12, 13–19, and 20+. These were used in previous research and in this paper. The 1991 PUMF Individual File has predetermined categories, that is, 0–14, 15–19, 20+, which are not comparable. The more recent ethnic-origin groups do not necessarily include all of the groups included by the authors in their request for 1981 special tabulations. Cases in point are the Middle Eastern origin group and the Indo-Chinese.

REFERENCES
▼

Anderson, A.B., & Frideres, J.S. (1981). *Ethnicity in Canada: Theoretical perspectives.* Toronto: Butterworths.

Boyd, Monica, Goyer, John, Jones, Frank, McRoberts, Hugh, Pineo, Peter, and Porter, John. (1985). *Ascription and achievement: Studies in mobility and status attainment in Canada.* Ottawa: Carleton University Press.

Darroch, A. Gordon, & Marston, Wilfred G. (1969). Ethnic differentiation: Ecological aspects of a multidimensional concept. *International Migration Review, 4,* 71–95.

Driedger, Leo. (1989). *The ethnic factor: Identity in diversity.* Toronto: McGraw-Hill Ryerson.

Economic Council of Canada. (1991). *Economic and social impacts of immigration.* Ottawa: Minister of Supply & Services.

Greeley, Andrew M. (1971). *Why can't they be like us?* New York: E.P. Dutton.

Inbar, M. (1977). Immigration and learning: The vulnerable age. *Canadian Review of Sociology and Anthropology, 14*, 218–234.

Jones, Frank E. (1987). Age at immigration and education: Further explorations. *International Migration Review, 21*(1), 70–85.

Kalbach, Warren E. (1970). *The impact of immigration on Canada's population.* Ottawa: Information Canada.

Kalbach, Warren E., & Richard, Madeline A. (1980). The differential effects of ethnoreligious structure on linguistic trends and the economic achievement of Ukrainians. In W.R. Petryshyn (Ed.), *Changing realities: Social trends among Ukrainian Canadians* (pp. 78–96). Edmonton: Canadian Institute of Ukrainian Studies.

———. (1985a). Ethnic-connectedness: How binding is the tie? *Heritage Review* (Germans from Russia Heritage Society), *15*(2), 49–54.

———. (1985b). The significance of age at immigration for assimilation. Paper presented at the 8th Biennial Conference of CESA, 17 October.

———. (1988). Ethnic-religious identity, acculturation, and social and economic achievement of Canada's post-war minority populations. *Review of Demography and Its Implications for Economic and Social Policy, 5*, 62–64.

———. (1990). Ethnic and religious identity and acculturation of Canada's post-war minority populations. In Leo Dreidger, Shiva Halli, & Frank Trovato (Eds.), *Ethnic demography* (pp. 179–198). Ottawa: Carleton University Press.

———. (1991a). Ethnic-religious identification and generation as correlates of acculturation and socio-economic attainment. In Robin Ostrow, Jürgen Fijalkowski, Y. Michael Bodeman, & Hans Merken (Eds.), *Ethnic structured inequality, and the state in Canada and the Federal Republic of Germany* (pp. 29–48). Frankfurt am Main: Peter Lang.

———. (1991b). The religious dimension of minority group assimilation in Canada. In Jürgen Fijalkowski, Hans Merken, & Folker Schmidt (Eds.), *Dominant national cultures and ethnic identities* (pp. 145–155). Berlin: Freie Universitat Berlin.

Kornacker, Mildred. (1971). Cultural significance of intermarriage: A comparative approach. *International Journal of the Sociology of the Family,* Special Issue, 147–156.

Li, Peter S. (1988). *Ethnic inequality in a class society.* Toronto: Wall & Thompson.

Porter, John. (1965). *The vertical mosaic: An analysis of social class and power in Canada.* Toronto: University of Toronto Press.

Richard, Madeline A. (1991). *Ethnic groups and marital choices.* Vancouver: UBC Press.

Richmond, A.H., & Kalbach, W.E. (1980). *Factors in the adjustment of immigrants and their descendants.* Ottawa: Minister of Supply & Services.

Ryder, N. (1955). The interpretation of origin statistics. *Canadian Journal of Economic and Political Science, 21*(4), 466–479.

Statistics Canada. (1982). *Census Dictionary.* Ottawa: Statistics Canada.

Yinger, Milton J. (1985). Ethnicity. *Annual Review of Sociology, 11*, 151–180.

PART FOUR

POWER AND INEQUALITY

INTRODUCTION

The study of ethnic stratification involves the examination of inequalities among ethnic groups. Part Four addresses inequality in terms of access to the power structures of Canadian society in a relatively general sense, and to the power structure of the Canadian economy. Chapter Thirteen deals with Aboriginal peoples, and Chapter Fourteen examines the ways in which ethnicity or race plays a role in how income becomes distributed in Canadian society. In Chapter Fifteen, Danielle Juteau examines the emergence of Quebec in terms of nation-ness. Chapter Sixteen examines the differences in prestige accorded some ethnic groups not only by themselves, but also by the majority group, in Montreal, Quebec.

James Frideres (Chapter Thirteen) examines what he calls "fault lines" in Aboriginal–white relations. He argues that the study of Aboriginal people not only provides an understanding of them as a people, but also broadens one's understanding of minority groups in general. Frideres begins with a historical overview of Aboriginal–white relations, then proceeds to a demographic profile of Aboriginals in Canada and an analysis of the activities both within Aboriginal communities, and between Aboriginals and the dominant society. Frideres reveals the complexity of the relationship between Aboriginals and the latter. He compares reserve Aboriginals with those who have become urbanites. He looks at the role of government regarding land claims, the lack of access Canada's Aboriginals have to the power structure of the Canadian economy.

Ellen Gee and Steven Prus (Chapter Fourteen) use the 1994 Survey of Labour and Income Dynamics to examine the relationship between income inequality and ethnicity. They use multiple indicators of ethnicity, including ethnicity/race, mother tongue, and place of birth, in order to ascertain whether differences in income can be attributed to ethnocultural background. In addition, they examine differences in income levels within groups. Other factors such as occupation, education, and labour-force participation were examined to see whether these characteristics influenced income inequalities. Gee and Prus are able to show that Canada's mosaic has been rearranged since the 1960s, following Porter's research.

Danielle Juteau (Chapter Fifteen) looks at Quebec and its struggle for nation-ness. In the process, she discusses and defines the concept of "nation" and the types of nationhood with reference to their effects on Canadian thinking, and in particular in the case of Quebec. She takes us through Quebec's quest for a societal model that suited its uniqueness. She argues that both Canada and Quebec have taken the "pluralist turn."

The final chapter in this section explores how members of various minority groups perceive themselves, believe they are perceived, and are actually perceived by majority group members in Quebec in terms of an inclusive label (Quebecer) and two exclusive labels (foreigner, immigrant). The respondents were 293 junior college students in Montreal. They represented French Quebecers (a majority group) and five immigrant groups, including European francophones, Jews, Latin Americans, Southeast Asians, and Haitians. European francophones were found to be most accepted by majority-group members, while visible minorities were the least accepted. Minorities in the group saw themselves more as "Quebecers" and less as "foreigners" and "immigrants" than they actually were. The reverse was shown for Haitians. The potential role of intergroup misperceptions in the marginalization of minorities is also discussed.

13

▼

REVELATION AND REVOLUTION: FAULT LINES IN ABORIGINAL—WHITE RELATIONS

JAMES S. FRIDERES

INTRODUCTION
▼

Few legal or political issues have lasted as long or remained so central to Canadians as Aboriginal issues. While all parties agree that issues such as Aboriginal rights are entrenched in our legal system, so many new documents dealing with Aboriginal people have appeared in recent years that the issues appear unresolvable. From what few agreements have been made with Aboriginal peoples, governments and courts have tried to draw out the implications and use these decisions as a basis for future agreements. However, it has been an elusive course, because courts and governments change over time and differ in their understanding of the legal and moral context of Aboriginal issues (Henderson, 1995). In the end, it is difficult to separate myth from reality, fact from fiction. Moreover, increasing alienation from their natural and social environments has nearly overwhelmed the ability of Aboriginal people to effectively function in Canadian society (Borrows, 1997). Over the years, there has been an incoherence, an instability, and a set of contradictions embodied in the approach of various British and Canadian administrators toward the issue of Aboriginal rights (Kulchyski, 1994). There has not been a progressive, linear development of philosophy regarding Aboriginal people by Canadians over the past two centuries.

Kulchyski (1994) argues that, over the past century, Aboriginals in Canada have been subjected to a process of "totalization." This is a process by which people are "ordered" in accordance with a set of principles conducive to the accumulation of capital and the logic of the commodity form, for example, capitalism. Government and courts have thus interpreted documents and defined, fixed, and circumscribed the rights of Aboriginal people as they developed within the new social order. However, it is clear that, in doing so, the courts and the government have not taken Aboriginal interests into account when they have acted. In fact, Macklem (1993) identifies the opportunistic and racist way the state chooses to identify, emphasize, and act upon similarities and differences between Aboriginal and non-Aboriginal peoples. He concludes that government acts in a manner that systematically disadvantages and maintains the marginality of Aboriginal people. As a result, the actions by governments have typified, and continue to do so, a Eurocentric perspective to the exclusion of an alternative worldview.[1] Macklem goes on to argue that having an alternative worldview is not only viewed negatively, but viewed as a hostile stance and one that requires punitive action. As a result, Aboriginal people have been assigned a marginal social niche in Canadian society, and their culture and values have systematically been denigrated. This displacement has come about through time, by intended and fortuitous events, by changing government policy, and by the actions of Aboriginal people themselves.

ABORIGINAL PEOPLE
▼

Why study Aboriginal people? What will be gained by focussing on one specific ethnocultural group? How can the analysis of one group add to the knowledge base of ethnic relations? The answer is multifaceted. First, the study of this group will provide the reader with a description of the conditions of Aboriginal people in Canadian society. Thus, comparisons with other ethnocultural groups can be made. Second, the study of Aboriginal people aids our understanding of historical processes that impinge upon minority groups. Third, it is instructive to discover the extent to which a group of people can be impoverished and forced to live at the margins of society without presenting a threat to the operation of the larger society. Fourth, the lack of any serious conflict between Aboriginals and other Canadians for over a century suggests that social-control mechanisms implemented by the dominant group have been successful. Finally, by focussing our attention on Aboriginal peoples, we are able to examine the nature, process, and extent of factionalization within an ethnic group, for example, the tension among Indians, Métis, and Inuit, and the implications. For example, we can look at the differences between urban and rural Aboriginals, between status and non-Status Indians, between treaty and non-treaty, and the differences among Aboriginals who live near urban areas versus those who live in isolated, rural communities. We will find within Aboriginal communities those who have obtained positions of power and those who have not. All these differences have, at times, come to play an important part in their relationship with the dominant society and the actions taken by Aboriginals. In summary, the study of Aboriginal people will allow us to understand the importance of history, comparative analysis, and the dynamics of both intra- and intergroup interaction in understanding ethnic relations.

To facilitate our analysis, we will begin with a brief historical review of Aboriginal–white relations. This will be followed by a demographic profile that will characterize the group within Canadian society. Finally, we will analyze the activities both within Aboriginal communities, and between Aboriginals and the dominant society.

HISTORICAL BACKGROUND
▼

Aboriginals living on the eastern seaboard of Canada were the first to experience contact when Europeans first arrived in North America. The initial contact was sporadic and symbiotic, with some tension, but both parties benefitting from the initial interaction, However, as Europeans continued to intrude on the lives of Aboriginals, they attempted to establish formal social relations with them. As a result, several Treaties of Peace and Friendship were negotiated between Indians and the French and English,[2] and this approach to Indian–white relations was carried on into the eighteenth and nineteenth centuries as both the French and the English courted Indians as allies.

After the conflict between the English and French subsided and more Europeans began to settle the land, Aboriginals became less important or influential in Canadian politics. In fact, Indians began to be viewed as a threat to further Euro-Canadian settlement and development of the land. It was at this time the young government of Canada took a more colonial perspective when dealing with Aboriginals. There also was a debate as to whether Indians should be isolated or integrated, and social experiments reflecting both philosophies were undertaken. In the end, it was agreed that isolation (the creation of reserves) was the preferred strategy, with the mistaken belief that if Indians were placed on isolated land areas, they would disappear (both literally and figuratively) in a generation or two, which in turn would free up all the land set aside for further development by new immigrants. To orderly and peacefully enact this philosophy, a series of numbered treaties were established with Indians.

In the beginning (1850s), the treaties focussed on small land areas in southern Ontario. However, given the size of Canada and the need to obtain major land areas for immigrant settlement, eleven major treaties were signed with Indians. These eleven treaties, over a time span of 50 years (1875–1921), covered most of the area of Canada between Ontario and Alberta, as well as much of the Mackenzie valley of the Northwest Territories. In addition, parts of Yukon and northern B.C. were included. Since much of the Atlantic provinces were covered by "Peace and Friendship" treaties, and Quebec was dealt with by the Royal Proclamation of 1763, only British Columbia, Yukon, and the Northwest Territories remained unclaimed by the government of Canada.

Once established, the treaties in Ontario became templates for those that followed, with some notable differences. For example, in some treaties, land allocation was 640 acres per family, while in others it was much less. Nevertheless, the overall content of the treaties is remarkably similar. On the one hand, the government of Canada would provide land, social and medical services, some financial compensation, and a variety of other services. In return, the Indians would give up their ownership to much of the land, maintain peace and good order, and carry out their daily lives within a Canadian political and economic framework. In addition to the formal written texts of the treaties, there were verbal promises made by the spokesperson for the government of Canada and chief of the tribe, promises never written down. The specifics of these promises remain unknown. Needless to say, many Aboriginal issues hinging on claims of "verbal promises" have become major points of concern for Aboriginal people today.

DEALING WITH ABORIGINALS

▼

The federal government has utilized many different strategies to deal with Aboriginal people over the past century. Starting with a belief in assimilation, they soon moved to a policy of segregation. This was followed by a period of wardship and protection that lasted a century, ending in the mid-twentieth century. For example, in 1888, Aboriginal title became constrained because of the courts, interpretation that the Crown "owned" all the land, and Aboriginal people merely have some undefined legal interest in it. After World War II, a new policy of democratization and integration was implemented. This period was highlighted by the government's introduction of the 1969 White Paper that attempted to do away with Indian status, and the Department of Indian Affairs, and treat all Aboriginals as though they were equal to other Canadian citizens. The subsequent reaction to this proposal by Aboriginal people, and a consortium of religious groups, civil rights organizations, and concerned citizens, stopped the implementation of such a policy. Today, we have moved to a "self-government" model in which the federal government is prepared to give some measure of control to Aboriginal communities in selected areas, for example, by-laws, provision of some social services, building permits. However, the extent to which Aboriginals will be given more control remains to be seen.

The federal government has taken the position that Aboriginals do not know what is in their best interest and thus has developed strategies to regulate all aspects of Indian life. This perspective and underlying assumption of the federal government has meant that the state has implemented a form of coercive tutelage designed to control and effect the social, economic, and cultural transformation of Aboriginal peoples and their communities. The goal was, and continues to be, to rid Indians of their Indianness and make them indistinguishable from other Canadians (Dyck, 1997). This system of tutelage has been resisted by Aboriginals and has not been successful. Moreover, today, Aboriginal leaders use the legacy of tutelage in negotiations with government as a moral suasion force to obtain their objectives. At the same time, the government of Canada uses the "rule of existing law" as their major tool in negotiating with Aboriginal people.[3]

THE SOCIAL DEMOGRAPHY OF ABORIGINALS
▼

This section presents a brief demographic profile of Aboriginal people in Canada. Today there are about 600 000 registered Indians, 100 000 Métis, and 40 000 Inuit in Canada. If we add to that the number of non-official Aboriginal people, the number exceeds 1.5 million.[4] Registered Indians are dispersed throughout Canada, and many reside on the 2326 reserves, which comprise about 2.75 million hectares of land. Another group, the Métis, are likewise spread across the country, but only Alberta recognizes them as legal entities. Table 13.1 reveals the total number of registered Indians (on and off the reserve) as well as the average annual growth rates over the past decade. Two major trends about residence emerge from the data that require further comment. First, we find that today fewer than six out of ten registered Indians now live on a reserve, compared with nine out of ten in the 1960s. Second, there is a very high growth rate for the off-reserve population, particularly between 1986 and 1990. This high rate is a result of the passage of Bill C-31 in 1985, which restored Indian status and membership rights to many individuals and their children.

TABLE 13.1
▼
REGISTERED INDIAN POPULATION AND AVERAGE ANNUAL GROWTH RATES (AAGR) ON/OFF RESERVE, CANADA, 1997–1995 (REVISED)

Year	On Reserve[a]			Off Reserve			Total		
	Number	Percent	AAGR	Number	Percent	AAGR	Number	Percent	AAGR
1977	214 216	72.4	1.92	81 682	27.6	3.40	295 898	100	2.34
1982	235 640	70.9	2.64	96 538	29.1	8.84	332 178	100	4.60
1987[b]	268 474	64.6	1.97	147 424	35.4	15.39	415 898	100	6.73
1988	273 766	61.7	2.16	170 118	38.3	9.73	443 884	100	5.06
1989	279 671	60.0	4.84	186 666	40.0	5.52	466 337	100	5.11
1990	293 204	59.8	3.94	196 974	40.2	5.11	490 178	100	4.41
1991	304 759	59.5	3.58	207 032	40.5	5.20	511 791	100	4.23
1992	315 663	59.2	3.42	217 798	40.8	4.17	533 461	100	3.72
1993	326 444	59.0	3.12	226 872	41.0	4.47	533 316	100	3.68
1994	336 643	58.7	3.35	237 014	41.3	3.42	573 657	100	3.38
1995	347 919	58.7	—	245 131	41.3	—	593 050	100	—

a On reserve includes Crown lands and settlements.
b In 1985, *The Indian Act* was amended to allow, through Bill C-31, the restoration of Indian status to those who had been enfranchised as a result of clauses in the *Indian Act*.

Source: Department of Indian Affairs and Northern Development, Indian Register, various years.

Figure 13.1 identifies the population by region. It shows that, in most regions of the country, the Aboriginal population has doubled over the past two decades. Nearly one quarter of the Indian population reside in Ontario, half are in the Prairies, and about 17 percent in British Columbia. The remainder are dispersed throughout the other regions. Today, over one third of registered Indians live in urban centres, while about 45 percent are considered rural. The remainder live in remote or special-access areas.[5]

Figure 13.2 reveals the age–sex distribution of the Aboriginal population as well as the general Canadian population. It demonstrates the youthfulness, and the demographic and economic potential of the Aboriginal population over the next decade. Today, nearly half of the Aboriginal population is less

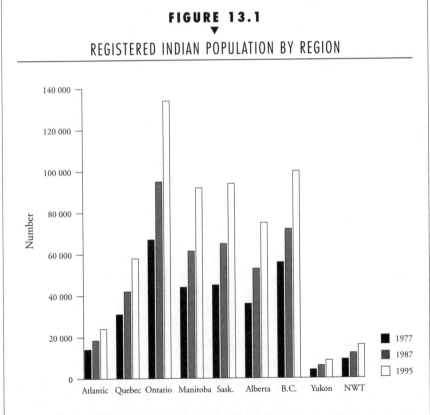

FIGURE 13.1
▼
REGISTERED INDIAN POPULATION BY REGION

Source: Department of Indian Affairs and Northern Development. *Basic Departmental Data, 1996* (Ottawa: Information Quality and Research Directorate, Information Branch, January 1997), Table 3, p. 9. Reproduced with the permission of the Minister of Public Works and Government Services Canada, 1999.

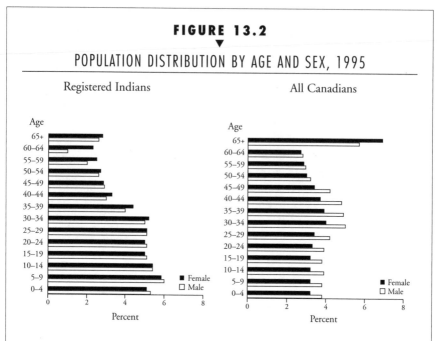

FIGURE 13.2

▼

POPULATION DISTRIBUTION BY AGE AND SEX, 1995

Source: Department of Indian Affairs and Northern Development. *Basic Departmental Data, 1996* (Ottawa: Information Quality and Research Directorate, Information Branch, January 1997), Table 8, p. 21. Reproduced with the permission of the Minister of Public Works and Government Services Canada, 1999.

than 25 years of age, and less than 5 percent are over the age of 65. This finding should be viewed in comparison with the general population, of which about one third are less than 25, and more than 12 percent are over 65. Life expectancy is clearly affected by these figures: it is true that Aboriginal men live about ten years less (die at age 69) than the average Canadian male, while females live about six years less (76) than the average Canadian female. These disparate figures result from mortality rates that reveal higher rates for Aboriginals in every "cause" of death with the exception of certain kinds of cancer.

The educational profile of Aboriginal people reveals major strides in educational attainment. Today nearly 80 percent of the registered Indian population between ages 4 and 18 are attending kindergarten, elementary, or secondary schools. About 75 percent of students remain in school until Grade 12, whereas, in 1960, the proportion was about 3 percent. At the same time, Indians are gaining control over their elementary and secondary schools. In the early 1970s, fewer than 50 schools were controlled by bands. Today, more than 400 schools are band operated. The number in post-secondary educational institutions also reveals major changes. In 1977, about 5 percent of the registered Indian and Inuit population were enrolled in post-secondary education institutions. Today, about one quarter are enrolled in post-secondary educational programs. We find that the post-secondary enrollment rate for registered Indians aged 17–34 continues to increase (6.0 percent to 6.5 percent from 1993 to 1995). However, the general Canadian population rate has increased from 10.1 to 10.4, revealing an increasing disparity in post-secondary education enrollment.

The achievement of a minimum quality of life depends upon an individual's ability to participate in the labour force and obtain fair market compensation for his or her contribution. In 1991, the latest set of data available, we find that fewer than half of the registered Indians in Canada, aged 15 and older, participated in the wage labour force. We also find major discrepancies between the income of Aboriginal and non-Aboriginal people.[6] It also is known that Aboriginal labour force participation is part-time and seasonal in nature. The incomes for individuals reflects both the type and the extent of involvement in the labour force. Given these findings, it is no surprise to find that the median income for on reserve males and females was $8933 and $10 403, while for the general Canadian population the respective figures were $25 571 and $13 565 (Statistics Canada, 1994).

THE ROLE OF CAPITALISM AND THE EMERGENCE OF TRANSNATIONAL CORPORATIONS
▼

SOCIAL DOMINATION

When treaties were signed, Indians were relegated to areas of land set aside for them by the federal government. In addition, the Indian Act was created as a policy document by which relations with Indians would be carried out. It started out by defining who was and was not an Indian, and then moved to documenting how the government would treat Indians in every aspect of their lives.

Thus, the current social location of Aboriginal people in Canadian society is a result of historical events, both planned and fortuitous. However, it should be clear that the current emergent world capitalist economy has achieved a hegemony unprecedented in human history. Through a series of planned and fortuitous events, an economic reality has been created, capable of spontaneous regeneration, of expansion through time and space, that has grown unchecked into the worldwide sphere of economic control

(Goehring, 1993). While Europeans have had the opportunity to accommodate themselves to the assumptions and philosophy of capitalism over time, Aboriginal people had no time to adjust to the new worldview and as a result, have found the new ideology frustrating and difficult to internalize. For example, it is hard to believe that all Aboriginals over the age of 38 experienced the time in Canada's history when Aboriginal people were prevented from voting in federal elections.

Today's capitalism represents the consequence of structural arrangements of Canadian society that placed Aboriginals in a peripheral position. While, at the time of contact, Aboriginal people had much to offer the colonists, within a few years the symbiotic relationship would change to one of domination–oppression. As Canada developed its land and resources, Aboriginal people were placed outside the economic and political framework, and prevented from entering the mainstream system. For example, in the early twentieth century, various agricultural lobbying groups representing white farmers convinced the government that providing support for Aboriginals in the area of agriculture would be unfair competition. Consequently, the government withdrew its financial and technical support for Aboriginal people and kept them out of the agricultural arena as possible competitors of white farmers (Carter, 1990). The impact of this early exclusion continues today, and most land controlled by Aboriginals is either pasture, unimproved land, or agricultural land that is leased by non-Aboriginals.

Moreover, over time the inequalities between Aboriginals and non-Aboriginals are becoming larger. The distance that separated the standard of living in Aboriginal communities from that of the dominant group in the mid-nineteenth century was smaller than the socio-economic distance that separates them today. Aboriginal communities will need to grow more rapidly economically if they are to maintain their current position. However, today the old-style colonialism is no longer necessary, as economic penetration into the reserves has been complete. Dependency is a situation with which Aboriginal communities have to deal every day. Their economy is controlled by the development and expansion of another economy, to which Aboriginals must adjust (dos Santos, 1968). To illustrate this, we note that 28 percent (167/585) of the Indian bands have entered into remedial management agreements with the government, with a cumulated debt of nearly $140 million.

Investments that are made on reserves can be either direct (private investment on the reserve, which gives them ownership and control of the process of production) or indirect (through social-welfare programs). The federal government has vacillated between the two strategies, although the latter is perhaps the most prominent today. Moreover, reserves have always been subjected to the process of "backwash effects" as market forces have drained them in terms of both physical and social resources. This results in reserves having a dependent relationship with the dominant society. Dependency is a result of three processes: exploitation, structural distortion, and suppression of autonomous policies (Chase-Dunn, 1975). Today, any investment by private capital ensures that any surplus created will be drained from the reserve back to the source of the investment. For example, the placement of a charter bank on the reserve may provide some jobs for local residents, but it also increases the bank's profit, and removes savings from the local community. This decapitalization ensures a dependency position for Aboriginal people.

The second process of structural distortion occurs through the development of an outward-oriented economy, especially those that specialize in the production of raw materials. This means that major developments on reserves today usually involve raw materials that are removed from the reserve, for example, timber, gas, and gravel. Since all other goods must be purchased from vendors outside the reserve, this reinforces an imbalance of trade for Aboriginal communities. This imbalance retards the integration of reserves into the national economy and keeps them dependent upon the larger economy. Finally, through the suppression of autonomous policies on reserves, local Aboriginal leaders are unable to achieve balanced development.[7]

Because Aboriginal communities are spread throughout Canada, it is nearly impossible for individual band councils to cope with the negotiating power of major national and international corporations as well as the domestic monolithic bureaucratic structures, for example, the Indian Affairs department. Direct investments in reserves have followed a pattern of exploitation of natural resources to be utilized as raw materials by the industries of the dominant society. When economic ventures in Aboriginal communities developed the infrastructure that would produce profits, they have been exported back to the dominant society, whence the capital originally came. In short, when investments in Aboriginal communities are made by outside corporations, they are done to maintain the economic and political influence of those corporations, and they present a major obstacle to the economic development of these communities. The federal government's rejection of providing funds for Aboriginals to become involved in the agricultural sector in the late nineteenth and early twentieth centuries is ample evidence that the process of domination was early and effective.

The federal government continues to balk at investing in Aboriginal enterprises. Thus, a second strategy employed by capital investors is to establish a common interest between themselves and the Aboriginal elite. If benefits are possible for Aboriginal elites, investments by external parties are encouraged and sustained. As such, certain factions within Aboriginal communities establish and maintain relations with the private sector. This places an additional burden on the community in that the elites control and benefit from such a relationship, while the remainder of the community has little say in the process and gains no benefit. The consequence of this has been the creation of a two-tiered class system on the reserves: a very small, elite group and a large, poor group. The alliance of the corporate interests with those of "leaders" of the community enables the system to continue.

To maintain control over subordinate groups, the state uses both positive and negative sanctions. Among the positive forces is the co-optation process by which the elites of an Aboriginal community are allowed to participate marginally in existing power structures and derive a reward, in exchange for "modernization" (Etzioni-Halevy, 1990). Various strategies have been employed to facilitate such investments, for example, joint ventures and management contracts. These strategies have been facilitated and supported by the federal government, since it decreases their fiscal commitment to Aboriginal people, increases the dependency of Aboriginals on the dominant economy, and thus facilitates assimilation, providing indicators that demonstrate Aboriginals are integrating into the dominant economy. Under all of these structural arrangements, formal authority continues to be concentrated in the administrative structures of the dominant economy, and local residents have less say in the future developments of their community.

One consequent of such an economic relationship is the sustainability of an Aboriginal elite that brings about patron (elite)–client relationships. For example, clients must continually support the actions of the patron if they are to expect continued support. If jobs are available, only clients that actively support the patron will be eligible. This ultimately fragments the community into those who support the elite and external development agents and those who do not. In the end, there is considerable tension and conflict within Aboriginal communities as different factions compete for scarce rewards. In the case of the elites, the conflict is not based upon issues, but on the pursuit of personal ambition. Further complicating are the federal government and the courts, which intervene on a regular basis and attempt to mediate the self-interests exhibited by the elites and the private sector. The recent investigations of Aboriginal communities and their fiscal activities reflect the active intervention of the state. At the same time, the state needs the elites to accomplish their goals of providing Aboriginals some necessities of life because someone has to take leadership positions within the community.

There has been a constant, although not consistent, policy by the government to "proletarianize the Aboriginal" in that they have worked at severing the ties with the traditional sector. This has been facilitated by developing a wage or money economy on the reserve. This means they must ensure that incomes derived from wage employment (or through social-welfare subsidies) are high enough to make the Aboriginal uninterested in the maintenance of reciprocal obligations in the traditional sector. Until recently, the private sector was not interested in investing on reserves and, even today, the investments are a result of unique opportunities in which the corporations feel they can profit. To facilitate that development, the federal government has provided incentives to both the private sector and the Aboriginal elites. Today's developments involve an implicit assumption that the new investments are capital-intensive and thus will not require the labour services of the resident population.[8] In many developments, the lack of need for unskilled workers has made Aboriginals a nonentity in the labour force.

Aboriginal communities on reserves remain economically and politically weak. Yet as we have noted, today's government is poised to provide more autonomy for local Aboriginal communities. Why? Is this a way of reducing dependency? The answer is no. First of all, the intervention of the courts has given Aboriginal communities more control over their natural resources. Second, new technology is once again making reserves irrelevant in today's economy. Finally, the movement of over half the Aboriginal population into urban centres means that reserves are becoming of less and less interest economically to major economic institutions. Aboriginals are no longer important because of their ethnicity, but are important because of their contribution to the secondary labour reserve. As such, new strategies will come to bear on urban Indians that are quite different from those used with rural Aboriginals.

Aboriginals continue to be peripheral to centres of economic and political power in Canada. There are two major mechanisms that continue to support the structure. First, there is an asymmetrical relationship in benefits. Second, there is a lack of integration of the reserves, which means they cannot co-ordinate their activities when dealing with the centre. As a result, they are marginal in almost every aspect of Canadian society, ranging from economic to political. They occupy the lowest rungs of the stratification system in having low educational attainments and low occupational status, and remain outside the primary labour force. This marginal existence has been thoroughly analyzed by social scientists, and they have demonstrated its debilitating influence in higher death rates, lower educational attainments, more illness, and shorter life (Boldt, 1993; Frideres, 1998; Satzewich & Wotherspoon, 1993).

CHANGING FORCES IN CANADIAN SOCIETY
▼

Until the 1970s, the federal government steadfastly held the position that Aboriginal land claims were gestures of symbolic importance only to Aboriginal people. The Canadian government successfully argued that the claims had no legal force, and only on rare occasions were Aboriginal claims accepted by the courts. However, this would all change in the early 1970s, when a group of Nisga'a Indians in British Columbia, pursuing their land rights for nearly a century, were able to have the Supreme Court of Canada hear their case. The 1973 *Calder* decision saw the Supreme Court rule, for the first time in our history, that Aboriginal title existed in law. As a result of this decision, the government was forced to reassess its position and develop a new limited "Aboriginal rights" policy. This landmark ruling forced the government of Canada to negotiate with Aboriginals across Canada over a variety of claims, further opening up the issue of Aboriginal rights. By 1982, Aboriginal "existing rights" were enshrined in the Canadian Constitution, which is now the basis for determining what those rights are.

Since the 1973 Supreme Court ruling, a series of legal cases have been dealt with by a range of courts, most of whom have sided with the Aboriginal peoples. These court decisions have bolstered the confidence of Aboriginal people with regard to their challenge of government. However, it is also clear to many Aboriginal people that the use of the courts to settle disputes with federal or provincial governments will take years, often more than the lifetime of any single individual. In addition, using the courts is an expensive procedure in which the outcome is unknown. This was made clear in the recent *Delgamuukw* decision. Moreover, the courts themselves are reluctant to hear these cases and have noted that many Aboriginal concerns should be dealt with through the political process and not through the courts. On the other hand, there is no doubt in the minds of most Aboriginal people that major court decisions such as the *Calder, Sparrow, Guerin, Nowegijick,* and *Sioui* have established the legitimacy of Aboriginal claims and forced the government to negotiate with them.

On the other hand, many Aboriginal people believe that their best chance for survival and obtaining the goals they have set out is by working within the existing political system. The actions of Elija Harper, a Cree and member of the Manitoba legislature, typify this belief. He was, through the withholding of his vote in the provincial legislature, able to defeat the federal government's attempt to pass a new constitutional amendment — The Meech Lake Accord (Mallea, 1994). While this example is extreme, it supports the belief of some Aboriginals that it is possible to effect change from within the

BOX 13.1
▼
LAND-CLAIMS SETTLEMENTS IN BRITISH COLUMBIA

In 1996, the B.C. government established the Treaty Negotiation Advisory Committee to provide input and advice to the government with regard to settling land claims by the Nisga'a, a claim that had begun over 100 years ago, when, in 1887, Nisga'a leaders travelled to Victoria to plead for a treaty giving them assured access to land they had occupied for millennia. This 31-member advisory committee, comprised of individuals from business, tourism, labour, recreation, and local government, provided advice for the government as it carried out negotiations with the Nisga'a.

The agreement has been ratified by the Nisga'a and B.C. legislature, but the federal government must also agree to it before the agreement is binding. Should this agreement be acceptable, 51 other bands currently in negotiations with the B.C. government (B.C. Treaty Commission) will likely use this as a model. The treaty gives the Nisga'a a central government with the authority to make laws concerning social services (including child and family issues), adoption, and health services, as well as tribal jurisdiction over education (from preschool to post-secondary). The laws to be created by the Nisga'a will have to be in agreement with the provincial laws and comparable to existing B.C. standards. The laws enacted by the Nisga'a will have standing in any court dispute, which means that the B.C. courts will consider Nisga'a law in determining a settlement.

In addition, the Nisga'a will administer and deliver federal and provincial social services. The specific manner in which this will take place has yet to be determined, and will require the agreement and support of the provincial and federal governments.

The land area involved in this agreement (nearly 2000 square kilometres of land) covers an area about half the size of Nova Scotia, but one tenth of what the Nisga'a wanted. Because one half of the Nisga'a live outside the Lower Nass valley, they will receive fishing and forestry rights as well as the right to set up their own government, policing, and courts. In addition, nearly $200 million will be provided, as well as an additional $40 million for road construction into and within the Lower Nass valley.

Under the agreement, the Nisga'a will continue to provide the services they have been taking over, but will now have full jurisdiction over them. The services will be funded through federal transfer payments. As soon as the Nisga'a begin to generate their own income through taxation and other fees, the amount of federal funds will be commensurately decreased. While, on the face of it, the agreement suggests that the Nisga'a will be a municipality, the fact that they will have control over social services, health, and education makes them different from a municipality, and thus provoked considerable debate in the country. For example, section 27 of the agreement (focussing on language and culture of the Nisga'a) notes that, in the event of an inconsistency between the Nisga'a laws and federal and provincial laws of general application, Nisga'a laws will prevail. The agreement also stipulates that voting rights on Native territory will be restricted to people of Nisga'a descent.

system. Thus, participation in politics and other mainstream institutions is viewed as necessary to obtain the results desired.

One of the most important areas where Aboriginal people have achieved some success is in their land claims. Prior to the 1970s, few land claims were taken seriously, and even fewer were settled. However, after the Supreme Court's ruling, the government and the courts began to deal with the claims. Figure 13.3 reveals the status of specific and treaty land-entitlement claims. The data show that, over the past two decades, one quarter have been settled, while many more are in the process of being settled. It also shows that less than 20 percent have been rejected, thus giving some credence to the claims being put forward by Aboriginals. Nearly 400 additional claims are still under review or under negotiation, and it is estimated that, in British Columbia alone, the value of the claims exceeds $10 billion. In a recent case (1997), the Supreme Court of Canada confirmed (in the Gitxsan and Wet'suwet'en — including the Delgamuukw — clans in British Columbia) the existence in prin-

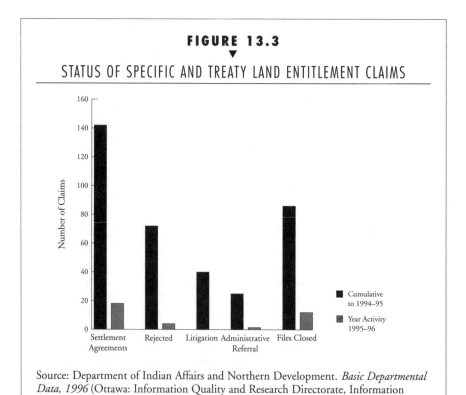

FIGURE 13.3
▼
STATUS OF SPECIFIC AND TREATY LAND ENTITLEMENT CLAIMS

Source: Department of Indian Affairs and Northern Development. *Basic Departmental Data, 1996* (Ottawa: Information Quality and Research Directorate, Information Branch, January 1997), Table 47, p. 3. Reproduced with the permission of the Minister of Public Works and Government Services Canada, 1999.

ciple of Aboriginal title to traditional territories. It ruled that Aboriginal title does exist. However, it went on to say that specific claims must be proven on a "case-by-case" basis.

As the court decisions and political agreements begin to take effect, Aboriginal people are developing strategies to achieve self-determination and implement self-government,[9] establishing new organizations and structures as a path to this goal. However, given the paucity of funds available to them, band councils are attempting to find novel structures to facilitate the process. Before these structures can be put in place, a clear definition, and an agreement by all parties, of what "rights" are needs to be established.

ABORIGINAL RIGHTS
▼

Aboriginal rights can be thought to have two sources: from Aboriginal people's prior and immemorial occupancy of the Americas, or from the Royal Proclamation of 1763.[10] While the first criterion needs little additional support, the second does. Legal documents such as the Royal Proclamation, the British North America Act, the Indian Act, and various treaties, are crucial for developing legal arguments respecting the nature and origins of Aboriginal rights. The courts consistently refer to these legal documents as well as to a new document, the Constitution Act, 1982, that has recently been added to this list. There is little question by either historians or the courts that, historically, Aboriginal peoples had their own forms of government, social organization, and economies (Isaac, 1995). As such, the Supreme Court of Canada has decided that Aboriginal title was not dependent upon legislative enactments, executive orders, or treaties. Rather, Aboriginal title is a legal right derived from the Indians' historic occupation and possession of their tribal lands. However, Aboriginal title is an issue for debate only in those areas where treaties have not been signed or where the issue of extinguishment of Aboriginal title is still in question, for example, British Columbia and the Northwest Territories (Isaac, 1995).

THE ROYAL COMMISSION ON ABORIGINAL PEOPLES
▼

In 1991, the Royal Commission on Aboriginal Peoples was established with a mandate to examine the treatment and position of Aboriginals in Canadian society, both past and present, in all aspects of their life. They were asked to make recommendations as to how Aboriginal Canadians could be more fully integrated into Canadian society.[11] Five years later, the commission completed its assignment and reported to the Canadian people. In the meantime, several special reports were commissioned to deal with issues such as suicide and justice. In the end, the commission made nearly 500 recommendations to the federal government.

The recommendations are wide-reaching and touch upon all aspects of Aboriginal life. However, some of these recommendations were viewed as having high priority and, unless they were undertaken, other actions recommended would not be successful. What were these high-priority recommendations? By far the most important recommendation was the call for an increase in the resources allocated to Aboriginal affairs. Even though today's federal allocation is nearly $6 billion annually, the commission noted that a substantial increase in budget was required. It noted that Aboriginals' lack of economic integration, for example, lost productivity, lost income, lost potential taxes, and increased health risks, cost the Canadian government about $7 billion per year, or $140 billion over a twenty-year period. Moreover, they noted that, if nothing was done to deal with Aboriginal poverty, the annual bill would escalate to $11 billion per year in twenty years. Thus, their recommendation for an additional $1.5 billion in spending for each of the next seven years, and $2 billion for each of the remaining thirteen years, would add $36.5 billion to the budget over twenty years. Nevertheless, it would substantially reduce the current projected outlay of at least $140 billion.

The commission went on to recommend a first ministers' conference with Aboriginal people to best determine how these funds might be allocated. The commission also suggested that community infrastructure and education be dealt with before other issues could be satisfactorily solved. They recognized that other issues, such as consultations, research, land claims negotiations, and the development of a youth strategy, could take place only if Aboriginal people had sufficient education and an infrastructure established to ensure a minimum quality of life. It was felt that, unless these recommendations were accepted, many other recommendations would be in jeopardy.

The second-highest-priority recommendation of the commission was that the government of Canada draft a Royal Proclamation (supplementing the Constitution and updating the Royal Proclamation of 1763) and develop a new Aboriginal–government framework. At this time, it is unknown how the government has responded to the first recommendation, but it has tried to address the second through the publication of a document *Gathering Strength — Canada's Aboriginal Action Plan.*

The royal commission also recommended new organizations and legislation to support Aboriginal organizations. For example, it recommended the establishment of an Aboriginal Parliament that would provide advice to the House of Commons and Senate. In addition, it recommended the abolition of the Department of Indian Affairs and Northern Development while simultaneously creating two new structures: the Department of Aboriginal Relations and the Department of Indian and Inuit Services. Within the first new department, two new offices would emerge — the Crown Treaty office and the Aboriginal Lands and Treaties Tribunal.

To bring about the above changes, new legislation and government structures would be required. In addition to the new Royal Proclamation, new legislation such as the Companion Treaty Legislation (a statement of how historical treaties are to be interpreted), and the Aboriginal Nations Recognition and Government Act (to identify how Aboriginals can advance to "nation status") would have to be passed. Other minor pieces of legislation addressing issues such as heritage sites, cultural artifacts, protection of intellectual property, and Aboriginal-language broadcasting rights also are recommended. All the above pieces of legislation would lead to the recognition of Aboriginal people as a "distinct society" and one that can exercise self-determination and self-government.

The commission also felt that a new morality for Canadians would result if the new proposed structures and legislation were put in place. These new structures would influence the values and ideologies of Canadians with regard to how they treat Aboriginal people. These new "laws" would be educational in nature and help Canadians see the wisdom of ensuring justice and fairness for Aboriginal people. In the end, the commission felt that, if the recommendations were accepted, there would be a reallocation of resources that would allow Aboriginal people to integrate into Canadian society. As the commission noted, if new institutional structures were put in place, three aspects of social change would be able to take place in Aboriginal communities: healing, improvements in economic opportunities, and human resource development.

THE GOVERNMENT'S RESPONSE
▼

Thus far, the government argues it will not increase the base budget for Aboriginal affairs but will add to the overall budget through "envelope" funding targetted for specific and limited-term activities. However, the federal government published *Gathering Strength — Canada's Aboriginal Action Plan* (1998) as a result of the recommendation of the Royal Commission on Aboriginal Peoples. In addition, the Assembly of First Nations and the government of

Canada agreed to embark upon a renewed relationship, captured in the document *An Agenda for Action with First Nations,* which parallels those identified in the *Gathering Strength* document.

The central objective of the *Agenda* is to renew the federal government's relationship with Aboriginal peoples. It also wishes to recognize and strengthen Aboriginal governments, establish a new fiscal relationship, and provide support for Aboriginal communities and individuals. The two parties agree to:

1. develop a trilateral relationship (First Nations, federal, and provincial governments) with regard to new treaties. These new treaties would establish integrated processes on a regional level to deal with governance and jurisdictional issues;
2. develop a national and regional protocol with the Assembly of First Nations that would involve a tripartite process;
3. develop a strategy to deal with the legacy and intergenerational effects of abuse at Indian residential schools;
4. develop a Federal–First Nations Aboriginal Languages program that would preserve and protect First Nations languages, heritage, and cultures;
5. develop an action plan for communication and public education to maintain and build support for the themes and initiatives identified in the *Agenda.*

The federal government seems committed to work out a "government-to-government" relations program that is acceptable to Aboriginal people. These relationships will be consistent with the treaties and recognize the inherent right of self-government, Aboriginal title, and Aboriginal and treaty rights under section 35 of the Constitution Act, 1982. To effectively achieve the goals identified above, the government of Canada has agreed to establish the following initiatives:

a. develop ways to recognize Aboriginal self-government and to establish a framework for working out jurisdictional and intergovernmental relations;
b. develop a Governance Transition Centre to support Aboriginals in developing governance structures, and support capacity-building in Aboriginal communities;
c. create organizational structures to deal with justice and disputed issues as well as create an independent claims body;
d. review current comprehensive claims policy and develop a new process for expediting the process;

e. partner with Aboriginal groups to develop a strategy to deal with lands and resource issues, which would include the exploration of possible methods other than surrenders or extinguishments of Aboriginal rights.

The federal government is also interested in developing equitable and sustainable fiscal relationships with Aboriginal people. This new policy would involve government-to-government transfer of funds that would further legitimate the existence of Aboriginal government. There would also be some revenue-sharing by the provincial governments, which would increase the funds available to Aboriginal communities.

Along with this fiscal restructuring, the federal government is also looking at ways to enhance economic development within Aboriginal communities. This would involve new ways to reduce welfare dependency and increase employability. It would also involve investing in Aboriginal education and training, particularly among the youth. To implement such a strategy, the federal government is planning to work jointly with Aboriginals, industry, the provinces, and municipalities to develop a national "partnering strategy."

At the same time these documents were released, the Minister of Indian Affairs and Northern Development released a "Statement of Reconciliation" on behalf of the government of Canada. The Statement of Reconciliation expresses regret over the way in which the government of Canada treated Aboriginal peoples, including the victims of sexual and physical abuse at residential schools. Along with this statement was a commitment by the government to give Aboriginal communities support for the development of community-based "healing activities." The minister of Indian Affairs acknowledged that the government may have acted in ways and condoned actions by others that injured Aboriginal people. Moreover, the government was sorry for those who experienced the tragedy of physical, sexual, and psychological abuse. A "healing fund" of $350 million was established to help communities develop programs to facilitate the healing process.

Individuals who wish to pursue individual claims against the government, or its agents, must take the government to court and relive the personal and painful matter in a public and adversarial forum. Nevertheless, the litigation approach has been taken by hundreds of former students who have joined class-action suits or have filed individual lawsuits against the federal government. Facilitating this action is the landmark British Columbia court ruling, in June 1998, that declared for the first time that both the federal government and the United Church are legally liable for widespread sexual and physical abuse in a federal Indian school. In the judgement, the federal government and the Church were ordered to compensate about 30 former students.

SELF-GOVERNMENT
▼

The issue of sovereignty and self-government have been on the agenda of Aboriginal peoples for many years. However, as noted previously, it would not be until 1973 that Canada officially agreed that Aboriginal rights are a contested issue and one that had to be dealt with. The government's initial response to the Supreme Court's ruling was to allow the courts to interpret the judgement and see if other cases would stand up under the scrutiny of the courts. Generally speaking, the courts have supported the Supreme Court's interpretation, and thus a political decision has to be made as to what level of self-government can be achieved by Aboriginal communities.

Self-government is usually defined as the basic international legal status of a state that is not subject, within its territorial jurisdiction, to the government of a foreign state or to foreign law other than public international law. Aboriginal self-government means the right to make decisions that are important to the community, not to constituents outside. Aboriginal peoples feel they have the right to make decisions for themselves that are appropriate to their cultural values since they have never surrendered their right to control their own destiny (Kulchyski, 1994). They feel that, whereas decisions made on the basis of the dominant society's ethos draw Aboriginal people further away from their culture, each decision made by Aboriginal people contributes to Aboriginal culture. Because politics has taken on larger-than-life proportions in the lives of Aboriginals, much of the contact between themselves and the government is based upon political issues. As a result, political control has become the major concern of most Aboriginal leaders and almost all other issues now being discussed by either party derives from the struggle over politics (Kulchyski, 1994).

The basis for their claim to self-government resides in the early signed treaties, and Aboriginal peoples argue that these treaties were considered international commitments by participating nations. However, as the social structure of society has changed over time, the authority of treaties has been redefined by the dominant society, from that of binding international agreements to that of domestic ones. Aboriginals argue that, even though this has diminished the status and legal force of treaties, it does not abrogate the promises made by government. Moreover, the federal courts have held that many of these treaties give the Tribes implied protection (Leonard, 1995).

Indigenous peoples who have higher levels of self-government retain most of their natural-resource rights, while those who accept a lower status generally lose jurisdiction over their human and natural resources. The extent to which Aboriginal people have sovereignty reflects their power to protect and preserve their sovereign rights.

Based on the attributes in Table 13.2, Table 13.3 reveals a quantification of the level of sovereignty or self-government of Aboriginal groups around the world. As one can see, there are few truly sovereign Aboriginal peoples.

However, when a national constitution, such as the Constitution Act, 1982, of Canada, contains articles defining a relationship with Aboriginal people, courts are compelled to recognize such relations and to resolve violations. Thus, having constitutional status elevates the status and degree of entrenchment of Aboriginal rights. Another way of defining the relationship between national and Aboriginal governments is through the conferring of authority for national legislature to protect Aboriginal rights. This is particularly the case where Aboriginal rights are not part of the country's constitution.[12]

Lesser levels of sovereignty are found in countries where agreements or contracts are signed between the government and Aboriginal peoples with regard to certain principles, objectives, or expenditures. Similarly, in such situations Aboriginal people may strike agreements with states, provinces, municipalities, or organizations. However, these agreements are limited by the power each political subdivision has relative to the delegated powers derived from the national government, and virtually no sovereignty is derived from these agreements. For example, the province of Ontario has issued an accord that recognizes Tribal Nations as sovereign entities and has agreed to work with Aboriginal communities on a government-to-government basis. However, these types of agreements have no legal force and can be changed any time. (See Figure 13.3 for national statistics on land claims.)

TABLE 13.2
▼
HIERARCHY OF SELF-GOVERNMENT AND CHARACTERIZING ATTRIBUTES

Level of Self-Government	Characterizing Attribute
Highest	sovereign status
	treaty status
	constitutional status
	national legislative status
	agreement/contract status
	sub-federal agreements/legislation
Lowest	no designated political status

TABLE 13.3

1998 INTERNATIONAL INDIGENOUS SOVEREIGNTY GEOGRAPHICS
ELEMENTS OF SOVEREIGNTY (SCALE 1-10)*

	United States	Canada	Mexico	New Zealand	Australia	Hawaii	Russia	Western Samoa	Totals	% of Sovereignty
Spirituality	10	10	10	10	10	10	10	10	80	100
Indigenous Membership	10	8	0	10	0	0	0	10	40	50
Creation of a Government	10	8	0	2	0	0	0	10	30	38
Power to Make Laws	10	6	0	1	0	0	0	10	29	36
Power to Tax	7	7	0	1	0	0	0	10	25	31
Control of Appropriations	7	7	0	4	4	2	0	10	34	43
Administration of Justice	7	1	0	0	0	0	0	10	18	23
Control of Domestic Relations	8	4	0	2	1	0	0	10	25	31
Defence of Sovereignty	2	2	5	2	2	4	1	10	28	35
Regulation of Commerce	5	4	2	1	1	0	0	10	23	29
International Relations	2	3	0	2	2	4	1	10	24	30
Land/Resource Base	10	10	5	2	4	2	2	10	45	56
Monetary System	0	0	0	0	0	0	0	10	10	13
Total	88	70	22	37	24	22	14	130	–	–
% of Sovereignty	68	54	17	28	18	17	11	100	–	–

*Revised from its original 1994 scores established by Lenoard.

Source: D. Leonard, "Indigenous Nature of Water," *The DLA Financial,* 2(3), (1995), 24.

BOX 13.2
▼
CRITERIA FOR NATION RECOGNITION

- Evidence of common ties of language, history, culture and a willingness to associate. Must have sufficient population size to support the exercise of a broad, self-governing mandate.

- Evidence of a fair and open process for obtaining agreement by citizens to embark on a nation-recognition process.

- Implementation of a citizenship code that is consistent with the Canadian Charter of Rights and Freedoms and international human rights codes.

- Implementation of impartial procedures to deal with appeals with regard to citizenship eligibility.

- Evidence that laws and constitutions are drawn up through consultation with citizens.

- Evidence that all citizens of the nation are permitted to ratify the proposed laws and/or constitution.

Source: Privy Council Office, *Royal Commission on Aboriginal Peoples* (1996), 165–166. Reproduced with the permission of the Minister of Public Works and Government Services.

CONCLUSION
▼

Because of different perspectives and worldviews, Aboriginals and Euro-Canadians sometimes have conflicting expectations. Sometimes these are real, while at other times they are a product of myths and reconstructions of history. For example, a real difference would be that Aboriginal burial sites are not considered burial sites in conventional "Western" ways and are considered by the Cemeteries Act to be "unproved Aboriginal cemeteries." This gives the provincial Director of Cemeteries the sole discretion to determine how to treat the remains of those interred in such places. On the other hand, the claim that Aboriginal people never engaged in conflict among themselves is not supported by historical analysis, nor is the claim that Aboriginals were always environmentally friendly in their relationship to the land. As the interaction between the two groups continues, the complexity of the relationship increases.

The new emphasis on "devolution" or "decolonialization" is another way in which the private sector can more easily enter and exploit Aboriginal communities that have, until recently, been controlled by the federal government. Why would businesses be interested in entering Aboriginal communities if they are as poor and undercapitalized as noted earlier? As pointed out, both the population and resource base are large and hold considerable economic potential. As noted previously, policies about Aboriginal people enacted by the government are nearly always directed toward rural Aboriginals, with little attention being paid to urban Aboriginals. This action is consistent with the policy by the government to move Aboriginals away from their homelands and into urban centres.

Today, the federal government is in the process of negotiating different forms of self-government with about 90 different Aboriginal groups across Canada. These negotiations range from major comprehensive claims to those which focus on specific jurisdictional authority, for example, the right of a band to enact a by-law (see Table 13.3). To achieve devolution and the urbanization of Aboriginals, alternative funding arrangements have been established with bands that allow new and flexible financial and administrative structures. These new arrangements allow band councils to take on more responsibility and become more accountable to residents of the Aboriginal community. For example, by 1996, more than 150 agreements with 235 bands were signed. While most of these agreements are with individual bands, 25 are with tribal councils or other First Nations organizations. This represents nearly 20 percent of all program expenditures directed toward Aboriginals by Indian and Inuit Affairs. In addition, more than 400 community economic-development organizations on reserves across Canada have taken on responsibility for the delivery of programs and services directed toward First Nations people. In summary, considerable devolution of authority is taking place as First Nations take over more control of their lives.

At one level, this devolution reflects a positive move by the federal government and places Aboriginal leaders in positions of power and trust within their community. Thus, when decisions are made, they are made with the support of the community. However, the nature and the level of funding are not within the final jurisdiction of most Aboriginal communities, as nearly all funding and decisions are ultimately controlled by the federal government through the Indian Act. Thus the ability of Aboriginal communities to truly exercise their decision-making ability is substantially reduced. Moreover, when unpopular decisions are made because of a lack of funds or because funds cannot be allocated to certain activities, the focus of discontent is directed toward the community leaders, not the ultimate source of power—the federal government.

In 1994, the Assembly of Manitoba Chiefs and the Minister of Indian Affairs, after several years of negotiations, agreed to dismantle the existing departmental structures of the Department of Indian Affairs and Northern Development as they affect Indians in Manitoba. The agreement also would recognize Indian governments in Manitoba as legally empowered to exercise the authorities required to meet the needs of Indian people and provide some forms of Indian self-government. This new agreement will recognize the rights of the Indians of Manitoba over the government, management, and control of their own lives, as recognized in the principles of self-government (Canada, 1994). Indians in other provinces are looking toward this agreement as a basis for renegotiating their relationship with the federal and provincial governments. Aboriginals also look to Greenland's Indigenous peoples for a model of how new processes can work in which Aboriginals can have their own government separate from the national government. This "Home Rule" seems to be working well for both the Danish government and the Aboriginal peoples, and continues to be a role model for Canadian Aboriginals.

We have discussed the internal tension between the elites and the rest of the Aboriginal community that poses problems for both the residents and government. However, other factions within the community also add to the complex dynamics of Aboriginal life. For example, the plight of Aboriginal women within their communities has been systematically ignored. However, we know they have played an important role in such actions as changing the Indian Act, which had stripped them of their legal status (and their children's) if they married a non-Indian person, while a "white" women who married an Aboriginal man became "Indian" (as did their children) and the man did not lose his "status." While the efforts of Aboriginal women have been influential in repealing this section of the Indian Act through the passage of Bill C-31, the change itself has not been totally successful.[13] Moreover, they have faced considerable hostility from male Indians, who argue this change will not allow Indians to define who is an Indian. While Aboriginal women rank among the most severely disadvantaged in Canada, having triple jeopardy — female, visible minority, Indian (Fleras & Ellliott, 1992) — they occupy a distinct niche in their community. For example, because of their higher educational achievements, they occupy most occupations requiring specific technical skills. Moreover, their influence in Aboriginal communities is noted both formally and informally, depending upon the lineage system. However, considerable tension exists between males and females regarding many important social issues in the community.

If the federal and provincial governments were serious about enhancing the standard of living of Aboriginals, it should be reflected in their quality of life. However, when we compare the statistics presented in the federally commissioned *Hawthorn Report* (1966–67) with those of today, we find there has been little change relative to other Canadians. Of course, incomes went up by $10 000 per year, but other Canadians saw their incomes increase by $30–40 000. In the end, the difference in socio-economic status between Aboriginals and other Canadians today is greater than 40 years ago.

We must conclude that the federal and provincial governments have not undertaken long-term programs that would allow Aboriginal peoples to become more fully integrated into Canadian society while at the same time maintaining cultural elements they feel are important. The recent Royal Commission on Aboriginal Peoples has tried to present a series of strategies for development of Aboriginal communities, but without the support of government these recommendations will never be enacted. Moreover, the federal and provincial governments have competed with each other and not collaborated to deal with the continued marginalization of Aboriginal peoples.

Today, we find few reserves integrated into the larger social structure of Canada. Those few that are reflect an integration with the outside economy attributable to economic development of the primary labour resource pool within each community, for example, lumber or oil. These conditions remind us of the duality of economies and culture (modern and traditional) in many Aboriginal communities.

We conclude this essay with a discussion of the generating and resilience capacity of a culture, and its linkage to a group's ability to integrate into the larger society. Resilience factors are those that affect the degree to which the economy is resilient to changes taking place in the rest of the world; generating factors are those affecting the degree to which the economy depends on the rest of the world to maintain increased internal levels of employment, output, demand. Because Aboriginal communities are dependent economies (dependent upon the larger Canadian economy for their production, for imports onto the reserves, for transfer of income and capital, for banking and financial services, and for business and technical skills), they have little capacity to develop their generating capacities; at the same time, their resilience ability continues to decrease.

While the government recognizes limited powers for Aboriginal people, it has not created any mechanisms to allow them to successfully implement these powers. Moreover, with no federal legislation to compel others to consider the interests of Aboriginals, they have little power to oblige parties to consider alternatives that may affect their culture or environment. Thus, in political contexts, Aboriginal peoples use blunt instruments to make their point, such as highly charged political demonstrations, blockades, and litigation. This often increases hostility and intransigence on the other side, and escalates the conflict (Borrows, 1997).

NOTES
▼

1. Over the past two decades, most Aboriginal languages experienced a steady erosion in linguistic vitality. Today, only Algonquian, Inuktitut, and Athapaskan are thriving linguistic families. Erosion of languages can be difficult to resist if an individual does not have the support of a closely knit community and is immersed in the language and culture of the dominant society.
2. The exact interpretation of these "treaties" has yet to be determined, and the courts have yet to establish the rights and responsibilities of both parties.
3. Even when the Supreme Court of Canada shows leadership in cases involving Aboriginal people, lower courts have lessened the impact of the decision. Mallea (1994) argues that it is partly as a result of this intransigence by the legal system that Aboriginal people are moving to dealing directly with governments in order to resolve issues.
4. There are many different types of "Aboriginals." The term "Indian" is a legal term and is to be used to identify only those individuals who are officially on the federal government "roll" of Indians. The term "registered" or "Status" Indian is sometimes used to identify "legal" Indians. However, many people are of Indian ancestry but have been struck from the roll for many different reasons, for example, completed university degree, mother married a non-Indian, voluntarily or involuntarily enfranchised. "Métis" and "Inuit" are other legal terms used to identify specific subgroups of Aboriginal people.
5. "Remote" refers to an Indian community that is more than 350 kilometres from the nearest service centre with year-round road access. "Special access" refers to an Indian community that has no year-round road access to the nearest service centre.
6. Nevertheless, it is clear that, in the past 25 years, Aboriginal people have not changed their position in Canadian society. In fact, statistics show that the gap between the poor and the wealthy has increased.
7. The intervention of government through the implementation of the Indian Act as well as other policies has, for well over a century, kept autonomous social, economic, and political action well beyond the reach of Aboriginal communities.
8. "Capital intensity of production" means that wages are only a small proportion of total costs.
9. Some of the new and radical proposals are outlined in the recent *Royal Commission on Aboriginal Peoples,* 5 vols. (1996)
10. Aboriginal rights are of two types — property and political. Property rights may involve land or resources, for example, hunting, fishing, while political rights involve a complex of laws, doctrines, and philosophy.

11. While rural communities are seen as the core of Aboriginal identity, self-determination and sovereignty, nearly all policy and politics of the federal government focus on rural, land-based issues. Yet about half of the Aboriginal population now reside off-reserve, many in large urban areas. What has been said or done with regard to this group? The Royal Commission on Aboriginal Peoples has little to say, other than recommending that governments support "community building" in the urban context, particularly around similarities of interest.

12. In one respect, national legislation is easier to enact and confers some elements of a sovereign nation, but it also means that it can easily be amended, changed, or removed.

13. Individuals who become Indians under the provisions of Bill C-31 can pass on their Indian status only to one more generation, at which time this generation loses its Indian status and becomes non-Indian.

REFERENCES
▼

Boldt, M. (1993). *Surviving as Indians.* Toronto: University of Toronto Press.

Borrows, J. (1997). Living between water and rocks: First Nations, environmental planning and democracy. *University of Toronto Law Journal, 47*(14), 417–468.

Canada. (1994). *The dismantling of the Department of Indian Affairs and Northern Development, the restoration of jurisdictions to First Nations peoples in Manitoba and recognition of First Nations governments in Manitoba. Framework agreement, workplan, memorandum of understanding.* Ottawa: Indian Affairs and Northern Development.

———. (1996). *Royal Commission on Aboriginal Peoples,* 5 vols. Ottawa: Minister of Supply & Services Canada.

———. (1997). *Basic departmental data.* Ottawa: Indian and Northern Affairs Canada, Department of Statistics Section.

Carter, S. (1990). *Lost harvests.* Montreal and Kingston: McGill-Queen's University Press.

Chase-Dunn, C. (1975). The effects of international economic dependence on development and inequality: A cross-national study. *American Sociological Review, 40,* 720–738.

dos Santos, T. (1968). *La crisis de la teoria del desarrollo y las relaciones de dependencia en America Latina.* Santiago: Boletin del Centro de Estudios Socio-Economics, University of Chile.

Dyck, N. (1997). Tutelage, resistance and co-optation in Canadian Indian administration. *Canadian Review of Sociology and Anthropology, 34*(3), 333–348.

Etzioni-Halevy, E. (1990). The relative autonomy of elites: The absorption of protest and social progress in Western democracies. In J. Alexander and P. Sztompka (Eds.), *Rethinking progress: Movements, forces, and ideas at the end of the twentieth century* (pp. 202–225). Boston: Unwin Wyman.

Fleras, A. & Elliott, J. (1992). *The "Nations Within": Aboriginal–state relations in Canada, the United States, and New Zealand.* Toronto: Oxford University Press.

Frideres, J. (1998). *Aboriginal peoples in Canada: Contemporary conflicts.* Scarborough, ON: Prentice-Hall Allyn & Bacon Canada.

Goehring, B. (1993). *Indigenous peoples of the world.* Saskatoon: Purich.

Henderson, J.Y. (1995). Mikmaw tenure in Atlantic Canada. *Dalhousie Law Journal, 18*(2), 196–294.

Isaac, T. (1995). *Aboriginal law.* Saskatoon: Purich.

Kulchyski, P. (1994). *Unjust relations: Aboriginal rights in Canadian courts.* Toronto: Oxford University Press.

Leonard, D. (1995). Indigenous nature of water. *The DLA Financial, 2*(3), 15–27.

Macklem, P. (1993). Ethnonationalism, aboriginal identities and the law. In M. Levin (Ed.), *Ethnicity and aboriginality: Case studies in ethnonationalism* (pp. 9–28). Toronto: University of Toronto Press.

Mallea, P. (1994). *Aboriginal law: Apartheid in Canada?* Brandon, MB: Bearpaw.

Satzewich, V., & Wotherspoon, T. (1993). *First Nations.* Scarborough, ON: Nelson Canada.

Statistics Canada. (1994a). *Profile of Canada's Aboriginal population,* Cat. no. 94-325. Ottawa: Statistics Canada.

14

▼

INCOME INEQUALITY IN CANADA: A "RACIAL DIVIDE"

ELLEN M. GEE AND STEVEN G. PRUS

INTRODUCTION
▼

Nearly 35 years ago, John Porter (1965), in his now-classic *The Vertical Mosaic*, argued that ethnic origin played an important role in the formation of classes in Canadian society. His basic thesis was that ethnic groups are "vertically arranged" in our society; members of northwestern European groups (especially the British) are more likely to be at the top, and persons of non-European origins are more likely to be at the bottom. He attributed this pattern to ethnic and racial prejudice, reflected and buttressed by Canadian immigration laws.

But, times have changed since Porter's research — multiculturalism has become institutionalized and a part of accepted ideology (Angus Reid Group, 1991); Canadian immigration policy has undergone substantial revisions and is, on the face of it, non-discriminatory — or at least less racist than it used to be (Simmons, 1998); employment equity legislation designed to protect visible minorities[1] and persons of Aboriginal background (as well as women and persons with disabilities) is in place [the Employment Equity Act of 1986] (Mentzer & Fizel, 1992). Other things being equal, then, we would expect Canadian society to be less structured on racial/ethnic lines.

However, changes in the economy have occurred as well — in the mid-1960s, economic growth was the order of the day (Dodge, 1998); we were prosperous and viewed our future economic prospects optimistically; nobody had ever heard of "recessions" or "inflation." In contrast, we are now part of a post-industrial global economy; companies are "downsizing/rightsizing"; youth unemployment is high; and Canadians no longer believe that the material lives of their children will be better than theirs; and, over the last decade, there has been some decline in real (adjusted for inflation) household income. At the same time, the ethnic and racial backgrounds/characteristics of immigrants to Canada have changed. Immigrants are more likely to be members of visible-minority groups; increasingly, the major source countries of immigrants are in Asia. The uncertainties of the present-day economy could create or magnify ethnic/racial prejudices in ways that operate to keep ethnic inequalities alive (Li, 1995; Waters & Eschbach, 1995). This is especially likely to occur in a country such as Canada with its long legacy of racist attitudes and practices (see Anderson, 1991, and Li, 1998a, with regard to Chinese in Canadian history). In addition, the ascendancy of the Reform Party both reflects and reinforces racist views, as discussed by Kirkham (1998). In other words, economic and political factors, along with the changing ethno-racial background of immigrants, may counteract initiatives to eliminate the structural allocation of persons on the basis of ascribed criteria.

PREVIOUS RESEARCH
▼

In the years since Porter's book, Canadian social researchers have conducted a considerable amount of research on the relationship between ethnicity and socio-economic status. However, the overall picture we get from this body of research is not very clear. Indeed, Yasmin and Abu-Laban (1992: 205) characterize the research area as one of "ongoing debate," with the debate centring on the *degree* to which ethnicity and race determine socio-economic status. Some studies show that the influence of ethnic variables on socio-economic status is quite weak (e.g., Darroch, 1980; Reitz, 1980; Stelcner & Kyriazis, 1995; Yasmin & Abu-Laban, 1992). Others show a fairly strong relationship (e.g., Herberg, 1990; Lautard & Loree, 1984; Richmond & Kalbach, 1980; Satzewich & Li, 1987).

We argue that the degree to which ethnicity/race and socio-economic inequality are related is not the key issue; rather, what is important are the *ways* in which ethnic/racial factors play out in socio-economic outcomes. Unlike in Porter's day, there is ample evidence that British-origin Canadians are no longer economically advantaged compared with other European-origin Canadians (Geshwender & Guppy, 1995; Ogmundson & McLaughlin, 1992). Also, research evidence is mounting that "race" is what matters (Herberg, 1990; Li, 1992; Lian, 1997; Satzewich & Li, 1987).

Social scientists no longer hold to the concept of "race"; there is no evidence that people can be divided into categories on the basis of physical/biological criteria. Nevertheless, it is still possible to find (far too many) situations where people are categorized on the basis of "race" (or socially constructed biological differences). When that categorization involves negative attitudes about, and negative treatment of, others, we can say that racism exists. In other words, while the concept of race itself may not be "real" (i.e., have empirical validity), but, rather, is socially created, the consequences of a belief in race — racism — may be very "real" (Satzewich, 1998).

Thus, to say that "race" matters is to say that some socially identified racial groups are subject to negative treatment in society on the basis of biological criteria that are believed to be important; they are subject to racism. But for what does "race" matter? For education, for occupation, for income, or for only some economic-related outcomes? And does "race" have similar economic consequences for men and women?

In this chapter, we focus on the distribution of income in Canada, examining the ways in which ethnicity and/or "race" play a role. We already know that the "vertical mosaic," as outlined by Porter in 1965, has changed — as has government policy and legislation in key areas related to it, our economy, and our ethnic composition. Let us in turn examine the shape of today's "vertical mosaic," paying particular attention to evidence that might show the role of racism in the determination of economic outcomes

DATA AND METHODS
▼

DATA SOURCE

Data used in this chapter come from the Survey of Labour and Income Dynamics (SLID), an ongoing, longitudinal household survey developed by Statistics Canada to study changes in, and determinants of, economic well-being in the same group of individuals and families over time. Data on labour market experiences, income, and personal characteristics are collected (Statistics Canada, 1997), making the SLID a useful resource in the study of income inequality. These data also provide the most recent information that is available to researchers outside the federal government.[2] Statistics Canada releases waves of information to the public in the form of longitudinal and cross-sectional data. The data here are derived from the 1994 cross-sectional files of the second wave, which consists of approximately 15 000 households/31 000 adults. The sample data are weighted to provide meaningful population estimates.

The SLID collects information from Canadians over the age of 16, except for people in the Yukon or Northwest Territories, persons living on reserves, members of the Canadian Armed Forces, and residents of institutions (Statistics Canada, 1997). People aged 20 to 54 are selected for analysis here, since our main goal is to examine income inequality and ethnocultural variables during the working years.

MEASUREMENT

Some measures used in this chapter are concrete and require no operational definition. For example, educational attainment is measured by the total numbers of years of formal schooling. Other variables are not as straightforward; they are briefly discussed below.

Multiple indicators of ethnicity/race are used, as is highly recommended in order to capture the fullest possible range of effects (e.g., Yasmin & Abu-Laban, 1992). The first ethnocultural indicator is the respondent's *ethnic origin*. In the SLID data base, this variable is categorized as British, French, Other European, Canadian,[3] Aboriginal,[4] or visible minority. While this categorization protects the confidentiality of respondents, it causes difficulties for researchers since the groups are varyingly heterogeneous. This is a particularly significant problem for the visible-minority category, which, as Hou and Balakrishnan (1996) remind us, contains a very wide range of persons in terms of colour, countries of origin, time of immigration, and so on. *Mother tongue*, defined as "the language that the respondent first learned at home in childhood and still understands," is the second measure of ethnicity/race (Statistics Canada, 1997: 106). Categories available in the SLID are English, French, and Other or Allophone (i.e., neither English nor French). A limitation of this variable is that the ability to speak an official language among Allophones is not assessed. That is, some in this category will be fully fluent in English and/or French; others will be partially fluent; and still others will be completely unable to speak an official language. Therefore, the Allophone category contains an unknown portion of persons whose functional inability in English/French prevents equal employment and income chances. The third measure, *place of birth,* is a straightforward variable, that is, Canadian-born or foreign-born.

Income is operationalized in two ways: total annual earnings and after-tax income. Total earnings are defined as the sum of wages/salaries and self-employment income, before taxes, in 1994. After-tax income (i.e., disposable income) is total income — money from wages, salaries, self-employment, investments, and government transfers — minus taxes payable in 1994. The latter measure provides a more accurate indication of economic well-being.

The SLID provides economic data at both the individual and the family level. Since this chapter is concerned with the relationship between ethnocultural characteristics and income, we use the individual as the unit of analysis. Hence, the earnings of individuals are used to measure the economic well-being of workers (both part-time and full-time) aged 20–54. The economic well-being of all people (workers and non-workers) aged 20–54 is measured with the after-tax income of individuals.

We also calculate Gini coefficients, which are one of the most widely used measures of income disparity. Gini coefficients allow us to look at income inequality in a different light; at how much inequality exists within an ethnocultural group (rather than across groups). The coefficient is a single index number, indicating the overall level of inequality in a given distribution. If everyone had the same income, for example, the Gini coefficient would be zero; conversely, if all incomes were held by just one individual, the coefficient would be one. Hence, the higher the Gini, the more inequality exists. For our purposed, Gini coefficients of .25 and .49 indicate moderate inequality; values of .50 or more indicate high inequality.

Occupation is measured using the Pineo–Porter–McRoberts socio-economic classification of occupations scale. This scale classifies jobs according to skill and management levels (Statistics Canada, 1997). Sixteen ranked occupational categories, ranging from professionals to unskilled workers/farm labourers, are included in the Pineo–Porter–McRoberts measure. For the purposes of descriptive overview, these sixteen categories are aggregated into three.

DATA ANALYSIS

Multiple Classification Analysis (MCA) is the primary statistical tool used here. Differences in income across ethnocultural groups are measured in average income deviations from the grand or overall mean (i.e., the estimated mean for all cases in the analysis). A group's estimated deviation/distance from the overall mean is computed before and after control variables are introduced. In this chapter, a gross deviation refers to a group's average distance from the mean before controls are introduced, while a net deviation refers to a difference after controls. For example, a gross deviation of – 4985 for Aboriginal men indicates that the average income among this group is $4985 below the overall mean; a net deviation of –1653 means that the average income of Aboriginal men is only $1653 below the mean, after eliminating the effects of selected control variables (e.g., age, region, education) by holding them constant.[5]

DESCRIPTIVE OVERVIEW
▼

INCOME

Table 14.1 presents data on median[6] incomes[7] along the three dimensions of ethnic background, mother tongue, and place of birth. The most striking feature here is the low incomes of Aboriginal men and women and of visible-mi-

TABLE 14.1

▼

MEDIAN TOTAL EARNINGS* AND TOTAL AFTER-TAX INCOME,** AND GINI COEFFICIENTS, PERSONS AGED 20–54, BY SEX, FOR ETHNIC-ORIGIN, MOTHER-TONGUE, AND PLACE-OF-BIRTH GROUPS

	Men						Women					
	Number	Total $ Earnings	Gini	Number	After-Tax ($)	Gini	Number	Total $ Earnings	Gini	Number	After-Tax ($)	Gini
Ethnic Origin												
British	3 724 002	31 000	0.40	4 430 713	23 960	0.35	3 335 043	20 000	0.44	4 486 275	15 500	0.41
French	721 210	29 000	0.40	859 645	23 000	0.34	603 514	17 000	0.44	830 303	14 680	0.40
Other European	1 724 584	30 000	0.38	2 004 377	24 880	0.34	1 559 659	18 000	0.44	2 074 144	15 471	0.41
Aboriginal	120 536	22 000	0.42	183 900	17 030	0.37	151 055	13 000	0.52	229 238	13 400	0.44
Visible-Minority	443 675	24 000	0.44	616 731	17 300	0.41	418 391	18 000	0.43	627 257	15 000	0.42
Mother-Tongue												
English	3 934 299	32 000	0.40	4 636 911	25 080	0.35	3 471 100	20 000	0.44	4 585 426	16 250	0.41
French	1 543 080	30 000	0.38	1 835 832	23 000	0.32	1 271 286	18 000	0.42	1 830 161	14 020	0.40
Other	753 982	27 000	0.41	969 772	21 100	0.37	701 785	19 000	0.44	1 037 861	14 740	0.43
Place-of-Birth												
Canada	5 278 909	30 000	0.39	6 242 694	24 000	0.34	4 577 351	19 000	0.44	6 172 677	15 200	0.41
Other	928 523	32 000	0.41	1 180 184	23 700	0.37	880 038	21 000	0.43	1 271 525	17 020	0.42

* Income from wages, salaries, and self-employment, before taxes (for all workers).
** Income from employment, investments, and government transfers, after taxes (for all persons).

Source: Statistics Canada, 1994. Survey of Labour and Income Dynamics, Merged Cross-Sectional Persons and Job Data Files.

nority men. The data in Table 14.1 also support other research that shows that British origin is no longer associated with high income (although English mother tongue wields some income advantage). We can see that persons born in Canada make less than the foreign-born; this difference is not large, however, and may be attributed in part to the younger average age of the Canadian-born (Beaujot, Basavarajappa, & Verma, 1990). Also of note is a pattern of small differences across groups for women compared with men, and that men's earnings are clearly race-related. These findings accord with that of Li (1992), who reports that the effects of race are greater for men's earnings than for women's.

Table 14.1 also presents Gini coefficients that measure the degree of income inequality within a category. Overall, we see that income inequality is quite high for all groups (recall that coefficients of .25 to .49 represent moderate inequality, and coefficients of .50 and over show high inequality). In general, differences in inequality across groups along the three ethnocultural domains are not large. However, looking at the Ethnic Origin dimension, we again see that First Nations persons (particularly women) and visible minorities stand out for somewhat higher levels of income inequality. Thus, the groups with the lowest incomes (within each gender) have the highest degree of income inequality. This pattern or relationship has not been researched to date, but it does suggest that "race" is a determinant of income inequality. That is, while racial minorities overall have low income levels, some of their members are what may be termed "exceptional," able to overcome income racial barriers. A related finding is that, overall, women, who have much lower incomes than men, have higher levels of income inequality — also suggestive of an "exceptionality" factor. However, the fact that some women and some racial-minority persons are able, as individuals, to overcome income barriers does not take away from the fact that those barriers exist, and most are blocked by them. Indeed, the existence of a few noticeable exceptions operates to entrench existing ascribed-based systems; the exceptions are used as examples, illustrating that things "really" do function fairly. One can go so far as to say that exceptions are needed for the maintenance of the status quo in societies, like Canada, that are ideologically committed to equality of opportunity. Too much rigidity would strain that ideology, and enlarge the discrepancies between the ideal and the actual.

EDUCATION

One could reasonably suggest that income variation might be attributable to differences in education attainment. To examine this, Table 14.2 provides data on education across the three ethnocultural domains. In contrast to

TABLE 14.2

▼

PERCENT OF POPULATION, 20–54 YEARS OF AGE, FOR RELATED LEVELS OF UNIVERSITY EDUCATIONAL ATTAINMENT, BY SEX, FOR ETHNIC-ORIGIN, MOTHER-TONGUE, AND PLACE-OF-BIRTH GROUPS

	Men		Women	
	Less than high school graduation	University degree	Less than high school graduation	University degree
Ethnic Origin				
British	20.0	18.9	15.9	16.9
French	21.6	16.2	17.6	15.8
Other European	18.6	16.7	13.3	17.9
Aboriginal	28.0	7.5	28.2	5.1
Visible-Minority	15.3	27.9	16.8	17.8
Mother-Tongue				
English	17.4	19.5	13.4	17.5
French	25.3	18.6	21.7	16.6
Other	22.9	17.8	18.9	17.5
Place-of-Birth				
Canada	20.5	18.2	16.4	16.9
Other	17.4	23.9	15.3	19.6

Source: Statistics Canada, 1994. Survey of Labour and Income Dynamics, Merged Cross-Sectional Persons and Job Data Files.

their low income levels, visible-minority men have by far the highest levels of education — approximately 28 percent of visible-minority men have at least one university degree, which is about 10 percent higher than for the three categories of European-origin men. Also, they are less likely not to be high school graduates (e.g., 15 percent compared with 20 percent of British-origin men). On the other hand, women of visible-minority groups have about the same educational attainment (and income level) as European-origin women.

The high level of education among visible-minority men should not be viewed as a straight function of immigration policy favouring the more highly educated. Table 14.2 also shows that immigrant (i.e., "other" place of birth) men (about 44 percent of whom are visible minorities), while exhibiting higher educational attainment levels than Canadian-born men, are not as likely to have a university degree as are visible-minority men. In other words, Canadian-born visible-minority males are particularly likely to get a degree. It appears, then, that a combination of immigration policy effects and educational accomplishments among Canadian-born men accounts for the high education levels of visible-minority men. However, this high education does not translate into high-income jobs for them.

In significant contrast to visible-minority men, Aboriginal men (who have a slightly higher median after-tax income than visible-minority men)[8] have very low levels of educational attainment. Similarly, First Nations women, who have the lowest income level, have a low level of educational attainment. The myriad reasons for low educational attainment among Aboriginals are beyond the focus and scope of this chapter; however, it does appear that their low income can, at least in part, be accounted for by education.

It is also worth noting that the French-origin and French-mother-tongue groups have low levels of education compared with other European-origin groups, although the difference is not large. Also, foreign-born men and women have a higher education level than their Canadian-born counterparts. These two facts are not unrelated; to some degree, the lower levels of education among French Canadians (the vast majority of whom are born in Canada) works to deflate the average education of the Canadian-born. However, immigration policy that favours the more highly educated is also an important factor. The lower income of French Canadians relative to other European-origin Canadians and the higher income of the foreign-born correspond with their relative education levels, thus further demonstrating the relationship between education and income — a relationship that appears to hold for all groups except men of visible-minority origins.

OCCUPATION

The occupational distribution of persons in the three ethnocultural domains is presented in Table 14.3. As with education, one can hypothesize that income differences could be accounted for by differences in occupation. There are insignificant differences in occupational distribution across the three European-origin groups and across the three mother-tongue categories for both men and women, although French-origin persons are, in keeping with their lower education levels, somewhat more likely to be employed in semi-skilled and unskilled jobs (although this does not really hold along the mother-tongue dimension, for reasons that are not clear).

Foreign-born men have a "better" occupational distribution than the Canadian-born, which accords with their higher average incomes. For women, the differences are smaller, but the general pattern is similar to that of men. The occupational distribution of Aboriginals stands out in Table 14.3; for both men and women, more than one-half are in semi-skilled and unskilled work, and a very small percentage, especially of men, are employed in professional, semi-professional, and higher management jobs. Again, this sug-

TABLE 14.3

▼

PERCENTAGE OCCUPATIONAL DISTRIBUTION, PERSONS AGED 20–54, WHO WORKED IN 1994, BY SEX, FOR ETHNIC-ORIGIN, MOTHER-TONGUE, AND PLACE-OF-BIRTH GROUPS

	Men			Women		
	Professional*	Skilled**	Semi- and Unskilled***	Professional*	Skilled**	Semi- and Unskilled***
Ethnic Origin						
British	22.2	38.9	38.8	28.5	28.6	42.9
French	21.2	36.6	42.2	23.5	27.1	49.5
Other European	18.4	41.4	40.3	28.1	25.1	46.8
Aboriginal	9.5	39.0	51.5	14.9	24.3	60.9
Visible-Minority	28.1	32.2	39.8	26.4	20.1	53.4
Mother-Tongue						
English	22.2	39.6	38.3	27.5	27.6	44.9
French	20.7	38.6	40.7	29.2	27.2	43.6
Other	20.1	38.0	41.9	26.7	31.7	48.4
Place-of-Birth						
Canada	21.0	39.6	39.3	27.6	27.6	44.9
Other	25.1	37.8	37.2	29.5	26.1	44.4

* Includes professional, semi-professional, high- and middle-level management, and technical workers.
** Includes supervisors, foremen/forewomen, skilled workers, and farmers.
*** Includes semi-skilled workers, unskilled workers, and farm labourers.

Source: Statistics Canada, 1994. Survey of Labour and Income Dynamics, Merged Cross-Sectional Persons and Job Data Files.

gests a relationship between occupation and income, given the low income levels of First Nations persons. However, this relationship breaks down for visible-minority men. They are the most likely (28 percent) to be in professional/semi-professional/higher management jobs — even higher than foreign-born men who have been "selected" by immigration policy for such jobs — and they do not have a higher likelihood of working in semi-skilled and un-skilled employment; yet, they, as we have already seen, have very low income levels. This suggests that access to "good" jobs is not the problem; rather, the issue seems to be one of getting "equal pay for equal work" and, perhaps, of blocked upward mobility within an employment situation. Also, Herberg (1990: 218) suggests that "racial discrimination prevents awarding wages equivalent to credentials."

LABOUR FORCE PATTERNS

Income may be affected by different patterns of labour force participation. For example, a portion of women's low income profile is due to their greater likelihood of working part-time.

Table 14.4 gives data on the labour force participation patterns of ethnocultural groups in Canada. As expected, women are less likely to work full-time, and this is especially true for Aboriginal women (34 percent). Part-time employment is uncommon for men of all groups. Full-time employment for men is generally in the 65 percent range, except for Aboriginal men (43 percent) and men of visible-minority groups (52 percent). Given the latter's high education, this low level of full-time work is surprising, and may indicate obstacles in securing full-time work based on "race." Their high level of unemployment/non-involvement in the labour force (17 vs. 8 percent for British-origin men, for example) and their relatively high "interrupted job pattern" similarly point to racial discrimination in the labour force. Visible-minority women also display comparatively high levels of unemployment/non–labour force participation, but it is difficult to ascertain how much cultural norms and expectations regarding women working outside the home may be operative.

The most "privileged" labour force participation pattern belongs to men of Other European origins — they are the most likely to be employed full-time, and the least likely to have an interrupted job history and unemployment/non-involvement in paid work. The least "privileged" pattern occurs for Aboriginal men and women, with well over one-half falling into the categories of interrupted job and unemployed/non-involvement in the labour force. There is no evidence of British advantage à la Porter, but English mother tongue seems to yield some benefits for both men and women.

TABLE 14.4
▼

PERCENTAGE LABOUR FORCE DISTRIBUTION, PERSONS AGED 20–54, BY SEX, FOR ETHNIC-ORIGIN, MOTHER-TONGUE, AND PLACE-OF-BIRTH GROUPS

	Full-Time	Part-Time	Interrupted Patterns*	Unemployed/Not in Labour Force	Self-Employed
MEN					
Ethnic Origin					
British	66.6	2.5	23.1	7.7	10.2
French	63.9	3.0	24.1	9.0	16.0
Other European	70.0	3.3	21.2	5.5	23.1
Aboriginal	42.6	3.6	32.3	21.3	10.1
Visible-Minority	52.2	4.1	26.7	16.9	14.0
Mother-Tongue					
English	68.8	3.2	21.3	6.7	19.5
French	63.5	2.3	25.5	8.7	17.2
Other	64.8	3.6	20.6	11.0	25.7
Place-of-Birth					
Canada	67.3	3.0	22.3	7.5	19.2
Other	64.9	3.2	21.6	10.4	23.0
WOMEN					
Ethnic Origin					
British	45.4	15.0	20.1	19.8	10.8
French	45.3	12.6	24.1	19.2	11.2
Other European	44.9	16.1	21.3	17.9	18.3
Aboriginal	33.9	13.1	26.4	26.6	13.3
Visible-Minority	43.6	10.0	22.2	24.3	6.7
Mother-Tongue					
English	46.3	14.4	21.9	17.4	12.0
French	41.6	13.8	19.6	25.0	9.0
Other	45.3	14.1	16.6	24.0	10.7
Place-of-Birth					
Canada	44.5	15.0	20.9	19.6	11.7
Other	47.1	10.5	19.9	22.9	9.4

*Includes persons who worked, either full-time or part-time, and did not work in 1994.

Source: Statistics Canada, 1994. Survey of Labour and Income Dynamics, Merged Cross-Sectional Persons and Job Data Files.

Self-employment varies quite considerably across ethnocultural groups. Overall, men are more likely to be self-employed than women (except among persons of British and aboriginal origins). Self-employment is highest amongst the Other European origins for both men and women. Also, men with an "other" mother tongue have a high likelihood of being self-employed, as do immigrant men. Assuming that a certain amount of capital is necessary for most self-employment ventures, it is likely that the recent "immigrant entrepreneur" policy is playing some role in these results (Wong, 1993).

These data go some way in accounting for the lower incomes of visible-minority men and Aboriginal men and women. All three groups are less likely to be engaged in full-time work and have comparatively high levels of job interruption and unemployment/non-participation in the paid labour force.

ASSESSING THE "MARKET VALUE" OF RACE[9]

Up to now, we have seen that ethnic/racial inequalities in the incomes of Canadians exist, and we have looked, one by one, at some of the factors that might account for differences in income. Now, we apply a more systematic analysis to the data, using the MCA technique (see Table 14.5). The gross income figures refer to actual deviations (for all persons who worked in 1994) from the mean after-tax income for men ($27 346) and for women ($19 975). A slight income advantage for persons of British origins, those with English mother tongue, and the foreign-born can be observed. We can also see the huge disadvantage of Aboriginal persons, and visible-minority men, as previously observed in Table 14.1. Some of these variations can be explained by differences in education, and other individual and market characteristics. In order to assess the simultaneous effect of such factors, we have computed net income deviations, that is, the amount that incomes would deviate from the mean if other relevant factors are held constant (as listed at the bottom of Table 14.5).

Basically, we are "pretending" that ethnocultural groups have identical sociodemographic profiles, and thus should have identical income levels. Any negative net deviations measure, in dollars, the "cost" of ascribed characteristics. Also, the gap between gross and net income deviations portrays the direction and magnitude of racial/cultural characteristics for income.

The net income deviations in Table 14.5 are much greater for men than for women, suggesting that ethnocultural characteristics play a bigger role in the "male labour market." However, among women, two pieces of data are noteworthy. First, Aboriginal women lose almost all of their income disadvantage; this means that their actual lower income levels can be largely attributed to factors such as their lower levels of education, their younger age, their lower likelihood of working full-time, and so on, and not to their "racial" origin. Second, immigrant women would make approximately $3000 more than the average fe-

TABLE 14.5
▼

GROSS AND NET INCOME DEVIATIONS (AFTER-TAX INCOME), PERSONS AGED 20–54, WHO WORKED IN 1994, BY SEX, FOR ETHNIC-ORIGIN, MOTHER-TONGUE, AND PLACE-OF-BIRTH GROUPS

	Men (grand mean = $27 346)		Women (grand mean = $19 975)	
	Gross Deviation ($)	Net Deviation* ($)	Gross Deviation ($)	Net Deviation* ($)
Ethnic Origin				
British	273	54	60	-139
French	-1 153	-238	-225	143
Other European	-47	53	-560	-546
Aboriginal	-4 985	-1 653	-2 924	-18
Visible-Minority	-3 529	-3 971	170	495
Mother-Tongue				
English	976	297	469	24
French	-1 650	170	-1 004	200
Other	-1 694	-1 932	-458	-474
Place-of-Birth				
Canada	-109	-942**	-245	-560**
Other	647	5 588	1 296	2 964

* Controlling for age, education, full-time versus part-time employment, occupation, and region.
** Additional controls for age at immigration and period of immigration.

Source: Statistics Canada, 1994. Survey of Labour and Income Dynamics, Merged Cross-Sectional Persons and Job Data Files.

male income, other things (i.e., the controlled variables) being equal. However, in reality, they earn only about $2300 more. In other words, immigrant women are not able to parlay their "human capital" into the income that they would receive, given their social characteristics, if they were not immigrants.

For men, we see that the net income deviation for visible minorities is nearly $4000, indicating that they lose a considerable amount of money yearly because, and only because, they are not white. In contrast, Aboriginal men, while still at a net income disadvantage, are less poorly off (hypothetically); their lower levels of education, lesser involvement in the labour force, and so on, account for a considerable amount of their actual low income level. Among immigrant men, the pattern is an exaggeration of the one for women:

they would earn about $5600 more than the male average, other things being equal; in reality, they earn only $647 more.

Also, a mother tongue other than English or French works to the income disadvantage of men (and women to a lesser degree). Lastly, lower levels of gross income among the French (as assessed by both ethnic origin and mother tongue) disappear among the net income deviation data, and actually become positive figures for women and for men with French mother tongue. This means that their lower actual earnings are due to sociodemographic factors, and not to "being" French Canadian or speaking French.

CONCLUSION
▼

The data in this chapter show that Canada's vertical mosaic has been rearranged or transformed since the time of Porter's (1965) research. At least in terms of income, Canada displays a "racial divide" between whites and non-whites, the latter including Aboriginals and members of visible-minority groups. This finding supports a prediction made in 1987 that race will become more important than ethnicity in the structuring of inequality in Canada (Satzewich & Li, 1987). This racial divide cannot be accounted for by educational (and other sociodemographic) differences in the case of visible minorities, and can only be partially so for Aboriginals. Education, and especially occupational, differences are less racially related, although Aborginals stand out for low educational attainment. Thus, in answer to our question posed earlier — "For what does race matter?" — it matters for income equality. It matters less for education and occupation, but it also does factor into labour force patterns. We have seen that non-whites are less likely to be full-time workers, and more likely to be unemployed or out of the paid labour force. Therefore, it seems that a "colour barrier" exists in terms of securing employment. Also, the fact that occupational distributions are quite similar, in conjunction with large income differentials by race, means that racial minorities face obstacles in getting "equal pay for equal work."

Our data show that this racial divide in income operates much more for men than for women. This finding has been reported by Pendakur and Pendakur (1996) and Li (1992), as well as in work from the 1973 Canadian Mobility Study (Goyder, 1981). Given that women systematically make less money than men, it is possible that a "floor effect" operates in women's incomes. Race does not matter so much when pay is at low levels — there is not much "room" for variation.

However, we cannot ignore the finding here that moderate to high levels of income inequality (as measured by Gini coefficients) exist within each ethnocultural/gender group. In other words, the structure of incomes in Canada (by ethnicity/race and gender) is not rigid — in even highly disadvantaged groups, some individuals earn a lot (although generally less than members of privileged groups). We have already discussed how such "flexibility" in income allocation is necessary in democratic societies in order to maintain the overall structure of the "racial divide."

In what policy directions do our findings lead? Our analysis does not accord with the conclusions of Mentzer and Fizel (1992) that income inequality can be erased by raising the educational level of low-income ethnic groups — at least with regard to visible minorities. Rather, our findings point to the importance of public policy interventions regarding job acquisition and equal pay. These policy suggestions are not new; in fact, they were made by the Abella Royal Commission on Equality in Employment fifteen years ago (Abella, 1984). However, it is safe to say that the Canadian public has not embraced employment equity or "affirmative action," and without public support such initiatives are probably doomed. As our economy hobbles along, and as Canadians do not feel secure about their economic futures, public support for employment equity is a pipe dream. Although economic decline did not cause the racial divide, we will need sustained economic recovery to overcome it.

NOTES
▼

1. For legislative, census, and other government purposes, visible-minority groups include: Chinese, Japanese, Filipinos, Koreans, South Asians (Indo-Canadians), Southeast Asians and West Asians, Other Pacific Islanders, Blacks, Arabs, and Latin Americans.
2. As of this writing, the public microdata file for the 1996 census is not available for academic researchers.
3. The Canadian category is not included in our analysis; most respondents who provided a Canadian response also characterized themselves as a member of one of the other four ethnic origins, and were placed in those categories.
4. The exclusion of on-reserve Aboriginals from the SLID sampling frame means that all data referring to Aboriginals are incomplete, based on an off-reserve sample only.
5. Age is controlled only in the Multiple Classification Analysis, presented in Table 14.5. In the preceding descriptive tables, the data are given for the age grouping 20–54 without taking into account differences across groups in age distribution within this grouping. In fact, the mean age of the sample is 36, and it varies from 34 for Aboriginal women (and 35 for Aboriginal men) to 39 for immigrant women (and 38 for immigrant men). Since income is age-related (i.e., within the working-age population, older persons tend to make more money than younger

persons), income comparisons will show somewhat higher levels for immigrants and lower levels for Aboriginals — due to this age factor alone.

6. The median is a more accurate measure of average than the more commonly used mean, when, as is the case with income, distributions are not normal (the bell curve).

7. The total earnings data apply to persons aged 29–54 who worked for all or some portion of 1994, either full-time, part-time (or both). Separate breakdowns for full-time and part-time workers are not possible; the numbers for part-time workers are too small to be reliable, when broken down along the three ethnocultural dimensions. The total income data apply to all persons aged 20–54.

8. The higher after-tax income of First Nations men, compared with visible-minority men, is not a function of First Nations exemption from federal income taxes. That exemption applies only to on-reserve Aboriginals (working on-reserve), and they are not included in the SLID.

9. This phrase is taken from Li 1998b.

REFERENCES
▼

Abella, R.S. (1984). *Equality in employment: A royal commission report.* Ottawa: Ministry of Supply & Services.

Allahar, A.L., & Côté, J.E. (1998). *Richer and poorer: The structure of inequality in Canada.* Toronto: Lorimer.

Anderson, K.J. (1991). *Vancouver's Chinatown: Racial discourse in Canada, 1875–1980.* Montreal and Kingston: McGill-Queen's University Press.

Angus Reid Group (1991). *Multiculturalism and Canadians: Attitude survey 1991, National survey report.* Ottawa: Multiculturalism and Citizenship Canada.

Beaujot, R., Basavarajappa, K.G., & Verma, R.P.B. (1990). *Income of immigrants in Canada: A Census data analysis. Current demographic analysis, 1988,* Cat. No. 91-527E. Ottawa: Statistics Canada Catalogue No. 91-527E.

Darroch, A.G. (1980). Another look at ethnicity, stratification and social mobility in Canada. In J.E. Goldstein & R.M. Bienvenue (Eds.), *Ethnicity and ethnic relations in Canada* (pp. 203–230). Toronto: Butterworths.

Dodge, D. (1998). Reflections on the role of fiscal policy: The Doug Purvis memorial lecture. *Canadian Public Policy, 24,* 275–289.

Geschwender, J.A., & Guppy, N. (1995). Ethnicity, educational attainment, and earned income among Canadian-born men and women. *Canadian Ethnic Studies, 27,* 67–83.

Goyer, J.C. (1981). Income differences between the sexes: Findings from a national Canadian survey. *Canadian Review of Sociology and Anthropology, 18,* 321–342.

Herberg, E.N. (1990). The ethno-racial socioeconomic hierarchy in Canada: Theory and analysis of the new vertical mosaic. *International Journal of Comparative Sociology, 31,* 206–221.

Hou, F., & Balakrishnan, T.R. (1996). The integration of visible minorities in contemporary Canadian society. *Canadian Journal of Sociology, 21,* 307–326.

Kirkham, D. (1998). The Reform Party of Canada: A discourse on race, ethnicity, and equality. In V. Satzewich (Ed.), *Racism and social inequality in Canada* (pp. 243–267). Toronto: Thompson Educational.

Lautard, E.H., & Loree, D.J. (1984). Ethnic stratification in Canada, 1931–1971. *Canadian Journal of Sociology, 9,* 30–40.

Li, P. (1992). Race and gender as bases of class fractions and their effects on earnings. *Canadian Review of Sociology and Anthropology, 29,* 488–510.

———. (1995). Racial supremacism under social democracy. *Canadian Ethnic Studies, 27,* 1–18.

———. (1998a). *The Chinese in Canada* (2nd ed.). Toronto: Oxford University Press.

———. (1998b). The market value and social value of race. In V. Satzewich (Ed.), *Racism and social inequality in Canada* (pp. 115–130). Toronto: Thompson Educational.

Lian, J.Z. (1997). Ethnic earnings inequality in Canada. *Dissertation Abstracts International, 57,* 4552.

Mentzer, M., & Fizel, J.L. (1992). Affirmative action and ethnic inequality in Canada: The impact of the Employment Equity Act of 1986. *Ethnic Groups, 9,* 203–217.

Ogmundson, R., & McLaughlin, J. (1992). Trends in the ethnic origins of Canadian elites: The decline of the Brits? *Canadian Review of Sociology and Anthropology, 29,* 227–242.

Pendakur, K., & Pendakur R. (1996). *Earnings differentials among ethnic groups in Canada.* Ottawa: Strategic Research and Analysis, Department of Canadian Heritage.

Porter, J. (1965). *The vertical mosaic: An analysis of social class and power in Canada.* Toronto: University of Toronto Press.

Reitz, J. (1980). *Survival of ethnic groups.* Toronto: McGraw-Hill Ryerson.

Richmond, A.H., & Kalbach W.E. (1980). *Factors in the adjustment of immigrants and their descendants,* Cat. No. 99-761. Ottawa: Statistics Canada.

Satzewich, V. (1998). Race, racism and racialization: Contested concepts. In V. Satzewich (Ed.), *Racism and social inequality in Canada* (pp. 25–45). Toronto: Thompson Educational.

Satzewich, V., & Li, P. (1987). Immigrant labour in Canada: The cost and benefit of ethnic origin in the job market. *Canadian Journal of Sociology, 12,* 229–241.

Simmons, A. (1998). Racism and immigration policy. In V. Satzewich (Ed.), *Racism and social inequality in Canada* (pp. 87–114). Toronto: Thompson Educational.

Statistics Canada (1997). *Survey of labour and income dynamics: Microdata user's guide* (70M0001GPE). Ottawa: Ministry of Industry.

Stelcner, M., & Kyriazis, N. (1995). An empirical analysis of earnings among ethnic groups in Canada. *International Journal of Contemporary Sociology, 32,* 41–79.

Waters, M.C., & Eschbach, K. (1995). Immigration and ethnic and racial inequality in the United States. *Annual Review of Sociology, 21,* 419–446.

Wong, L.L. (1993). Immigration as capital accumulation: The impact of business immigration to Canada. *International Migration, 31,* 171–190.

Yasmin, M., & Abu-Laban, B. (1992). Ethnicity and occupational inequality: A reconsideration. *Alberta Journal of Educational Research, 38,* 205–218.

15

▼

CHANGING FORMS OF NATION-NESS IN THE CANADIAN CONTEXT: THE QUEBEC CASE[1]

DANIELLE JUTEAU

INTRODUCTION
▼

Twenty-five years ago, Canadian sociologist John Porter (1965) aptly defined Canada as a huge demographic railway station: almost as many millions were leaving the country as were pouring in. The time has come to change the metaphor, as Canada now resembles a busy construction site, where not only one but many nations are being constructed, deconstructed, and reconstructed.

Nations-building in Canada has involved a series of interrelated and, at times, competing national projects: first of all, the ongoing but as yet unrealized goal of achieving an integrated and overarching Canadian nation-state;[2] second, the construction of the French-Canadian nation, its eventual dissolution, and the reformulation of a national project specific to Quebec; and, finally, the recent political emergence of the First Nations.[3]

This essay focusses on three aspects of the question: (1) the concept of nation; (2) models of nation-building; and (3) nations-building in Canada, with special attention given to the production and consolidation of a pluralist model in Quebec as well as to the challenges and tensions that arise in this context.

THE CONCEPT OF NATION
▼

Nations involve shared history, dreams, goals, projects, and consciousness (Juteau & McAndrew, 1992). As communities of history and destiny, they can be examined in terms of the following elements: nationality and national consciousness, specific project, and historical trajectory.

The concept of nationality "shares with that of the 'people' the vague connotation that whatever is felt to be distinctively distinct must derive from common descent," although in reality "persons who consider themselves members of the same nationality are often much less related by common descent than are persons belonging to different and hostile nationalities" (Weber, 1978: 395).

The concrete reasons for the belief in joint nationality and the resulting social action vary greatly; common language, religion, common customs, or political memories come to mind. Furthermore, this belief does not rest on the existence of common characteristics or qualities, nor even on common feelings for the same qualities; it rests on the mutual orientation of behaviour of those sharing such characteristics, which usually occurs in the context of economic, political, and cultural inequality.

What is specific to "the nation"? What the term uniformly refers to, is "the idea of a powerful political community of people," a state that may already exist or may be desired. The concept of nation seems to refer to a specific kind of ethos that is linked to political power; and the more power is emphasized, the closer the link between nation and state appears to be (Weber, 1978: 397–398).

This national consciousness and this specific project are elaborated in the context of a given historical trajectory. For the nation is also a *product*, resulting from the conditions of the struggle for existence that constitutes itself in the context of the constant reciprocal interaction of those sharing a common destiny (Bauer, 1987). This community of destiny, also known as a "national" community of character, should not be apprehended in a static and essentialist way; it forms a system, since the elements defining a community — origin (common ancestors), mores, customs, historical past, laws, religion — maintain a clear relation among themselves. A community's common history creates common mores and customs, common laws, and common religion, and thus — to preserve our linguistic usage — the community of cultural tradition (Bauer, 1974: 250).

In short, different nations, such as the French, the German, and the Canadian, are the products of distinct trajectories; they develop distinct visions of what they were, of what they are, and of what they ought and want to be. It follows, therefore, that their representations and projects are anchored in specific collective histories that give birth to specific practices, policies, and ideologies. The latter usually rest upon an organicist conception of the nation or a territorial one; but they can also rest upon a pluralist model, of various types: multicultural, intercultural, transcultural, and so on. We shall now examine the types of nationhood.

TYPES OF NATIONHOOD
▼

There exists a general tendency in the European literature to present a binary model of the nation, opposing the nation based on ancestry to the nation of citizens (Juteau & McAndrew, 1992) — on the one hand, a nation based on blood ties, and on the other, a nation based on territoriality and political history; an organicist versus a voluntaristic approach. Germany and France represent these two conceptions.

Each one of these approaches presents problems. To base nationality on common ancestry and blood ties is to mask the processes of ethnicization responsible for the social production of ethnicity and nationality; it situates in the biological domain what is essentially a cultural and a political question.

France comes closer to the statist model since it emphasizes territoriality, "le droit du sol." Nevertheless, the realization of this model is problematic; first, access to citizenship remains restricted, since not all those born on French territory are French nationals; second, acquiring French citizenship requires a strong level of assimilation. It seems that, in France, citizenship is linked to the possession of French culture. Although the French disassociate the political sphere from the biological, they establish an equation between a political identity and a cultural one. For example, Dominique Schnapper, in her book *La France de l'intégration* (1990), writes: "On est français par la pratique d'une langue, par l'apprentissage d'une culture, par la volonté de participer à la vie économique et politique." [One is French by practice of a language, by the learning of a culture, by the will to participate in economic and political life.]

Actually, things are not as simple as this binary opposition lets us think. First, each of these models contains its share of voluntarism and of organicism. As A.D. Smith reminds us (1986), both the territorial and the ethnic type of model exhibit characteristics belonging to the other. Second, there exists at least another model, this one emerging mainly in settler societies and constituting a pole distinct from the other two; the pluralist model is found, for example, in Australia, Canada, and the United States. Territorial rights really exist; that is, being born in the country gives you citizenship. Furthermore, citizenship is relatively easy to acquire for newcomers. A necessary link between the political community and common ancestry is not postulated; furthermore, integration into the political community does not require complete cultural assimilation. Multiple cultural identities co-exist with a national identity; it is sometimes seen as the essence of national identity. It has been suggested that this pluralist model may be the first postmodern national model. But it also includes, as do the other two, organicist, voluntarist, and assimilationist trends that counteract the dominant orientation.

We will now see that Canada and Quebec, like other nations, are the products of distinct historical trajectories; it is within this context that they developed different visions of what they are, what they were, and what they should become. As such, their representations and projects are anchored in a collective history that includes relations with other collectivities and gives birth to specific practices, policies, and ideologies — a passage from an organicist model in French Canada and a statist model in English Canada to the adoption of similar pluralist models.

FORMS OF NATION-NESS IN THE CONTEXT OF QUEBEC AND CANADA

▼

LA STAATSNATION CANADIENNE

Canada is a country characterized by various immigration waves that took the form of a double colonization. Let us not forget that the colonizers called themselves "the founding peoples," that the actual founding peoples were called "Indians" and "Natives," and that all others were called "immigrants" and "ethnics."

Each of the two "founding peoples" clung to its respective vision of a homogeneous nation; by excluding, economically, politically, and culturally, the First Nations (or by trying to assimilate them) and by trying to reserve the French fact for Quebec or to keep Quebec as French as possible.

Because of their different positions within the system of ethnic social relations, their strategies will differ. French Canadians will develop an organicist model: one is born a French Canadian, one does not become one; ancestry, language, and culture become central elements of the nation. English Canada develops a national model akin to that of France, a *Staatsnation:* strongly assimilationist, it favours nativism and Anglo-conformity. The symbolic and cultural construction of the nation is oriented in the direction of a Canadian society of a British type; Canadianization implies speaking English within a British-type institutional system, and it was quite successful on the whole (Breton, 1984: 127–28).

During the century following Confederation, the two founding nations do not blend into each other, nor are they capable of building a strong national Canadian identity. The conflict opposing them led to the Royal Commission on Bilingualism and Biculturalism in 1963. This commission was given the mandate to propose a new model and a new *entente* between the two groups.

Meanwhile, important social changes are restructuring Quebec society. The election of the Liberal Party of Quebec in 1960, which had campaigned under the slogan "Il faut que ça change" [It is necessary that this change] is now recognized as constituting a watershed. What was to be called "The Quiet Revolution" had begun. Given that the Quebec state could not claim control over the life and destiny of French Canadians living across Canada, the ensuing modernization, expansion, and bureaucratizion of the Quebec state apparatus gave way to a growing emphasis on territory. The Quebec government's plans, reforms, and interventions affected everyone living in that province and highlighted a territorial basis of identification. It was acting on behalf of the French Canadians of Quebec, and its gradual consolidation soon gave rise to the emergence and development of a new community: *les Québécois*, a community excluding all French-Canadians living outside Quebec (Juteau-Lee, 1980). But what about the other residents of Quebec? Were they included or excluded? The answer is not so simple.

TOWARD INCLUSIVENESS: EXTENDING THE QUÉBÉCOIS SOCIETAL BOUNDARIES

▼

Despite the emergence of new words, new boundaries, new projects, and a new political consciousness, the Québécois nation had yet to be forged. The discarding of the French-Canadian identity, associated with domination and colonialism,[4] led to a national struggle focussed initially on achieving economic, political, and cultural sovereignty vis-à-vis the Anglo-American environment.

While the Quiet Revolution accelerated the demise of the Church, it also increased the administrative and political power of the new technocrats, who needed the state as an instrument of development. By promoting the state as the only tool controlled by the national community, bureaucrats successfully argued that it also constituted a tool of national liberation (Cloutier & Latouche, 1979). Furthermore, these bureaucrats could count on the substrate necessary to the formation of the new state, that is, the indestructible national community of character. Thus, the nation became the foundation of the state, which in turn both protected the community (Bauer, 1987: 208) and redefined it. The intelligentsia, sensitive to matters of national honour and pride, became its ally. The composition of these classes (the bureaucracy interacting and intermingling with the intelligentsia) affected the orientation of the national struggle: some economic reform; ongoing political battles with the federal government; strong and quite successful measures dealing, as could be expected, with language and culture (Juteau-Lee, 1974, 1979).

These changes were accompanied by demands for greater economic, political, and cultural autonomy; at the political level, one finds projects going from new forms of federalism to sovereignty to associate states and special status. This led other groups in Canada to demand recognition of their material and symbolic contribution to nation-building in Canada.

They questioned the idea of a bilingual and a bicultural Canada excluding them from the processes of restructuring Canada. Binationalism was replaced by bilingualism (1969), and biculturalism by multiculturalism (1971). In their efforts to achieve greater control over the economic, political, and cultural boundaries of the Québécois nation, the dominant elites became active in the definition of a new blueprint for Quebec society. Interestingly enough, the consolidation of the Québécois societal community followed a course not unlike the one unfolding in the broader Canadian context. The French Language Charter (Bill 101) had unintended consequences; Quebec language policies altered the boundaries between the various ethnic groups and favoured increased relations between immigrants and Québécois of French-Canadian ethnicity in various areas such as schools, and social and health services.

The multiplication of the links between immigrants and members of the host society has heightened the "visibility" of the immigrants themselves as well as the centrality of the "ethnic" question. From a situation in which immigrants lived for the most part within institutions established by members of their own community (Laferrière, 1983) and, linguistically speaking, integrated themselves into the English-Canadian millieu, that is, a situation in which immigrants and French Canadians lived side by side rather than together, there has been a proliferation of interactions between immigrants and social actors often employed by the federal, provincial, and municipal bureaucracies. These agents, often bureaucrats and community organizers, are directing their attention to the forms of individual and collective relations that need to be developed between immigrants and non-immigrants, and between Quebec's various ethnic groups.

Quebec thus began its quest for a societal model; in spite of the fears manifested by several groups, it did accept the pluralist idealogy. The new model would differ from the old model of a *Kulturnation* based on blood ties and common ancestry, and the nation was to be defined in terms of the population of an economic region and a state. It also tended to distance itself from the model of the *Staatsnation* as it was developed in France: this model emphasizes, as we have seen, a nation based on collective will, and recognizes the primacy of individual rights of citizenship based on territoriality. In France, as I mentioned, the adoption of this model has also been accompanied by a conception of a culturally homogeneous nation combined with strong assimilationist pressures. The Québécois nation wants to construct a nation based on citizenship rather than on ancestry, as the following review of the evolution of pluralist ideologies in Quebec will reveal (GRES, 1992).

Already in 1975, the Quebec Charter of Rights and Freedoms recognized that persons belonging to ethnic minorities have the right to maintain and develop their own cultural life. Stating that there can be no culture without minorities, the White Paper *La Politique québécoise du développement culturel* stipulated that all have a right to expect from the state those cultural tools and the collective equipment necessary to their full development (1978: 64). For its part, the Quebec government, in its publication *Autant de façons d'être québécois* (1981), proposed a vision that rejected the American model of the melting-pot, and the Canadian model of multiculturalism perceived as the juxtaposition of diverse groups. It wanted to avoid the pitfalls of cultural homogeneity without adopting the principles of multiculturalism. This document differentiates between two categories of individuals: members of the "Québécois" nation and those of "cultural communities"; it also states that the development of Quebec's various cultural groups requires the vitality of Quebec as a French society. In other words, cultural pluralism will be encouraged within the context of a French-speaking society, and its acceptance will not preclude the adoption of measures ensuring the strengthening of the French language in Quebec.

In December 1990, the government publication *L'Énoncé de politique en matière d'immigration et d'intégration au Québec* proposed a policy of intercultural rapprochement and, to this end, introduced the expression "Québécois des communautés culturelles." "Québécois" and "cultural community" would no longer designate mutually exclusive categories; the category "Québécois" was henceforth more inclusive. The policy of integration and the measures stemming from it were framed by three principles: a society in which French was the common language of public life; a democratic society in which the contribution and participation of all are expected and privileged; a pluralist society open to multiple expressions within the limits imposed by the respect for fundamental democratic values and the necessity of intercultural exchange (1990: 15).

This document also expresses a preference for interculturalism over the multicultural approach favoured in Canada (Laperrière, 1985). Multiculturalism is viewed as overemphasizing minority cultures as isolated and static entities while ignoring their relationship to the majority. It is also argued that the requirement of equal status for all cultural groups masks the political and historical differences between various ethnic groups and favours the mobility of some groups at the expense of others. Interculturalism implies not the protection of minority cultures, but the fostering of a dynamic interaction between minorities and the majority. Interculturalism is viewed as the desirable form of pluralism because it allows societies and groups to achieve an increased level of adaptive capacity, as individuals will acquire a more complex and equilibrated cognitive capacity. Actually, as the ideologies of interculturalism and multiculturalism evolve, what differs is more their representation than their actual content.

In hindsight, acceptance by the Quebec state of cultural pluralism and its adoption of normative pluralism should not come as a surprise; many factors pointed in this direction. First, the complex articulation of ethnic relations in Canada has engendered, in the century following the British North America Act, an unresolved conflict between the two "founding" peoples, the occlusion of their respective status as colonial powers dominating the First Nations, and a blindness to the contribution of groups other than English or French to the construction of the Canadian nation. This unresolved conflict has led to the erosion of the two existing models of nation, the *Kulturnation*, based on common ancestry, and the *Staatsnation*, based on the citizenship rights of people who become culturally similar. The opposition in Canada between two powerful national groups and conceptions of the nation has rendered impossible the actualization of an assimilationist model. Second, the ensuing adherence of the federal state to normative pluralism and the articulation of policies aiming at its implementation exerted a strong influence in the direction of increased pluralism; the rivalry between the provincial and the federal states, each one wooing the same groups in order to secure their allegiance, led to the development of a positive attitude toward pluralism by the Quebec state (Juteau, 1986). Third, the Québécois nation, while it incorporated pre-existing ethnic elements, is now defined in territorial terms. As such, it can both imagine and realize itself as a voluntarist and political nation; one can, in principle at least, become a Québécois.

The presence of government support does not mean that pluralism as an ideology is accepted and endorsed by all. The furor over Opposition leader J. Parizeau's political "blunder" represents a good example. You will remember that he affirmed that Quebec could realize sovereignty without the aid of non-francophones. Although mathematically correct, this statement indicates how deep the boundaries opposing "we" and "they" still remain for some Québécois — and therefore how much work remains to be done in order to break down the boundaries of the French-Canadian nation, which is still often considered to represent the core of the Québécois nation. Finally, this process of inclusion is further slowed down by the confrontation between two collectivities claiming national status with the same territory. It is interesting to see how "les Autochtones" are now redefining themselves as First Nations. In this context the word "nation" is not innocent, since it does imply the legitimate right to self-determination.

CONCLUSION
▼

The consolidation of the Québécois nation followed a course not unlike that of Canada as a whole. In its effort to regulate the relations between the various ethnic groups living within its boundaries, the Quebec state gradually adopted and developed a pluralist model of the nation, one that emphasizes greater inclusion and diversity while it simultaneously is contested. Now that both Quebec and Canada have taken the pluralist turn, we are faced with two competing national communities, each engaged in a process of consolidation, integration, and maintenance of a culturally diverse national community. What is less clear, however, is whether Canada has the capacity to integrate two projects that are not necessarily incompatible, or the capacity to implement this model in the face of growing opposition. Now that the acceptance of cultural and normative pluralism seems to have led to the questioning of some of the centre's symbols, there seems to be growing support for a return to an assimilationist model. In Quebec, this is reinforced in academic circles by our numerous contacts with French intellectuals. For them, accepting pluralism inevitably leads to the adoption of an ethnic model closely linked to racism.

What is crucial, obviously, is to reinforce our message regarding the social construction of ethnicity. For recognizing the existence of ethnicity and nationality creates in the long run fewer problems than burying it.

It allows for the implementation of a broader basis of inclusion and for the rejection of the idea of the homogeneity of the nation. Politics and culture must be disassociated from genetics. But in Quebec, as in Canada and elsewhere in the world, inclusion requires the institutionalization of the legal, political, and social components of citizenship, a goal that represents a considerable challenge in a world traversed by socio-economic inequalities and characterized by the re-emergence of neo-fascist movements and the reinforcement of sexist and racist ideologies.

NOTES
▼

1. This essay takes as its starting point my article "The Production of the Québécois Nation" published in the *Humboldt Journal of Social Relations, 9/2* (1993), pp. 79–108.
2. For A.D. Smith, "state-nations" represent "political formations with de facto sovereignty i.e. states, which do not [yet] possess ... cultural differentiae and ingroup sentiment" (1971: 189).
3. "First Nations" refers to the Aboriginal peoples.
4. As "Coloured" became "Blacks" in the United States, "French Canadians" in Quebec became "Québécois."

REFERENCES
▼

Bauer, Otto. (1974). Le concept de nation. Le socialisme et le principe de nationalité. Différenciation croissante entre les nations dans la société socialiste. In G. Haupt, M. Lowy, & C. Weill (Eds.), *Les Marxistes et la question nationale, 1848–1914* (pp. 233–274). Montreal: L'Etincelle.

———. (1987). *La Question des nationalités et la social-démocratie,* vol. 2. Montreal: Guérin Littérature; Paris: Etudes et Documentations Internationales.

Breton, Raymond. (1984). The production and allocation of symbolic resources: An analysis of the linguistics and ethnocultural fields in Canada. *Revue canadienne de sociologie et d'anthropologie, 21*(2), 123–244.

Cloutier, Edouard, & Latouche, Daniel. (1979). *Le système politique québécois: recueil de textes*. LaSalle, QC: Hurtubise HMH.

Government of Quebec. (1978). *La Politique québécoise du développement culturel.* Quebec: Editeur officiel.

———. (1990). *L'Énoncé de politique en matière d'immigration et d'intégration au Québec. Pour bâtir ensemble.* Montreal: Ministère des Communautés Culturelles et de l'Immigration.

Government of Quebec/MCCI. (198)1. *Autant de façons d'être québécois. Plan d'Action du gouvernement du Québec á l'intention des communautés culturelles.* Montreal: Government of Quebec/MCCI.

GRES. (1992). Immigration et relations ethniques au Québec: un pluralisme en devenir. In G. Daigle (Ed.)., *Le Québec en jeu. Comprendre les grands défis* (pp. 451–481). Montreal: Les Presses de l'Université de Montréal.

Juteau, Danielle. (1986). L'Etat et les immigrés: de l'immigration aux communautés culturelles. In Pierre Guillaume et al. (Eds.), *Minorités et etat* (pp. 35–51). Bordeaux: PUB et Presses Universitaires de Laval.

Juteau, Danielle, & McAndrew, Marie. (1992). Projet national, immigration et intégration dans un Québec souverain. *Sociologie et sociétés, 24*(2), 161–180.

Juteau-Lee, Danielle. (1974). The impact of modernization and environmental impingements upon nationalism and separatism: The Quebec case. Unpublished Ph.D. Thesis, University of Toronto.

———. (1980). Français d'Amérique, Canadiens, Canadiens-Français, Franco-Ontariens, Ontarios: Qui sommes-nous? *Pluriel,* no. 24, 21–43.

Laferrière, Michel. (1983). L'éducation des enfants des groupes minoritaires au Québec: de la définition des problèmes par les groupes eux-mêmes á l'intervention de l'etat. *Sociologie et Sociétés, 15*(2), 117–133.

Laperrière, Anne. (1985). *Les Idéologies et pratiques d'intervention britanniques concernant l'intégration sociale des immigrantes et minorités ethniques.* Rapport de recherche présenté au Conseil scolaire de l'Ile de Montréal et au Conseil de la langue français. Montreal: Université du Québec á Montréal.

Porter, John. (1965). *The vertical mosaic: An analysis of social class and power in Canada.* Toronto: University of Toronto Press.

Schnapper, Dominique. (1991). *La France de l'intégration. Sociologie de la nation en 1990.* Paris: Gallimard.

Smith, A.D. (1986). *The ethnic origins of nations.* Oxford: Basil Blackwell.

Weber, Max. (1978). *Economie et société.* Paris: Plon. [First edition 1921–22].

16

▼

THE WARPED LOOKING GLASS: HOW MINORITIES PERCEIVE THEMSELVES, BELIEVE THEY ARE PERCEIVED, AND ARE ACTUALLY PERCEIVED BY MAJORITY-GROUP MEMBERS IN QUEBEC, CANADA

FATHALI M. MOGHADDAM, DONALD M. TAYLOR, PEGGY TCHORYK PELLETIER, AND MARC SHEPANEK

INTRODUCTION
▼

A central feature of North American societies is the growing demographic importance and increased collective mobilization of ethnic minorities (Bienvenue & Goldstein, 1985; Fleras & Elliott, 1992; Maldonado & Moore, 1985; Olsak, 1983). Perhaps partly in response to these changes, social psychologists have shown greater concern for the issues of contact between ethnic groups (Miller & Brewer, 1984), racism (Dovidio & Gaertner, 1986; Katz & Taylor, 1988), justice (Lind & Tyler, 1988), and cultural diversity (Moghaddam, Taylor, & Wright, 1993). In the Canadian context, specifically, the integration patterns of ethnic minorities, and majority attitudes toward minorities, have received greater research attention (Berry, 1984, 1991; Berry, Kalin, & Taylor, 1977; Lalonde, Taylor, & Moghaddam, 1992; Moghaddam, 1994; Moghaddam & Taylor, 1987; Moghaddam, Taylor, & Lalonde, 1987, 1989; Reynolds, 1992).

In a major national survey, Berry et al. (1977) found that majority-group Canadians differentially evaluated membership in different minority groups, and that their preferences implied a "hierarchy of acceptance" (see Berry et al., 1977: 106). The position of different minorities in this hierarchy seemed to be associated with how similar the minority is to majority-group members. Thus, minorities of Western European origin appeared at the top half of the hierarchy and those of Asian or African descent were situated at the bottom half. This pattern of results is consistent with a long line of research on "social distance" and similarity-attraction (Bogardus, 1925; Byrne, 1971), suggesting that similar others are more likely to be accepted into the category of "in-group." Also indicative of majority-group perceptions is the growing literature on racism in Canada (see Henry & Tator, 1985), which serves to highlight the idea that minority groups are differentially accepted by majority-group Canadians.

There is still need, however, for more research on the self-perceptions of ethnic minorities themselves. Central to such self-perceptions are the labels immigrants have available to them after arrival in the host society. Some such labels imply that the individual remains outside the majority group, while others imply that the individual has moved closer to gaining entrance to the majority group. For example, in the context of the Canadian province of Quebec, the labels "foreigner" and "immigrant" imply less progress in gaining entrance to the majority group, thus "exclusion," than the label "Quebecer," which implies "inclusion" to a greater extent.

Clearly, ethnic minorities adopt labels such as "foreigner" and "Quebecer" through interactions with others (Weinreich, 1983,1986). Thus, in addition to exploring how individuals perceive themselves, it is also important to examine how individuals view majority groups as perceiving the self. In examining this latter topic, Moghaddam and Taylor (1987) conducted a study of visible-minority women in Montreal, and found that these women perceived themselves more as "Canadians" and less as "immigrants" than they believed majority-group Canadians perceive them. Importantly, the longer these women lived in Canada, the more they felt that they were viewed by majority-group members as outsiders. This unexpected finding was interpreted by Moghaddam and Taylor (1987) as reflecting the experiences of visible-minority women with discrimination, so that women who have lived in Canada longer have greater opportunities to experience discrimination and, consequently, are more likely to believe they are perceived as outsiders. Related to this is the finding of Lalonde et al. (1992) that ethnic minorities believe Canadian society positively values the label "Canadian" more than that of "immigrant." Thus, labels such as "Canadian" and "immigrant" seem to imply different levels of "inclusion" and "exclusion."

This line of research focussing on the perceptions of minority groups is limited in an important way, however, because it fails to provide information about the accuracy of such perceptions. If society, and majority groups in particular, can act as a mirror for the "looking glass self" (Cooley, 1902), we must also address the question "how accurately do individuals see what is in the mirror?"

An important next step, then, is to assess how majority-group members actually perceive minority groups (actual-out-group perceptions). Do majority-group members actually perceive members of different minority groups as "immigrants" and "foreigners," more than they perceive them as majority-group members, or are they only assumed to do so? This question is, we believe, of theoretical importance, because discrepancies between believed and actual-out-group perceptions are likely to be systematically associated with similarity. Because majority-group members place more similar outgroups higher in the status hierarchy (Berry et al., 1977), the more similar minority groups are more likely to assume that majority-group members see them as "in-group" rather than as "outsiders." In contrast, dissimilar minority groups are more likely to see themselves as being placed in "outsider" categories.

If this pattern of intergroup perceptions was to emerge, then a number of potentially frustrating consequences might arise. For instance, Western Europeans might be over-confident about how much they are accepted, and be unexpectedly frustrated at what they may see as their "cool" reception. On the other hand, visible-minority-group members who perceive themselves to be outsiders, and also believe they are perceived by majority-group members as outsiders, may be misjudging how majority groups actually perceive them. In some conditions, majority-group members may be more accepting of minority groups than minority groups believe them to be.

In order to explore "own," "believed-out-group," and "actual-out-group" perceptions, we undertook a study of intergroup attitudes in the context of a francophone junior college in Montreal. The respondents included samples of majority-group members (French Quebecers), "non-visible"-minority-group members (European francophones), and a variety of "visible" minority-group members (Jews, Latin Americans, Haitians, and Southeast Asians).

The focus for the research was perceptions on the basis of group labels implying "exclusion" ("immigrant," "foreigner") and "inclusion" ("Quebecer") in terms of: (1) the actual perceptions that majority-group members have of various minority groups; (2) the perceptions of minority-group members in terms of their own category memberships; and (3) the perception of minority-group members in terms of how they believe majority-group members perceive them. We ventured three hypotheses.

The first hypothesis was based on the notion of "cultural distance" and predicted that acceptance by majority-group members would be in order of intergroup similarity (Bogardus, 1925; Byrne, 1971). It was hypothesized that majority-group members (French Quebecers) would perceive the non-visible-minority group (European francophones) more as "Quebecer" and less as "immigrant" or "foreigner" than the other four visible-minority groups. Following Moghaddam and Taylor (1987) and Lalonde et al. (1992), our second hypothesis was that minority-group respondents would perceive themselves less as "immigrant" and "foreigner" and more as "Quebecer" than they believed French Quebecers perceive them. Hypothesis three predicted that the beliefs that minority groups hold about majority-group perceptions would be systematically biased, so that there would be an exaggeration of "being rejected" by visible-group minorities, and an exaggeration of "being accepted" by European immigrants. The testing of this third hypothesis, which was the main innovation of this study, required the contrasting of how minority groups perceived themselves and believed they are perceived by majority-group members, with how they are actually perceived.

METHOD
▼

SUBJECTS

The respondents for this study were 293 junior college students from an ethnically diverse college in Montreal. The average age of the students was approximately 18 years. Four immigrant groups were represented in the sample: 30 European francophones, the majority from France, with 8 from Belgium and 1 from Switzerland; 45 Haitians; 45 Southeast Asians representing the nations of Vietnam, Thailand, Laos, and Cambodia; 23 Jewish students, 17 of whom were Sephardic from North Africa (we use the labels "European francophones," "Jews," "Latin Americans," "Haitians," and "Southeast Asians," because pilot work demonstrated that the respondents clearly understood these labels). For one particular analysis a sample of 150 Caucasian French Quebecers from the same college were also included.

MATERIALS AND PROCEDURE

The present research was part of a large-scale project dealing with ethnic relations at a multi-ethnic junior college. Respondents were recruited by soliciting their participation in school classes, with the co-operation of school authorities. In the case of the ethnic-minority respondents, our goal was to achieve as large a sample as possible. Thus, we attempted to be as inclusive as possible, achieving about a 70 percent return rate. The French Quebecers were randomly selected from the total school population by using school lists.

Questionnaires were completed individually by respondents in their classes during school hours; but there was no communication between respondents while they completed questionnaires. Since their classes are all in French, respondents completed a questionnaire in French. The questionnaire comprised the following sections of relevance to the present study.

- *Demographic Information:* A series of demographic questions focussed on age, sex, and details of ethnic background.
- *Intergroup Perceptions:* Respondents' perception of themselves and how they believe they are perceived by French Quebecers were assessed through three sets of questions. The first set of questions required respondents to rate the extent to which they thought of themselves as a member of a variety of group labels. Respondents were presented with the following labels: "immigrant," "foreigner," and "Quebecer."[1] After the presentation of each label, respondents indicated the extent to which they saw themselves as members of that particular category. The labels were presented in a fixed order, based on our previous research experience using these labels (e.g., Lalonde et al., 1992; Moghaddam & Taylor, 1987), which indicated no order effect. Responses to each question took the form of a nine-point scale, where one (1) represented "definitely no" and nine (9) represented "definitely yes." For the second set of questions, the interviewer asked the respondent to rate the same groups again, adding "... only this time rate, not how you think of yourself, but how most French Quebecers think of you." For the third set of questions, 150 French Quebecers were asked how they actually perceived members of the other five groups in terms of the labels "immigrant," "foreigner," and "Quebecer."
- *Actual Perceptions:* Ratings made by French Quebecers on the three labels were analyzed by a 3 x 5 (status by ethnic group) NOVA, with repeated measures on both factors, resulting in a significant interaction, $F(8,144) = 35.65$, $P < .001$. Post-hoc comparisons of means (Newman-Keuls) revealed that French Quebecers perceived European francophones and Jews less as "immigrants" than Haitians, Latin Americans, and Southeast Asians (see Figure 16.3). Compared to the Jews, the Latin Americans, and the Haitians, the European francophones were perceived less as "foreigners" and more as "Quebecers." The Jews were also perceived more as "Quebecers" than the Southeast Asians.
- *Self-Perceptions:* Own and believed-out-group perceptions were analyzed using a 2 x 3 x 5 ANOVA, perception type (own / believed other) by status label (immigrant/foreigner/Quebecer) by ethnic groups (European francophones/Jewish/Latin American/Haitian/Southeast Asian), with repeated

measures on the first two factors. The three-way interaction was not significant. When a 2 (perception type) x 3 (status label) ANOVA was run for each of the five ethnic groups separately, significant interaction effects were found for the Haitians $F(2,86) = 13.05$, $p < .001$, the Latin American sample $F(2,62) = 5.09$, $p < .01$, and the Jewish sample $F(2,56) = 7.9$, $p < .001$. Post-hoc comparisons of means (Neuman-Keuls) revealed the source of the interaction to be a trend found for all three groups, showing own perceptions to be lower than believed-out-group perceptions on the "immigrant" and "foreigner" labels, but higher on the "Quebecer" label (see Figures 16.1 and 16.2).

- *Self versus Actual-Out-group Perceptions:* One-way ANOVAs were computed across own, believed-out-group, and actual-out-group perceptions for each group's rating on each status label. Post-hoc tests (Neuman-Keuls) were used to examine the sources of significant differences, and three distinct patterns emerged. First, European francophones perceived themselves and believed they are perceived less as "immigrants," $F(2,217) = 26.03$, $p < .001$, and "foreigners," $F(2,219) = 10.45$, $p < .001$, than they actually are; and more as "Quebecer" than they actually are, $F(2,218) = 3.51$, $p < .01$. This is contrasted by a second pattern, evident to different degrees in the responses of the Jewish, Latin American, and Haitian samples, but most clearly apparent in the case of the Haitians. The Haitians believed that they are perceived more as "immigrants," $F(2,232) = 7.68$, $p < .01$, and "foreigners," $F(2,233) = 11.49$, $p < .01$, than they actually are, and less as "Quebecer," $F(2,230) = 3.52$, $p < .01$, than they actually are. A third pattern is evident in the responses of the Southeast Asians. There were no differences between own, believed-out-group, and actual-out-group perceptions on any of the three status labels (see Figures 16.1–16.3).

CONCLUSION
▼

The main innovation of this study was to assess the accuracy of beliefs minority-group members hold about how majority-group members perceive them. We addressed this question by examining the relationships among how minority groups perceive themselves, believe they are perceived by majority-group members, and are actually perceived by majority-group members on the labels "immigrant," "foreigner," and "Quebecer."

Our first hypothesis was that the actual perceptions held by majority-group members would reflect a "hierarchy of acceptance," so that, because of their greater similarity to French Quebecers, European francophones would

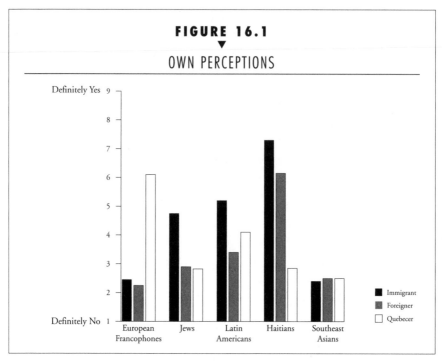

FIGURE 16.1
▼
OWN PERCEPTIONS

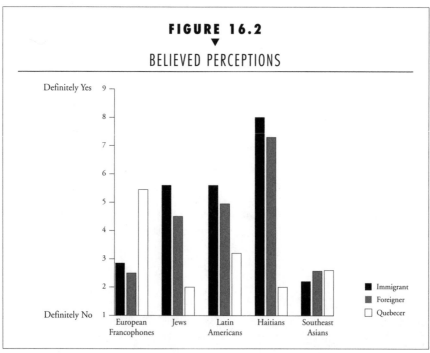

FIGURE 16.2
▼
BELIEVED PERCEPTIONS

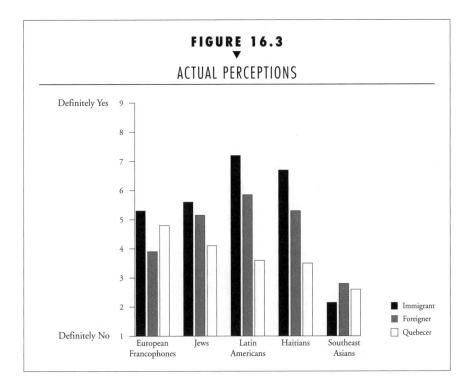

FIGURE 16.3

▼

ACTUAL PERCEPTIONS

be perceived as "Quebecers" and less as "immigrants" and as "foreigners" than the other groups. The findings clearly support this hypothesis, although the "hierarchy of acceptance" is not as clear-cut as we had predicted. The European francophones clearly were perceived more as "Quebecers" and less as "foreigners" than the other groups, but the Jews were perceived to be similar to the European francophones on the "immigrant" label. Also, the Jews were seen more as Quebecers than one of the other minorities, the Southeast Asians.

The general trend of our findings is consistent with those of Berry et al. (1977), and suggest that majority-group members differentiate between minority groups and are more accepting toward some than toward others. Interestingly, this study comes fifteen years after Berry et al. (1977), and shows very similar patterns of preferences. Some ambiguity remains with respect to the Jews. Although most of our sample were Sephardic Jews, and although it was they who interacted with the majority-group sample on a daily basis at school, we cannot exclude the possibility that in making their ratings the majority-group sample were thinking of the long-established community of European Jews in Quebec. Thus, what seems to be more accepting attitudes toward Jews, relative to the visible-minority groups, may have been influenced by the

Jews' being conceived as "European," and thus more similar to majority-group Canadians than to visible minorities.

The second hypothesis was that minority-group respondents would perceive themselves less as "immigrants" and "foreigners," and more as "Quebecers," than they believe majority-group Canadians perceive them. The previous studies that we are aware of which reported this trend focussed on visible-minority-group members (Lalonde et al., 1992; Moghaddam & Taylor, 1987). In the present study, this hypothesis was fully confirmed in the cases of the Haitian, Latin American, and Jewish samples, but not in the case of the Southeast Asians. Responses among the Haitians, Latin Americans, and Jews seem to reflect the general belief that they are perceived by majority-group members as outsiders, and as "belonging" less than they themselves believe they belong in Quebec.

The perception that one "belongs" more than majority-group members see one as "belonging" was not shared by European francophones. This is perhaps because European francophones are treated as being more similar to French Quebecers by French Quebecers.

Thus, the findings provide general support for the first two hypotheses. On the one hand, majority-group members seem to have a "hierarchy of acceptance." They perceive European francophones more as "Quebecers" and less as "outsiders." Correspondingly, Haitians, Latin Americans, and Jews believe that majority-group Canadians see them less as "Quebecers" and more as "outsiders" than they see themselves. European francophones do not perceive such a rift; and this can be explained, it seems to us, with reference to the high status they enjoy.

But in the realm of intergroup perceptions, perhaps the most important rift that can arise is between how majority-group members actually perceive minorities and how they are assumed to perceive minorities. In support of the third hypothesis, the findings of this study indicate that such rifts exist and, second, that the existing rifts are systematically associated with status differences between groups. The "non-visible" minority-group, the European francophones, acted in an "over-confident" manner, in that they assumed that they are "accepted" as Quebecers more than they actually were, and seen less as "outsiders" than they actually were. In contrast, the Haitians, a representative "visible"-minority group, lacked confidence completely, since they assumed that they are perceived more as "outsiders" and less as "Quebecers" than they actually were.

These misperceptions are bound to exacerbate the potential for intergroup conflict. In the case of over-confidence, group members believe they are accepted when in fact the majority has reservations. Members of the over-confident group will not be taking steps to overcome the majority group's reservations, and indeed are likely to be presumptuous in the context of interactions with members of the majority group. Such a posture is likely to make integration with the majority group more problematic.

For members of visible-minority groups who exaggerate the extent to which they are not supported by the majority group, a defensive posture is likely. This tends to exacerbate the potential for conflict and also prevent members of visible minorities from taking advantage of the available good will that actually exists in the larger society.

Also, the question arises as to why one visible-minority group, the Southeast Asians, did not follow the predicted pattern and generally responded in a way that was different from the other groups. There was no difference between own, believed-out-group, and actual-out-group perceptions among the Southeast Asian sample on any of the three labels. One possibility is that the Southeast Asians genuinely are more accurate in assessing and matching how they see themselves, as compared to how they are seen by majority-group Canadians. But a more plausible explanation is that, because they are a newly arrived refugee population, the Southeast Asian respondents themselves and members of the majority group were uncertain about their own role in Canadian society and as yet unclear about how they should describe themselves. This would explain why consistently low ratings were given to all three labels, relative to ratings given by the other minority groups who have been in Canada longer and have probably developed a clearer picture of their place in Canada.

Finally, we should raise a methodological issue that might have a bearing on our findings. Our respondents were junior college students, and the question arises as to how these results might be pertinent for other sectors of the population. We specifically chose a junior college as the context for our study because of the importance the school context has in the socialization of intergroup relations. This is a context in which future adults from diverse ethnic backgrounds have an opportunity to interact with one another and form relationships across ethnic boundaries. It is also a context in which there are, presumably, ample opportunities for minority-group members to accurately assess how majority groups view them. The discovery of inaccuracies in intergroup perceptions in this school context raises the possibility that such perceptions will be even more biased among adults. This should be a topic for future research in multicultural societies such as Canada.

NOTES
▼

1. We used the category "Quebecer" rather than "French Quebecer" because the former is more inclusive.

REFERENCES
▼

Berry, J.W. (1984). Multiculturalism policy in Canada: A social psychological analysis. *Canadian Journal of Behavioural Science, 16,* 353–370.

———. (1991). Sociopsychological costs and benefits of multiculturalism. Working Paper No. 24. Ottawa: Economic Council of Canada.

Berry, J.W., Kalin R., & Taylor, D.M. (1977). Multiculturalism and ethnic attitudes in Canada. Ottawa: Supply & Services Canada.

Bienvenue, R.M., & Goldstein, J.E. (Eds.) (1985). *Ethnicity and ethnic relations in Canada* (2nd ed.). Toronto: Butterworths.

Bogardus, E.S. (1925). Measuring social distance. *Journal of Applied Psychology, 9,* 299–308.

Bolaria, B.S., & Li, P.S., (1988). *Racial oppression in Canada.* Toronto: Garamond.

Byrne, D. (1971). *The attraction paradigm.* New York: Academic.

Cooley, H.C. (1902). *Human nature and the social order.* New York: Scribner.

Dovidio, J.F., & Gaertner, S.L. (Eds.) (1986). *Prejudice, discrimination, and racism.* New York: Academic.

Fleras, A., & Elliott, J.L. (1992). *Multiculturalism in Canada.* Scarborough, ON: Nelson.

Henry, F., & Tator, C. (1985). Racism in Canada: Social myths and strategies for change. In R.M. Bienvenue & J.E. Goldstein (Eds.), *Ethnicity and ethnic relations in Canada* (pp. 321–335). Toronto: Butterworths.

Katz, P.A., & Taylor, D.A. (Eds.) (1988). *Eliminating racism.* New York: Plenum.

Lalonde, R.N., Taylor, D.M., & Moghaddam, F.M. (1988). Social integration strategies of Haitian and Indian immigrant women in Montreal. In J.W. Berry & R.C. Annis (Eds.), *Ethnic psychology* (pp. 114–124). Amsterdam: Swets & Zeitlinger; Berwyn, P.A.: Swets North America.

Lalonde, R.N., Taylor, D.M., & Moghaddam, F.M. (1992). The process of social identification for visible immigrant women in a multicultural context. *Journal of Cross-Cultural Psychology, 23,* 25–39.

Lambert, W.E., Mermegis, L., & Taylor, D.M. (1986). Greek Canadians' attitudes towards own group and other Canadian ethnic groups: A test of the multicultural hypothesis. *Canadian Journal of Behavioural Science, 18,* 35–51.

Lind, E.A., & Tyler, T.R. (1988). *The social psychology of procedural justice.* New York: Plenum Press.

Maldonado, L., & Moore, J. (Eds.) (1985). *Urban ethnicity in the United States.* Beverly Hills: Sage.

McConahay, J.B., & Hough, J.C. (1976). Symbolic racism. *Journal of Social Issues, 32,* 23–45.

Miller, N., & Brewer, M. (1984). Groups in contact: *The psychology of desegregation.* New York: Academic.

Moghaddam, F.M. (1992). Assimilation et multiculturalism: Le cas des minorites au Québec. *Revue québécoise de psychologie, 13*, 140–157.

Moghaddam, F.M. (1994). Ethnic segregation in a multicultural society: A review of recent trends in Montreal and Toronto and reconceptualization of causal factors. In Frances Frisken (Ed.), *The changing Canadian metropolis*, Vol. 1 (pp. 237–258). Toronto: Canadian Urban Institute.

Moghaddam, F.M., & Taylor, D.M. (1987). The meaning of multiculturalism for visible minority immigrant women. *Canadian Journal of Behavioural Sciences, 19*, 121–136.

Moghaddam, F.M., Taylor, D.M., & Lalonde, R.N. (1987). Individualistic and collective integration strategies among Iranians in Canada. *International Journal of Psychology, 22*, 301–313.

Moghaddam, F.M., Taylor, D.M., & Lalonde, R.N. (1989). Integration strategies and attitudes toward the built environment: A study of Haitian and Indian immigrant women. *Canadian Journal of Behavioural Science, 21*, 160–173.

Moghaddam, F.M., Taylor, D.M., & Wright, S.C. (1993). *Social psychology in cross-cultural perspective*. New York: Freeman.

Olsak, S. (1983). Contemporary ethnic mobilization. *American Journal of Sociology, 9*, 355–374.

Reynolds, A.G. (Ed.) (1992). Bilingualism, multiculturalism, and second language learning: The McGill conference in honor of Wallace E. Lambert. Hillsdale, NJ: Lawrence Erlbaum.

Sears, D.O. (1988). Symbolic racism. In P.A. Katz & D.A. Taylor (Eds.), *Eliminating racism* (pp. 53–84). New York: Plenum.

Sears, D.O., & Kinder, D.R., (1985). Whites' opposition to busing: On conceptualizing and operationalizing group conflict. *Journal of Personality and Social Psychology, 48*, 1141–1147.

Weinreich, P. (1983). Psychodynamics of personal and social identity. In A. Jacobson-Widding (Ed.), *Identity: Personal and socio-cultural* (pp. 159–185). Stockholm: Almqvist & Wiskell International.

Weinreich, P. (1986). The operationalisation of identity theory in racial and ethnic relations. In J. Rex & D. Mason (Eds.), *Theories of race and ethnic relations* (pp. 299–320). Cambridge: Cambridge University Press.

PART FIVE

PREJUDICE AND DISCRIMINATION

INTRODUCTION

Part Five is concerned with prejudice and discrimination not only in Canada, but also on a global scale. Frances Henry and Carol Tator look at some of the forms racism can take, but focus on a form they call "democratic racism." Agnes Calliste's article is a case study of women of colour in the nursing profession vis-à-vis prejudice and discrimination. Anthony Richmond's article adds a global dimension to prejudice and discrimination that very much includes Canada. Reginald Bibby's chapter brings Part Five, and the book itself, to a fitting end, one that suggests that harmony in a pluralistic or multicultural society such as Canada is there for the taking.

In Chapter Seventeen, Henry and Tator examine a relatively new and more invisible form of racism that they call "democratic racism." They define it as a tension that arises from the "clash between the reality of pervasive racism, and, at the same time, a commitment to the ideology of democratic liberalism." In essence, Henry and Tator examine the theory and the practice of democratic racism in Canada by examining the relationship between ideology and discourse and how they produce individual, institutional, and systemic forms of racism within the framework of a democratic liberal society.

In Chapter Eighteen, Agnes Calliste presents a case study of "women of colour" in the nursing profession in the province of Ontario. Calliste interviewed registered nurses, officers of the nurses' union, and members of community organizations as a basis for her analysis. She also analyzed data records of the Ontario Human Rights Commission and other secondary sources. Her chapter discusses the history and the conditions under which female nurses of colour have become targets of discriminatory behaviour by the actions of others, such as their superiors in the nursing profession. Calliste found that discrimination occurred in many different areas, including the process of accreditation of immigrant nurses, oversupervision by supervisors, and unfair disciplinary practices instituted against them but not against others.

In Chapter Nineteen, Richmond reminds us that prejudice and discrimination exist elsewhere in the world besides Canada. He ponders the question of whether we are creating a system of global apartheid based on discrimination against migrants from developing countries or, alternatively, whether our actions are simply rational ways of protecting our social system. His discussion centres around the concept and practice of apartheid, and to this end he uses South Africa as an example of a country where there is now social and political reform, but where apartheid was once the order of the day.

Richmond notes the emergence of intolerance through stricter immigration controls worldwide, including Canada, as various nation-states seek to have greater control over who gets in. He argues that the world must learn to live with ethnic diversity, mass migration, and social change.

In Chapter Twenty, Reginald Bibby expresses hope ... hope for the future of Canada's mosaic. This chapter brings our discussion full circle and asks us to consider how we as Canadians of many ancestries can co-exist. The hope, as Bibby sees it, is a society where madness gives way to sanity.

17

▼

THE THEORY AND PRACTICE OF DEMOCRATIC RACISM IN CANADA[1]
FRANCES HENRY AND CAROL TATOR

This paper examines a relatively new form of racism in Canadian society that we have called "democratic racism" (Henry et al., 2000). This contemporary form of racism is linked to previous theoretical models known as "symbolic" (Sears, 1988) or "aversive" racism (Gaertner & Dovidio, 1986) The concept of democratic racism refers to a deep tension in Canada and other democratic states such as the United Kingdom and the United States that arises from two competing value systems: the clash between the reality of pervasive racism and, at the same time, a commitment to the ideology of democratic liberalism. The paper begins with a brief examination of the function of ideology as the basis of social behaviour and inequality, and then explores the nature of racist ideology. Ideology provides the foundation for understanding the racist attitudes and behaviours of individuals, the maintenance of racist policies and practices in Canadian institutions, and the promulgation of racist doctrines and laws by the state. The last section of the paper examines the discourse of democratic racism; the common expressions of racist discourse cloaked in liberal sounding principles, values, and beliefs that support and reinforce racism as ideology and practice. The authors examine the relationship between ideology and discourse and how, together, they serve to reproduce individual, institutional, and systemic forms of racism within the framework of a democratic liberal society.

INTRODUCTION
▼

INDIVIDUAL, INSTITUTIONAL, AND SYSTEMIC FORMS OF RACISM

One of the most complex aspects of racism is its elusive and changing nature. The most commonly accepted concept of racism in Canada is one that refers to the individual expression of overtly negative feelings or actions. "Racism," in this sense, is understood to refer to physical assaults that have been perpetrated by bigoted individuals, racial slurs and harassment in schools or in the workplace, defacing property with racial graffiti, and similar aggressive anti-social acts. However, individual racism is not limited to the beliefs and be-haviours of social deviants.

Individual racism is rooted in the individual's belief system and has been defined as the attitude, belief, or opinion that one's own racial group has su-perior values, customs, and norms, and, conversely, that other racial groups possess inferior traits and attributes. Prejudiced attitudes are largely uncon-scious, and as such go unrecognized by most people (Hebdige, 1993). Racist attitudes are derivative in nature and grow out of and are sustained by the structure of social relations of which they are a mere reflection (Henry et al., 2000; Goldberg, 1993; Parekh, 1995).

Essed (1990) describes individual racism experienced by people of colour as the everyday glances, gestures, encounters, and actions that may not register in the consciousness of its perpetrators, but are immediately and painfully felt by the victims — the empty seat on the crowded bus next to a person of colour; the inability to make direct eye contact with a Black person; the racist joke told in a meeting; and the ubiquitous question "Where are you from?" This form of racism has also been identified as existential racism (Amit-Talai & Knowles, 1996).

The last decade or more has seen the emergence of a growing field of in-quiry analyzing and documenting institutional forms of racism. This form of racism is manifested in the policies, practices, procedures, values, and norms that operate within an organization or institution (e.g., a school and a board of edu-cation). For example, manifestations of institutional racism in education refer to racially biased attitudes and practices of teachers and administrators, Eurocentric curriculum, racial harassment of minority students, streaming of minority stu-dents into non-academic programs, the assimilationist culture of the school (Dei, 1996; D'Oyley & James, 1998; Alladin, 1995). In the media, racism is mani-fested by stereotypical portrayal and misrepresentation, invisibility of people of colour, lack of representation at all levels of media organizations, racialization of people of colour as social problems, reproduction of white Eurocentric values and images, biased attitudes and practices by media professionals, and so on (Fleras & Elliot, 1996; Henry et al., 2000; Tator et al., 1998; van Dijk, 1991). In em-ployment, racism is manifested in racial harassment in the workplace; disparities in salaries between white employees and those of colour with the same levels of job experience and education; higher levels of underemployment; lack of recog-nition of foreign credentials; or inflated educational requirements for a position (Abella, 1984; Jain, 1988; Reitz, 1990; Pendakur & Pendakur, 1995).

Systemic racism, although similar to institutional racism, refers more broadly to the laws, rules, and norms woven into the social system that result in the unequal distribution of economic, political, and social resources and rewards among various groups. For example, the history of immigration policies in Canada is marked by racist, discriminatory, exclusionary policies lasting over 100 years (Bolaria & Li, 1988; Calliste, 1994; Creese, 1993/94; Malarek, 1987; Abella & Troper, 1991). Kobayashi (1990: 40) contends that the systems of governance and the law itself have been used to create a "common-sense justification of racial differences" and to reinforce common understandings deeply embedded with the Canadian cultural system of values.

Systemic racism is the denial of access, participation, and equity to people of colour for services such as education, employment, and housing. Although institutional or systemic racism may be invisible or unwittingly practised, regardless of intent, these forms of racism have the consequence of promoting, sustaining, or entrenching differential advantage or privilege for white people. What all these manifestations of racism share in common is that they are rooted in ideology.

THE NATURE OF IDEOLOGY

Ideology is a set of beliefs, perceptions, assumptions, and values that provide members of a group with an understanding and an explanation of their world. At another level, ideology provides a framework for "organizing, maintaining and transforming relations of power and dominance in society" (Fleras & Elliot, 1992: 54).

Ideology influences the ways in which people interpret social, cultural, political, and economic systems and structures, and it is linked to their perceived needs, hopes, and fears. Ideological formations are not static, but organic and constantly evolving, often as a result of contradictory experiences (Hall, 1993; Hebdige, 1993). The function of ideology is to normalize the status quo and to present as immutable aspects of the human condition, the particular social condition (e.g., racism) which currently exists (Khenti, 1996).

Within everyday ideological constructs, ideas about race, gender, and class are produced, preserved, and promoted. These ideas form the basis for social behaviour. Therefore, understanding ideology is crucial to an understanding of the marginalization, exclusion, and domination of people of colour in Canadian society.

THE DEFINITION AND FUNCTION OF RACIST IDEOLOGY

Racist ideology provides the conceptual framework for the political, social, and cultural structures of inequality and systems of dominance based on race, as well as the processes of exclusion and marginalization of people of colour that characterize Canadian society.

The cognitive dimensions of racism are located in collective patterns of thought, knowledge, and beliefs, as well as in individual attitudes, perceptions, and behaviours. "Racism as ideology includes the whole range of concepts, ideas, images and institutions that provide the framework of interpretation and meaning for racial thought in society" (Essed, 1990: 44). Racist ideology therefore organizes, preserves, and perpetuates the power structures in a society. It creates and preserves a system of dominance based on race and is communicated and reproduced through agencies of socialization and cultural transmission, such as the mass media; schools and universities; religious doctrines; symbols; master narratives and images; art, music, and literature; and the courts and law enforcement agencies. It is reflected and regenerated in the very language that is read, written, and spoken.

Racist ideology forms part of "common sense." Racist thinking, according to this view, is natural and forms part of the ways in which ordinary people view the world — they do not need to have specialized knowledge about minority groups to be racist. "Common sense" racism is not based on theory, nor does it have a unified body of knowledge to support it; it contains a "storehouse of knowledge" that guides the thinking of "the practical struggle of everyday life of the popular masses" (Lawrence, 1982: 49).

The construction of and belief in a racist ideology helps people to understand the increasingly complex societies in which they live. Thus, recently unemployed people can easily blame the new immigrants who have taken their jobs away. People who are fearful in their homes and on the streets can now blame all the Black or Asian people, who, they believe, commit the crimes. Teachers whose Black students are underachieving can believe that it has nothing to do with their own racial attitudes or classroom practices. The corporate manager is able to justify a refusal to hire those who are racially, and often culturally, "different" on the basis of not wanting to disrupt the harmony of the workforce. These forms of everyday racism are part of what has been called the "new racism," which also includes forms identified as aversive or symbolic racism (noted above). The so-called new racism manifests itself in more subtle and indirect ways. It is often expressed discursively through "text, talk, ... board meetings, job interviews, policies, laws, parliamentary debates, political propaganda, textbooks, scholarly articles, movies, TV programs and news reports in the press, among hundreds of other genres" (van Dijk, 2000) Although the new racism rarely demonstrates itself in violence or overt behaviour, its consequences for minorities are just as severe: it limits and constrains their life chances.

"Democratic racism" is a particular form of the new racism identified by the authors. It refers both to an ideology that emphasizes racism and to a set of discursive policies and practices that regulate behaviour in specific institutions and settings.

THE CONCEPT OF DEMOCRATIC RACISM

Despite the ideological foundation of democratic liberalism and a legislative state framework based on the policies of multiculturalism, employment equity, the Canadian Human Rights Code, provincial human rights codes, and the Charter of Rights and Freedoms, racism continues to operate and penetrate all levels of Canadian society (Henry & Tator, in press; Tator, Henry, & Mattis, 1998; Razack, 1998; St. Lewis, 1996; Henry et al., 2000; Cannon, 1995). Thus, there is a fundamental tension in Canadian society between the ideology of Canada as a democratic liberal state and the racist ideology that is reflected in the collective belief system operating within Canadian cultural, social, political, and economic institutions.

Democratic racism results from the retention of racist beliefs and behaviours in a "democratic" society. Obfuscation and justificatory arguments are deployed to demonstrate continuing faith in the principles of an egalitarian society while at the same time undermining and sabotaging those ideals. Democratic racism is an ideology in which two conflicting sets of values are made congruent. Commitments to democratic principles such as justice, equality, and fairness *conflict* but *co-exist* with attitudes and behaviours that include negative feelings about minority groups and differential treatment of and discrimination against them (see Henry et al., 2000; Goldberg, 1993).

One of the consequences of this conflict is a lack of support for policies and practices that might improve the relatively low status of some people of colour. These policies and practices tend to require changes in the existing social, economic, and political order, usually by state intervention. The intervention, however, is perceived to be in conflict with, and a threat to, liberal democracy. Thus, democratic racism holds that the spread of racism should be dealt with only — if at all — by leaving basic economic structures and societal relations essentially unchanged (Gilroy, 1987). Efforts to combat racism that require intervention to change the cultural, social, economic, and political order will lack political support. More important, they will lack legitimacy, according to the egalitarian principles of liberal democracy.

THE DISCOURSE OF DEMOCRATIC RACISM[2]
▼

How is democratic racism manifested in the daily lives, opinions, and feelings of people? What are the values, assumptions, and arguments of democratic racism? As Wellman (1977) has noted, the maintenance of a wide array of myths and misconceptions about racism has permitted a pattern of denial that has led to a wholly inadequate response to racism. These myths attempt to explain, rationalize, and resolve insupportable contradictions and tensions in society. Myths arise at particular historical moments in response to a perceived need within society.

Democratic racism in its ideological and discursive form is deeply embedded in popular culture and popular discourse. It is located within what has been called society's "frames of reference" (Hebdige, 1993). These frames of reference are a largely unacknowledged set of beliefs, assumptions, feelings, stories, and quasi-memories that underlie, sustain, and inform perceptions, thoughts, and actions. Democratic racism as racist discourse begins in the families that provide nurturance; the community that helps in the socialization process; the schools and universities whose role it is to educate; the media that communicate ideas and images; and the popular culture that entertains. People learn this discourse from the very same sites in which every other form of learning is provided.

Goldberg (1993) contends that racist discourse covers a wide spectrum of expressions and representations, including a nation's recorded history; biological/scientific explanations of racial difference; economic, legal, and bureaucratic forms of doctrines; cultural representations in the form of national narratives, images, and symbols. Racist discourse refers to the ways in which society gives voice to racism (Wetherell & Potter, 1992). Fiske (1994: 5) notes that "there is a discourse of racism that advances the interests of Whites and that has an identifiable repertoire of words, images and practices through which racial power is applied...."

The conflict between the ideology of democratic liberalism and the racist ideology present in the collective belief system of the dominant culture is reflected in the racist discourse that operates in the school, media, the courts, law enforcement agencies, arts organizations and cultural institutions, human services, government, bureaucracies, and political authorities. The school, university, newspaper, television station, courtroom, police headquarters, hospital, government office, and House of Parliament are all discursive spaces. Within these spaces, controlled mainly by a dominant white culture, there exists a constant moral tension: the lived reality and everyday experiences of people of colour, juxtaposed against the perceptions and responses of those who have the power to redefine that reality, such as educators, journalists, editors and broadcasters, judges, police, cultural critics, writers, artists, arts managers, cultural funders, and government officials and politicians, among others.

Many people resist antiracism and equity initiatives because they are unwilling to question *their* own belief and value systems, *their* discursive practices, *their* organizational and professional norms, and *their* positions of power and privilege within the workplaces and society in general. Thus, they are unable to explore the relational aspects of cultural and racial differences, and the power dynamics that are constructed around ideas about differences. Acknowledging that ethnoracial differences and racism make a difference in the lives of people is to concede that Euro-Canadian hegemony continues to function and organize the structures within which mainstream programs and services operate (Dei, 1996). In each of these discursive spaces (e.g., the school, museum, courtroom), there is tension and resistance in relation to how multicultural and antiracism ideologies and policies are "imagined, internalized and acted upon" (Yon, 1995: 315). Resistance may manifest itself as active opposition to addressing racial barriers that is expressed openly. But, more commonly, it is articulated in more subtle forms of discourse. Discourses on race and racism converge with concerns about Canadian identity, national unity, ethnicity, multiculturalism, and so on. Discourse provides the conceptual models for mapping the world around us and incorporates both social relationships and power relations (Goldberg, 1993). Michel Foucault (1980) uses the term "discourse" to refer to the ways in which language and other forms of communication are used as a vehicle of social processes. However, dominant discourse is an elusive concept because it hides within the mythical norms that define "Canadianness" as being white, male, Christian, heterosexual, and English-speaking. It is the elusive nature of the rhetoric of racism that allows it to mask its racialized ideas so easily.

Yon (1995) demonstrates this point in an important ethnographic study carried out with students and teachers in a Toronto high school. In his research, he shows how discourse about identity and nation that never mentions the word "race" can also be read as racist discourse. Increasingly, in education, media, and politics, the discourse of liberalism is juxtaposed with popular conservative ideology, and individuals slide ambivalently between the two. As Yon (1995: 315) points out: "Resistance and accommodation can be present in the same moment." Discourse often reveals ambivalence, contradiction, and subtleties in relation to the issues of difference. For example, discussions about culture by teachers, journalists, or politicians are often framed in the context of being "tolerant," "sensitive," and sufficiently enlightened to appreciate and respect the diverse cultures of the "others." Culture discourse tends to cover up the "unpleasantness" of domination and inequity (Wetherell & Potter, 1992).

The next section examines some of the prevailing myths that constitute discourse of dominance associated with "democratic racism." This includes the myths, explanations, codes of meaning, and rationalizations that have the effect of establishing, sustaining, and reinforcing democratic racism. This discourse is contextualized within democratic liberal, humanistic values. The analysis illustrates Goldberg's (1993) view that the central values of liberal ideologies carry different meanings and connotations, depending on the context. Tolerance, equality, and liberty, central concepts in liberal discourse, have immensely flexible meanings. Mackey (1996: 305) contends that these liberal principles often become "the language and conceptual framework through which intolerance and exclusion are enabled, reinforced, defined and defended."

It is the elusive nature of dominant discourse that allows it to mask its racialized ideas (Fiske, 1994). Within each of these liberal discourses are unchallenged assumptions or myths. The following are some of the prevailing myths and discourses that form the foundation of the thoughts, ideas, policies, and practices associated with democratic racism.

THE DISCOURSE OF DENIAL

Within this discourse, the principal assumption is that racism simply does not exist in a democratic society. There is a refusal to accept the reality of racism, despite the evidence of racial prejudice and discrimination in the lives, and on the life chances, of people of colour. "The New Racism wants to be democratic and respectable, and hence first off denies that it is racism. ... Real Racism, in this framework of thought, exists only among the Extreme Right" (van Dijk, 2000). The assumption is that, because Canada is a society that upholds the ideals of a liberal democracy, it can not possibly be racist. When racism is shown to exist, it tends to be identified as an isolated phenomenon relating to a limited number of social deviants, economic instability, or the consequence of "undemocratic" traditions that are disappearing from the Canadian scene. This discourse resists the notion that racism is systemic and inherently embedded in our cultural values and our democratic institutions.

THE DISCOURSE OF POLITICAL CORRECTNESS

The concept of political correctness is difficult to define because of its lack of tangible reference points (Fleras, 1996). It is neither an ideology nor a coherent social movement.

"Political correctness" is a term that, in recent years, has become a central part of the public discourse of the neo-conservatives as an expression of their resistance to forms of social change. Demands of marginalized minorities for inclusive language, and proactive policies (e.g., employment equity) and practices, are discredited as an "overdose of political correctness." Those opposed to proactive measures to ensure the inclusion of non-dominant voices, stories, and perspectives dismiss these concerns as the wailing and whining of radicals whose polemics (and actions) threaten the cornerstones of democratic liberalism. "Political correctness" is a term commonly used today by culturally conservative academics, journalists, politicians, writers, and cultural critics. It is commonly employed to deride the aspirations of minorities, and the pedagogical goals of liberal/radical professors in universities.

The political-correctness discourse is part of a larger and ongoing debate dealing with very different visions of society and diverse paradigms of social change. It is a rhetoric that has served to intensify and polarize positions with respect to issues of inclusion and representation (language and images in curricula, media, film, museums and galleries, literature), multiculturalism, equity, racism, and sexism in universities, schools, and human-services and government agencies (Srivastava, 1996). Toni Morrison (quoted in Miller, Swift, & Maggio, 1997), suggests that the label of political correctness is designed to stifle dissent. She goes on to say: "The political correctness debate is really about ... the power to be able to redefine. The definers want the power to name. And the defined are now taking the power away from them" (54).

THE DISCOURSE OF COLOUR BLINDNESS

Colour blindness is a powerful and appealing liberal discourse in which white people insist that they do not notice the skin colour of a racial-minority person. But as Gotanda (quoted in Crenshaw, 1991) suggests, this technique of observing but not considering "race" is a "technical fiction. It is impossible not to think about a subject without having first thought about it a little" (101). The refusal to recognize that race is part of the "baggage" that people of colour carry with them, and the refusal to recognize racism as part of everyday values, policies, programs, and practices, is part of the psychological and cultural power of racial constructions (James, 1994). Colour-blindness or colour evasion leads to power evasion (Frankenberg, 1993).

THE DISCOURSE OF EQUAL OPPORTUNITY

This discourse suggests that all we need to do is treat everyone the same and fairness will be ensured. This notion is based on an ahistorical premise; that is, we all begin from the same starting point, and everyone competes on a level playing field. Society merely provides the conditions within which individuals differentially endowed can make their mark. All have an equal opportunity to succeed and the same rights. Thus, individual merit determines who will be successful in the workplace, school, politics, and the arts.

This view ignores the social construction of race in which power and privilege belong to those who are white (among other social markers of privilege, including gender, class, sexual orientation, and able-bodiedness). Equal opportunity represents a passive approach and does not require the dismantling of white institutional power or the redistribution of white social capital (Crenshaw, 1997). This paradigm demands no form of proactive institutional or state intervention such as employment equity or antiracism policies.

THE DISCOURSE OF "BLAME THE VICTIM"

If equal opportunity and racial equality are assumed to exist, then the lack of success on the part of a minority population must be attributed to some other set of conditions. One explanation used by the dominant culture is the notion that certain minority communities themselves are culturally deficient (e.g., lacking intellectual prowess; more prone to aggressive behaviour or other forms of "deviant behaviour"). In this form of dominant discourse, it is assumed that certain communities (e.g., African Canadian) lack the motivation, education, or skills to participate fully in the workplace, educational system, and other arenas of Canadian society.

Alternatively, it is argued that the failure of certain groups to succeed and be integrated into the mainstream dominant culture is largely due to recalcitrant members of these groups refusing to adapt their "traditional," "different" cultural values and norms to fit into Canadian society, and making unreasonable demands of the "host" society.

THE DISCOURSE OF WHITE VICTIMIZATION

In this discourse, it is argued that white European immigrants have also experienced prejudice and discrimination in Canada. According to this view, the social system is open, but all immigrant groups must expect to start at the bottom of the social and economic ladder. It is only through their own initiative that they can expect to achieve upward mobility and thereby receive full and equal treatment. Therefore, there is no need for preferential policies or programs.

This assumption is based on the traditional view that race, ethnicity, and the immigrant experience are one and the same phenomenon. It does not recognize that genetic racial features such as skin colour do not simply disappear over time. It ignores the fact that second- and third-generation Canadian people of colour continue to experience the same prejudiced attitudes and discriminatory behaviour as their parents and grandparents. They continue to be severely impeded in their opportunities for upward mobility. Equating racial disadvantage and discrimination against the experiences of white European immigrants ignores the importance of the history of colonization, subjugation, and oppression of people of colour by Canadians of European origin.

THE DISCOURSE OF REVERSE RACISM

In a semantic reversal, those associated with the dominant culture contend that they are now the victims of a new form of oppression and exclusion. Antiracism and equity policies are seen as undemocratic, and thus discredited by those who suggest in strong, emotive language that such policies are nothing more than "apartheid in reverse," a "new inquisition," or "McCarthyite witch-hunts."

Positive and proactive policies and programs are thus aligned with creeping totalitarianism, incorporating the antidemocratic, authoritarian methods of the extreme Right. Those concerned with addressing racial inequalities have frequently been accused of belonging to radical extremist groups. The implication of these reproaches is that the issue of race is being used as a cover for promoting conflict in pursuit of other questionable political ends. Those concerned with racial injustice have been labelled as "radicals" who are using an antiracism platform to subvert Canada's fundamental institutions, values, and beliefs.

THE DISCOURSE OF BINARY POLARIZATION

The fragmentation into "we" and "they" is usually framed in the context of an examination of the relative values and norms of the majority-versus-minority populations. "We" represents the white dominant culture or the culture of the organization (police, school, workplace); "they" refers to the communities who are the "Other," possessing "different" (undesirable) values, beliefs, and norms. "We" are law-abiding, hardworking, decent, and homogeneous. We are the "Canadian Canadians" (Mackey, 1996) — "birthright Canadians" (Dabydeen, 1994). The "theys" are very different, and therefore undeserving (Apple, 1993). Those marked as "Other" are positioned outside of the "imagined" community (Anderson, 1983) of Canada and national identity of Canadians.

The discourse of "otherness" is supported by stereotypical images embedded in the fabric of the dominant culture. Although these stereotypes have little basis in reality, they nevertheless have a significant social impact. When minorities have no power to control, resist, produce, or disseminate other real and more positive images in the public domain, these images and generalizations increase their vulnerability in terms of cultural, social, economic, and political participation in the mainstream of Canadian society (Pieterse, 1992).

THE DISCOURSE OF "MORAL PANIC"

The economic and political destabilization and social dislocations experienced by societies such as Canada, the United States, the United Kingdom, and Germany have created a climate of uncertainty, fear, and threat. Some scholars have identified these phenomena as "moral panics" (Husband, 1994; Hall, 1978) in which those identified with the mainstream population or the dominant culture experience a loss of control, authority, and equilibrium. The country is described as in crisis, under siege. "We are not who we used to be" (McFarlane, 1995: 20).

This siege mentality is most evident in the public sphere (e.g., police, government, academia, and media). The antiracism initiatives of the late 1980s and early 1990s have been either significantly weakened or eliminated. Equality is being redefined — and is less and less considered the responsibility of the state. It is no longer linked to group oppression and systemic disadvantage and discrimination (Apple, 1993).

These new "moral panics" are based mainly on fears about cultural and racial differences, which imperil the national culture and identity. They take the form of "propaganda" campaigns in which a group is perceived, represented, and constructed as an imminent threat to "normal," "civilized society." The subtext in "moral panics" is almost invariably ethnic/racial exclusionism.

THE DISCOURSE OF MULTICULTURALISM: TOLERANCE, ACCOMMODATION, HARMONY, AND DIVERSITY

The concepts of tolerance, accommodation, sensitivity, harmony, and diversity lie at the core of multicultural ideology and are firmly embedded in multicultural policy and discourse (Li, in press; Henry et al., 2000; Tator et al., 1998). The emphasis on tolerance and sensitivity suggests that, while one must accept the idiosyncrasies of the "others," the underlying premise is that the dominant way is superior.

Within this minimal form of recognition of difference, the dominant culture and guardians of the social order create a ceiling of tolerance, that is, stipulating what differences are tolerable. This ceiling on tolerance is reflected in responses in public-opinion polls and surveys to questions dealing with multiculturalism (Mirchandani & Tastsoglou, 1998) in which a significant number of respondents take that position that "we" cannot tolerate too much difference as it generates dissent, disruption, and conflict. According to this view, paying unnecessary attention to "differences" leads to division, disharmony, and disorder in society. Where possible, the dominant culture attempts to accommodate *their* idiosyncratic cultural differences.

Declarations of the need for tolerance, diversity, and harmony tend to conceal the messy business of structural and systemic inequality, and the unequal relations of power that continue to exist in a democratic liberal society (Mohanty, 1993).

THE DISCOURSE OF LIBERAL VALUES: INDIVIDUALISM, TRUTH, TRADITION, UNIVERSALISM, AND FREEDOM OF EXPRESSION

As noted above, democratic liberalism is a philosophy and discourse that is distinguished by a set of beliefs, including the rights of the individual to supersede collective or group rights; the power of (one) truth, tradition and history, an appeal to universalism, the sacredness of the principle of freedom of expression, a commitment to human rights and equality, among many other ideals.

But as many scholars observe (Hall, 1986; Goldberg, 1993; Morrison & Brodsky Lacour, 1997; Apple, 1993; Winant, 1997), liberalism is full of paradoxes and contradictions, and assumes different meanings, depending on one's social location and angle of vision. As Parekh (1995: 82) argues, "liberalism is both egalitarian and inegalitarian." It simultaneously supports the unity of humankind and the hierarchy of cultures. It is both tolerant and intolerant.

From the perspective of the marginalized and excluded, traditional liberal values have been found wanting. In the interests of expanding democratic liberal principles and extending the promises of liberalism to those who have not enjoyed its benefits, minority communities are demanding an "affirmative" correction of historical injustices (Stam, 1993). However, those individuals and groups who invoke the validity of alternative voices, experiences, traditions, perspectives, and histories are seen to be violating a sacred body of principles, values, and beliefs. There is only one truth, a single "authentic" history, a noble Euro-American tradition, and a universal form of human understanding and expression that includes and transcends all cultural and racial boundaries.

THE DISCOURSE ON NATIONAL IDENTITY

Erasures, omissions, and silences mark the discourse of Canada's national identity. Ethnoracial minorities are placed outside the national project of Canada, excluded from the "imagined community" (Anderson, 1983) and culture of Canadian society. From Canada's earliest history, the idea of "hyphenated" Canadians was a fundamental part of the national discourse, but it has been limited to only two identities, that is, English Canada and French Canada. The Fathers of Confederation ignored the cultural plurality that existed even at that time. Aboriginal and other cultures were omitted from the national discourse, and thereby rendered invisible. Later, a category of "others" was added, but only two of these had constitutional rights.

National discourse constructs meanings and influences "our actions and our conceptions of ourselves" (Hall, 1992: 292). National culture defines identity by "producing meanings about the nation with which we can identify; these are contained in the stories that are told about it, memories that connect it with its past, and the images which are constructed of it" (1992: 282).

The debate over national identity is fundamental to Canadian discourse. Canada's search for national unity is really a search for cultural stability. The question of cultural identity is influenced by the politics of difference, a politics shaped by the interplay of history, culture, race, and power. In the struggle over national identity, the dominant culture is reluctant to include identities of "others" that it has constructed, perpetuated, and used to its advantage. To discard "otherness" would in a sense be to abandon the vehicles through which inequalities and imbalances are legitimated.

Many Canadians see themselves as egalitarian and have little difficulty in rejecting the more overt expressions of racism. They may make symbolic gestures of inclusivity. However, beyond these tokenistic efforts, the struggles of people of colour are met with arbitrary use of political, economic, and cultural institutional power in the interest of "maintaining democracy."

CONCLUSION
▼

In this paper, fundamental tensions embedded in Canadian ideology and discourse that reflect the dynamics of democratic racism have been examined. Within each of the above discourses are myths that attempt to explain, rationalize, and resolve the tension between the racism that is deeply embedded in the fabric of Canadian society, and the liberal ideals and values upon which Canada as a state is founded. This conflict provides one explanation for the relative lack of progress in dismantling individual, institutional, and systemic forms of racism. An ideology based on the policies and practices of antiracism, ethnoracial access, and equity requires a commitment to a different set of values, discourses, and practices, one in which the traditional democratic values which now function on a merely symbolic level are transferred and transformed into real behaviour and practice.

NOTES
▼

1. This paper provides an overview of a new and more invisible form of racism that is widely practised in Canada today. For a more in-depth analysis of democratic racism and the theory and practices of racist discourse, see Henry et al. (2000). This text also provides the reader with an understanding of how racism and racist

discourse operate in the state and in various institutions such as education, media, justice and law enforcement, and cultural institutions (e.g., theatre, museums, the literary establishment).

2. Discourse analysis goes beyond the social linguistic forms to include those sets of social relations ordered by a particular discourse. In addition to texts, there are values, norms, attitudes, and behavioural practices associated with a particular discourse. Discourse is language in social use. Discourses actually construct or define systems of beliefs and ideologies and position the players within it. For example, a dominant discourse of immigration can be identified in Canadian society today that differs markedly from earlier discourses. Moreover, there are also alternative discourses on this topic espoused by people of colour and other non-dominant groups in Canadian society. The discourse of the immigration officer and the would-be immigrant is positioned within the context of a particular set of power relations and the differing interests of each individual's discursive community (see Goldberg, 1993; van Dijk, 1991).

REFERENCES
▼

Abella, Irving, & Troper, Harold. (1991). *None is too many: Canada and the Jews in Europe 1933–1948* (3rd ed). Toronto: Lester & Orpen Dennys.

Abella, Rosalie. (1984). *Equality in employment: The report of the Commission of equality in employment.* Ottawa: Supply & Services.

Alladin, Ibrahim. (1996). *Racism in Canadian schools.* Toronto: Harcourt Brace.

Amit-Talai, Vered, & Knowles, Caroline. (1996). *Re-situating identities: The politics of race, ethnicity, and culture.* Peterborough, ON: Broadview Press.

Anderson, Benedict. (1983). *Imagined communities.* London: Verso.

Apple, Michael. (1993). Constructing the "Other": Rightist reconstructions of common sense. In C. McCarthy & W. Crichlow (Eds.), *Race, identity and representation in education* (pp. 24–39). New York & London: Routledge.

Bolaria, S., & Li, Peter. (1988). *Racial oppression in Canada* (2nd ed.). Toronto: Garmond.

Calliste, Agnes. (1994). Race, gender, and Canadian immigration policy: Blacks from the Caribbean, 1900–1932. *Journal of Canadian Studies, 28*(4), 131–148.

Cannon, Margaret (1995). *The invisible empire: Racism in Canada.* Toronto: Random House.

Centre for Contemporary Cultural Studies. (1982). The organic crisis of British capitalism and race. In *The empire strikes back: Race and racism in 70's Britain* (pp. 9–46). London: Hutchinson.

Creese, Gillian. (1993/94). The sociology of British Columbia. *BC Studies.* Special Issue no. 100 (Winter), 31–42.

Crenshaw, Kimberly. (1997). Color-blind dreams and racial nitemares: Reconfiguring racism in the post-civil rights era. In T. Morrison & C. Brodsky Lacour (Eds.),

Birth of a nation'hood: Gaze, script, and spectacle in the O.J. Simpson case (pp. 97–168). New York: Pantheon.

Dabydeen, Cyril. (1994). Citizenship is more than a birthright. *Toronto Star,* 20 September, A23.

Dei, George. (1996). *Anti-racism education: Theory and practice.* Halifax: Fernwood.

D'Oyley, Vincent, & James, Carl. (Eds.). (1998). *Re/visioning: Canadian perspectives on the education of Africans in the late 20th century.* North York, ON: Captus Press.

Essed, Philomena. (1990). *Everyday racism: Reports from women of two cultures.* Claremount, CA: Hunter House.

Fiske, John. (1994). Media matters: Everyday culture and political change. Minnesota: University of Minnesota Press.

Fleras, Augie, & Elliot, Jean. (1992). *Multiculturalism in Canada.* Scarborough, ON: Nelson.

———. (1996). *Unequal relations: An introduction to race, ethnic and aboriginal dynamics in Canada* (2nd ed.). Scarborough, ON: Prentice-Hall Canada.

Foucault, Michel. (1980). Two lectures. In Colin Gordon (Ed.), *Power/knowledge: Selected interviews and other writings* (pp. 78–108). New York: Pantheon.

Frankenberg, Ruth. 1993. *White women, race matters: The social construction of whiteness.* Minneapolis: University of Minneapolis Press.

Gaertner, S.L., & Dovidio, J.E. (1986). The aversive form of racism. In J. Dovidio & S. Gaertner (Eds.) *Prejudice, discrimination, and racism* (pp. 61–89). Orlando, FL: Academic.

Gilroy, Paul. (1987). *There ain't no Black in the Union Jack.* Chicago: University of Chicago Press.

Goldberg, David (Ed.). (1990). *The anatomy of racism.* Minneapolis: University of Minnesota Press.

———. (1993). *Racist culture: Philosophy and the politics of meaning.* Oxford: Blackwell.

Hall, Stuart. (1978). Racism and reaction. In *Five views of multi-racial Britain.* London: Commission for Racial Equality.

———. (1986). Variants of liberalism. In James Donald & Stuart Hall (Eds.), *Politics and ideology: A reader* (pp. 34–69). Buckingham, UK: Open University Press.

———. (1992). The question of cultural identity. In Stuart Hall, David Held, & Tony McGrew (Eds.), *Modernity and its futures* (pp. 274–326). Cambridge: Polity Press, in association with Open University.

———. (1993). Culture, community, nation. *Cultural Studies, 7*(3), 349–363.

Hebdige, Dick. (1993). From culture to hegemony. In S. During (Ed.), *The cultural studies reader* (pp. 357–367). London: Routledge.

Henry, Frances. (1978). *Dynamics of racism in Toronto.* North York, ON: York University.

Henry, Frances, & Tator, Carol. (In press). State policies and practices as racialized discourse: Multiculturalism, the Charter of Rights and Freedoms, and employment equity. In Peter Li (Ed.), *Race and ethnic relations in Canada* (2nd ed.). Toronto: Oxford University Press.

Henry, Frances, Tator, Carol, Mattis, Winston, & Rees, Tim. (2000). *The colour of democracy: Racism in Canadian society* (2nd ed.). Toronto: Harcourt Canada Ltd.

Husband, Christopher. (1994). Crisis of national identity as the "new moral panics": Political agenda-setting about definitions of nationhood. *New Community* (Warwick), *20*(2), 191–206.

James, Carl. (1994). The paradox of power and privilege: Race, gender and occupational position. *Canadian Woman Studies: Race and Gender, 14*(2), 47–51.

Jain, Harish. (1988). Affirmative action employment equity programs and visible minorities in Canada. *Toronto: Current Readings in Race Relations, 5*(1), 3.

Kobayashi, Audrey. (1990). Racism and the law. *Urban Geography, 11*(5), 447–473.

Khenti, Akwatu. (1996). A historical perspective on racism. In C. James (Ed.), *Perspectives on racism and the human services sector: A case for change* (pp. 51–75). Toronto: University of Toronto Press.

Lawrence, Eroll. (1982). Just plain common sense: The "roots" of racism. In Centre for Contemporary Cultural Studies, *The empire strikes back* (pp. 47–94). London: Hutchinson.

Li, Peter (Ed.). (In press). *Race and ethnic relations in Canada* (2nd ed.). Oxford: Oxford University Press.

Mackey, Eva. (1996). *Managing and imagining diversity: Multiculturalism and the construction of national identity in Canada.* D.Phil. thesis, Department of Social Anthropology, University of Sussex.

Malarek, Victor. (1987). *Heaven's gate: Canada's immigration fiasco.* Toronto: Macmillan of Canada.

McFarlane, Scott. (1995). The haunt of multiculturalism: Canada's multicultural act: The politics of incorporation and "Writing thru Race." *Fuse, 18*(3), 18–21.

Miller, C., Swift, K., & Maggio, R. (1997). Liberating language. *MS,* September-October, 51–54.

Mirchandani, Kiran, & Tastsoglou, Evangelia. (1998). Toward a diversity beyond tolerance. Unpublished paper submitted to the Journal of Status in Political Economy.

Mohanty, Chandra Talpade. (1993). On race and voice: Challenges for liberal education in the 1990s. In Becky W. Thompson & Sangeeta Tyagi (Eds.), *Beyond a dream: Deferred multicultural education and the politics of excellence.* Minneapolis: University of Minnesota Press.

Morrison, Toni, & Brodsky Lacour, Claudia. (Eds.). (1997). *Birth of a nation'hood: Gaze, script, and spectacle in the O.J. Simpson case.* New York: Pantheon.

Parekh, Bhikhu. (1995). Liberalism and colonialism. In Bhikhu Parekh & Nederveen Pieterse (Eds.). *The decolonization of imagination: Culture knowledge, and power* (pp. 81–98). London: Zed.

Pendakur, Krishna, & Pendakur, Ravi. (1995). The colour of money: Earnings differentials among ethnic groups in Canada. Ottawa: Strategic Research and Analysis, Department of Canadian Heritage.

Pieterse, Nederveen Jan. (1992). *White on black: Images of Africa and Blacks in Western popular culture.* New Haven & London: Yale University Press.

Razack, Shrene. (1998). *Looking white people in the eye: Gender, race and culture in the courtrooms and classrooms.* Toronto: University of Toronto Press.

Reitz, Jeffrey. (1990). Ethnic concentration in labour markets and their implications for ethnic inequality. In Raymond Breton, Wsevolod Isajiw, Warren Kalbach, & Jeffrey G. Reitz (Eds.), *Ethnic identity and equality: Varieties of experience in a Canadian city* (pp. 135–195). Toronto: University of Toronto Press.

Satzewich, Vic. (1993). *Deconstructing a nation: Immigration, multiculturalism and racism in 90s Canada.* Halifax: Fernwood.

Sears, D. (1988). Symbolic racism. In P. Katz & D. Taylor (Eds.). *Towards the elimination of racism: Profiles in controversy* (pp. 53–84). New York: Plenum.

Srivastava, Sarita. (1996). Song and dance? The performance of antiracist workshops. *Canadian Review of Sociology and Anthropology/Revue canadienne de sociologie et d'anthropologie, 33*(3), 291–315.

St. Lewis, Joanne. (1996). Identity and Black consciousness in North America. In James Littleton (Ed.), *Clash of identities: Essays on media, manipulation and politics of self* (pp. 21–30). Englewood Cliffs, NJ: Prentice-Hall.

Stam, Robert (1993). From stereotype to discourse. *Cine-Action, 23* (Fall), 12–29.

Tator, Carol, Henry, Frances, & Mattis, Winston. (1998). *Challenging racism in the arts: Case studies of controversy and conflict.* Toronto: University of Toronto Press.

Thompson, Neil. (1993). *Anti-discrimination practice.* London: Macmillan.

Turner, Terrence. (1994). Anthropology and multiculturalism: What is anthropology that multiculturalism should be mindful of it? In D. Goldberg (ed.)., *Multiculturalism: A critical reader* (pp. 406–425). Oxford: Blackwell.

van Dijk, Teun. (1991). *Racism and the press.* London and New York: Routledge.

———. (2000). New(s) racism: A discourse analytical approach. In Simon Cottle (Ed.), *Ethnic minorities: Changing cultural boundaries.* Buckingham, UK: Open University Press.

Wellman, David. (1977). *Portraits of white racism.* Cambridge: Cambridge University Press.

Wetherell, Margaret, & Potter, Jonathon. (1992). *Mapping the language of racism.* New York: Columbia University Press.

Winant, Howard. (1997). Behind blue eyes: Whiteness and contemporary U.S. racial politics. In Michelle Fine, Lois Weis, Linda C. Powell, & L. Mun Wong (Eds.), *Off white: Readings on race, power, and society* (pp. 40–56). New York and London: Routledge.

Yon, Dan. (1995). *Unstable terrain: Explorations in identity, race and culture in a Toronto high school.* Ph.D. thesis, Department of Anthropology, York University, Toronto.

18

▼

RESISTING PROFESSIONAL EXCLUSION AND MARGINALITY IN NURSING: WOMEN OF COLOUR IN ONTARIO[1]

AGNES CALLISTE

INTRODUCTION
▼

In October 1996, the Congress of Black Women of Canada (CBWC), Toronto Chapter, made a deputation to the Metropolitan Toronto Antiracism, Access and Equity Committee, asking it to call on the provincial government to adopt and implement 3 out of 32 recommendations from the CBWC's 1995 conference report, *End the Silence on Racism in Health Care* (Calliste, 1995; CBWC, 1996): first, that the provincial government establish a commission of inquiry into systemic racism within the health care sector; second, that health care institutions provide mandatory antiracism education and training to their personnel, boards of directors, and volunteers; third, that health care institutions develop, implement, monitor, and evaluate their employment policies and practices to ensure that racism and other forms of discrimination are eliminated. Moreover, the CBWC recommended that the penalty for health care institutions that refuse to implement antiracism training and fair employment policies should be loss of accreditation and provincial funding (CBWC, 1996: 1–2). The CBWC's deputation was supported by Nurses and Friends Against Discrimination (NAFAD) and the Ontario Nurses Association (ONA), the nurses' union (NAFAD, 1996; ONA, 1996).

Evidently, women of colour moved from exclusion from nursing in the late 1940s to marginality in the profession. Currently, it seems that they are being further marginalized and excluded in the 1990s, as economic restructuring and rapid downsizing of the health care system have been combined with new (and very old) forms of racism, racialization, and sexism that have a disproportionate impact on health care workers of colour, particularly

Black women who are assertive (Calliste, 1993, 1996; Hardill, 1993; McPherson, 1996). Women of colour were allowed into nursing as a floating reserve army of labour during the postwar expansion of industrial capitalism and severe nursing shortages. However, they are more likely than their white counterparts to be underemployed, to be denied access to promotions, and to be assigned heavy patient loads and duties involving mostly menial and back-breaking work (Caissey, 1994; Calliste, 1993, 1996; CBWC, 1995; Das Gupta, 1996; Head, 1986; OHRC, 1992a). During economic crises, they are the first to be suspended, demoted, and summarily dismissed, often for alleged incompetence, or for not following standard nursing procedures, or for "unacceptable behaviours," especially if they resist racism. As Cherrille Franklin, an employee relations officer with the ONA and former nurse manager, stated at the Ontario Hospital Association's antiracism conference,

> We [racial minority nurses] came here when Canada needed the expertise of professional nurses, and developed your organizations.... We have worked the night shifts and weekends when no one else would, at a time when salaries were very low. Now that salaries have increased, our positions are being terminated.... In some cases, the only restructuring that is going on is the restructuring of the personal lives of racial minority nurses. (Franklin, 1995: 3)

As a result of this inequity and injustice, racial-minority nurses and a few white nurses have been organizing themselves and have been demanding institutional and systemic change to address racism and the interlocking systems of social oppression (such as classism and sexism) in the health care system.

This study analyzes racial-minority nurses' organizing and resistance to exclusion and marginality in nursing in Ontario from the late 1970s to the 1990s from an integrative antiracist perspective. Marginality is a process in which "a sense of otherness and peripherality is perpetuated and encouraged" (Brandt, 1986: 104). Racial minorities are denied access to positions of power within institutions, and their experiences and perspectives are considered irrelevant. Ontario is chosen because there are large numbers of nurses of colour in this province (ONA, 1996). For instance, in 1981, Reitz, Calzavara, and Dasko (1981: 37) found that Caribbean women[2] in Toronto's workforce were overconcentrated in nursing (except in supervisory positions), in nursing aide and orderly work, and in other segregated occupations. The late 1970s demarcates the beginning of nurses' political organizing to combat increased racism during economic recession and cuts in health care budgets. The 1990s is characterized by racial-minority nurses' and communities' intense antiracism struggles.

THE INTEGRATIVE ANTIRACISM FRAMEWORK
▼

Integrative antiracism is a critical discourse of social oppressions (such as racism, sexism, and classism) through the lens of race. It is also "an educational and political action-oriented strategy for institutional and systemic change to address racism and the interlocking systems of social oppression" (Dei, 1996: 25). The emphasis on racism is not intended to prioritize oppressions. Instead, the antiracism discourse highlights that, though "race" is a "fundamental organizing principle of contemporary social life" (Winant, 1994: 115) in racialized societies, racism is continually negated by the status quo as an organizing logic of relations of production and labour. The logic of capital is not "race"- and "gender"-blind. Access to work and justice is constrained by relations of oppression such as racism, and gendered racism (Brandt, 1986; Essed, 1991). Gendered racism refers to the racial oppression of racial/ethnic minority women as structured by racist perceptions of gender roles and behaviour.

Some nurses of colour acknowledge that they experience multiple oppressions in the workplace (CBWC, 1991; Nurses, Woodlands Hospital, 1992). For instance, in 1991, the Coalition in Support of Black Nurses stated: "Traditionally, Black women have been singled out to bear the brunt of economic hardships in our society, especially during recessionary periods" (CBWC, 1991). However, nurses of colour emphasize racism because it is more visibly salient for them. Nursing is a female-dominated occupation and many of the oppressors of nurses of colour are white female nurses who collaborate with management in harassing nurses of colour (interviews, 25 May 1994, 8 September 1996).

Antiracism theory incorporates many theoretical perspectives and builds on critical race, class, and gender studies to provide an integrative understanding of oppression as well as individual and collective resistance. Antiracism goes beyond acknowledging the material conditions that structure social inequalities to question white power and privilege and its rationale for dominance (Dei, 1996; Frankenberg, 1993; McIntosh, 1990; Razack, 1998). Antiracism questions the role that the state (including human rights commissions and labour arbitration systems) and societal institutions (such as workplaces) play in producing and reproducing inequalities. Antiracism acknowledges that the state and societal institutions contain and manage the protests of oppressed groups (e.g., by individualizing grievances), but they do not interrogate the underlying causes of discrimination or challenge systemic racism and sexism, especially racism, unless they are pressured into doing so (Agnew, 1996; Bolaria & Li, 1988; Calliste, 1996; Henry et al., 1995). Thus, the state's response to antiracist and other minority struggles (whether it crushes, appeases, or co-opts them) varies in accordance with the groups' economic, political, and social power. Antiracism theory questions the devaluation of knowledge, credentials, and experience of subordinate groups (see Ontario Ministry of Citizenship, 1989a, 1989b), and the marginalization and silencing of certain voices in the workplace and in society. It recognizes the need to confront the challenge of social diversity and difference in Canadian society and the urgency for more inclusive and equitable workplaces and society (see Dei, 1995).

The integrative antiracism theoretical framework is relevant in explaining racial-minority women's resistance to exclusion and marginality in nursing. Black women, for example, are perceived as the antithesis of the Florence Nightingale image of the compliant, compassionate, nurturing, soft-spoken, feminine, and professional nurse (see Ehrenreich & English, 1973; Hine, 1989; Marks, 1994; McPherson, 1996). Black nurses are stereotyped as childlike, lazy, aggressive, emotional, uncommunicative, troublemaking, less competent, less skilled, and less disciplined than whites (CBWC, 1995; Doris Marshall Institute & Arnold Minors & Associates [hereinafter cited as Marshall & Minors], 1994; Ontario Ministry of Labour, 1994a, 1994b; interviews, 25–27 May and 1 July 1994, 24 June and 3 July 1996). Racial and class divisions between Euro-Canadian and racial-minority nurses, particularly African Canadians, have made for a "fractured sisterhood" (Marks, 1994: 3). Historically, the divisions between African-Canadian and Euro-Canadian women were most evident in the racist, sexist, and classist images of Black women as "mammies," "bad women," and "matriarchs" (see Barbee, 1993; Brand, 1988; Calliste, 1991, 1994; Thornhill, 1991). An African-Canadian nurse notes that "the Black nurse is still treated as the servant girl in the kitchen" (interview, 1 July 1994). Thus, in Canada, like in the United States and South Africa, the Black woman nurse becomes an "undesirable" entity in a traditional subordinate women's occupation, which is striving for an increase in the status of the profession (see Barbee, 1993; Glazer, 1991; Hine, 1989; Marks, 1994). Moreover, as some Toronto nurses contend, given the current economic crisis, Black nurses could be perceived as a liability in a competitive health care industry, where hospitals must portray an image of "the best care and the brightest staff" in order to attract international consumers (Hardill, 1993: 20; interview 3 July 1994).

In Canada, gender and class historically have been racialized in both nursing and the state's immigration policy (Calliste, 1991, 1993, 1994). For instance, the exclusion of racial-minority women from nursing in Canada before the late 1940s was rationalized by ideological constructions of racially specific femininity and sexuality, representing the opposite models of white, middle-class womanhood. McPherson (1996) argues that, because nurses wanted to protect their elite position, nursing relied on the image of feminine respectability and gentility, defined according to Eurocentric and middle-class standards. She notes:

> In the eyes of hospital administrators and nursing leaders, Canadian women of non-European heritage could not be relied on to reflect the morality of health at the bedside, to meet the standard of gentility demanded by elite patients, or to negotiate the tricky sexual terrain of patient care. (1996: 17).

When racial-minority women were allowed into nursing, they were initially encouraged to pursue nursing only to serve "their" communities (McPherson, 1996; see Calliste, 1993). Racial-minority nurses and practical nurses have helped to maintain a segmented nursing labour force that was initially based on class (see Doyal, Hunt, & Mellor, 1981; Gamarnikow, 1978).

Unlike antiracism theory, in which race is central, segmented labour market theory focusses on class (Edwards, 1979; Gordon, Edwards, & Reich, 1982; Piore, 1971). Antiracism theory can benefit from segmented labour market theory by incorporating an analysis of class exploitation of racialized minority men and women in the labour market while simultaneously according a separate analytical status to race. The latter theory contends that jobs and industries are readily divided into primary and secondary sectors, and this division is reinforced by barriers that make it difficult for workers to move from one sector to another. In the primary sector, jobs are characterized by higher wages and fringe benefits, greater employment stability with possibilities of promotion, a higher degree of unionization, superior working conditions, and due process in negotiating job rights. In contrast, the secondary sector includes work in "peripheral" industries. These jobs are characterized by weak unions, low wages, insecure employment, poor working conditions, minimal advancement, and arbitrary management practices. The secondary sector uses the groups with little bargaining power. Racialized/ethnic minorities and women are pushed into particular race- or sex-typed jobs to maximize profits and partly because of racism/ethnicism and sexism. Blacks are hired into the dirtiest, most physically demanding, and lowest-skilled occupations, while women are pushed toward "helping" and nurturing occupations (Edwards, 1979). The underlying argument is that capitalists create and sustain racism and sexism as part of a "divide and conquer" strategy to keep wages low and the workers' movement disorganized.

However, some feminists (Hartmann, 1976, 1981) argue that segmentation is also the result of exclusionary practices used by male-dominated trade unions and professional associations to prevent the entrance of women into male-typed occupations or industries in which male workers predominate. They contend that gender segregation in employment benefits men economically and emotionally by reducing low-wage competition from women workers and maintaining women in subordinate relations with men both at work and at home.

Segmented labour market theory helps to explain the segregation of women workers into female-typed jobs, and Blacks into race-typed jobs. However, there have been many criticisms of the theory (see Armstrong & Armstrong, 1990; Collins, 1990; Gannage, 1986; Phillips & Phillips, 1993). For example, segmented labour market theorists have not accounted for the interaction of race and gender operant in, for example, the differences between white women workers and racialized minority women workers, and how the former may support educational and workplace policies that result in the reinforcement of class and racialized/ethnic inequalities between themselves and other women. Moreover, racism and sexism are not merely epiphenomena or manifestations of class. Race and gender relations have the capacity to shape class relations. As Omi and Winant (1983: 61) argue in relation to race and working-class consciousness in the United States,

> [historically,] race [and gender have] ... not merely been an impediment to the development of working-class consciousness.... [They have] also shaped it.... The very nature and composition of the working class have been shaped by racial [and gender] projects.

Omi and Winant's statement is also relevant to Canada.

Although segmentation usually refers to distinctions between occupations, it includes differentiation within an occupation between professional and non-professional strata, for example, between registered nurses (RNs) and registered practical nurses (RPNs) (Glazer, 1991). Nurses of colour in Canada, like their counterparts in Britain, South Africa, and the United States, are concentrated at the lower levels of the nursing hierarchy as staff nurses and RPNs — a reflection of persistent inequalities in nursing and in the wider society (Doyal et al., 1981; Glazer, 1991; Head, 1986; Marks, 1994; Reitz et al., 1981).

As Glazer (1991: 352) argues with reference to the United States, national associations representing RNs and nursing educators historically have sought to prevent the displacement of RNs by RPNs and nurses' aides by using a variety of exclusionary strategies (such as limiting their work to non-technical health care tasks and restricting the training of these lower-level personnel) and practising institutional racism. The College of Nurses of Ontario's decision to abolish the classification of graduate nurse (i.e., trained nurses without registration) effective January 1997, which resulted in the dismissal of some graduate nurses also indicates the college's attempt to increase the status of the profession and to preserve RNs' jobs, given the rapid downsizing of the health care system (interviews, 11 June, 5 July 1996).

In addition to this formal segmentation to protect the class-based and racial/ethnic privileges of some nurses, there are informal ways of segmenting RNs to protect the racial privileges of white RNs. The Dunfermline Hospital serves as an illustration of the racially segmented nursing labour force. In 1992, its management was predominantly white, while 56 percent of its nursing staff were people of colour, of whom 30 percent were Black. However, 85 percent of the nurses in the Chronic Care Unit were people of colour (Das Gupta, 1993: 39; OHRC, 1992a: 3). Conversely, Black nurses were severely underrepresented in high-technology and high-status specialty areas (such as intensive care), where there are greater opportunities for further training and the nurses are encouraged to take courses (Caissey, 1994; Head, 1986; OHRC, 1992a; ONA, 1996). For instance, only 13 percent of the nurses in the Intensive Care Unit were Black, compared with 55 percent white and 32 percent other nurses of colour such as Canadians of Filipina descent (OHRC, 1992a: 9).

RESEARCH METHODS
▼

My discussion is based upon data drawn from 35 semi-structured interviews conducted mainly in 1994–1995. The sample consists of 26 registered nurses, 3 officers from nurses' unions, and 6 members of community organizations that assisted Black nurses in their antiracism struggles. The sample was drawn through snowball sampling and referrals, as well as from the membership list of a nurses' organization. I was also a participant observer at three conferences in Toronto on antiracism and/or integration and advancement of Black nurses in health care: the CBWC's "End the Silence on Racism in Health Care," the Ontario Hospital Association's (OHA) "Antiracism," and the University Hospital of the West Indies Graduate Nurses Association's (UHWIGNA) "Remembering the Past, Creating the Future, Making Changes, Taking Charge" conferences. The CBWC conference brought together nurses and health care workers, especially Blacks, who discussed their experiences in the workplace and strategies for institutional and systemic change. I wrote the conference report for the CBWC. The OHA conference was organized primarily for hospital administrators. The UHWIGNA conference was intended to focus on "integration and advancement" of Black nurses within the health care system (UHWIGNA, 1997: 1). However, some participants focussed on antiracism in health care as essential for integration and advancement of racialized minority nurses. The primary data were supplemented with analysis of records of the Ontario Human Rights Commission (OHRC) and labour arbitration cases, community organizations, and other secondary sources. The secondary data also served as checks for possible biases in the primary data. In order to maintain confidentiality, fictitious names are used to identify nurses and health care institutions, except those named in secondary sources.

EXCLUSION AND MARGINALITY IN NURSING
▼

In Canada, nurses of colour, particularly African Canadians, are streamed into the least skilled and least desirable areas, where the work is arduous; injurious to health; and considered to be low-status, boring, and dead-end. For instance, an investigation by the OHRC into systemic racism in Dunfermline Hospital in Toronto, in 1992, found that "streaming of nurses of colour" into the Chronic Care Unit seemed "to be a common phenomenon," irrespective of their qualifications and experience, because it was "the hospital's position that these women do not have the qualifications to work in other units" (OHRC, 1992b: 2). The differential assignment of nursing duties (e.g., night shifts and a heavy patient load) restricted some racialized minority nurses' chances of upgrading their skills and, in turn, restricted their chances for transfers and promotions into specialty areas. Moreover, some Black nurses, including some who work in specialty areas, argue that they are denied access to in-service and leadership training because of management's arbitrary distribution of training opportunities among nursing staff. For example, Joyce, a nurse with a Master's degree in nursing who works in a specialty unit in a Toronto hospital, alleges that her nurse manager tried to hinder her from advancing within the unit by denying her in-service and discouraging her from furthering her education. She notes: "When I told her I was going back for my Master's, she asked me: 'And what are you going to do with it?'" (interview 23 May 1997).

The central white labour force is "insulated" from the "peripheral" coloured labour force (Friedman, 1977: 105) since the latter tends to be passed over for further training, promotions, and transfers, sometimes by nurses whom they have trained (Bertley, 1985; Head, 1986; Marshall & Minors, 1994). As the ONA (Caissey, 1994: 2) points out, "It remains very rare to find a visible minority nurse in a middle or senior level management position, even in hospitals where 30 or 40 percent of the staff may be visible minority members."

The streaming of women of colour into Chronic Care Units makes them more vulnerable and powerless during economic restructuring and downsizing of the health care system, given that "peripheral" workers are the first to be laid off or displaced by cheaper labour. The ONA notes:

> More so than on other units, chronic unit nurses are being replaced by [low-skilled Unregulated Assistive Personnel or] generic workers, while at the same time these same nurses are told that they lack the skills to bump into other areas of the hospital, even if they have the seniority to do so. (ONA, 1996: 5; see also Landsberg, 1996)

Racially specific gender and classist ideologies (such as nurses of colour, particularly Blacks, are less professional than white nurses) have been used to justify the marginality and exclusion of racialized minority women from nursing (Calliste, 1996; Marshall & Minors, 1994; interviews, 1–2 July 1994). However, some nurses of colour argue that their work underutilizes their educational qualifications or training (Bertley, 1985; Head, 1986; Robertson, 1985; interviews, 1 July 1994, 3 July and 1 September 1996). For instance, in 1986, Wilson Head (1986: 50) found that only 37 percent of Black health care workers in Metropolitan Toronto (mainly RNs) compared with 68 percent of white health care workers in that location reported that their work fully utilized their educational qualifications. Conversely, Black health care workers were more likely than their white counterparts to report that their work only partly utilized their educational qualifications (56 vs. 29 percent). Some of the nurses I interviewed in 1994–96, also felt that they were underemployed because they were relegated to Chronic Care Units and menial work, or they were denied promotions (interviews, 23–25 May, 1 July 1994; 3 July, 1 September 1996). For example, Pat, a Black, experienced public health nurse with impressive credentials, including a Master's degree in Education, was confined to the performance of menial tasks (such as unpacking boxes of teaching materials and cleaning cupboards) in her health unit in Sudbury (Sudbury and District Health Unit and ONA, 1987; interview, 1 September 1996). Some nurses of colour, especially those who were trained in the third world, have experienced individual deskilling (Bakan, 1987; Calliste, 1993; Lee, 1982).[3]

The devaluation of overseas credentials and experience by the College of Nurses of Ontario and hospitals is a major factor in the individual deskilling and marginality of some racial minority nurses (Calliste, 1993; OHRC, 1992b; Ontario Ministry of Citizenship, 1989a, 1989b). In 1992, the OHRC found "extreme discrepancies in the way" a Toronto hospital "applied 'equivalency standards and overseas experience for white and nurses of colour'" for salary purposes. The commission notes:

> [The hospital's] system for determining equivalency appears arbitrary re-
> sulting in many immigrant nurses having to press the hospital for equiv-
> alent accreditation or waiting several years to be considered equal to a
> nurse trained in Canada. (OHRC, 1992b: 3)

Evidently, such biases influenced recruitment and placement, especially since
the same staff member was also responsible for pre-screening applications and
checking references. The OHRC found that the hospital's employment systems adversely affected the hiring of nurses of colour:

> ... generally more references were checked for nurses of colour during the
> recruitment process ... there was personal and irrelevant information doc-
> umented on their applications and on the files (information about fami-
> ly, proficiency in English, disability, place of origin). There were also
> comments regarding where a person obtained his/her education outside
> Canada.... Information about the number and age of ... [Maria's] children
> were recorded. (OHRC, 1992b: 4)

Maria, a Filipina nurse, made several unsuccessful attempts to have her past
work experience and courses recognized in order to be remunerated com-
mensurate with other nurses with similar experience.

ACCREDITATION OF IMMIGRANT NURSES
▼

Credentialism performs a gatekeeping function, and it has a disproportionately negative impact on members of racialized and ethnic minority groups,
who experience occupational closure (Collins, 1979; Ontario Ministry of Citizenship, 1989a; Parkin, 1979; Richmond, 1992). Although the primary
obligation of the College of Nurses of Ontario is to protect the public against
"incompetent or dishonest practitioners" (Ontario Ministry of Citizenship,
1989a: 61, quoting the Committee on Healing Arts, 1970; see Moloney,
1986), it also produces unintentional racism. The Task Force on Access to
Trades and Professions in Ontario's (TFATPO) findings confirm that there are
systemic barriers to access to the trades and professions, including nursing, because "the prior learning of foreign-trained applicants is not always being ad-
equately and fairly addressed" (Ontario Ministry of Citizenship, 1989a: xii).
With specific reference to nursing, the TFATPO found that between 25 and
30 percent of immigrant nurses were required to complete upgrading by the
College of Nurses of Ontario (Ontario Ministry of Citizenship, 1989b: 10).
Those whose qualifications are not accepted by the college can either retrain
and then write the RN examinations or immediately write the RPN examinations (Ontario Ministry of Citizenship, 1989a: 447). Given systemic and

situational access barriers to upgrading programs (such as lack of space, the cost of being a full-time student, and language-proficiency prerequisites), some immigrant nurses, especially racial minorities, have worked as RPNs and health care aides for many years. So, some health care institutions have benefitted from a trained and experienced low-paid workforce (Calliste, 1993; Farr, 1991; interview, 19 December 1991).

Some immigrant nurses and communities argue that the college's formerly "rigid" language testing requirements for overseas-trained nurses whose first language is not English were a major systemic barrier to the accreditation process (Farr, 1991; Ontario Ministry of Citizenship, 1989b; interview, 20 December 1991). The language prerequisites for the RN and RPN examinations as well as for upgrading programs are a minimum total score of 500 on the Test of English as a Foreign Language (TOEFL), with at least 50 in each of the three component parts, and a score of 200 on the Test of Spoken English (TSE) examinations (Farr, 1991: 10, 12; Ontario Ministry of Citizenship, 1989a: 192; interviews, 19 December 1991, 5 July 1996). Jane's case serves as an illustration of some immigrant nurses' complaints about the college's language requirements. For eighteen years, Jane, a woman of colour, was prevented from obtaining certification and upgrading from a nursing assistant to an RN because she "failed" the TOEFL at least 27 times even though, on 4 occasions, her score was 490 or higher (Farr, 1991: 10). In 1989, she filed a complaint with the Health Discipline Board. The board decided that, although there was "no bad faith" on the college's part, Jane had been "put through unnecessary stress, cost and delay" in trying to satisfy the college's rigid cut-off test score because they had either misinterpreted or not taken the time to read the test guidelines, which strongly discourage the use of rigid cut-off scores and instead advocate ranges because of the standard error of measurement (quoted in Farr, 1991: 10, 12).[4] She was granted certification shortly after.

The TFATPO also found that the TOEFL and TSE were inadequate and inappropriate for testing profession-specific language and they were weak predictors of performance. Moreover, the examinations are culturally biased against non–North American test takers because a significant segment of the content is related to U.S. culture and history, and the accent on the tapes is North American (Ontario Ministry of Citizenship, 1989a, 1989b). As a result of these criticisms, the Educational Testing Service, which administers these tests, is in the process of constructing occupational health specific examinations (B. Lewis, personal communication, 22 May 1997). In addition, the college began administering a revised TSE in 1995. It also became more flexible in determining the acceptable TOEFL scores, and considers four alternative tests (e.g., the Certificate of Proficiency in English) as proof of fluency (College of Nurses of Ontario, 1995a: 15).

The RN examination is another major systemic barrier to registration for some immigrant nurses. The failure rate for non-Ontario graduates is usually five times the failure rate for Ontario graduates. For example, in 1987, the failure rate for non-Ontario graduates on the RN examinations was 41 percent compared with 8 percent for Ontario graduates (Ontario Ministry of Citizenship, 1989b: 8; interview, 5 May 1997). However, in 1995, the failure rate for non-Ontario graduates who wrote the examinations for the first time increased significantly to 73 percent, while the failure rate for Ontario graduates was 8 percent (College of Nurses of Ontario, 1995b: 17). Although the college's reports do not provide the breakdown of failure rates by the countries where nurses were trained, the evidence suggests that a high proportion of the non-Ontario candidates are immigrant women (Ontario Ministry of Citizenship, 1989b; interview, 5 July 1996). In 1992–95, the largest source countries of non-Canadian trained nurses who applied for registration in Ontario were the Philippines, Poland, the British Isles, the United States, and Hong Kong, in descending order of magnitude. In that period, 70 percent of the 5607 non-Ontario trained applicants were non-Canadian trained. Of these, 34 percent were trained in the Philippines (College of Nurses of Ontario, 1994: 48; 1995b: 17).

The low pass rates of immigrant nurses may be attributed to several factors: a difference in focus of overseas nursing programs from Canadian programs, variations in nursing terminology, linguistic problems, and some immigrant nurses' lack of familiarity with multiple choice examinations. For instance, it has been argued that Canadian programs are more theoretical than Caribbean and British nursing programs. Moreover, the RN examinations focus on problem-solving and do not measure the candidate's nursing knowledge (Ontario Ministry of Citizenship, 1989b; interviews, 5 July 1996; 21 and 24 May 1997). The ONA also notes that the problem is not the nurses' competency, but their ability to write the examinations in all areas of nursing, given they usually work in one area, and they are working full-time. The college estimates that there are 650 graduate nurses in Ontario, most of whom are immigrants with many years of experience and a high level of seniority. Of these, 50 are ONA members. Many of the graduate nurses have been employed continuously as practising nurses in Ontario since at least 1981 (OHRC, 1996a: 19; ONA, 1998: 24; interviews, 5 July 1996, 20 May 1997).

In the 1980s and 1990s, some racial-minority nurses and communities organized themselves (e.g., the Chinese Nurses Association, and the Coalition of Visible Minority Women) and set up continuing education classes to assist immigrant nurses to overcome systemic barriers in the RN accreditation process, and to pass the language and RN examinations. For instance, the Filipino Nurses Association successfully lobbied the college to waive the language requirements for Filipina nurses in lieu of a letter that attests to the applicant's comprehension and verbal fluency (Ontario Ministry of Citizenship, n.d.; Project Health Care Workers/Team, 1985; interviews, 20 December 1991, 1 July 1994).

Given the rapid downsizing of the health care system and the college's decision to increase the professional status of nursing, graduate nurses have become expendable. Following the introduction in 1994, by Regulated Health Professions Act (RHPA), of controlled tasks that only RNs could perform (Ontario, 1995b), the college instituted deadlines for graduate nurses to pass the RN examinations or become unregulated. Graduate nurses who practised continuously in the same setting for at least five years were eligible to apply for the Provisional Certificate of Registration by January 1994.[5] This certificate is revoked after three years, or when the member has passed the RN examinations, whichever occurs first (College of Nurses of Ontario, 1995a; interviews, 5 July 1996, 8 and 20 May 1997). This decision to abolish the classification of Graduate Nurse, which became effective in January 1997, resulted in the displacement of some graduate nurses, mainly immigrant women of colour in their 40s and 50s, by cheaper junior RNs, RPNs, and generic workers who are mainly white (interviews, 10 June, 5 July 1996). As a result, some graduate nurses have filed grievances and human rights complaints alleging unfair layoffs, which they attributed to the college's "narrow interpretation" of the RHPA (interviews, 10 June, 5 July, and 21 October 1996). The ONA argues that revoking the registration of graduate nurses was an instance of "constructive discrimination against a group that consisted primarily of women of colour who had trained outside of Canada" (ONA, 1998: 25).

Moreover, the union contends that the college should have included a "grandparent" clause that would allow the graduate nurses who were in the system before 1997 to continue to work as graduate nurses. The ONA asked the OHRC to initiate a systemic complaint against the college on the bases of race, ethnic origin, and age. However, the OHRC decided to use an initiated-settlement approach, but the college withdrew from the process. The OHRC employed different strategies, such as asking the Minister of Health to use his legislative authority to override the college's decision, or the commission would lay a systemic complaint against the college (interviews, 21 October 1996, 2 May 1997). The minister's refusal to intervene forced the OHRC, in October 1997, to initiate a systemic complaint against the Ministry of Health and the college concerning their treatment of working graduate nurses and nursing assistants in Ontario. The outcome of this case could have implications for diploma-trained nurses when the B.ScN. becomes a requirement for the RN.

HARASSMENT OF NURSES OF COLOUR
▼

Overt racism, sexism, and ageism in nursing, as in other areas of employment, increased during the economic recession and cutbacks in health care budgets in the late 1970s to early 1980s, and intensified during the 1990s fiscal crisis (Bolaria & Li, 1988; Calliste, 1996; Hardill, 1993; Henry & Ginzberg, 1985). Moreover, it appears that, with increases in nurses' salaries in 1989–90, some hospital management began to harass assertive, senior nurses of colour, especially Blacks (interview, 20 December 1991). As I have discussed elsewhere (Calliste, 1996), harassment of nurses of colour by hospital management takes several forms, including targeting racial-minority workers for discriminatory treatment and oversupervision, and differential documentation and discipline for minor or non-existent problems for which white nurses are not disciplined. For instance, in the early 1990s, Lucy, an assertive Chinese-Canadian nurse and president of her union local, filed a series of grievances and a human rights complaint against Pearls Hospital in Toronto, alleging that she was harassed after she questioned management about its biased restructuring policies (Ontario Ministry of Labour, 1995, 1996b; interview, 1 July 1994). In her words:

> I got called into my resident manager's office.... He said ... you are a good nurse. Being the most senior nurse in the unit, do you ever think of leaving the unit?... So the junior nurse can have a job; she desperately needs the experience.... You can go to the community, like the rest of the Chinese people, to sell real estate.... Every time when I turned around, one of my co-workers was spying on me. When I did my charting, as soon as I left, someone would come and check over my chart.... They had different expectations of me compared to my white counterparts.... They accused me of not doing certain things. Thank God, we had written proof that I did do those things. (CBWC, 1995; interview, 1 July 1994)

Lucy experienced interlocking systems of oppression: racism, sexism, and ageism. She notes that senior RNs and RPNs of colour were harassed to take early retirement, in part to save labour costs;[6] meanwhile, the hospital was hiring white nurses and other health workers (interview, 1 July 1994; see Gray, 1994). Lucy was also harassed to control her assertive behaviour, to discourage solidarity, and to undermine her ability to influence others. Management's divisive strategy also served as a form of containment; at the same time, it was a factor in producing a "poisoned" work environment.

Management argued that Lucy misinterpreted its actions or statements as harassment when in fact they were innocuous. It attributed her concerns to "her personality or individual circumstances" (Ontario Ministry of Labour,

1995: 3). There are several cases of health care institutions reinforcing the marginality of nurses of colour by denying their experiences of racism. Instead, they focus on interpersonal dynamics such as "communication skills" and "personality problems," and blame nurses of colour for "their problems" rather than investigating the issue of racism (Martina v. North York General Hospital, 1986; Ontario Ministry of Labour, 1994a; interviews, 24 June, 3 July 1996). Management's denial of racism is also reflected in their lack of support for nurses of colour who are subjected to racism and sexism, and to physical assault by patients' families. Hospitals tend to deal with such incidents as crisis-management issues rather than dealing with the issue of racism (OHRC, 1992b; interviews, 27 May 1994, 3 July 1996). Mary, an indigenous African-Canadian nurse, notes:

> You have to be aware of the subtleties of racism, whether it is my pet peeve, communication. It seems it's not just blacks, it's Chinese, Filipinos, anybody that is a nurse of colour, who seem to have a communication problem.... They like to use communication as a way of targeting you, as a way of putting you down. (CBWC 1995)

Scapegoating racial-minority nurses (e.g., as having communication problems) diverts attention from a critical analysis of the structures and practices of the workplace, which treat racial-minority nurses inequitably and justify the status quo by blaming the victims.

In a labour arbitration case in 1994, Vickie, a Black psychiatric nurse at Gouyave Hospital in Toronto, alleged that she was targetted, wrongfully disciplined, suspended, and dismissed because of racial discrimination and harassment from Janice, her acting unit manager, and some nurses. Management claimed that she was dismissed because of personality conflicts and unprofessional behaviour (such as her loud talking), and some nurses felt that her behaviour was threatening to them (Ontario Ministry of Labour, 1994a: 73). The evidence suggests that, before Harry, the unit manager, decided to dismiss Vickie, he was aware of her claims of racial discrimination, but he did nothing to investigate her allegations. Instead, he was concerned with personality conflicts. The ONA argued that the hospital's actions against Vickie were discriminatory, especially since she was disciplined for incidents while white employees in similar circumstances were not disciplined. For example, white nurses who were "visibly shaken and very angry and upset" were not disciplined. Janice consoled them for losing their temper with Vickie, the alleged "troublemaker" (1994a: 55). The arbitration board found that, although on occasion Vickie's conduct warranted discipline, the penalty of discharge was too severe. Thus, the board ordered her reinstatement, with compensation and without loss of seniority or benefits (Ontario Ministry of Labour, 1994a, 1994b).

In 1992, Donna, an indigenous African-Canadian public health nurse, received her first unsatisfactory performance appraisal in fifteen years of employment at the Belair Health Unit, in part because of a "negative perception of her personality." However, she was not given a satisfactory explanation for the performance appraisal. She notes:

> When I inquired as to why I was not told about the negative perception of my personality and my work prior to this date, I was told I would have reacted negatively.... Most of the comments lack concrete data. (Donna, 1993: 1)

Donna argues that she began experiencing racial harassment in 1990 when she began to be more assertive, and to resist (gendered) racism and ageism in the workplace, such as her colleagues' "condescending manner" and "being treated like a child" (interview, 24 June 1996). In 1994, Donna filed several grievances and a human rights complaint of racial discrimination and harassment against her employer. However, she resigned in 1994, citing continuing discrimination. She felt that the stressful work environment was having a negative impact upon her health (Ontario Ministry of Labour, 1996a; Donna, 1994; interview, 24 June 1996).

Racial-minority women's assertiveness, and resistance (e.g., speaking out and "talking back" or "back-chatting") to the multiple oppressions they experience, are perceived as threatening to white patriarchal definitions of femininity. bell hooks (1988: 5, 8) defines "talking back" as "speaking as an equal to an authority figure" or dominant-group member; it entails making a statement "that compels listeners, one that is heard"; it aims at dialogue. Thus, "talking back" is "an act of resistance, a political gesture that challenges the politics of domination that would render [subordinate members] nameless and voiceless." Some racial minorities' cultural way of communicating in conflict situations (such as speaking frankly) clashes with some Euro-Canadians' "subtlety." One of the norms of the dominant Canadian culture is to be soft-spoken and calm, even under extreme pressure (such as being subjected to harassment from management and physical assault by patients' relatives). Moreover, as McPherson (1996: 165) notes, nurses are socialized to show social deference, and "to avoid insubordination or other emotions that put them out of control." Although she was writing about the pre-1970s period, some nurses argue that they are still being socialized to be submissive (Racism at McMaster, c. 1980; interviews, 1 July 1994; 24 June, 3 July 1996). Thus, some assertive racial-minority female nurses' behaviours are pathologized as aggressive and "crazy" in order to silence them (CBWC, 1995; hooks, 1992; Martina v. the College, 1985; Martina v. North York General Hospital, 1986; OHRC, 1992; interview, 3 July 1996). For instance, in the 1980s, a Toronto hospital and the college ordered Martina, an assertive South Asian nurse, to undergo a psychiatric examination because they interpreted her resistance to alleged racial discrimination and harassment as symptoms of mental incapacity (Martina v. the College, 1985; Martina v. North York General Hospital, 1986). This indicates some of the hidden injuries of racism and sexism, as well as the emotional and psychological costs of resistance. Martina's refusal to comply with the college's request resulted in the suspension of her licence.

Racial-minority nurses' everyday experiences reflect the systemic racism in the workplace (e.g., subjective recruitment, evaluation and promotion processes, as well as different work assignments) (Calliste, 1996). As I discussed above (see also Calliste, 1996), management practices and the employment systems in these hospitals adversely affect nurses of colour. The recruitment and promotion processes are often subjective and arbitrary, and lead to discriminatory treatment of applicants. For example, some hospitals recruit through employee referrals or word-of-mouth methods that tend to reproduce the status quo. Pre-screening of applications, checking of references, interviewing and internal transfers are often left to one person, a white manager. Moreover, no standard questions are consistently asked when interviewing for nursing staff. As a result, culturally laden questions could be asked as well as arbitrary, biased, and subjective decisions being made (Henry & Ginzberg, 1985; OHRC, 1992b). In sum, systemic and everyday racism produce and reproduce each other. This section of the paper has shown that nurses of colour moved from exclusion to marginality in nursing. Moreover, with economic restructuring and rapid downsizing of the health care system, racial-minority nurses are more likely than their white counterparts to be "structured out." The next section discusses racial-minority nurses' antiracism organizing and resistance between the late 1970s and the 1990s.

ORGANIZING, AND RESISTING EXCLUSION AND MARGINALITY IN NURSING

▼

Health care workers of colour in Ontario began organizing themselves and making formal as well as informal complaints of racial discrimination and harassment in the late 1970s and the early 1980s as racism and sexism increased with the downturn in the economy and cuts in health care budgets (Calliste, 1996; interview, 5 July 1994). For instance, in 1980, Eva, a Black nurse, filed a human rights complaint against a university hospital in Ontario, alleging racial harassment and wrongful dismissal. Several organizations (such as the local chapter of the International Committee Against Racism and the Afro-

Caribbean Students Association) demanded that the university and the hospital "end racist practices in employment and education, rescind the dismissal" of Eva, and "drop all charges before the College of Nurses" (Hathiramani, 1980; Quigley, 1980; Racism at McMaster, c. 1980: 1; interview, 5 July 1994).

In the early 1980s, health care workers of colour in Toronto organized the Visible Minority Health Care Team to provide personal and professional support for their members; to counsel and assist new immigrant nurses and health care workers in mobilizing their skills and fulfilling their career aspirations; and to combat racism in the workplace (Head, 1986; Visible Minority Health Care Workers, n.d.; interviews, 5–6 July 1994). The team, with a membership of 100 professionals, organized a conference, in 1985, to create antiracist awareness. It addressed topics of major concern to health care workers such as systemic racism, communication problems, and employment equity (Head, 1986; Project Health Care Workers/Team, 1985). It also sensitized the community to racism in the health care system by proposing and collecting data for Head's study (1986) on health care workers' perceptions of racism in the workplace. Although the OHRC commissioned the study and the Ontario Hospital Association promised to address its findings of everyday and systemic racism, its recommendations were not implemented (interview, 19 May 1997).

Although a few nurses of colour won individual cases in the 1980s, neither their organizations nor their communities had the power to pressure local governments and health care facilities for institutional and systemic changes. The status quo (sometimes including the ONA) was able to block resistance because economic and political power resources are unequally distributed. In the 1990s, antiracist movement organizers realized they needed a multilayered or multidirectional agenda to achieve institutional and systemic changes.

As I discussed elsewhere (Calliste, 1996), in 1994–95 the CBWC, with the support of several organizations, was instrumental in obtaining human rights settlements for some racial-minority nurses at two Toronto hospitals. The hospitals also agreed to adopt and implement policies and practices that would transform them into institutions free of racism. Emphasizing the need for effective networks and coalitions to combat racism in the health care system, Lucy told some participants at the "End the Silence on Racism" conference that the Chinese community, including the Chinese Nurses Association and NAFAD, were among those who assisted her in pressuring the ONA to process her grievance and to get an arbitration hearing (CBWC, 1995). These organizations also supported her during the arbitration process by attending the hearings and taking notes.

Lucy's labour arbitration case is significant because of its precedent-setting decision and partly because she subsequently filed a human rights complaint of racial discrimination against the ONA, alleging that her grievances were not addressed in a timely and effective manner (CBWC, 1995; Ontario Ministry of Labour, 1995; interviews, 11 June, 5 July 1996). Lucy alleges that in the early 1990s, she had difficulty filing a grievance and getting an arbitration hearing. She notes:

> [In 1992,] I had to wait at ONA's head office for three days to get the grievance language. I was being harassed.... The ... officer said she could not give me the grievance language because I was not disciplined yet.... ONA deliberately delayed my grievance. They tried to squash it. Another time, they tried to settle it in my absence.... They tried to intimidate me. (CBWC, 1995; interview, 1 July 1994)

This is not surprising, given that before the nurses' protests in the early 1990s, the ONA tended to reinforce racism in the workplace by denying or ignoring it; many nurses are still dissatisfied with ONA's performance in dealing with racism (Calliste, 1996; interviews, 22 October 1996, 27 May 1997).

Between 1992 and 1994, Lucy filed six grievances and a human rights complaint against Pearls Hospital, alleging systemic racial discrimination and harassment. The ONA argued that section 45(8)3 of the Labour Relations Act empowered the arbitration board to interpret and apply the Human Rights Code where appropriate in order to decide these grievances and any remedial relief. It sought to call evidence of other workers who had experienced racial discrimination similar to that reported by the grievor and to seek remedies both under the collective agreement and under section 41(1) of the Human Rights Code in order to redress the alleged systemic racial discrimination experienced by the grievor (Ontario Ministry of Labour, 1995). The board set a precedent by deciding to hear similar fact evidence in order to assist it in determining whether management's practices toward Lucy constituted racial discrimination and whether she was subjected to a poisoned work environment.

The nurses' individual and collective resistance have had some effects on the ONA, the Ontario Hospital Association (OHA), and some health care institutions that have since adopted some antiracism initiatives. For instance, the OHA's Antiracism Task Force developed policy guidelines and strategies for implementing antiracism organizational change in hospitals (Ontario Hospitals Antiracism Task Force, 1996). Similarly, Donna's grievances and human rights complaint against the Belair Health Unit propelled it to employ the Doris Marshall Institute, independent antiracism consultants, to investigate whether there was racism in the unit. The findings indicate that ten (15 percent) employees stated that they experienced some form of discrimination at the unit; and five of these employees argued that discrimination was ongoing. The consultants made 44 recommendations to combat racism in the workplace, and the Health Unit and the ONA agreed to provide antiracism training for all staff members (Kohli & Thomas, 1995; Ontario Ministry of Labour, 1996a).

However, some nurses and their allies doubt whether health care institutions are willing to make any fundamental changes, particularly since most have not even acknowledged that racism exists in their workplaces. It seems that the progress the nurses made in 1994 and 1995 is being eroded. Some of the human rights agreements made during that period have not been implemented, and some that were implemented are now being rolled back (interviews, 13 February, 3 July 1996; 26 March 1998). Moreover, the social agenda for antiracism and equity in the health care system and other organizational settings is threatened, given the neo-conservative political climate, fiscal restraints, and the rapid downsizing of the health care system. The ultra-Conservative government, with its hard-edged agenda, has gutted all antiracism and equity initiatives in the ministries, and the OHRC refuses to deal with human rights complaints of unionized workers in order to reduce its caseload (Calliste, 1996; OHRC, 1996b; ONA, 1997). The commission argues that unionized nurses' complaints of discrimination and harassment could be dealt with more efficiently by an arbitration board, given that section 48(12)(j) of the Labour Relations Act grants power to an arbitrator or chair of an arbitration board to interpret and apply human rights and other employment-related statutes (Ontario Court of Justice, 1998: 2). However, arbitration boards rarely deal with racism complaints.

Although the Metropolitan Toronto Anti-racism, Access and Equity Committee agreed to lobby the provincial government to implement some of the recommendations of the CBWC's conference report, *End the Silence on Racism in Health Care*, the committee was disbanded with the amalgamation of the municipalities into a megacity, Toronto. Despite these setbacks, some racial-minority nurses and their allies seem determined to mobilize support for their antiracist struggles. For instance, at the 1997 UHWIGNA's conference, some participants emphasized the need for Black nurses to organize and form strong coalitions with other racial-minority nurses' organizations to struggle for equity and to minimize reprisals.

CONCLUSION
▼

This study on resisting exclusion and marginality in nursing supports integrative antiracism theory by illustrating the relational aspects of social difference. It also demonstrates some of the emotional, psychological, and social costs of resistance. The OHRC's maximum compensation ($10 000) for mental anguish is grossly inadequate, given that some nurses are suffering from severe emotional, physical, and psychological effects from their experience with racism. For instance, a nurse who got a human rights settlement in 1994 is on long-term disability and may not be able to return to work. Some nurses also complain of a change of personality and fear of "being set up" (CBWC, 1995; interviews, 1 July 1994, 3 July 1996). In order to minimize reprisals for resisting, and to achieve institutional and systemic change, while at the same time addressing the politics of everyday racism, racial-minority nurses must take political action. They must unite and organize into a strong association as well as actively participate and get elected to the executive of the ONA, the Registered Nurses Association of Ontario, and the College of Nurses of Ontario, where they could influence policy. Moreover, racial-minority nurses must form meaningful coalitions and networks at the local, national, and international levels with other antiracist movements in nursing as well as in other institutions (such as universities and colleges) and workplaces. We cannot eliminate racism and other interlocking systems of social oppressions in the health care system without simultaneously combatting them in education and changing the social and economic institutions of capitalist society.

NOTES
▼

1. The author wishes to thank the nurses and their families; the Congress of Black Women of Canada, Toronto Chapter; Nurses and Friends Against Discrimination; the officers of the Ontario Nurses Association; the College of Nurses of Ontario; and others who shared information with her.
2. Although not all Caribbeans are people of colour, a large proportion are.
3. The concept of "individual deskilling" is borrowed from David Lee's critique of Harry Braverman's idea of skill. Lee differentiates between skills associated with one's job requirements and skills that reflect the worker's capabilities (Braverman, 1974; Lee, 1982). Bakan (1987) and Calliste (1993) show that the concept of "individual deskilling" is relevant in interpreting the experiences of individual Black Caribbean women whose previously acquired skills or potential to develop further skills was eliminated as a result of adapting their abilities to meet the needs of the Canadian labour market. Research in Britain also suggests that deskilling of nurses frequently occurs along both class and racial lines. Nurses of colour are more likely to be deskilled because of discrimination and their "educational disadvantage" (Doyal et al., 1981: 66). In the case of immigrants from the South, the deskilling process occurs not only as a feature of the process of capital accumulation on an international scale and discrimination, but also as a

direct result of the individual's experiences in migrating from an underdeveloped country to an advanced industrial one.

4. For example, a score of 500 is equal to 500 + or - 14.2, which is equal to any score between 485.9 and 514.1 (Ontario Ministry of Citizenship, 1989a: 192).

5. Graduate nurses who are eligible to write the General Certificate of Registration have six years, or six opportunities, whichever comes first. If candidates do not pass the examination within three years, or after they have had three opportunities to write the examination, whichever occurs first, the Registration Committee may require them to complete further study prior to being eligible to rewrite the examination. In most provinces, candidates have fewer opportunities to write the examination (College of Nurses of Ontario, 1996: 2).

6. Some nurses and their supporters argue that harassment of senior nurses in Ontario hospitals intensified after nurses received a salary increase (interview, 9 June 1997).

REFERENCES
▼

Agnew, V. (1996). *Resisting discrimination.* Toronto: University of Toronto Press.

Armstrong, P., & Armstrong, H. (1990). *Theorizing women's work.* Toronto: Garamond.

Bakan, A. (1987). The international market for female labour and individual deskilling. *North/South: Canadian Journal of Latin American and Canadian Studies, 12,* 69–85.

Barbee, E. (1993). Racism in U.S. nursing. *Medical Anthropology Quarterly, 7*(4), 346–362.

Bertley, L. (1985). Discrimination against Black nurses? *Afro-Can, 5*(2), 1, 5.

Bolaria, B., & Li, P. (1988). *Racial oppression in Canada* (2nd ed.). Second Edition. Toronto: Garamond.

Brand, D. (1988). A conceptual analysis of how gender roles are racially constructed. M.A. thesis, University of Toronto.

Brandt, D. (1986). *The realization of anti-racist teaching.* London: Falmer.

Braverman, H. (1974). *Labor and monopoly capital: The degradation of work in the twentieth century.* New York: Monthly Review Press.

Caissey, I. (1994). Presentation to the City of North York's Community, Race and Ethnic Relations Committee. Toronto, 13 October.

Calliste, A. (1991). Canada's immigration policy and domestics from the Caribbean: The second domestic scheme. *Socialist Studies, 5,* 136–168.

———. 1993. Women of "exceptional merit": Immigration of Caribbean nurses to Canada. *Canadian Journal of Women and the Law, 6*(1), 85–102.

———. (1994). Race, gender and Canadian immigration policy: Blacks from the Caribbean, 1900–1932. *Journal of Canadian Studies, 28*(4), 131–148.

———. (1995). *End the silence on racism in health care: Build a movement against discrimination, harassment and reprisals. Conference report.* Toronto: CBWC.

————. (1996). Antiracism organizing and resistance in nursing: African Canadian women. *Canadian Review of Sociology and Anthropology, 33*(3), 361–390.

CBWC [Congress of Black Women of Canada], Toronto Chapter. (1991). Press Conference, 27 March.

————. (1995). End the silence on racism in health care: Build a movement against racism, discrimination and reprisals conference. Toronto, 25–26 May.

————. (1996). Presentation to the Metropolitan Toronto Antiracism, Access and Equity Committee, 16 October.

College of Nurses of Ontario. (1994). *The college annual report.* Toronto: College of Nurses of Ontario.

————. (1995a). *A guide to the process for registration in the general class.* Toronto: College of Nurses of Ontario.

————. (1995b). *Vision: The college annual report.* Toronto: College of Nurses of Ontario.

————. (1996). Canadian Nurses Association Testing Division Registration Examination: Fact Sheet 1997, 9 August.

Collins, P. (1990). *Black feminist thought.* London: Unwin Hyman.

Collins, R. (1979). *The credential society.* New York: Academic.

Das Gupta, T. (1993). *Analytical report on the human rights case involving Northwestern General Hospital.* Unpublished paper. Toronto, September.

————. (1996). *Racism in paid work.* Toronto: Garamond.

Dei, G. (1995). Examining the case for African-centred schools. *McGill Journal of Education, 30*(2), 179–198.

————. (1996). *Antiracism education: Theory and practice.* Halifax: Fernwood.

Donna. (1993). Letter to F. White, 25 January.

————. (1994). Letter to F. Gallant, 23 September.

Doris Marshall Institute & Arnold Minors & Associates. (1994). *Ethno-racial equality: A distant goal? An interim report to Northwestern General Hospital.* Toronto: authors.

Doyal, L., Hunt, G., & Mellor, J. (1981). Your life in their hands. *Critical Social Policy, 1*(2), 54–71.

Edwards, R. (1979). *Contested terrain.* New York: Basic.

Ehrenreich, B., & English, D. (1973). *Witches, midwives, and nurses: A history of women healers.* Old Westbury, NY: Feminist Press.

Essed, P. (1991). *Understanding everyday racism.* Newbury Park, CA: Sage.

Farr, M. (1991). Discriminating matters. *The Registered Nurse,* February 9–14, 37.

Frankenberg, R. (1993). *White women, race matters: The social construction of whiteness.* Minneapolis: University of Minnesota Press.

Franklin, C. (1995). Presentation at OHA conference on antiracism. Toronto, 29 May.

Friedman, A. (1977). *Industry and labour.* London: Macmillan.

Gamarnikow, E. (1978). Sexual division of labour. In A. Kuhn & A. Wolpe (Eds.), *Feminism and materialism* (pp. 96–123). London: Routledge.

Gannage, C. (1986). *Double day, double bind: Women garment workers.* Toronto: Women's Press.

Glazer, N. (1991). "Between a rock and a hard place": Women's professional organizations in nursing and class, racial, and ethnic inequalities. *Gender & Society,* 5(3), 351–372.

Gordon, D., Edwards, R., & Reich, M. (1982). *Segmented work, divided workers.* London: Cambridge University Press.

Gray, S. (1994). Hospital and human rights. *Our Times, 13*(6), 17–20.

Hardill, K. (1993). Discovering fire where the smoke is: Racism in the health care system. *Towards Justice in Health, 2*(1), 17–21.

Hartmann, H. (1976). Capitalism, patriarchy, and job segregation by sex. *Signs, 1*(3), 137–169.

———. (1981). The family as the locus of gender, class, and political struggle: The example of housework. *Signs, 6*(3), 366–394.

Hathiramani, H. (1980). Tribunals study nurse dismissal at Mac-Chedoke. *Silhouette,* 18 September.

Head, W. (1986). *An exploratory study of attitudes and perceptions of minority and majority group health care workers.* Toronto: Ontario Human Rights Commission.

Henry, F., & Ginzberg, E. (1985). *Who gets the work: A test of racial discrimination in employment.* Toronto: Urban Alliance on Race Relations.

Henry, F., Tator, C., Mattis, W., & Rees, T. (1995). *The colour of democracy: Racism in Canadian society.* Toronto: Harcourt Brace.

Hine, D. (1989). *Black women in white.* Bloomington: Indiana University Press.

hooks, b. (1988). *Talking back.* Toronto: Between the Lines.

———. (1992). *Black looks.* Toronto: Between the Lines.

Kohli, R., & Thomas, B. (1995). *A time for change.* Toronto: Doris Marshall Institute for Education and Action.

Landsberg, M. (1996). Getting rid of nurses bad medicine for hospitals. *Toronto Star,* 19 May, A2.

Lee, D. (1982). Beyond deskilling. In S. Wood (Ed.), *The degradation of work? Skill, deskilling, and the labour process* (pp. 146–162). London: Hutchinson.

Marks, S. (1994). *Divided sisterhood: Race, class and gender in the South African nursing profession.* New York: St. Martin's Press.

Martina v. the College. (1985). Toronto: OHRC.

Martina v. North York General Hospital and the College. (1982). Toronto: OHRC.

Martina v. North York General Hospital. (1986). *Ontario Human Rights report,* Case No. 236. Toronto: Ontario Human Rights Commission.

McIntosh, P. (1990). White privilege: Unpacking the invisible knapsack. *Independent School, 49*(2), 31–36.

McPherson, K. (1996). *Bedside matters.* Toronto: Oxford University Press.

Moloney, M. (1986). *Professionalization of nursing.* Philadelphia: J.B. Lippincott.

NAFAD [Nurses and Friends Against Discrimination]. (1996). Presentation to Antiracism and Equity Committee, Metro Council. 16 October.

Nurses, Woodlands Hospital. (1992). Letter to the OHRC, 5 December.

OHRC [Ontario Human Rights Commission]. (1992a). Case report. Toronto.

———. (1992b). Dunfermline Hospital: Systemic analysis. Toronto.

———. (1996a). *Annual report*. Toronto: Ontario Human Rights Commission.

———. (1996b). Donna and Belair Health Unit, 15 November.

Omi, M., & Winant, H. (1983). By the rivers of Babylon. Part One. *Socialist Review, 13*(5), 31–65.

ONA [Ontario Nurses Association]. (1996). Presentation to the Metropolitan Toronto Antiracism, Access and Equity Committee. 16 October.

———. (1997). Judicial reviews filed for Human Rights Commission's refusal to investigate unionized workers' complaints. *The ONA News*, (June/July), 26.

———. (1998). Ontario Human Rights Commission takes up the fight for grad nurses. *The ONA News*, (Jan./Feb), 24–25.

Ontario. (1995a). Human Rights Code. *Revised Statutes of Ontario*, Chapter H. 19. Toronto: Queen's Printer.

———. (1995b). Nursing Act, 1991. *Statutes of Ontario*, 1991, Chapter 32. Toronto: Queen's Printer.

Ontario Court of Justice. (1998). *Three Nurses and the OHRC and Toronto Hospital*, file 342/96. Toronto, 5 February.

Ontario Hospitals' Antiracism Task Force. (1996). *Ontario hospitals anti-racism project report*. Toronto: Ontario Hospitals Anti-Racism Task Force.

Ontario Ministry of Citizenship. (1989a). *Access! Task Force on Access to Professions and Trades in Ontario*. Toronto: Queen's Printer for Ontario. Quoting the Committee on Healing Arts (1970).

———. (1989b). Nursing: Background study prepared by the TFAPTO. Toronto: Ontario Ministry of Citizenship.

———. (n.d.). These Ontarians are really outstanding. Toronto: mimeo.

Ontario Ministry of Labour. (1983). *Sudbury and District Health Unit and ONA*. Toronto: Ontario Ministry of Labour.

———. (1992). *Woodlands Hospital and ONA*, file A 9104985.

———. (1994a). *Gouyave Hospital and ONA*, file 921317. Toronto, 24 Jan.

———. (1994b). *Gouyave Hospital and ONA*, file 921317. Toronto, 20 June.

———. (1995). *Pearls Hospital and ONA*, file 930169. Toronto, May.

———. (1996a). *Belair Health Unit and ONA*, file 940354, July.

———. (1996b). *Pearls Hospital and ONA*, file M/9601179).

Parkin, F. (1979). *Marxism and class theory: A bourgeois critique*. New York: Columbia University Press.

Pearls Hospital. (1995). Anti-Discrimination and Anti-Harassment. November.

Phillips, P., & Phillips, E. (1993). *Women and work*. Toronto: Lorimer.

Piore, M. (1971). *The dual labor market*. Lexington, MA: D.C. Heath.

Project Health Care Workers/Team. (1985). *Workshop '85 program*. Toronto: Project Health Care Workers/Team.

Quigley, M. (1980). Racism: A growing problem at McMaster. *Silhouette*, 18 September.

Racism at McMaster. (*c.* 1980). Interview by author. Toronto, 11 August.

Razack, S. (1998). *Looking white people in the eye: Gender, race and culture in courtrooms and classrooms*. Toronto: University of Toronto Press.

Reitz, J., Calzavara, L., & Dasko, D. (1981). *Ethnic inequality and segregation in jobs.* Research paper no. 3. Toronto: Centre for Urban and Community Studies, University of Toronto.

Richmond, A. (1992). Immigration and structural change: The Canadian experience, 1971–1986. *International Migration Review, 26,* 1200–1221.

Robertson, M. (1985). A victory for Black nurses. *Afro-Can, 5*(5), 1, 11.

Sudbury and District Health Unit and ONA. (1987). *Labour Arbitration Cases, 28*(3), 196–211.

Thornhill, E. (1991). Focus on Black women! *Socialist Studies, 5,* 27–38.

UHWIGNA [University Hospital of the West Indies Graduate Nurses' Association], Canadian Chapter. (1997). Remembering the past ... creating the future, making changes ... taking charge. Conference. Toronto, 2–3 May.

Visible Minority Health Care Workers. (n.d.) *The professional communique.* Toronto: Visible Minority Health Care Workers.

Winant, H. (1994). *Racial conditions.* Minneapolis: University of Minnesota Press.

19

▼

GLOBAL APARTHEID: MIGRATION, RACISM, AND THE WORLD SYSTEM[1]

ANTHONY H. RICHMOND

INTRODUCTION
▼

It may seem strange to juxtapose terms such as "apartheid," "asylum," and "refuge" and to link them to concepts such as "ethnic cleansing," "reservation," "prison," and "hospital" (see Figure 19.1). However, from a sociological perspective, these are all actions, structures, and institutions associated with forcible isolation of people who are different. Because of these differences, they are perceived to have actual (or potentially) conflicting relationships. Distancing is used to deal with the conflict. When separation is imposed by a dominant group upon a less powerful one, the conflict is only temporarily resolved. In the long run, the opposition is generally exacerbated. Restitution and retribution may be delayed for generations, but the power struggle continues. As processes of structuration, apartheid, and asylum have much in common.

The word "apartheid" literally means "apart*hood*" (c.f., neighbour*hood*), that is, the separation of people into different areas. The term "asylum" (literally meaning "non-seizure") originated with the Church's refusal to allow wanted criminals and others sought by the authorities to be forcibly removed from the altar. Later the term was applied to mental hospitals, sanatoria, and other institutions where anyone who might contaminate others, disturb the peace, or in some way come into conflict with the general public, could be kept apart. As Michel Foucault (1973) showed in his study *Madness and Civilization*, the nineteenth-century insane asylum brought to bear on the mentally ill all the means of social control in the power of "keepers."[2] They used segregation, surveillance, subordination, and silencing as instruments. These replaced physical coercion with self-restraint, judgement, and the patriarchal authority of the medical profession.

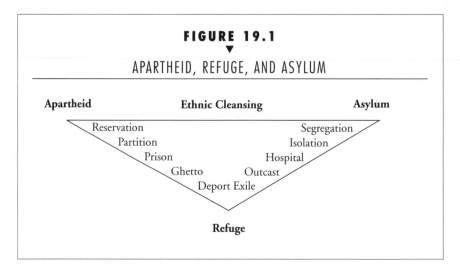

FIGURE 19.1
▼
APARTHEID, REFUGE, AND ASYLUM

| Apartheid | Ethnic Cleansing | Asylum |

Reservation   Segregation
Partition   Isolation
Prison   Hospital
Ghetto   Outcast
Deport Exile

Refuge

Totalitarian states have long used the device of exile or forcible confinement in prisons or hospitals as a means of dealing with dissidents and political enemies. Thus "asylum" acquired a dual meaning. On the one hand, it is a way in which a more powerful (or majority) group segregates "others" who do not conform or who are seen as threatening. On the other hand, the asylum offers sanctuary and some protection for the minority or outcast who might otherwise face death. The term "refugee" (from the Latin *regugium*, meaning "to flee back") was first applied to the Protestant Huguenots escaping the threat of death and persecution in France, following the revocation of the Edict of Nantes in 1685.

The principle of separation is widely used as a means of social control, and has a long history in Canada and elsewhere. The expulsion of the Acadians from the Maritimes in 1756; the separation of Upper and Lower Canada; the creation of Indian reserves; and, in some provinces, the formation of separate school systems for Catholics and Protestants are all examples of the principle of separation being used as a device to reduce tension and maintain control. When South Africa introduced its system of African reserves (later called Bantustans, or homelands), it was following a well-established precedent in colonial history. The English "Pale" in France and Ireland, the partition of Ireland, and later India (establishing Pakistan and later Bangladesh), the division of Cyprus —all are examples of the political application of the principle. The so-called ethnic cleansing of areas in former Yugoslavia is the latest example and one that comes close to genocide. Serbian, Crotian, and Muslim peoples who have lived together for centuries are being separated by military force in an attempt to create homogeneous ethnoreligious areas, expanding the power and territorial control of fanatical nationalist leaders. Numerous civilian casualties and vast refugee movements are the result.

Residential segregation by ethnicity and religion created the ghettoes of European cities and eventually led to the Holocaust. In the United States, the emergence of separate residential areas ("Black" ghettoes) and separate schools for "Blacks" and "Whites" is another example. In 1954, the American Supreme Court found separate schools and colleges for Afro-Americans "inherently unequal" and therefore unconstitutional, but, despite busing, de facto residential and educational segregation have persisted. In some cases, electoral boundaries have been redrawn in order to emphasize ethnic homogeneity, thereby giving a spurious legitimacy to residential segregation. In determining the legitimacy of any case of ethnic segregation, it is necessary to consider the extent to which it is voluntary on both sides, and examine how much of it results from coercion and domination by one group over another. The latter is nearly always the case.

As far as immigration is concerned, the question becomes: Are we creating a system of global apartheid based on discrimination against migrants and refugees from poorer developing countries? or are we simply acting rationally to protect the integrity of our social systems and harmonize our immigration policies? Will the emerging New World Order ensure justice and equality of treatment for immigrants and refugees, or will it create a system that privileges some and deprives others of their rights? In order to determine whether it is accurate to describe present trends as contributing to global apartheid, it is necessary to summarize the key elements in the South African experience concerning external and internal migration, in the context of state-legislated apartheid in that country.

APARTHEID IN SOUTH AFRICA
▼

When the Nationalist party came to power in South Africa in 1948, building on existing forms of discrimination and segregation, it proceeded to create the system that came to be known as "apartheid." In defending the South African Group Areas Act in 1951, then president Dr. Malan argued that it was essential to keep the groups apart in order to maintain "racial peace" (Richmond, 1961: 81–137). An integral element of the system was the control of internal migration, combined with the selective immigration to South Africa of people who were racially defined as "European." Forty-four years later, the system is gradually being dismantled, although South Africa is a long way from institutionalizing equality, democracy, and racial integration. Apartheid failed for a number of reasons, among which were the internal contradictions and conflicts within the system itself. Revolutionary change could be contained only by the use of excessive force, with consequent loss of legitimacy in the eyes of the world and its own people. Internal resistance to oppression was reinforced by pressure from outside the country. Externally imposed economic sanctions were used to symbolize disapproval of the regime and provide leverage for reform.

"White" South Africans are outnumbered by a ratio of six to one within the republic. They are an affluent and politically dominant minority enjoying a material standard of living comparable to that of middle-class Canadians, while the majority of the African population have average incomes that are only one-tenth of those of "Whites." This inequality has been maintained by systemic discrimination beginning with the Labour Regulation Act (1911), regulating the recruitment of labour, and the Native Lands Act of 1913, which created the "reserves," later to be described as "homelands," confining the African population to 13 percent of the total area of the country. Subsequent legislation, up to and including the Abolition of Influx Control Act (1986), regulated the movement of people into urban areas. Other measures included the Blacks (Urban Areas) Consolidation Act (1945); the Population Registration Act (1950), which required everyone to carry racially classified identification; the Group Areas Acts (1950 and 1966); and the Prevention of Illegal Squatting Act (1951). Added to these were a series of measures entrenching the dominant economic and political power of the "White" population by denying full citizenship and the franchise, suppressing political opposition, and restricting access to education and social rights (Adam, 1979).

The selective immigration of "White" settlers to South Africa was encouraged in part to compensate for the demographic imbalance between "White" and non-"White" and to provide a source of skilled labour. An immigrant to South Africa had to be "readily assimilable by the White inhabitants" and not a threat to "the language, culture or religion of any white ethnic group," according to the minister of immigration (Couper, 1990). In fact, more than 1 million immigrants of European ethnic origin were admitted to South Africa between 1945 and 1985. At the same time, South Africa forced into exile many opponents of apartheid and hunted down Mozambican refugees who crossed the border, deporting those they caught (U.S. Committee for Refugees, 1991: 53).

Notwithstanding these measures, the South African economy is dependent on a supply of temporary workers from within and outside the country. Agriculture, mining, manufacturing, and domestic services all rely heavily on migrant workers. These are drawn from neighbouring countries such as

Malawi, Mozambique, and Zambia, as well as from the homelands, such as Transkei and Ciskei. Such migrant workers were confined to separate townships or to hostels away from the "White" areas. A third of the "Black" population is now urban, but have no security of tenure. In 1981, it was estimated that 74 000 "Blacks" commuted daily from homelands into "White" areas to work, and a further 1.5 million worked for longer periods as contract labourers (Glavovic, 1987: 47).

The South African situation gives rise to numerous external refugees and internally displaced persons. Opponents of apartheid were often obliged to go to Swaziland or other neighbouring countries to avoid persecution. Compulsory removal to homelands, factional disputes within Bantustans and between tribal groups, together with squatter camps made up of those seeking employment, have created internal refugees, whose numbers may range from hundreds of thousands to millions (Mabin, 1987: 80–5). Despite some changes to the system, it seems that current trends represent "relatively insignificant changes from past apartheid policies" (Robertson, 1987: 116), but there is no guarantee that these will bring peace. Regional divisions remain, and the possibility of secession cannot be ruled out (Adam & Moodley, 1993). The African National Congress is pressing the all-"White" government to introduce more radical reforms that will enable the non-"White" majority to participate democratically in the political process. For the first time, democratic elections with universal franchise were held in 1994. Meanwhile, factional fighting between Zulus and other African groups vying for power, and armed reaction by "White" extremists demanding their own separate state, do not augur well for the future. Southern Africa will continue to generate its own refugees, "Black" and "White."

RACISM OUTSIDE SOUTH AFRICA
▼

However, as apartheid in South Africa is gradually giving way to political reform and social change, the rest of the world appears to be moving in a different direction. In eastern and central Europe, following the collapse of the Soviet empire, nationalism and irredentism have revived, causing widespread violence. Ethnic cleansing provides the ideological rationale for civil war in the former Yugoslavia. The idea that only one dominant racial or ethnoreligious group should be allowed to occupy a particular territory is precisely the meaning of apartheid. When military force is used to bring about such territorial separation, killing or displacing hundreds of thousands (possibly millions) of people in the process, it is no exaggeration to speak of "apartheid."

Faced with the prospect of mass migration from poorer to richer countries, from those where governmental systems have collapsed to those with more stable political environments (and with huge refugee flows from Bosnia–Herzegovina), co-ordinated efforts are being made to stem the potential flow into western Europe. The legislation used and the regulative institutions created have a remarkable similarity to those that South Africa adopted to control the movement of people from outside and within its borders. Furthermore, the ideological justifications used to defend these measures echo those adopted by the dominant "White" minority in South Africa to defend their actions in imposing the system of apartheid on the non-"White" majority. As well as explicit racism and claims to "superiority," they include an obligation to limit intertribal conflict, the need to preserve ethnic identity, expressions of religious fanaticism, the defence of existing cultural and social institutions, state security, the maintenance of law and order, preservation of economic privilege, and the need to regulate and manage population movements. These themes, which were constantly repeated by defenders of the South African system, are now recurring in the rhetoric of those who wish to restrict immigration into western Europe, North America, and Australia.

People in most countries have an ambivalent attitude toward questions of race, ethnicity, and migration. On the one hand, the United Nations Subcommission on Prevention of Discrimination and Protection of Minorities and the Commission on Human Rights condemn apartheid and, on the other, they note an upsurge in racism, discrimination, intolerance, and xenophobia in many parts of the world (*Human Rights Newsletter*, October 1990, April 1991). In Europe and North America, neo-Nazi and other right-wing extremist groups are gaining support. Recent riots in Los Angeles and lesser outbreaks of violence in Toronto serve to remind us how volatile interracial situations are. Public opinion surveys in many countries reveal a backlash against immigration and growing support for reactionary political parties. In France, the Front National, led by Jean-Marie Le Pen, mobilized 15 percent of the popular vote in recent elections, and demonstrations against non-"White" immigrant workers are frequent events, as are antiracist marches (Husbands, 1991; Singer, 1991). In Germany, a tenfold increase in racist attacks (from 200 to 2386) was reported in 1991 (*Migration News Sheet*, February 1992). There was a further escalation of ethnic violence in Germany in 1992, much of it instigated by neo-Nazi skinheads, targeted toward asylum applicants; gypsies; and other foreigners, including long-resident Turkish workers and their families. The government reacted by proposing stricter controls over immigration and an amendment to the constitutional right to asylum. The Republican party in Germany proposed mass repatriation of foreigners and the confinement of accepted refugees in camps away from cities.

IMMIGRATION CONTROLS
▼

There is a worldwide trend toward stricter immigration controls and attempts to limit the flow of refugees and asylum applicants. It is part of a growing nostalgia for a simpler world in which people felt secure in homogeneous communities where neighbours shared "traditional" values. It is also a reaction to the insecurity felt by many faced with a rapidly changing global society. This is evident in the growth of racism, zenophobia, and religious and ethnic conflict in various countries, including those that have traditionally been receptive to both political and economic migrants. Politically, it is expressed in the co-ordinated efforts of countries in western Europe, North America, and Australia to deter asylum applications and limit mass migration to these regions. There is a growing fear in Europe concerning the possibility of mass migration from east to west, and an equal concern about the potential flow from south to north, including from the Maghreb territories of the southern Mediterranean and Africa, to France and Germany.

The reunification of East and West Germany reduced the FRG's dependency on immigrant workers, while at the same time leaving the country vulnerable to mass migration from east and central Europe as well as from the former Soviet Union. Under the German constitution, "ethnic Germans," from wherever they may come, have privileged rights of entry and citizenship, although long-time residents of the country who are not of German descent (including their children born in Germany) are denied similar privileges. Recently, new immigration legislation was introduced in Germany that will severely restrict the number of asylum applicants accepted and allows the government to segregate them in camps. Britain introduced an asylum bill that will require refugees to be fingerprinted, restrict access by asylum applicants to public housing, permit deportation where an asylum claim has been refused, and require airlines or other carriers to ensure that travellers hold a visa to enter or even pass through the United Kingdom en route to another country.

Notwithstanding the European Economic Community's abolition of internal border checks, Britain, Ireland, and Denmark have expressed reservations and indicated exceptions. The U.K. intends to retain frontier controls for all non-EEC nationals, including those entering Britain via other EEC countries. A limit of three months' stay will be placed on non-U.K. nationals entering the country. Britain is one of the twelve European countries that signed the Dublin Convention in June 1990. Neither this nor the related Schengen Agreement has yet been ratified by all the countries involved, although the provisions of both are expected to come into force in 1994, having been delayed by preparation of a computerized data bank concerning immigrants. Meanwhile, France, Germany, Belgium, and other countries tightened their control over asylum applicants and refugee movements.

THE SCHENGEN AGREEMENT AND DUBLIN CONVENTION
▼

The Schengen Agreement was signed in 1985 by Belgium, Denmark, France, Germany, and Luxembourg. When the subsequent Dublin Convention and Maastricht Treaty are ratified, it will apply to all twelve EEC members. The agreement provides that persons with valid documents who can show that they have sufficient means to support themselves during their stay and to return to their country of origin will be allowed entry, but only if they are not considered a "threat to public policy, national security or international relations of the Contracting Parties." Once admitted, they may travel freely within the EEC, subject to any limitations that Britain or other dissenting countries may impose. In order to enforce the regulations, the countries in question may take any necessary steps to verify documents and may use mobile units to exercise surveillance at external borders. Every contracting party is obliged to supply the others with information concerning individuals requesting admission (including asylum applicants), and this information may be computerized.

As well as extending the provisions of the Schengen Agreement to all countries in the EEC, the Dublin Convention also deals specifically with the question of asylum applicants and determines who is responsible for processing them. It reiterates the 1951 Geneva Convention's definition of a refugee, as amended by the 1967 New York Protocol. In order of precedence, the state responsible for hearing an asylum application is the one that issued either a residence permit or an entry visa; when no visa is required, the state that first admitted the person into the EEC territory is responsible. The other EEC states are bound by the decision of the one that processes the application.

Critics of the Schengen Agreement and Dublin Convention note that there is no recognition of the growing numbers of cases of de facto humanitarian refugees who may not meet the 1951 convention definition. It is felt that the effect of visa requirements, entry regulations, and carrier sanctions will be to deter or exclude many legitimate claimants and those trying to escape wartorn countries. It will also increase the traffic in forged documents.

Third-country nationals (i.e., non-EEC citizens) residing in the EEC will find their right to travel and work in other countries restricted. These agreements must also be considered in the context of increasing co-operation within and between European countries and others in matters of international policing and security. The Trevi Group is an intergovernmental body that co-ordinates efforts to combat terrorism and organized crime. Among the measures it has recommended (and that are being widely adopted) are uniform documentation of travellers; the fingerprinting of migrants and asylum applicants; the creation of a computerized database and information exchange on criminals, deported persons, and unwanted persons; training of police officers and border guards for surveillance; and the harmonization of legislation governing immigrant and security measures at borders. The Maastricht Treaty, when ratified, will create a European Union with even greater co-ordination of immigration controls. A provisional list of countries whose nationals will require visas to enter any European Union country covers most third-world states, including many Commonwealth countries whose citizens do not at present require a visa to visit Britain, although they will do so in the future.

It is probably not a coincidence that many of these measures have been incorporated into the new Canadian legislation on immigration (Bill C-86). Canada is one of the sixteen states participating in the Inter-governmental Consultations on Asylum, Refugee, and Migration Policies in Europe, North America, and Australia. Described as "informal," these consultations enable governments to be kept informed of developments in other countries and facilitate the harmonization process. The participating states acknowledge the value of co-operation, endorse the principles established in the Dublin Convention, and seek to intensify co-operation in combatting illegal immigration. The aim is to adopt a concerted approach that will also include the countries of eastern Europe, so that they will adopt policies that correspond with those in western Europe.

Canada's new Immigration Act enables this country to harmonize its immigration law and practice with that of other countries. As in the McCarthy era in the United States, guilt by association with allegedly subversive organizations or a criminal record, however minor, will be sufficient to exclude potential immigrants and asylum applicants. Asylum applicants will be fingerprinted, and the use of forged documents will be grounds for exclusion. Immigrants may be required to work in particular places, and to remain in such employment for two years after arrival, as if they were indentured. Business immigrants and investors will be given top priority for admission. Officials will have greater control over numbers admitted annually in various categories. As at present, the extensive use of temporary employment visas will enable the government to limit the number of people allowed to settle permanently. None of these measures, in itself, appears particularly draconian. However, the combined effect will be to give considerable advantage to the wealthy and well educated over "your tired, your poor, your huddled masses yearning to breathe free." The delayed reaction of Canada and many other countries to the prolonged plight of refugees in Somalia and other regions of Africa, compared with the response to those in former Yugoslavia, suggests that the "huddled masses" should preferably be "White" if they are to receive much help at all. The United States (in the Bush and Clinton administrations) has applied a double standard in its treatment of Cuban as compared with Haitian asylum applicants. "Fortress Europe" is matched by "Fortress North America."

AFRICA AND THE MIDDLE EAST
▼

The African continent has experienced large population movements induced by economic conditions and political instability. South Africa has always relied on a flow of workers from neighbouring countries who are employed on a contract basis in mining and other industries. Reliable statistics are difficult to obtain, but the number of people living and working outside their country of birth runs into millions. The situation is summarized by Aderanti Adepoju (1988) as follows:

> International migration in West Africa is dominated by clandestine or undocumented migration of unskilled persons. In southern Africa migration is temporary and oscillatory, conditioned largely by South African immigration laws. Refugee migration is a major feature in Central and especially East Africa. Clandestine migrations are most frequent among nomads — especially between Somalia, Kenya and Tanzania. (Adepoju, 1988: 78)

The growing number of refugees and others displaced by war and ecological disasters is a disturbing feature of the African scene, particularly in the region of the Horn and Sudan, where more than 5 million people live under the most primitive conditions in and outside organized camps (Harrell-Bond, 1986; Mazur, 1988).

The Middle East and the Gulf region are experiencing the combined effects of economic and political instability. Israel has always been a country of immigration and has welcomed Jewish settlers from any country. In recent years, the numbers of Soviet Jews emigrating to that country has grown more rapidly than the regular immigration and settler assistance system can handle.

Israel is reported to have budgeted for 400 000 Soviet Jewish immigrants in 1991 and still more in 1992. Meanwhile, the Palestinian problem and the *Intifaddah* continued to exacerbate an already prolonged refugee crisis in the region throughout the 1980s and early 1990s (Abu-Lughod, 1988). It remains to be seen whether the PLO/Israel peace accord of 1993 will reduce the bloodshed and relieve the refugee problem in Jordan and elsewhere.

The oil-rich Gulf region always attracted professional, skilled, and managerial personnel from Britain, Europe, and the United States, but, after 1970, the number of Asian workers in the region rose to over 3 million. They provided much-needed remittances to their countries of origin, and because the two-way flow of contract labour has a profound influence on families in the sending countries, they also made a significant cultural impact. The average length of a contract is two to three years. The reintegration of return migrants has caused problems for the countries of origin. The war between Iraq and Iran led to some diminution in the flow of migrants, but when it ended, the numbers began to increase again until the Kuwait crisis and the war in the Persian Gulf (Amjad, 1990; Seccombe, 1988). This resulted in more than half a million workers being forced to leave (Curmi, 1993). Some were trapped in Jordan, where they spent months in makeshift camps. In the aftermath of the war, a major refugee crisis occurred as thousands of Kurds tried to escape to Turkey or Iran.

ASIA
▼

Asia has long been a source of permanent and temporary migration to the rest of the world. This is particularly true of east and south Asia (especially China, India, and Pakistan) whose emigrants now form permanently established minorities in Britain, North America, Australia, and elsewhere. Asia has a large refugee problem involving people from Tibet, Afghanistan, Bangladesh, Sri Lanka, Vietnam, and Kampuchea. Many have sought asylum in neighbouring countries, as well as farther away (Centlivres & Centlivres-Dumont, 1988; Zolberg, 1989).

In recent years, the NIE counties, together with those that have become part of the ILE, have experienced net inward migration as well as outward flows. There is a growing interdependence of the economies of Asia, as well as cross-national labour migration, particularly within and between Thailand, Malaysia, Singapore, Brunei, Indonesia, the Philippines, and the leading ILE countries such as Japan and Hong Kong (Gunasekaran, 1990). It is impossible to document the detailed flows, but the multiway nature of the movements must be emphasized. Hong Kong is losing some of its wealthiest and best-qualified people, who are emigrating as a result of mainland China's repossession in 1997 but, at the same time, it has more than 2 million foreign-born residents, mainly from China, but also from ILE countries such as Britain, the United States, and Japan (Abella, 1990). Hong Kong, Thailand, and other Asian countries also have a serious refugee problem.

Some Asian countries, such as Singapore, rely heavily on temporary workers from Thailand and elsewhere. There are strict controls to deal with illegal migrants. Malaysia supplies labour to Singapore, but is also a receiver of labour migration from other countries. Brunei is an oil-rich country that makes use of migrant workers (including women working as domestics) from the Philippines and elsewhere. Indonesia is a net exporter of labour. Appleyard (1988: 159) noted that many of the issues relating to international migration in Asia also apply to the Pacific islands, where there is a proportionally greater outward flow, thus reflecting the poverty and deteriorating economic conditions on the islands compared with the relative prosperity of some Asian countries. Nevertheless, as in other regions, remittances from nationals working abroad are important. Throughout Asia, as elsewhere, these multiway flows of population create severe strains on sending and receiving areas alike, sometimes exacerbating existing ethnic tensions and cultural clashes (Appleyard, 1989; Claval, 1990; Stahl, 1988).

CONCLUSION
▼

We are living in a global society, although we still lack effective world governmental institutions. Nevertheless, the most economically developed and affluent countries are banding together to protect their privileged position in much the same way that Afrikaners and others of European descent sought to maintain their dominance in South Africa. Europeans and those of European descent in the Americas and Oceania are outnumbered in the world in a ratio of four to one. This leads to fear that they will lose their power and territorial control as the people of Africa and Asia restructure their economies and participate in a global postindustrial society where mass migration is the norm. As the senior legal adviser to the UNHCR has stated, even if the developed countries "were prepared to betray the very values on which their societies are based, by building new iron curtains and Berlin Walls around their common territory, the human flood would still find its ways" (von Blumenthal, 1991). In other words, a system of global apartheid is bound to fail.

What then is the alternative? The director of the agency for intergovernmental consultations echoes the view of many experts that uncontrolled, large-
scale international migration threatens social cohesion, international solidarity,
and peace (Widgren, 1991). Co-ordinated efforts to deter irregular movements, encourage voluntary repatriation, harmonize immigration and asylum
policies, and promote economic development in the third world are seen as essential. But the economic, political, and social costs of effective measures to
deal with root causes are enormous. They would involve long-term developmental assistance, large-scale planned migration, and concerted efforts to promote human rights and equality in sending and receiving countries alike. Contrary to the view that economic growth will itself remove the need for
migration, it must be recognized that the emerging global economic and social
system is one in which population movements will continue to increase rather
than decline. A comprehensive, non-exodus approach, such as that advocated
by the intergovernmental committee and its advisers, will be self-defeating.
Global apartheid will collapse as surely as the South African version has done.
In the postmodern world, we must all learn to live with ethnocultural diversity, rapid social change, *and* mass migration. There is no peaceful alternative.

NOTES
▼

1. This is a revised version of an article published in *Refuge, 13*(1) (April 1993).
   Pages 339–340 are from my article "International Migration and Global
   Change" in O.J. Hui, C.K. Bun, & C.S. Beng (Eds.), *Asian Transmigration* (Singapore: Prentice-Hall, 1994).
2. Foucault (1973: 241–78) compared the humanitarian efforts of the Religious Society of Friends and Samuel Tuke at the Retreat in York, England, with those of
   Scipion Pinel at Bicêtre near Paris, France. Although the former was based on religious ideals and the latter on secular, rational principles, they had in common
   the imposition of self-discipline, order, and justice to modify behaviour in conformity with majority expectations.

REFERENCES
▼

Abella, M. (1990). *Structural change and labour migration within the Asian region.*
   Nagoya: U.N. Centre for Regional Development, Expert Group Meeting on
   Cross-National Labour Migration in the Asian Region.
Abu-Lughod, J.L. (1988). Palestinians: Exiles at home and abroad. *Current Sociology,*
   36(2): 61–70.

Adam, H. (1979). *Ethnic power mobilized: Can South Africa change?* New Haven, CT: Yale University Press.

Adam, H. & Moodley, K. (1993). *The opening of the apartheid mind: Options for the new South Africa.* Berkeley: University of California Press.

Adepoju, A. (1988). International migration in Africa south of the Sahara. In R. Appleyard (Ed.)., *International migration today,* Vol. 1: *Trends and prospects* (pp. 17–88). Paris: UNESCO.

Amjad, R. (1990). *Asian labour in the Middle East: Lessons and implications.* Nagoya: U.N. Centre for Regional Development, Expert Group Meeting on Cross-National Labour Migration in the Asian Region.

Appleyard, R. (Ed.). (1988). *International migration today,* Vol 1: *Trends and prospects.* Paris: UNESCO.

Centlivres, P., & Centelivres-Dumont, M. (1988). The Afghan refugees in Pakistan: A nation in exile. *Current Sociology, 36*(2), 71–92.

Claval, P. (1990). *Cultural dimension of cross-labour migration.* Nagoya: U.N. Centre for Regional Development, Expert Group Meeting on Cross-National Labour Migration in the Asian Region.

Couper, M.P. (1990). *Immigrant adaption in South Africa.* Unpublished Ph.D. thesis, Rhodes University, South Africa.

Curmi, B. (1993). Gestation de la crise des refugies au detour de la crise du gulfe: le role des organizations internationales. In *International Union for the Scientific Study of Population,* vol. 2 (pp. 59–67). Montreal: International Population Conference, August.

Foucault, M. (1973). *Madness and civilization: A history of insanity in the age of reason.* New York: Vintage.

Glavovic, P.D. (1987). State policy, agriculture and environmental values. In A.J. Rycroft, L.J. Boulle, M.K. Robertson, & P.R. Spiller. (Eds.), *Race and the law in South Africa* (pp. 41–51). Cape Town: Juta.

Gunasekaran, S. (1990). *Cross-national labour migration within Asia: Patterns and problems.* Nagoya: U.N. Centre for Regional Development, Expert Group Meeting on Cross-National Labour Migration in the Asian Region.

Harrell-Bond, B. (1986). *Imposing aid: Emergency assistance to refugees.* Oxford and New York: Oxford University Press.

Human Rights Newsletter. (October 1990). Geneva: U.N. World Campaign for Human Rights.

———. (April 1991). Commission on Human Rights Concludes Annual Session. Geneva: U.N. World Campaign for Human Rights.

Husbands, C.T. (1991). The support for the Front National: Analyses and findings. *Ethnic and Racial Studies, 14*(3), 382–416.

Mabin, A. (1987). Unemployment, resettlement and refugees in South Africa. In J.R. Rogge (Ed.), *Refugees: A third world dilemma* (pp. 80–85). Totowa: Rowman & Littlefield.

Mazur, R.E. (1988). Refugees in Africa: The role of sociological analysis and praxis. *Current Sociology, 36*(2), 43–60.

Migration News Sheet. (February 1992). Brussels: European Information Network.

Richmond, A.H. (1961). *The colour problem* (Rev. ed.). Harmondsworth: Penguin.

Robertson, M.K. (1987). Orderly urbanization: The new influx control. In A.J. Rycroft, L.J. Boulle, M.K. Robertson, & P.R. Spiller. (Eds.), *Race and the law in South Africa* (pp. 107–118). Cape Town: Juta.

Seccombe, I.J. (1988). International migration in the Middle East: Historical trends, contemporary patterns and consequences. In R. Appleyard (Ed.), *International migration today,* Vol. 1: *Trends and prospects* (pp. 180–209). Paris: UNESCO.

Singer, D. (1991). The resistable rise of Jean-Marie Le Pen. *Ethnic and Racial Studies, 14*(3), 368–381.

Stahl, C. (Ed.). (1988). *International migration today,* Vol. 2: *Emerging issues.* Paris: UNESCO.

U.S. Committee for Refugees. (1991). *World refugee report, 1991.* Washington: American Council for Nationalities Service and U.S. Committee for Refugees.

von Blumenthal, U. (1991). Dublin, Schengen and the harmonization of asylum in Europe. Paper presented at the First European Lawyers Conference.

Widgren, J. (1991). The management of mass migration in a European context. Statement at the Royal Institute of International Affairs, London.

Zolberg, A. (1989). *Escape from violence: Conflict and the refugee crisis in the developing world.* New York: Oxford University Press.

20

▼

MOSAIC MADNESS
REGINALD W. BIBBY

I'm a fairly typical Canadian. My grandparents on my father's side were Americans from Pennsylvania and Missouri, a generation removed from England. My mother's parents were from small Welsh villages. The Welsh link has been dominant — with some regularity I venture back to Cardiff and wander around rural Wales, imagining what the past may have been like. I also feel at home in the United States. I have lived there for two stretches of three years each, and frequently visit.

But while I cherish my national heritages, I am a Canadian, which for me means much more than being a Welsh–American hybrid who attends Welsh song festivals and watches American sports on TV. Living in Canada means more than merely sharing common geographical turf with an assortment of other cultural hybrids and purebreds who are all encouraged to give pre-eminence to the national cultures of their origins.

Why? For one thing, I have only a slight grasp of my Welsh past, and my American heritage was never really cultivated. Moreover, what I know of both leaves me with an appreciation for the aspects of each that are positive, but with no desire to perpetuate the features that need improvement.

So where does that leave me, and thousands — no, millions — of other Canadians, in a country that tells us that our national end is to live out our cultural heritages? The answer lies in taking a closer look at our ancestral past.

THE DREAM THAT CREATED DIVERSITY
▼

The vast majority of our parents, grandparents, and great-grandparents came to Canada not to live out the old life here, but to find a new life, one much better than what they had known in the countries of their birth.

In May 1990, as I drove up the winding narrow road that leads to the village of Nasareth in northern Wales and again looked at the rolling, sheep-dotted hillsides, I thought of the risk that my grandfather — then only a young man in his early twenties — had taken embarking on that long voyage to Canada, never to return. As I walked down the narrow little main street of Corris in central Wales, where my grandmother had walked as a child, I was moved to think of the risk she had taken as a young woman heading off to the distant and unknown land of Canada. She, too, would never see her homeland again.

They and so many other hundreds of thousands of immigrants came to Canada because they had a dream of a better life. Historically, there is perhaps no single characteristic more common among those varied new arrivals than that dream. Our relatives who preceded us from Britain and France, from the rest of Europe and Asia and Africa and the Americas, came because they saw hope of better things. It is not an exaggeration to say that the dream of a better life is the very source of our cultural diversity.

That dream needs to be re-emphasized in our time. We, like they, want to stay alive and live well. That's why it's so important that we resolve the issue of co-existence, so that we who have come to Canada and those who were here when we arrived together can give our energies to pursuing the best existence possible in this land.

Our cultural diversity is one of our richest assets. Our dream of well-being — along with a willingness to work for it — is a goal that brings cohesion to that diversity. Social sanity lies in refocussing on the dream that created a multinational Canada.

WHAT IT WILL TAKE
▼

A question of motivation emerges from this analysis: What will it take for Canadians to move on to better things? What will lead people to become more concerned about a balance between individualism and the group, more concerned about pursuing the best of available choices? What will lead institutions to encourage such emphases, when they have thought it to be in their best interests to stress individualism and relativism?

One can appeal to altruism, urging Canadians to have a greater concern for the social good. I would like to believe that there are large numbers of people from Newfoundland to British Columbia who would respond to such a plea. While individualism is rampant, there is, I believe, a growing recognition of some of its destructive results. Many of us feel a certain revulsion when individuals and organizations experience success at the expense of others. We certainly applaud winning; but little affirmation is given to those who win with callous disregard for those who lose. Many, I think, are attracted to the idea of a Canada that values individuality while emphasizing themes like problem-solving and communication as means to better group life.

Similarly, the importance of pursuing the best of available possibilities is not "a hard sell." To call Canadians to be discerning is to ask them to think more, not less.

Many of these "reflective altruists" are, of course, already well aware of the need for balance and pursuit of the best. The hope is that they will be joined by other people who have aspired to good personal and group life, but just now are beginning to catch a glimpse of what it is going to take to make it happen.

The appeal to altruistic concern for the well-being of the entire society of course has definite limits. Philosophers provide the arguments, and sociologists and psychologists the data, that make the conclusion clear: significant numbers of Canadians are guided by self-interest, plain and simple. Egoism is alive and well in this country. That leaves us with the tough question: What will it take to bring these people around?

Fortunately, there is an answer: their very self-interest! As Freda Paltiel, a senior policy adviser to Health and Welfare Canada, recently put it, when people who have power are asked to share it, they tend to have three typical responses. The first is, "Gee, Ma, do I have to?" The second is, "Are you going to make me?" And, if the first two fail, the third is, "What happens to me if I don't?" (Paltiel, 1990). We now are at the "what happens to me" stage. It would be preferable for Canadians to opt for balance and pursuit of the best out of concern for the society as a whole; however, the truth of the matter is that, in the long run, no one has much choice.

If we continue to insist on individualism at the expense of society as a whole, at best we are simply going to co-exist and subsist, nationally, institutionally, relationally. At worst, we are going to experience ever-increasing social disintegration. Large chunks of the nation are going to be snapped off; the possible secession of Quebec, rather than being the end of a problem, will only be the beginning of many more. Other parts — the Atlantic region, the West, the Territories — could just as readily follow suit. Organizationally and interpersonally, excessive individualism and relativism will make group life and personal relationships all the more difficult.

Where does it all end? That's hard to say. Where does sanity begin? That's easy to say: it begins with Canadians, whether motivated by concern for others or concern for self, finding a balance between the individual and the group, and together pursuing the best kind of life possible. The alternatives lie before us like a divided highway that is coming up fast. One side is marked with a "proceed" arrow, the other with a circled X. I hope we will opt for sanity.

THE MORAL OF THE CANADIAN STORY
▼

And so we return to where we began. A world that is intent on freedom and increasingly open to individualism, pluralism, and relativism would do well to watch the drama being produced in Canada. Former British Columbia Supreme Court justice Thomas Berger goes so far as to say that "the idea of two linguistic communities living and working together is something that *has* to succeed. If we can't do it in this country," he says, "what hope do they have in countries like Israel, Ireland or Pakistan? We have an educated population, a tolerant population and we have a high standard of living. If we can't make it work, who can?" (Vancouver Sun, 1990).

We may well see not only Canada but our *world* slip increasingly into social chaos. Still, that's the worst scenario. Many times in our history and world history, when compassion and reason have failed, a residual resource has surfaced: necessity. It's almost as if the gods let us "mess things up" close to the point of self-annihilation, and then say, "Enough's enough, the game is over; it's time to get serious and tidy up."

In Canada and elsewhere, the altruist and egoist alike may soon have little choice but to give up the luxury of their differences and give increased attention to balance and best. The alternative is not attractive. The times call for people to make social life work, to embark on problem-solving and the conscious pursuit of the best kind of existence possible. Whether born of virtue or expediency, there is still much hope. Nationally and globally, madness can yet give way to sanity. But it's time to make our move.

REFERENCES
▼

Editorial, *Vancouver Sun.* (1990). 26 May: B1.

Paltiel, Freda L. (1990). *Status of women in Canada: Zeitgeist, process, and personalities.* Paper presented at the annual meeting of the Canadian Sociology and Anthropology Association, Victoria, May.

CREDITS

We wish to thank the authors, publishers, and copyright holders for permission to reprint the selections in this book, which are listed below in order of appearance.

Statistics Canada information is used with the permission of the Minister of Industry, as minister responsible for Statistics Canada. Information on the availability of the wide range of data from Statistics Canada can be obtained from Statistics Canada's regional offices; its World Wide Web site, at http://www.statcan.ca; and its toll-free access number, 1-800-263-1136.

"Explaining Canada's Ethnic Landscape: A Theoretical Model" by Alan B. Anderson and James S. Frideres. Written especially for the text.

"Does 'Race' Matter? Transatlantic Perspectives on Racism after 'Race Relations'" by Robert Miles and Rudy Torres. Reprinted from Vered Amit-Talai and Caroline Knowles (Eds.) *Re-situating Identities: The politics of race, ethnicity and culture.* (Peterborough, ON: Broadview, 1996), pp. 24–46. Reprinted by permission.

"Social Networks and Institutional Completeness: From Territory to Ties" by Sheldon Goldenberg and Valerie A. Haines. Reprinted from *Canadian Journal of Sociology, 17*(3) (1992), 301–312. Reprinted by permission.

"Conceptualizing Gender, Race, and Ethnicity as a Field of Study" by Edit Petrovic. Written especially for the text.

"Ethnic Diversity: Canada's Changing Cultural Mosaic" by Warren E. Kalbach. Written especially for the text.

"Patterns of Ethnic Identification and the 'Canadian' Response" by Ravi Pendakur and Fernando Mata. Reprinted from *Canadian Ethnic Studies, 30*(2) (1998), 125–137. Reprinted by permission.

"Ethnic and Civic Self-Identity in Canada: Analyses of 1974 and 1991 National Surveys" by Rudolf Kalin and John W. Berry. Reprinted from *Canadian Ethnic Studies, 27*(2) (1995), 1–15. Reprinted by permission.

"Ethnicity and the Altar" by Madeline A. Kalbach. Written especially for the text.

"Residential Segregation and Canada's Ethnic Groups" by T.R. Balakrishnan. Written especially for the text.